A Guide to Innovative Public-Private Partnerships

Utilizing the Resources of the Private Sector for the Public Good

Thomas A. Cellucci

Government Institutes
An imprint of
The Scarecrow Press, Inc.
Lanham • Toronto • Plymouth, UK
2011

**Government
Institutes**

Published by Government Institutes
An imprint of The Scarecrow Press, Inc.
A wholly owned subsidiary of The Rowman & Littlefield Publishing Group, Inc.
4501 Forbes Boulevard, Suite 200, Lanham, Maryland 20706
http://www.govinstpress.com

Estover Road, Plymouth PL6 7PY, United Kingdom

British Library Cataloguing in Publication Information Available

Library of Congress Cataloging-in-Publication Data

Cellucci, Thomas A., 1958–
  A guide to innovative public-private partnerships : utilizing the resources of the private sector for the public good / Thomas A. Cellucci.
    p. cm.
  Includes bibliographical references and index.
  ISBN 978-1-60590-745-1 (cloth : alk. paper)—ISBN 978-1-60590-746-8 (electronic)
  1. United States. Dept. of Homeland Security. 2. Public-private sector cooperation—United States. I. Title.
  HV6432.4.C446 2011
  363.34'5250973—dc22
                                    2010051315

Contents

	Preface	v
1	It's Not Business as Usual at DHS	1
2	Commercialization Office	9
3	DHS Sees Value in Commercialization	21
4	Using Commercialization to Develop Solutions Efficiently and Effectively	29
5	Public-Private Partnerships	67
6	Creating Opportunities for the Private Sector	101
7	Offering Transformational Change beyond DHS	111
8	Conservative Estimates of Potential Available Markets	119
9	Bridging the "Communications Gap" between the Public and Private Sectors: Making It Easier to Do Business with DHS	123
10	The Capstone IPT and Beyond	133
11	It's All about Putting Theory into Practice	143
12	FutureTECH in Action	259
13	"Change Ain't Easy"—But It's Possible	303
	Appendix A: Infrastructure Geophysical Division (IGD) Overview	309

Appendix B: Typical New Product Development Process Used
in the Private Sector   319

Appendix C: Product Realization Guide   321

Appendix D: DHS's Private Sector Resources Guide   325

Bibliography   421

Index   429

About the Author   435

Preface

This book is the culmination of efforts aimed to demonstrate that both the public and private sectors can leverage their respective competences, resources, and experience to create a new paradigm in the way we develop technologies, products, and services—all to the benefit of the taxpayer. We have shown that the commercialization model described in this book works in practice and is extendable throughout the federal government in the Unites States and elsewhere.

Commercialization and public-private partnerships are not new concepts. However, we have applied these ideas to create a long sought-after condition in which the taxpayer, public sector, and private sector can excel through "win-win-win" interactions that may in fact change the way governments and the private sector work in the future.

This manuscript would not have been possible had it not been for the encouragement and support from colleagues at the U.S. Department of Homeland Security, dedicated men and women from the private sector who put "country before profit," and first responders who really do "rush in when others rush out." Of special mention are: Mark Protacio, Caroline Greenwood, Ryan Policay, Morgan Motto, Amy Scheuer, Sara Jett, Steve Roberts, Steve Dennis, Rich Kikla, Roger McGinnis, Rolf Dietrich, Jay Cohen, Janet Napolitano, Michael Chertoff, Paul Schneider, Don Dayton, Todd Keil, Douglas Smith, Al Martinez-Fonts, Jim Plehal, Aneesh Chopra, the Council on Competitiveness, Tara O'Toole, Brad Buswell, Tom Foley, Harry Timmons, C. Reed Hodgins, Robert Perthuis, Don Bliss, John McSheffrey, Quintin Kelly, Greg Maultsby, Bob Toups, Linda Vasta, Stewart Baker, Regina Duggan, Elaine Duke, John Higbee, Jay Grant, Scott Charbo, Stephen Heifetz, Soraya Correa, Dan Cotter, Lee

Smith, Jane Holl Lute, Adam Price, Bob Hooks, Daniel Hooks, Mark Kirk, Sam Francis, George Atkinson, Don Ducey, Ed Grekoski, Marshall Caggiano, Mark Rosen, Bob Coyle, Don Hiett, Tom Manson, Steve King, Bob Stephan, Beth Windisch, Tim Del Monico, Arch Turner, Rosemary James, Jake Olcott, Devin O'Brien, Bennie Thompson, Peter King, James McGee, Nabil Adam, Chad Evans, Chad Holiday, Ray Johnson, Vicki Looney, and James Woods.

This work is a reflection of my professional experiences as a senior business executive, Board member, professor, consultant and leader in both the private and public sectors. I am grateful to all of the partners, customers and mentors I have been lucky enough to interact with throughout my career. It is said that the greatest gift one can give to another is time—and these folks were tremendously generous.

Finally, I'd like to take this opportunity to thank my lovely wife, Julie, and our children (Jared, Laura, Emily, Katie, Brad, and Drew) for letting me leave the corporate world to give back to our country and society—which has been a true honor and privilege. I am indebted to them for all of their love and support and hope I am worthy of their profound generosity.

Chapter 1

It's Not Business as Usual at DHS

The U.S. Department of Homeland Security (DHS) is comprised of many organizational elements with a single purpose: to enable, support, and expedite the mission-critical objectives of DHS's seven operating components (OCs)—Transportation Security Administration (TSA), U.S. Customs and Border Patrol (CBP), U.S. Secret Service (USSS), U.S. Citizenship and Immigration Service (USCIS), U.S. Immigration and Customs Enforcement (ICE), Federal Emergency Management Agency (FEMA), and the U.S. Coast Guard (USCG). See figure 1.1.

In these unprecedented times, there is an immediate need for DHS to provide these operating components with the products and services they require, using efficient and cost-effective product development methods. DHS is working proactively to attract the private sector to develop, produce, test, and evaluate products and services that meet the requirements of DHS operating components (OCs), first responders (FRs), and critical infrastructure and key resource (CIKR) owners and operators.

Why would the private sector be inclined to develop products using their own resources at their own expense? This initiative's high probability for success lies in the following principles and guidelines:

1. DHS operating components determine clearly defined capability gaps and operational requirements that can be addressed effectively with existing or developed commercial-off-the-shelf (COTS) items.
2. The private sector wants knowledge of and access to large potential available markets (PAMs) that comprise the DHS operating components and ancillary markets (such as FRs and CIKRs), as it enables a presumably strong business opportunity.

1

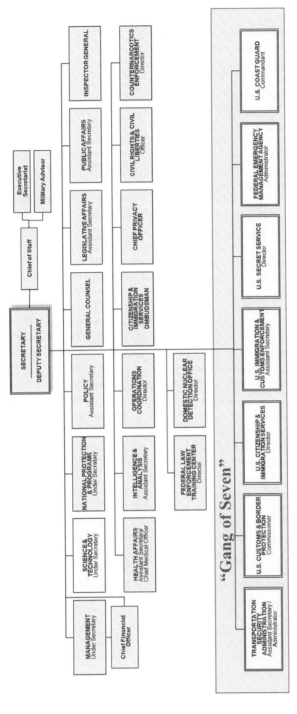

Figure 1.1. DHS Organizational Structure. The U.S. Department of Homeland Security (DHS) is comprised of many organizational elements. The vast majority of resources are contained in the seven operating components (OCs) highlighted in yellow. All other elements within DHS are chartered with enabling, supporting, and enhancing the mission-critical objectives of the OCs, first responders (FRs) and critical infrastructure/key resource (CIKR) owners and operators, which are major responsibilities of FEMA and the Office of Infrastructure Protection respectively.

3. Taxpayer cost savings will be realized by the "win-win" private–public sector partnership. Figure 1.2 outlines a market-potential template, used in various private sector outreach processes by DHS, showing the critical elements to attract the private sector's interest in partnering with DHS.

"WIN-WIN" STRATEGIC PARTNERSHIPS

One often overlooked cost-effective vehicle to efficiently commercialize technology is the formation of a win-win strategic partnership. The relationship between the public and the private sectors can be mutually beneficial in many ways, as each has something of value that the other desires. DHS has substantial potential available markets and direct knowledge of the operating requirements of its large "customer base" as well as detailed information on the unmet needs and wants of ancillary market customers found in state, regional, local, and tribal first responder communities.

Requirements development is one of the cornerstones of the commercialization process. DHS's Science & Technology Directorate (S&T) has led in the development of clear, detailed, commercialization-based operational requirements documents (C-ORDs) and intends to publish them on what would be a public web portal accessible by all private sector and nongovernment entities who believe they have the ability to meet those published requirements and demonstrate that they possess third-party, independent operational test and evaluation performance data. Further benefits that DHS has to offer private sector entities come in the form of grants and Small Business Innovative Research (SBIR) programs as well as other programs geared toward potential partners.

C-ORDs are based on discussions, surveys, and market research conducted by DHS with persons found throughout DHS operating components, the first responder community, the critical infrastructure owners and operators community, and private sector/industry contacts, which are then vetted thoroughly by DHS.

Conversely, the private sector has skills, expertise, capital, established sales channels, and the integrated marketing programs necessary to produce and distribute technically advanced products and services. The private sector appreciates a conservative estimate of the potential available

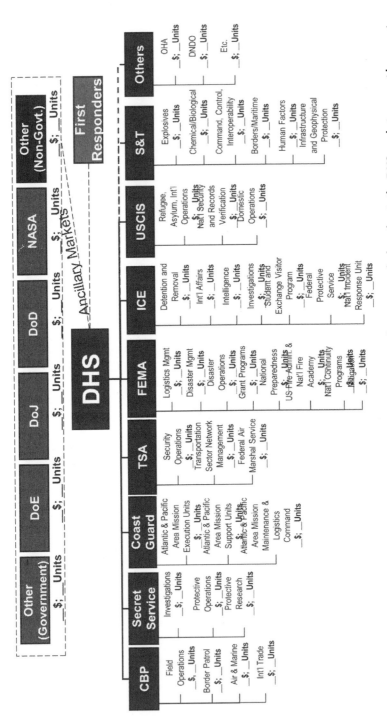

Figure 1.2. This graphic delineates a market potential template or map used to conservatively estimate the DHS market segment by operating components, as well as demonstrate how DHS is a conduit to other large ancillary markets throughout the public and private sectors.

markets within DHS's operating components and/or ancillary markets, as well as clear, detailed operational requirements. With these two items in hand, the private sector can verify supplied estimates and generate business cases to determine if it is feasible to conduct research and development to develop and distribute products or services. This relationship enables substantial benefits given the ever-changing nature of the needs of established and potential new security applications. The private sector will need to continue its innovation as DHS adjusts to address new, emerging threats.

SYNCHRONIZATION

The execution of a radically different methodology to develop, produce, and distribute new products and services for use by DHS operating components does not come without its challenges. For many years, the U.S. government was indoctrinated and accustomed to the acquisition process of commissioning a custom-made product or service to perform a specific objective. The government would oversee the creation of the requirements, concept and technology development, system capability development, testing and evaluation, and production and deployment—paying for each step of the process. The concept of transferring responsibility for many of the steps in the process to the private sector ultimately removes control by the government. Not only is this a new way of thinking about developing and procuring products, it necessitates clear and precise communications between the public and private sectors.

In its new commercialization model, S&T acts as a facilitator between its customers, DHS's operating components and ancillary markets, and the private sector entities potentially developing products. S&T must work with its valued customers in the creation of C-ORDs as well as conduct market surveys and technology scans to ensure that needed technical capabilities and/or products exist within firms accessible for distribution of these C-ORDs. Oftentimes, private sector entities have products in development that are closely aligned with current homeland security capability gaps. In these situations, it is important to determine the exact level of development for the product.

As previously stated, clear and precise communications are paramount. To that end, the lexicon of product development was different in the public versus the private sectors (see figure 1.3). Notice that DHS utilizes Basic Research, Innovation, and Transition nomenclature with Technology Readiness Levels as a "backbone" language, while the private sector utilizes Science, Technology Development, and then Product Development as the phases of developing a product from a concept. In

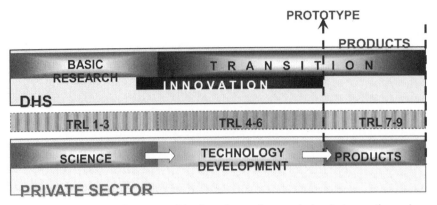

Figure 1.3. Lexicon differences. This chart shows the correlation between the various nomenclatures to delineate differing levels of product development. The Technology Readiness Levels (TRLs) serve as a standardized lexicon for enhanced communications.

order to ensure effective communications, the Technology Readiness Levels (TRLs) model is used to standardize communication for all parties involved (see figure 1.4). With the TRL system in use, all parties are able to assess quickly the development stage of a given product and determine an anticipated timeline for product deployment. Later on, we'll describe the use of MRLs-Manufacturing Readiness Levels as an additional communication tool between the public and private sectors.

TRLs are NASA-generated and Used Extensively by DoD

Basic principles observed and reported	1	Basic
Technology concept and/or application formulated	2	
Analytical and experimental critical function and/or characteristic	3	
Component and/or breadboard validation in laboratory environment	4	Advanced
Component and/or breadboard validation in relevant environment	5	
System/subsystem model or prototype demonstration in a relevant environment	6	
System prototype demonstration in a operational environment	7	Applied
Actual system completed and 'flight qualified' through test and demonstration	8	
Actual system 'flight proven' through successful mission operations	9	

TECHNOLOGY MATURITY

Figure 1.4. Technology Readiness Levels. TRLs are used to assign a numerical value to a corresponding stage in a technology's development and maturity. This system of standardization is useful to communicate effectively between entities that may have used varying technology-maturity lexicons.

OPEN, TRANSPARENT, AND FAIR COMPETITION LEADS TO COOPERATIVE NEW PRODUCT DEVELOPMENT

Once DHS has fulfilled its obligation to create realistic C-ORDs and conducts technology scans and market surveys to ensure that capabilities exist, the department then posts pertinent requirement information on the proposed publicly available, open-access website. This web portal is the vehicle by which private sector and nongovernment entities would engage DHS to find capability gaps/detailed requirements for which solutions exist or can be produced quickly and efficiently. Given this information, private sector entities could develop or enhance a given product or service in cooperation with S&T to enable or improve upon currently fielded DHS solutions. Close alignment with the detailed requirements are critical in this process.

In theory, in order for a company to be considered by S&T for cooperative development, it should be able to:

1. Demonstrate they possess technology at TRL-5 (i.e., applied or advanced R&D) or above and possess the resources to invest in the commercialization of its technology to TRL-9 (i.e., fully field deployable product)
2. Propose a technology development effort that has clear and substantial alignment with published DHS requirements

A simple, straightforward and binding agreement such as a CRADA (Cooperative Research and Development Agreement) could then be executed whereby the private sector entity would detail milestones with dates to develop its technology to a TRL-9 state (if not already at that level). Once the private sector entity has successfully achieved TRL-9, it will perform independent third-party operational testing and evaluation (T&E) on the product/service to ensure it meets all required previously agreed-upon specifications. DHS then would review and evaluate the accuracy of the third-party T&E data and publish its factual summary on the proposed website. The free market system should yield several companies producing similar products, as is often seen in commercial markets. DHS customers and ancillary markets stand to benefit from this system by which a "clearinghouse" of products and services is created.

MEASURABLE RESULTS

The ultimate goal of any commercialization initiative is to produce products that are better, faster, and less expensive compared to what is currently available. DHS hopes to leverage the private sector's endless pursuit of this idea and marry it with the vast demands created by an organization whose mission is to protect a nation. DHS S&T has a critical role acting as the facilitator between sets of markets and a willing and able private sector looking for large, stable markets to purchase and use advanced technologies. A program like this can result in a demonstrable increase in the quality and quantity of technologies, products, and services to assist not only DHS in carrying out its mission objectives, but customers engaged in many other related security applications. It is indeed expected that taxpayers will observe a significant and demonstrative increase in the amount of private sector funding used for the timely development of new and reliable products to help thwart the threat of terrorism.

CONCLUSION

The U.S. Department of Homeland Security through its Science & Technology Directorate is forging a new paradigm that can have far-reaching positive consequences for its customers, its private sector partners, and the U.S. taxpayers through the rapid, cost-effective, and efficient development and deployment of products and services to protect the United States. The relatively recent formation of DHS (its seventh anniversary was on March 1, 2010) is advantageous in many ways, particularly in that it enables flexible and forward thinking in its long-term goals and processes. This commercialization initiative is a groundbreaking and innovative approach to foster a mutually beneficial relationship between the public and private sectors, both of whom stand to benefit greatly from this new partnership created in open and free competition. The future of this initiative looks bright; we have already experienced an overwhelmingly positive response to the initial private sector outreach. S&T will continue to monitor and measure the benefit this program stands to provide.

Chapter 2

Commercialization Office

OVERVIEW

The DHS commercialization efforts are headed by the chief commercialization officer (CCO), a position created in summer 2007 within DHS S&T. Commercialization is broadly defined as the process of developing markets and producing and delivering products or services to meet the needs of those markets. There are four major pillars of the Commercialization Office: requirements development initiative; commercialization process; innovate public-private partnerships, and private sector outreach.

The CCO is responsible for creating initiatives that identify, evaluate, and commercialize technology for the specific goal of rapidly developing and deploying products and services that meet the specific operational requirements of the Department of Homeland Security's operating components and its other stakeholders, such as first responders and critical infrastructure/key resources owners and operators, mostly found in the private sector. Developing and driving the implementation of DHS S&T's outreach with the private sector to establish and foster mutually beneficial working relationships to facilitate cost-effective and efficient product/service development efforts is also a critical job responsibility. Recognizing that many DHS solutions require widely distributed products or services, the CCO works to leverage the private sector's resources to develop COTS products aligned specifically to meet DHS stakeholders' operational requirements for later potential procurement.

The CCO assists the private sector by enabling them to learn about DHS business opportunities, and plays a vital role internal to DHS in coaching, teaching, and assisting project managers, technology transition

managers, and division heads in developing detailed operational requirements through recently published books, tutorials, and teaching materials
spearheaded by DHS S&T. In addition, the CCO works closely with DHS
senior executives and operating components on initiatives and programs
to identify and define the operational needs for capability gaps throughout the entire department.

Mission

The mission of the CCO is to develop and execute programs and
processes that identify, evaluate, and commercialize widely distributed
products or services that meet the operational requirements of the Department of Homeland Security's operating components, first responder
community, and other department stakeholders when required. Developing and managing DHS S&T's outreach effort with the private sector to
establish and foster mutually beneficial working relationships leading to
the fielding of technologies to secure the nation is a primary, day-to-day
function of the CCO.

Major Policy/Program Initiatives

Below is a listing of some of the major activities and resources developed for DHS's commercialization initiative:

- *Developing Operational Requirements* (Version 2.0) is a 353-page
  book that assists in the development and communication of needs
  throughout the department and externally to the private sector when
  appropriate. The development of detailed operational requirements
  for DHS programs and projects will ensure that efficacious products,
  systems, or services, are developed to address specific, well-articu-
  lated needs.
- The development and implementation of a commercialization process for DHS combines the benefits of a pure government acquisition
  process and a pure private sector commercialization process into a
  hybrid process that guides product development in a cooperative
  strategic partnership between the public and private sector in which
  all parties benefit, resulting in positive benefits for the taxpayers—in
  terms of both dollars savings and an increase in the speed of execution of government programs and projects.
- The SECURE (System Efficacy through Commercialization, Utilization, Relevance and Evaluation) Program is an efficient and cost-effective program to foster cooperative win-win partnerships between

DHS and the private sector. This innovative program has received positive response from taxpayers, the private sector, and DHS. It is also starting to be recognized as a groundbreaking public-private partnership useful in many areas of the federal government. The private sector works to develop products and/or services aligned to the needs of DHS operating components and other DHS stakeholders such as the first responder communities because the department posts detailed operational requirements and a conservative estimate of the potential available market (PAM) of a given product, system, or service on the DHS website. See www.dhs.gov/xres/programs/gc_1211996620526.shtm.

- The FutureTECH Program is reserved for those critical research/innovation-focus areas that could be inserted eventually into Department of Homeland Security acquisition or commercialization programs when development reaches TRL-6 based on metrics and milestones more specific than those of a broad technology need statement alone, yet not as specific as a detailed C-ORD. The objective of the FutureTECH program is to establish mutually beneficial partnerships with the private sector, national laboratories, university community, and other research and development (R&D) organizations to develop technologies/capabilities that address the long-term needs of the department and its stakeholders. See www.dhs.gov/files/programs/gc_1242058794349.shtm.
- Public relations and outreach efforts inform the public on "How to Do Business with DHS." These are receiving positive feedback from the private sector and media. Outreach efforts center on notifying the private sector about opportunities that exist for partnership and business development to address the needs of the department. Several articles have been written about DHS commercialization efforts. Outreach efforts are conducted through invited talks to trade conventions, reaching small, medium, and large businesses. Efforts also extend to meet with minority, disadvantaged, and HUBZone (Historically Underdeveloped Business Zone) groups on a regular basis.
- A detailed company overview database containing nonproprietary information about companies' capabilities, technologies, and products aligned to DHS needs has been created. The database provides a given company's alignment to specific capability gaps and is published regularly by DHS S&T. This information has been compiled from responses received as part of our private sector outreach efforts and is useful to identify possible solution providers for a known set of requirements.

REQUIREMENTS DEVELOPMENT INITIATIVE

The goal of this initiative is to improve the articulation and communication of detailed operational requirements to facilitate efficient and cost-effective product development and procurement activities.

Background

The mission of the development of operational requirements across the department is to ensure the accurate and timely development and deployment of products and services to aid in the implementation of the mission-critical objectives of the operating components, first responders, and others. Requirements define the detailed problems and needs that will close existing capability gaps.

Requirements provide criteria against which solutions can be tested and evaluated, ensuring ultimately informed purchasing decisions on products, systems, or services that achieve the stated operational goals. A detailed requirements analysis can uncover hidden requirements as well as discover common problems across programs and various DHS components. Detailed operational requirements will guide product development so that a given solution's specifications actively solve the stated problem(s). This analysis also facilitates market and technology scans to determine if feasible solutions currently exist, saving DHS significant time and money on unnecessary new product development efforts.

Current Status

The requirements development initiative has yielded to date the publication of six books to assist in the development of requirements.

- *Requirements Development Guide*
- *Developing Operational Requirements*
- *Developing Operational Requirements (Version 2.0)*
- *Harnessing the Valuable Experience and Resources of the Private Sector for the Public Good: DHS's Entry into Commercialization*
- *First Responder Capstone IPT: Delivering Solutions to First Responders*
- *Critical Infrastructure Key Resources: Using Commercialization to Develop Solutions Efficiently and Effectively*

These books were written, published, and approved for public release as a resource on requirements hierarchy, elicitation, and the role that requirements play in the product development life cycle. The books are being distributed throughout DHS by the CCO, Private Sector Office, Office of Public Affairs, and the DHS librarian.

In addition to the requirements development books, training courses with a detailed curriculum and background materials have been created for instructor-led learning opportunities for DHS employees.

Commercialization processes and programs are being developed for inclusion in future Acquisition Management Directive MD102-01 editions.

SECURE PROGRAM

The SECURE Program—DHS Science and Technology's innovative business initiative—enables collaboration of public and private entities to develop products and services rapidly to protect the homeland to the benefit of the American taxpayer, private sector, and DHS. The goal of the SECURE Program is to leverage the resources of the private sector to develop solutions aligned with and tested against detailed operational requirements of DHS, first responders, and critical infrastructure and key resource owners and operators. DHS stakeholders can make better-informed purchasing decisions on products or services specifically aligned to their operational needs. The SECURE Program is managed by the chief commercialization officer and operates under the budget for Science and Technology's Directorate. See www.dhs.gov/xres/programs/gc_1211996620526.shtm.

Background

With the initiation of the SECURE Program in June 2008, the department began posting detailed operational requirements documents on its website that provide information outlining specific operational needs and a conservative estimate of the potential available market of a given product, system, or service to private sector entities. Private sector entities can make a business case for development of solutions and conduct third-party independent operational test and evaluation (OT&E) by recognized labs against the given C-ORD at their cost, and DHS will validate the company's OT&E results. DHS components and first responders, for example, will be able to make informed purchasing decisions on successful products or services aligned to the given C-ORD.

The benefits of this program are far-reaching. DHS benefits from gaining a better understanding of its needs and by leveraging the free-market system to have multiple private sector entities offering possible solutions, all aligned to DHS's specific needs at a speed-of-execution not typically seen in the public sector. The private sector receives from DHS critical information in order to develop business cases to begin development of solutions to a given DHS-sponsored C-ORD with the possibility of gaining access to significant potential available markets found throughout DHS and its ancillary markets. The American taxpayer also benefits when DHS components receive technology solutions to enhance their mission capabilities, developed in a cost-effective and efficient manner.

Current Status

The SECURE Program completed its pilot phase and has resulted in the development of eight C-ORDs, which are posted on www.dhs.gov, outlining detailed operational needs for DHS end users. On a similar note, over forty additional C-ORDs are in the process of being developed, and eighty-three potential private sector partners have expressed interest in the SECURE Program for the eight C-ORDs currently posted on www .dhs.gov.

The CCO continues to meet with DHS operating components and first responders and others to identify capability gaps and develop C-ORDs that detail the requirements to fill those needs. The CCO has also coordinated efforts with economists in the Private Sector Office (PSO) to begin development of PAM estimates, as well as efforts with DHS members and partners regarding evaluation by recognized third parties testing data related to proposed solutions.

The SECURE Program already appears successful despite its infancy, operating ahead of schedule with greater-than-expected impact. The program has been embraced by senior DHS management, including executives from both the Bush and Obama administrations.

The Commercialization Office has conducted a series of SECURE Program Working Group meetings to develop the detailed process for the execution of the SECURE Program. These productive meetings provided useful feedback and comments to improve the flow process for the program. Detailed work flows, "swim lanes," and roles and responsibilities were discussed and approved by the Working Group. Supporting documents were also compiled in a library of resources to assist those proposed to be involved in the SECURE Program process for final approval at DHS.

FutureTECH PROGRAM

The FutureTECH Program's objective is to establish mutually beneficial partnerships with the private sector, national laboratories, university community, and other research and development organizations to develop technologies/capabilities that address the long-term needs of the Department of Homeland Security and its stakeholders. FutureTECH identifies and focuses on the future needs of the department, as fully deployable technologies and capabilities, in many cases, are not readily available in the private sector or federal government space.

FutureTECH outlines focus areas for which current technology only exists at earlier stages on the technology readiness scale (TRL 1–6). Its "sister program" SECURE (System Efficacy through Commercialization, Utilization, Relevance and Evaluation) is for fully deployable TRL-9 products and services. See www.dhs.gov/files/programs/gc_1242058794349.shtm.

Background

With the initiation of the FutureTECH Program in May 2009, DHS S&T is able to efficiently and cost-effectively leverage the resources, skills, experience, and productivity of the private sector and other non-DHS entities to develop technologies/capabilities in alignment with research/innovation focus areas obtained from DHS S&T. These technologies/capabilities can ultimately be used by DHS, the first responder community, critical infrastructure/key resources owners/operators, and other DHS stakeholders. In essence, FutureTECH provides a "window of visibility" or "preview" of research/innovation focus areas that DHS and its stakeholders believe are essential in future products and services where detailed operational requirements documents cannot be fully developed at this time. The program also provides insight into areas where independent research and development (IRAD) monies could be spent by firms possessing funding to address DHS research/innovation focus areas.

To state it simply, the SECURE Program focuses on product/service development to create products and services to protect our nation in the shorter term, while FutureTECH will focus on critical research/innovation focus areas at lower TRLs for eventual deployment. Like all of the Commercialization Office's programs, all parties win in the FutureTECH Program. The private sector and others win by receiving valuable insight into future research/innovation focus areas needed by DHS and its stakeholders. DHS wins because it will leverage the valuable skills, experience, and resources of the private sector and other non-DHS entities to expedite efficient and cost-effective technology development; the non-DHS entities win because they receive valuable information useful for their own strategic plans. Most importantly, all American taxpayers win because this innovative partnership yields valuable technologies/capabilities aligned with research/innovation focus areas developed in a more cost-effective and efficient way saving taxpayer money.

Current Status

As of July 2010, the FutureTECH Program is still in its pilot phase and ten research/innovation focus area documents have been drafted, approved, sponsored, and placed on the DHS website. All ten focus on technologies that detect or prevent the detonations of improvised explosive devices. On a similar note, more than twenty-five potential private sector partners have expressed interest in the FutureTECH Program and the research/innovation focus area documents currently posted on dhs.gov.

The FutureTECH Program has experienced moderate success despite its infancy. The program has again been embraced by Senior DHS management, with the CCO spearheading the development of research/innovation focus area documents with others at DHS S&T based on needs for additional possible commercial technologies/capabilities from the private sector.

Due to the success of the SECURE Working Group, the Commercialization Office received feedback on this "sister program." Like SECURE, FutureTECH's primary focus is on the nonfederal first responders and critical infrastructure/key resources (CIKR) owners and operators. The FutureTECH Program is reserved for those research/innovation focus areas that could be inserted eventually into DHS acquisition or commercialization programs when development reaches TRL-6, which is often described as a representative model system that is tested in a relevant environment. The Commercialization Office is responsible for the management and oversight of the program and will work closely with all participants in the process.

The objective of the FutureTECH Working Group was to develop an established process for the following:

- Technical subject matter experts (SMEs) can review basic research/innovation focus area documents
- Review statements of work and developmental test plans (potentially insert into a CRADA agreement between DHS and private sector entity)
- Review private sector T&E data to validate that a "technology/capability does what it claims to do" and that the technology/capability meets or exceeds the stated needs in the basic research/innovation focus area

The Commercialization Office believes that a working group should strike a balance between satisfying legitimate needs for a detailed, defendable, and fair process (one that "breathes" to allow for creativity) and one that assists (not burdens) project managers as an additional "tool in their toolbox."

The Commercialization Office will engage the assistance of FFRDCs (Federally Funded R&D Centers) or potential contractors in order to expedite the timely review of T&E data to efficiently and effectively develop technologies and capabilities at minimum cost to the department.

The CCO continues to meet with DHS operating components, first responders, and others to identify capability gaps and develop research/innovation focus area documents that detail the preliminary requirements to fill those needs. The CCO has also coordinated efforts with economists in the Private Sector Office (PSO) as well as efforts with other members of DHS for optimal evaluation methods of testing data related to private sector or non-DHS-proposed technologies/capabilities.

The voluntary participation and contribution to the program by DHS and the private sector who view the FutureTECH Program as a "best practice" reflects the enormous benefits that the program brings to DHS, the private sector, and the American taxpayer.

COMMERCIALIZATION PROCESS OVERVIEW

The development and implementation of a commercialization process for DHS, led by the S&T Commercialization Office, combines the benefits of a pure government acquisition model and a pure private sector commercialization model into a process that guides product development in a cooperative strategic partnership between the public and private sector in which all parties benefit, resulting in positive benefits for the taxpayers.

Background

The development and implementation of a commercialization process for DHS is an opportunity for DHS to work closely with the private sector to develop widely distributed products/services aligned to the needs of DHS and its ancillary markets such as first responders and CIKR owners and operators. DHS leverages the significant potential available markets for homeland security, along with detailed operational requirements from DHS stakeholders to encourage private sector investment and development of products/services for potential procurement by DHS and its stakeholders. The benefits of this partnership extend to both the public and private sectors, who receive considerable resources from one another; DHS receives products/services aligned to its needs through a highly competitive open market system, and the private sector receives detailed information on requirements and market potential. In addition, American taxpayers benefit as product development costs are borne by the private sector, saving DHS money and delivering quality products used in protecting the homeland.

Current Status

The commercialization process has begun to create a "commercialization mind-set" at DHS in which S&T program managers actively seek opportunities to articulate the needs of their customers (DHS operating components, first responders, CIKR owners and operators, etc.) for the purpose of providing that information to the private sector along with a conservative estimate of the potential available market associated with a given need/requirement. Through the execution of the SECURE and FutureTECH Programs, the Commercialization Office has created a vehicle by which DHS can present information on requirements and potential available markets to potential solution providers in a free-market system. The Commercialization Office has been working to incorporate its practices into an upcoming Management Directive to affect the Department's acquisition processes.

H.R. 4842, released in March 2010, will authorize appropriations for DHS S&T for fiscal years 2011 and 2012, and for other purposes. This bill also authorizes the formal establishment of an Office of Public-Private Partnerships, which will fall under DHS S&T. Objectives of the Office of Public-Private Partnerships include:

- Provide guidance on how to pursue proposals to develop or deploy homeland security technology, including persons associated with small business
- Coordinate with components of the department to issue announcements seeking unique and innovative homeland security technology
- Promote interaction between homeland security researchers and private sector companies to accelerate transition research or a prototype into a commercial product
- Conduct technology research assessment and market place analysis

PRIVATE SECTOR OUTREACH OVERVIEW

The private sector outreach efforts of the Commercialization Office in the Science and Technology Directorate are designed to provide information to the public on "How to Do Business with DHS." Efforts demonstrate the value of engaging in mutually beneficial relationships to provide business opportunities to produce products/services to DHS components and ancillary markets such as first responders and critical infrastructure/key resources owners and operators.

Background

The private sector outreach efforts of the Commercialization Office center on notifying the private sector about opportunities that exist for partnership and business development to address the needs of the department. Outreach efforts are conducted through invited talks to trade conventions, reaching small, medium, and large businesses. Efforts also extend to meet with minority, disadvantaged, and HUBZone groups on a regular basis. As of July 2010, the Commercialization Office has written eight books on requirements development and commercialization that have been released to the public and over twenty articles. Several articles have been written about the commercialization efforts in domestic and international publications. The Commercialization Office maintains two websites, one of which is open to the public for information dissemination.

Current Status

Current private sector outreach efforts have yielded significant positive feedback from the private sector interested in learning more about business opportunities that exist at DHS. As of July 2010, a database of company overviews submitted to the Commercialization Office has collected and aligned over 500 companies offering over 3,500 technologies/products/services aligned to DHS needs. The chief commercialization officer speaks regularly at conferences, engages with regional business development networks, and continues to spread the word about commercialization efforts both to public audiences, as well as with internal DHS operating components and leadership. In addition to internal and external DHS websites, the Commercialization Office has a presence on business-oriented social networking sites such as LinkedIn as well as video sharing websites such as YouTube.

As of July 2010, the Commercialization Office conservatively estimates that over 60,000 organizations/entities have been exposed to DHS commercialization outreach efforts; over 12,000 "Full Response" packages have been sent to private sector and non-DHS entities; with over 2,500 Full Response packages closely reviewed by private sector and non-DHS entities; and over 500 completed company profiles received by the Commercialization Office. Please note that these numbers do not include the millions of people who are made aware of commercialization activities through various forms of media such as television, print media, websites, and so on.

In late August 2009, Los Angeles County faced its largest wild land fire in recorded history, and the Commercialization Office visited and worked with the CAL FIRE deputy chief in order to better understand the challenges faced in fighting wild land fires, especially in the urban interface. Due to the wealth of information received from the visit, the Commercialization Office has continued to work closely with CAL FIRE and other first responder groups and organizations around the United States to write and edit operational requirements documents to help first responders describe a number of problems that technology could solve. The voluntary participation and contribution to our innovative public-private partnership programs by DHS and the private sector, who view the SECURE Program as a "best practice," reflects the enormous benefits that the program brings to DHS, the private sector, and the American taxpayer.

Chapter 3

DHS Sees Value in Commercialization

It is undeniable that the U.S. Department of Homeland Security (DHS)—like many government agencies—possesses a deeply ingrained "Acquisition mind-set." While the Acquisition model has been utilized effectively in developing custom, one-off products such as aircraft carriers, it is not particularly germane to the vast majority of needs at DHS—namely, the development of lower-priced, widely distributed products for both DHS operating components (TSA, FEMA, CBP, ICE, USCIS, USSS, and U.S. Coast Guard) and ancillary markets such as the first responder communities. Recognizing this fact, the department recently developed and started implementing a "commercialization mind-set" in order to leverage the vast capabilities and resources of the private sector through innovative "win-win" private-public partnerships.

DHS has faced several challenges attempting to amalgamate twenty-two disparate organizations into a cohesive organization with a unified mission and culture. Those familiar with merger and acquisition (M&A) activities realize that while integration of organizations poses difficulties, it also represents opportunities to infuse new processes and values into a newly created organization. Through both a "bottom-up" and "top-down" approach, DHS has been successful in developing, socializing, and now implementing an innovative commercialization framework that has started to gain traction throughout the agency. The creation of a "commercialization mindset" has caught the attention of DHS managers and employees and has been embraced by senior management because of its apparent and significant benefits to the department's internal and external activities.

Why is there a need for a commercialization process? DHS requirements, in most instances, are characterized by the need for widely distributed COTS (commercial-off-the-shelf) products. Oftentimes, the need is for thousands, if not millions, of products for DHS's seven operating components and the fragmented, yet substantial, first-responder market and more fragmented and even more substantial CIKR market. Figure 3.1 shows the major differences between a "pure" acquisition versus "pure" commercialization processes, along with the recently developed and implemented DHS "hybrid" commercialization process.

Figure 3.2 provides an overall description of DHS's new commercialization model and its first innovative public-private partnership program, called SECURE (System Efficacy through Commercialization, Utilization, Relevance and Evaluation) Program to develop products and services in a mutually beneficial "win-win" way, recently announced in June 2008 by DHS and described in detail at www.dhs.gov/xres/programs/gc_1211996620526.shtm. Briefly, the SECURE Program is based on the premise that the private sector has shown that it is willing and able to use its own money, resources, expertise, and experience to develop and produce fully developed products and services for DHS if significant market potential exists. The private sector has shown remarkable interest in devoting its time and money to such activities if and when an attractive business case can be made related to large revenue/profit opportunities,

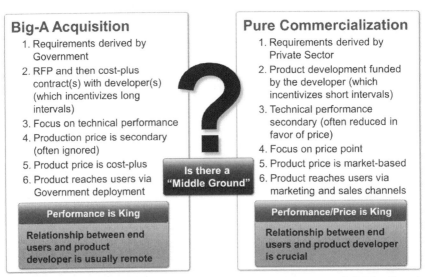

Figure 3.1.   Comparison of "pure acquisition" versus "pure commercialization" models for product/system development and the resultant hybrid model implemented by DHS.

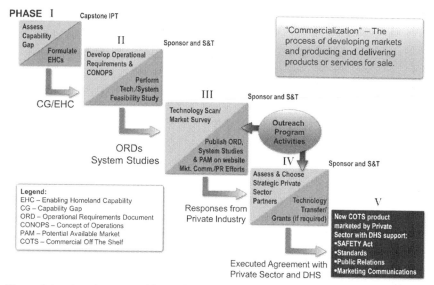

Figure 3.2. Step-by-step guide to the commercialization process developed and adopted by DHS with a brief summary of the popular SECURE Program.

which certainly exist within DHS and its ancillary markets. The private sector requires two things from DHS: (1) detailed operational requirements, and (2) a conservative estimate of potential available market(s). This information can then be used to generate a business case for possible private sector participation in the program.

To augment the commercialization process, DHS has undertaken the task of developing an easy-to-use comprehensive guide to assist in developing commercialization-based operational requirements. This guide now enables DHS personnel to articulate, in detail, a given system's requirements and communicate those needs to both internal and external audiences. This effort addresses a long-standing need for DHS to fully articulate its requirements.

Early response related to this guide and programs like SECURE from groups within DHS and in the private sector has been very favorable. The department plans to regularly update its website with Commercialization-based Operational Requirements Documents (C-ORDs) to continually expand this innovative private-public partnership.

DHS's newly developed and recently implemented commercialization process offers long-awaited benefits to the rapid execution of cost-effective and efficient development of products and services to protect our nation and its resources. And it is a model that every other federal agency can adopt—either on its own or in conjunction with other agencies—to boost potential available market sizing.

Commercialization, broadly described as "the development of markets and the production and delivery of products/services to meet the unsatisfied needs/wants of these markets," represents a key process that the U.S. Department of Homeland Security can use to effectively create capabilities for the first responder community and other members of the Homeland Security Enterprise (HSE). Commercialization allows DHS to develop and deliver products/services to the first responder community, for example, in a more cost-effective and efficient manner as compared to a traditional governmental acquisition process, to the benefit of the first responder and, just as importantly, to the benefit of the American taxpayer. Through this commercialization process, DHS is fostering new partnerships with the private sector to participate in cooperative product/service development efforts aligned to DHS needs. It should be noted that commercialization is not a new concept to the private sector (see figure 3.5).

In a relatively short amount of time, DHS has developed and is now implementing a "commercialization mind-set" in its approach to responding to the needs of its stakeholders. These stakeholders include DHS's seven operating components (TSA, CBP, FEMA, ICE, USCIS, U.S. Secret Service, and U.S. Coast Guard), the first responder community, and the critical infrastructure/key resources (CIKR) owners/operators. The idea of utilizing a commercialization process at DHS is a much-needed and significant departure from the commonly employed acquisition model

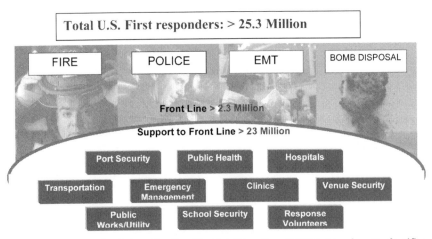

Figure 3.3. Homeland Security Presidential Directive (HSPD) Number 8 classifies those individuals considered first responders in the United States. A conservative estimate shows that over 25.3 million people work or volunteer as first responders. For a complete segmentation of the first responder market map, please refer to Appendix I of the Developing Operational Requirements book available online at www.dhs.gov/xlibrary/assets/Developing_Operational_Requirements_Guides.pdf.

because it has the potential to yield significant benefits in terms of reducing research and development costs, as well as realizing a much more rapid time-to-market for newly developed commercial products/services for DHS. Rather than have DHS pay for the development of custom "one-off" systems, which is frequently the case in military applications, it is apparent that DHS has much to offer the private sector in terms of potential available markets that can be addressed in a more "commercial" fashion with firms competing for sales in an open and free-market system. As previously mentioned, figure 3.1 shows the major differences between a "pure" acquisition versus "pure" commercialization process, and our resultant DHS "hybrid" commercialization process.

While the development of highly specialized products is still relevant to the department, DHS itself represents a substantial potential available market for widely distributed products; in many instances requiring thousands, if not millions of product or service units to address unsatisfied needs. Couple to this the fact that DHS has responsibility for an array of ancillary markets: namely, first responders and CIKR owner/operators, representing large potential available markets in their own right; it is evident that substantial business opportunities exist for the private sector. Figure 3.3 shows those groups of individuals classified as first responders according to Homeland Security Presidential Directive Number 8. While these groups represent a highly fragmented market, the size of the market is nonetheless attractive enough that many companies seek to capture portions of it (represent many niche markets).

There is a new concentrated focus in understanding the requirements of members of the first-responder community in an effort to close their mission-critical capability gaps. Given the fragmented nature of the first-responder communities, DHS, through the Science and Technology

S&T Transition IPT Members and Function

Figure 3.4. The First Responder Capstone IPT is derived from the general Capstone IPT model above and will bring together end users, scientists, and program managers to discuss mission-critical capability gaps and requirements.

Figure 3.5. New product development process typically implemented in the private sector. Courtesy of Cellucci Associates, Inc.

	FEASIBILITY PHASE	OPTIMIZATION PHASE	DEVELOPMENT PHASE	PILOT PHASE	SALES RELEASE PHASE
OVERVIEW	Objective: To investigate new product ideas (or technologies) when market and/or engineering risks are significant. Inputs: A value proposition statement and concise objectives, strategies and tactics of the investigation. Output: A written report of findings and recommendations.	Objective: To develop a detailed product plan. Input: A preliminary product plan. Output: A detailed product plan.	Objective: To complete the design and development of the product through the release of an engineering documentation package and manufacturing plan. Input: A detailed product plan. Outputs: Engineering documentation package release and manufacturing plan.	Objective: Demonstrate that the product can be manufactured within cost and on schedule. Inputs: Completed engineering documentation and manufacturing plan. Outputs: Completed manufacturing plan release package and manufacturing plan release package.	Objective: Prove that a defect-free product can be promoted, sold, manufactured and tracked according to its product plan. Input: Completed manufacturing plan release package Outputs: Commercially available defect-free product and finalized product plan.
RESEARCH & DEVELOPMENT	• Establish technical objectives and milestones (including go / no-go decision points) • Conduct preliminary IP review • Select team and estimate required resources	Develop Engineering Plan to include: • Detailed performance specifications (agreed to by Marketing and Sales) • Product Cost Estimate • User interface(s) • Packaging considerations • Accessories • Detailed schedule and budget • Technology Risks • Standards / Safety Compliance • Workhorse Patent considerations • Potential hazardous technologies • Potential technology platforms • Trade-secrets	Complete the following: • Design product to specifications with several design reviews • Prepare and complete engineering documentation • Build engineering prototypes • Design and build support tooling and test fixture(s) • Demonstrate ease-of-manufacturability • Build Alpha and Beta units • Aid in supplier identification and evaluation • Provide environmental specifications (vibration, EMI, etc.) • Design shipping / packaging • Demonstrate conformance to requirements • Create "design freeze"	Complete the following: • Support required testing and assembly training • Support manufacturability (design changes) • Offer assistance in other functional areas when required (e.g., help in finalizing sales literature or tools)	Complete the following: • Any ECOs implemented • Ensure application engineering / technical support trained and tested • Assist other functional areas if required
PRODUCTION	• Provide list of any potentially required tools, materials or new processes • Act as an advisor on subjects such as "design for test", "manufacturability" and ways to cost-effectively produce a product / technology platform	Develop Manufacturing Plan to include: • Product Cost Estimate • Manufacturability issues • Detailed schedule and budget • Capital / facilities requirement • Product structure / architecture	Complete the following: • Aid in ease-of-manufacturability • Identify critical paths / processes • Develop product structure • Schedule prototype and pilot runs • Design and test assembly procedures • Conduct "make vs. buy" analysis • Set up product routings • Design and fabricate process tooling • Order long-lead items • Develop and test assembly procedures • Finalize manufacturing plan	Complete the following: • Finalize tooling and set up manufacturing routings • Measure and track pilot engineering changes • Ensure material and production control • Provide productivity feedback to R&D • Train applications engineering personnel	Complete the following: • All QA / testing finalized • All tooling and processes frozen • Final manufacturing and assembly routines / procedures are frozen
MARKETING & SALES	• Establish marketing objectives and milestones (including market size(s) and forecasts) • Estimate required resources and select team from Marketing and Sales • Develop rough draft of features, benefits and "reasons to buy" • List potential derivative products / technologies • Provide draft of prospective customers	Develop Marketing Plan to include: • Detailed schedule and budget • Application(s) overview • Detailed competitive analysis • Alpha and Beta site plan • Product launch plan • Features, benefits and "reasons to buy" • Detailed market research (primary and secondary) • Trademarks • "Monopoly creation" • Branding strategy	Complete the following: • Develop sales / distribution plan • Manage and report on Alpha and Beta sites • Develop first draft of User's Manual • Develop integrated marketing communications strategy • Finalize product structure • Develop sales training plan • Solicit sales force's feedback • Update marketing plan	Complete the following: • Initiate worldwide sales training • Approve user manual • Prepare sales release package • Update / distribute product to corporate literature / web site / etc. (demo only) • Review / edit promotion strategy	Complete the following: • All integrated marketing activities are finalized • Worldwide sales materials, tools and training are complete (internal and external) • All corporate materials are updated • Finalize marketing plan
QUALITY CONTROL	• Ensure the qualification of tools / materials / processes and suppliers as required	Develop Quality Plan to include: • Standards Conformance • Calibration requirements • Packaging / shipping testing • Lifetime / reliability testing • Safety training and testing • Development of new procedures / processes / metrics • Monitoring progress against goals	Complete the following: • Develop and implement test plan • Define regulatory requirements • Design and build inspection tooling • Conduct shipping tests • Develop preliminary QA test procedures • Audit key suppliers • Edit and approve manuals	Complete the following: • Obtain yield data • Verify and update QA / test procedures based on quality requirements	Complete the following: • Finalize all QA / test procedures • Finalize all QA / test tooling • Finalize quality plan
FINANCE	• Provide team with any financial data or information required	Complete a Financial Analysis to include: • NPV / ROI • Cash flow • Sensitivity / Scenario Analysis	Complete the following: • Conduct preliminary cost roll-up	Complete the following: • Complete cost roll-up	Complete the following: • Ongoing shipment process(es) have been verified and tested for new product
REVIEW OF CORPORATE "DELIVERABLES"	Review of Corporate "Deliverables": 1. The written report of findings and recommendations (preliminary product plan) is to be distributed to corporate reviewers at least one week prior to the scheduled review meeting. 2. The Feasibility Review meeting will be attended by each corporate officer, the "product / technology champion" and a designated representative of each functional area. 3. Results / follow-up actions of the review meeting will be communicated to the organization by the champion. Approved preliminary product plans continue to the Optimization Phase and approved new technology roadmaps are given to the CTO and / or VP R&D for further development and implementation.	Review of Corporate "Deliverables": 1. The written product plan is to be distributed to corporate reviewers at least one week prior to the scheduled review meeting. 2. The Optimization Review meeting will be attended by each corporate officer, "the product champion" and a designated representative of each functional area. 3. Results / follow-up actions of the review meeting will be communicated / coordinated by the champion.	Review of Corporate "Deliverables": 1. The engineering documentation package release and manufacturing plan is to be distributed to corporate reviewers at least one week prior to the scheduled review meeting. 2. The Development Phase review will be attended by each corporate officer, the "product champion" and a designated representative of each functional area. Note: Ample time must be allocated for deep probing of details of not only the engineering and manufacturability plan, but also of progress / updates from the functional areas. 3. Results / follow-up actions of the review meeting will be communicated / coordinated to the organization by the champion.	Review of Corporate "Deliverables": 1. The manufacturing plan release package is to be distributed to corporate reviewers at least one week prior to the scheduled review meeting. 2. The Pilot Phase review will be attended by each corporate officer, the "product champion" and a designated representative of each functional area. 3. Results / follow-up actions of the review meeting will be communicated / coordinated to the organization by the champion.	Review of Corporate "Deliverables": 1. The finalized product plan sales release package is to be distributed to corporate reviewers at least one week prior to the scheduled review meeting. 2. The Sales Release Phase review will be attended by each corporate officer, the "product champion" and a designated representative of each functional area. Note: Ample time must be allocated to the processes to ensure flawless execution of the acceptance, shipment and after-sales support of the new product. 3. Results / follow-up actions of the review meeting will be coordinated / communicated to the organization by the champion.

Directorate (S&T) has formulated a crosscutting Capstone Integrated Product Team (IPT) to focus solely on the needs and requirements of the first responders. Figure 3.4 shows the general organization of a Capstone IPT along with the appropriate functions of each member. The First Responder Capstone IPT reaches out to the various first-responder associations and organizations across the country to gain valuable insight into their needs and requirements and provide a forum for them to be discussed and addressed.

The Capstone IPT process[1] ensures that quality, efficacious products are developed in close alignment with customer needs. Through a network of communication channels, Capstone IPTs bring together S&T division heads, management personnel and end users (operating components, field agents, and supporting first responders and/or CIKR owner/operators) involved in research, development, testing, and evaluation (RDT&E). Working collaboratively, the First Responder IPT collects,

Table 3.1. Benefit Analysis—"Win-Win-Win"

The SECURE Program is viewed positively by DHS stakeholders. The success of the program lies in the fact that all participants receive significant benefits.

Taxpayers	Public Sector	Private Sector
1. Citizens are better protected by DHS personnel using mission-critical products	1. Improved understanding and communication of needs	1. Save significant time and money on market and business development activities
2. Tax savings realized through private sector investment in DHS	2. Cost-effective and rapid product development process saves resources	2. Firms can genuinely contribute to the security of the nation
3. Positive economic growth for American economy	3. Monies can be allocated to perform greater number of essential tasks	3. Successful products share in the "imprimatur of DHS"; providing assurance that products really work.
4. Possible product "spin-offs" can aid other commercial markets	4. End users receive products aligned to specific needs	4. Significant business opportunities with sizable DHS and DHS ancillary markets
5. Customers ultimately benefit from COTS produced within the free-market System—more cost-effective and efficient product development	5. End users can make informed purchasing decisions with tight budgets	5. Commercialization opportunities for small, medium, and large business

evaluates, and prioritizes requirements to enable new mission-critical capabilities.

In providing critical information to the private sector in terms of the collection and articulation of detailed operational requirements and a conservative estimate of the potential available market, DHS has laid the foundation for cooperative product development with the private sector, because this is the kind of information used by the private sector for its new product development processess (see figure 3.5). These relationships drive the commercialization process and ensure that end users such as first responders receive needed products/services in a timely manner at minimal costs to DHS. Given these relationships, it is relatively easy to make a case for commercialization at the department (see table 3.1) as it results in "wins" for the American taxpayer and both the public and private sectors.

In conclusion, a commercialization process is ideal to match, for example, the detailed requirements of the collective first-responder community with product development efforts undertaken by the private sector, who seek access to the large potential available markets represented by the first responders. Commercialization is not only an attractive method by which DHS can develop products/services for first responders, but it is also beneficial to both the public and private sectors and—most importantly—to the American taxpayers at large.

NOTE

1. Richard V. Kikla and Thomas A. Cellucci, "Capstone IPTs: Even in Government the Customer Comes First," April 2008.

Chapter 4

Using Commercialization to Develop Solutions Efficiently and Effectively

Protecting the nation's critical infrastructure and key resources (CIKR) is a key Department of Homeland Security mission established in 2002 by the National Strategy for Homeland Security and the Homeland Security Act.

The department's Office of Infrastructure Protection (IP) within the National Protection and Programs Directorate (NPPD) leads the coordinated national program to reduce risks to the nation's CIKR posed by acts of terrorism and to strengthen national preparedness, timely response, and rapid recovery in the event of an attack, natural disaster, or other emergency.

IP addresses these needs through the National Infrastructure Protection Plan (NIPP). The NIPP establishes a partnership structure for coordination across eighteen CIKR sectors and a risk-management framework to identify assets and systems whose loss or compromise poses the greatest risk.

Within the sector framework, IP works with public and private partners to protect CIKR and provide CIKR information to strengthen incident response. IP initiatives fall into six programmatic areas:

- Partnerships, Outreach, and Training
- Contingency Planning and Incident Management
- Chemical Facility Security and Compliance
- CIKR Protective Security and Field Operations
- Infrastructure Analysis, Research, and Development
- Infrastructure Information Collection and Protection

IP relies on regular interaction with CIKR owners and operators to ensure the ability of infrastructure protection personnel to conduct their missions successfully. IP also assists in addressing the needs and concerns of those infrastructure protection communities to maintain high levels of operational readiness.

The U.S. Department of Homeland Security (DHS) is comprised of many organizational elements with a single purpose: to enable, support, and expedite the mission-critical objectives of DHS's seven operating components and directorates to protect our most valuable asset—our citizens. Transportation Security Administration (TSA), U.S. Customs and Border Protection (CBP), U.S. Secret Service (USSS), U.S. Citizenship and Immigration Service (USCIS), U.S. Immigration and Customs Enforcement (ICE), Federal Emergency Management Agency (FEMA), U.S. Coast Guard (USCG), and NPPD are the major organizations chartered within the department to coordinate the transition of multiple agencies and programs into a single, integrated agency focused on protecting the American people and their homeland.

The operating components and directorates work closely with, support, and are supported by a large network of first responders at the state, local, tribal, and territorial levels, along with the critical infrastructure and key resources (CIKR) owners and operators. These groups comprise DHS's stakeholder community and play critical roles in planning, preparedness, response, and recovery efforts of DHS. The DHS stakeholders rely on the support of its many organizational elements to ensure mission success and address challenges confronting these stakeholders. Among the challenges facing DHS is how to gather and refine the needs and requirements of its various stakeholders, who represent a wide variety of mission spaces and operating environments, in a cost-effective and efficient manner.

The purpose of this chapter is simple and straightforward: to enable the reader to effectively engage with the Department of Homeland Security in a simple and straightforward way. This resource will facilitate methods to articulate detailed operational requirements and define mission problems effectively, specifically those of the CIKR community. Readers will be able to better understand stakeholder interaction channels through various organizational elements and learn how to improve the communication of their needs and requirements to others in DHS, other federal agencies, or the private sector.

Requirements form the cornerstone of understanding challenges faced in providing the capabilities necessary to complete mission-critical objectives. Requirements further enhance one's ability to communicate those challenges to those who can best begin to address them. We can improve this situation by implementing some fundamental practices in a disciplined manner so that requirements are both gathered and disseminated through the proper channels at the department and external audiences, when appropriate.

A well-written requirements document or articulation can be an effective tool to relay the needs of a given group in an easily understood format. Clear and consistent communications help to avoid the extra hours, money, and other resources spent guessing about needs that are not clearly defined. Research conclusively shows that the foremost reason programs or projects do not succeed is a lack of detailed requirements at the initiation of a program or project. Delays in bringing needed capabilities to the hands of those who need them most are not acceptable for those whose missions are critical to the protection of the American people and the critical infrastructure and key resources that support our everyday lives. Efforts invested early to develop a clear understanding of requirements pay dividends in the positive outcome of programs—not to mention the savings in both time and money in corrective actions needed to get a program back on track (if it is even possible).

The Office of Infrastructure Protection (IP) and the Science and Technology Directorate (S&T) work together to understand and address the needs and problems of CIKR communities. To that end, we have provided in this book an introduction to working with DHS and its organizational elements responsible for assisting CIKR owners and operators and an easy-to-follow template that will enable the generation and articulation of detailed operational requirements. We have also included several real-world examples of well-written operational requirements documents (C-ORDs) that show how complex challenges can be articulated. In the numerous appendixes accompanying this book, you will find articles and briefings that provide additional context to the role that creating detailed operational requirements plays in effective product realization. It is our goal that this resource opens communication between DHS's stakeholders and the department through positive interaction that leads to actions taken to address the needs and requirements of all stakeholders, whether they be direct DHS field agents, our nation's first responders, or critical infrastructure and key resources owners and operators.

NATIONAL PROTECTION AND PROGRAMS DIRECTORATE AND THE OFFICE OF INFRASTRUCTURE PROTECTION

The National Protection and Programs Directorate (NPPD) manages many aspects of the planning and preparedness functions of the department. NPPD comprises a number of offices that effectively outreach and connect with several functional areas across the homeland security mission space important in the daily operations of the country. NPPD oversees the coordinated operational and policy functions of the directorate's subcomponents—Cyber Security and Communications (CS&C), Infrastructure Protection (IP), Risk Management and Analysis (RMA), the Federal Protective Service (FPS), and the United States Visitor and Immigrant Status Indicator Technology (US-VISIT) program—in support of the department's critical mission.

IP leads the coordinated national program to reduce risks to the nation's CIKR posed by acts of terrorism and to strengthen national preparedness, timely response, and rapid recovery in the event of an attack, natural disaster, or other emergency. This is a complex mission. Critical infrastructure can range from the nation's electric power, food, and drinking water to its national monuments, telecommunications and transportation systems, chemical facilities, and much more. The vast majority of national CIKR is privately owned and operated, making public-private partnerships essential to protect CIKR and respond to events.

IP manages mission complexity by breaking it down into three broad areas: (1) identify and analyze threats and vulnerabilities; (2) coordinate nationally and locally through partnerships with both government and private sector entities that share information and resources; and (3) mitigate risk and effects (encompasses both readiness and incident response).

National Infrastructure Protection Plan and the Public-Private Partnership Model

The National Infrastructure Protection Plan (NIPP) was created to codify the nation's action plan to provide for CIKR resiliency, protection, and preparedness (see appendix A). The goal of the NIPP is to build a safer, more secure, and more resilient America by enhancing protection of the nation's CIKR to prevent, deter, neutralize, or mitigate the effects of deliberate efforts by terrorists to destroy, incapacitate, or exploit them and to strengthen national preparedness, timely response, and rapid recovery in the event of an attack, natural disaster, or other emergency. The NIPP structure provides a foundation for enhancing critical infrastructure protection and resilience. The CIKR Support Annex to the National Response Framework (NRF) provides a bridge between the NIPP "steady-state" processes for infrastructure protection and the NRF unified approach to domestic incident management. These documents provide the overarching doctrine that ensures full integration of the two vital homeland security mission areas—critical infrastructure protection and domestic incident management. The ways in which CIKR are interdependent create additional challenges from cascading effects in the event of a disruption to sectors of CIKR.

Critical infrastructure protection is a shared responsibility among federal, state, local, and tribal governments and the owners and operators of the nation's CIKR. Partnership between the public and private sectors is essential, in part because the private sector owns and operates approximately 85 percent of the nation's critical infrastructure, while government agencies have access to critical threat information and each controls security programs, research and development, and other resources that may be more effective if discussed and shared, as appropriate in a partnership setting.

The NIPP partnership model provides a forum through which the diverse community of infrastructure protection providers can collaborate and share information to discuss requirements identification, planning, and policy coordination. This unique set of infrastructure protection providers encompasses groups of CIKR owners and operators along with government officials at all levels. See figure 4.1 for the structure of the NIPP partnership model.

Under the NIPP, a Sector-Specific Agency (SSA) is the assigned federal agency to lead a collaborative process for infrastructure protection tailored to the specific risk landscape of each of the eighteen CIKR sectors. The NIPP allows IP to provide the cross-sector coordination and collaboration needed to set national priorities, goals, and requirements for

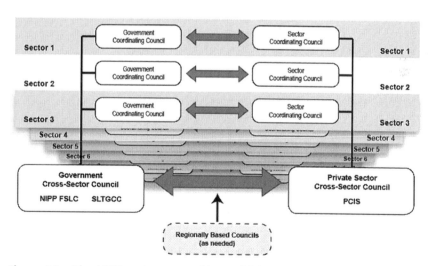

Figure 4.1. The NIPP sector partnership model is a collaborative forum whereby government and private sector entities at federal, state, regional, local, tribal, and territorial levels responsible for infrastructure protection can share information and ideas on requirements.

effective allocation of resources. More importantly, the NIPP integrates a broad range of CIKR public and private protection activities.

The SSAs provide guidance about the application of the NIPP to state, local, tribal, and territorial homeland security agencies and personnel within their specific sectors. They coordinate NIPP implementation within their sector, which involves developing and sustaining partnerships and information-sharing processes, as well as assisting with contingency planning and incident management.

IP serves as the SSA for six of the eighteen CIKR sectors. IP works closely with SSAs of the other twelve CIKR sectors to implement the NIPP. This frequently involves addressing cross-sector vulnerabilities and working to achieve cross-sector program efficiencies. The eighteen CIKR sectors are as follows (the six for which IP serves as the SSA are italicized):

Agriculture and Food
Banking and Finance
Chemical
Commercial Facilities
Communications
Critical Manufacturing
Dams
Defense Industrial Base
Emergency Services
Energy
Government Facilities
Healthcare and Public Health
Information Technology
National Monuments & Icons
Nuclear Reactors, Materials and Waste
Postal and Shipping
Transportation Systems
Water

An important facet of the sector partnership model is the creation of cross-sector councils and working groups. The many ways in which CIKRs are interrelated create additional challenges from cascading effects in the event of a disruption to various CIKR sectors. The collaborative nature of cross-sector councils and working groups not only facilitates the gathering of information on those cascading effects and interdependencies but also offers insight into commonly shared requirements that may be addressed by similar solutions. This information provides significant details of the problem description to solution developers as well as opens opportunities for the deployment of multi-use technologies and a reduction in redundant programs that solve similar problems.

Working through these sectors, IP assists NIPP stakeholders in identification and articulation of strategic R&D needs. IP oversees the collection, analysis, and prioritization of sector requirements for all eighteen CIKR sectors. IP also facilitates the coordination of addressing the needs of these stakeholders with other department organizational elements to address identified capability gaps. An analysis of the stakeholders of these CIKR markets shows that there are many CIKR owners and operators who need to be able to engage with DHS to convey their requirements. These sectors also represent large user groups that often require widely distributed products and services to meet their needs nationwide. See figure 4.2 for a breakdown of the sectors and their component stakeholders.

These sectors play a critical role in the understanding of capability gaps and requirements experienced by the CIKR owners and operators. The direct interaction between the Government Coordinating Council (GCC) and Sector Coordinating Council (SCC) for each sector provides opportunities for these groups to develop a common understanding of current challenges facing the sectors. The sector partnership model allows for "bottom-up requirements gathering" that can be shared through the well-defined process and reach those groups that are able to act upon the gathered information. IP has a close relationship with several organizational elements throughout the department to not only find common requirements and capability gaps but also to work with those best able to develop and deploy technological solutions to those in need.

DHS SCIENCE AND TECHNOLOGY DIRECTORATE

Advances in science and technology continue to spur the development of new and innovative products focused on the homeland security market. As this marketplace expands, it becomes increasingly important for homeland security personnel to assist in guiding product development to match their various needs. Delivering these customer-driven products and technologies is a primary objective for DHS.

For many organizational elements within DHS, the primary focus is to assist in policy management, preparedness planning, and crisis mitigation efforts. These support functions are critical to component field agents, first responders, and infrastructure protection personnel. As department stakeholders perform their missions, they inevitably are faced with situations where their current capabilities are not sufficient to carry out their objectives. Ever-changing threat dynamics often require new,

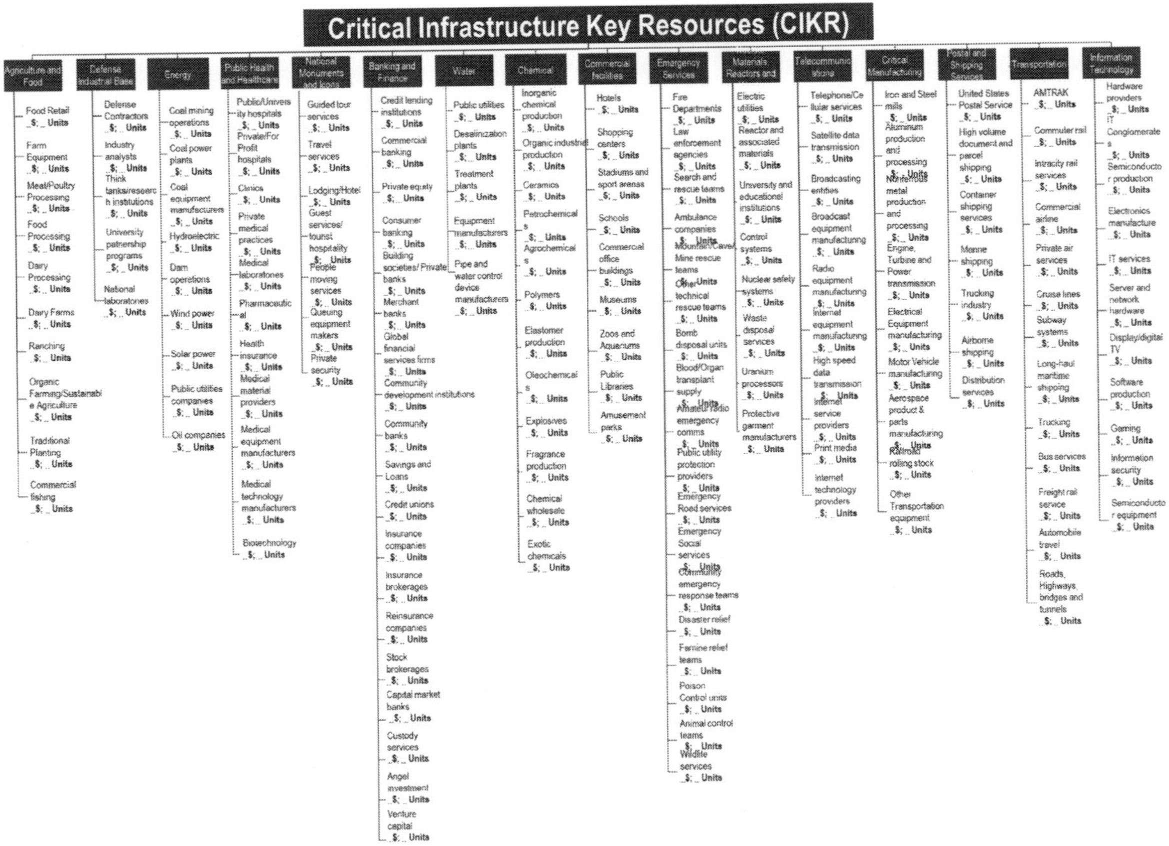

Critical Infrastructure Key Resources (CIKR)

Figure 4.2. Market potential template for the CIKR Market

innovative technology-based solutions in order to prevent or mitigate the potential effects of current and future dangers, not to mention the numerous challenges faced by these groups on a daily basis that are integral to providing security for all citizens. Chief among the organizational elements charged with delivering new products and capabilities is the DHS Science and Technology Directorate (S&T). DHS S&T is unique in that it is the organizational element within the department whose primary mission is to provide department stakeholders with the technologies, products, and services needed in order to perform their objectives.

DHS S&T is organized into several divisions to address stakeholder requirements in the fields of basic research, high-risk/high-reward innovation projects, and product transition activities that serve to get products into the hands of stakeholders to enhance their mission capabilities. In today's dynamic homeland security environment, delivering customer-driven products and technologies is a primary objective for DHS. DHS S&T manages DHS's diverse group of operating components and supporting elements, whose missions address a wide variety of terrorist and natural threats to our homeland.

DHS S&T works to understand, document, and offer solutions to current and anticipated threats faced by these partners/stakeholders, our "customers" and our "customers' customers" (i.e., first responders and CIKR owners and operators). DHS S&T, through the Capstone Integrated Product Team (IPT) process, ensures that quality, efficacious products are developed in close alignment with detailed customer needs. The Capstone IPT process represents the requirements-driven, output-oriented portion of DHS's technology development investments geared toward providing DHS stakeholders with the necessary tools to protect America's most valuable asset—its people.

Capstone Integrated Product Teams

The Capstone Integrated Product Teams (IPTs) are chartered to ensure that technologies and products are engineered and integrated into systems aligned to the needs of DHS customers. Consistent with the Homeland Security Act of 2002, Capstone IPTs establish a lean and agile world-class S&T management team that delivers the technological advantage necessary to ensure DHS agency mission success. The Capstone IPT process is the framework used to determine whether developed capabilities meet operational needs, analyze gaps in strategic needs and capabilities, develop operational requirements, and develop programs and projects to close capability gaps and expand mission competencies. This process is a customer-led forum through which the identification of functional capability gaps and the prioritization of these gaps across the department are formalized. The Capstone IPTs manage the research and development efforts of DHS S&T and enable the proper allocation of resources to the highest priority needs established by the DHS operating components.

The Capstone IPT process is a model that requires participation and input from several DHS stakeholders. This collaborative effort centers on the principle that the customer is "the focus" of this process. The product and technology outputs of the Capstone IPT process are driven by customer requirements from start to finish. The customer is involved throughout the process to ensure that they receive products and technologies specifically aligned to their detailed operating requirements. Ultimately, our customers receive quality products that effectively deliver the necessary, mission-critical capabilities to secure our nation.

Led by the DHS S&T customer, Capstone IPTs bring together DHS S&T division heads, acquisition partners, and end users (operating components, field agents, and supporting first responders—customers of DHS) involved in the research, development, testing, evaluation (RDT&E), and acquisition activities. Working together, the Capstone IPT members identify, evaluate, and prioritize the operational requirements necessary to complete missions successfully. Based on information gained from Capstone IPT meetings, DHS S&T providers assess the technological and system development of products that will ultimately be deployed into the field. Figure 4.3 shows the general organization of a Capstone IPT. The figure also contains the specific members of the Infrastructure Protection IPT. The Office of Infrastructure Protection chairs the Infrastructure Protection IPT on behalf of the Sector Coordinating Councils. The formalization of efforts between the Office of Infrastructure Protection and the Capstone IPT process at an early stage allows key stakeholders to identify and address critical capability gaps.

The Capstone IPTs are currently structured to focus on functional, department-level requirements and deal with programmatic and technology issues within the six DHS S&T divisions: Explosives (EXD), Chemical/ Biological (CBD), Command Control and Interoperability (C2I), Borders and Maritime Security (BMD), Human Factors (HFD), and Infrastructure and Geophysical (IGD). Capstone IPTs have been created across thirteen major homeland security core functional areas: Information Sharing/ Management, Cyber Security, People Screening, Border Security, Chemical/Biological Defense, Maritime Security, Counter–Improvised Explosive Devices, Transportation Security, Incident Management, Interoperability, Cargo Security, Infrastructure Protection, and First Responders.

Each Capstone IPT is chaired or cochaired by senior leadership from a DHS operating component or federal organizational element with corresponding needs within a specific functional area. The chair/cochair, representing the end users of a delivered capability, engage throughout

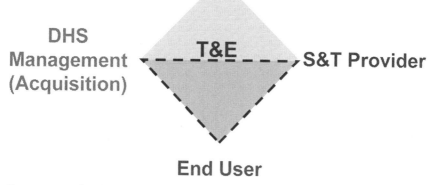

Figure 4.3a. The above "diamond" shows the structure of the Capstone IPT model.

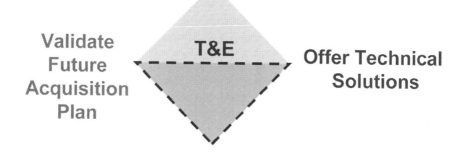

Figure 4.3b. The above "diamond" shows the model's output functions carried out by each IPT member.

Infrastructure Protection IPT

Office of Infrastructure Protection (Requirements Sponsor)

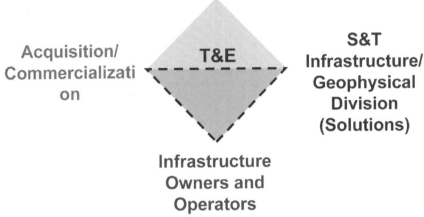

Acquisition/ Commercializati on

T&E

S&T Infrastructure/ Geophysical Division (Solutions)

Infrastructure Owners and Operators

Figure 4.3c.   The above "diamond" shows the actual organization of the Infrastructure Protection IPT.

the process to identify, define, and prioritize current and future requirements and ensure that planned technology and/or product transitions and acquisition programs, commercialization efforts, and standards development are optimally suited to their operational requirements. Operating components, field agents, first responders, and other noncaptive end users with an interest in the core functional areas of a Capstone IPT are welcome to participate and contribute throughout the Capstone IPT process. See figure 4.3 (b) for the captive members for each IPT.

Capstone IPTs purposefully cover very broad core functional areas. This broad focus aids in reducing the duplication of efforts geared toward various operating components of DHS. It is often the case that a given capability gap is experienced by numerous operating components and stakeholders simultaneously and can thus share in the capabilities provided. Technology development is functionally aligned to allow technologies to be used in support of multiple operating components and customer sets within DHS. The effective management and communication of capability gaps ensures that similar efforts are either combined or developed in concert so that required capabilities are provided to as many stakeholders sharing similar capability gaps, reducing overall technology development costs and accelerating the time-to-market for certain capabilities.

DHS S&T Capstone IPTs
Gathering Mechanism for Customer Requirements:

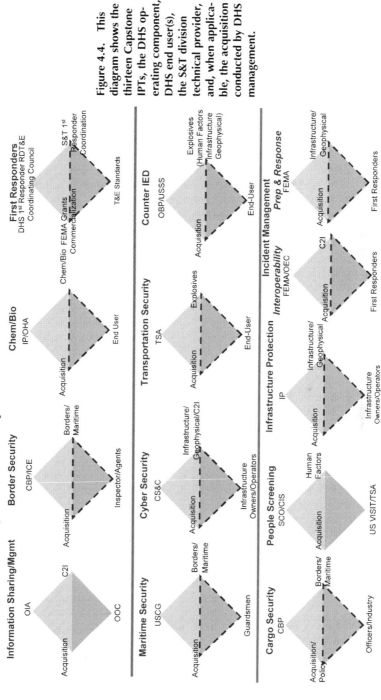

Information Sharing/Mgmt
OIA
Acquisition — C2I
OOC

Border Security
CBP/ICE
Acquisition — Borders/ Maritime
Inspector/Agents

Chem/Bio
IP/OHA
Acquisition
End User

First Responders
DHS 1st Responder RDT&E Coordinating Council
Chem/Bio FEMA Grants Commercialization — S&T 1st Responder Coordination
T&E Standards

Maritime Security
USCG
Acquisition — Borders/ Maritime
Guardsmen

Cyber Security
CS&C
Acquisition — Infrastructure/ Geophysical/C2I
Infrastructure Owners/Operators

Transportation Security
TSA
Acquisition — Explosives
End-User

Counter IED
OBP/USSS
Acquisition — Explosives (Human Factors Infrastructure Geophysical)
End-User

Cargo Security
CBP
Acquisition/ Policy — Borders/ Maritime
Officers/Industry

People Screening
SCO/CIS
Acquisition — Human Factors
US VISIT/TSA

Infrastructure Protection
IP
Acquisition — Infrastructure/ Geophysical
Infrastructure Owners/Operators

Incident Management
Interoperability
FEMA/OEC
Acquisition — C2I
First Responders

Prep & Response
FEMA
Acquisition — Infrastructure/ Geophysical
First Responders

Figure 4.4. This diagram shows the thirteen Capstone IPTs, the DHS operating component, DHS end user(s), the S&T division technical provider, and, when applicable, the acquisition conducted by DHS management.

The mission of the Infrastructure/Geophysical Division (IGD) is to improve the nation's preparedness and response to natural and man-made threats by developing technology to enhance situational awareness, emergency response capabilities, and critical infrastructure protection. The Infrastructure/Geophysical Division supports federal, state, local, tribal, territorial, and private sector entities for all-hazards events that impact both the U.S. population and critical infrastructure.

IGD conducts research and development (R&D) activities for the eighteen critical infrastructure and key resource (CIKR) sectors identified in the NIPP. The NIPP provides the overarching approach for integrating the nation's many CIKR protection initiatives into a single national effort.

- IGD receives the highest-priority capability gaps from the eighteen CIKR sectors as identified in the Sector Annual Reports. IGD works with the Office of Infrastructure Protection, R&D Project Office, to analyze, organize, and prioritize the gaps.
- IGD gathers customer requirements through the Capstone Integrated Product Team (IPT) process, which is chaired by the Office of Infrastructure Protection. The Infrastructure Protection Capstone IPT comprises staff from the Office of Infrastructure Protection, IGD, as well as the R&D provider and the ultimate end users (infrastructure owners and operators). The Capstone IPT is customer driven and user oriented and provides a mechanism by which owners and operators gain visibility into the R&D development life cycle from inception to completion.
- IGD and IP have formed the Committee on Requirements (CoRe), which focuses on reviewing unfunded and new gaps submitted by the sectors and developing recommendations for a way ahead with these gaps.

Capability Gaps and Enabling Homeland Capabilities

Capstone IPTs generate several outputs that guide the development and fielding of technologies and systems for DHS's stakeholders. The primary role of the Capstone IPTs is to conduct strategic needs analyses to determine and prioritize the capability gaps that exist within a given functional area. Capability gaps are broad descriptions of department-level-identified mission needs that are not met, given current products and/or standards. Capability gaps catalog opportunities for enhanced mission effectiveness or address deficiencies in national capability. Capability gaps often start with "We need to be able to do . . ." statements that identify mission needs rather than suggested solutions. See figure 4.5 for the requirements hierarchy diagram.

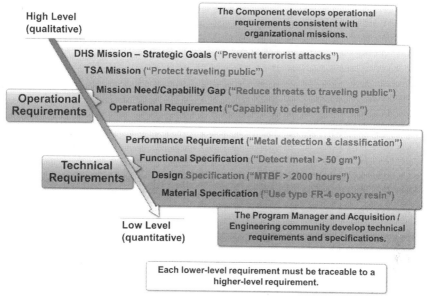

Figure 4.5.   This "requirements hierarchy" shows the evolution of requirements from a high-level macro set of operational requirements to a low-level micro set of technical requirements. Note that each lower-level requirement stems directly from its higher requirement so that all requirements are traceable to the overall DHS mission.

Led by their IPT chairs/cochairs, Capstone IPTs are responsible for the analysis, identification, and prioritization of their capability gaps. Capability gaps can come in several forms. Gaps may appear in the form of modified personnel and resource allocation, training, standards, plans/protocols/procedures, resources, technology, systems, and so on. For those capability gaps requiring technology-based solutions, a grouping of technology components is identified by DHS S&T to address the various needs delineated in the capability gaps. These grouped technology solutions, or Enabling Homeland Capabilities (EHCs), collectively deliver new gap-closing capabilities to the customers. EHCs focus on the technology pieces that develop, mature, and are delivered to DHS acquisition programs; are commercialized; or are validated as a standard within a three-year period or less. DHS S&T develops EHCs that contain quantifiable metrics that allow for effective management of development progress. These metrics define how the EHC will address/close the related capability gap, outline the cost and schedule over the life of the EHC, identify the specific S&T efforts addressed by the EHC, and provide endorsements and recommendations of proposed EHCs and corresponding deliverables by the relevant Capstone IPT. EHCs enable customers and

DHS S&T engineers to focus on discussions related more broadly to overall capability needs and operational requirements rather than discussions simply about potential solutions to problems.

Project-IPTs: Managing the Day-to-Day Development of Capabilities

The Capstone IPT process enables the DHS S&T divisions to interact regularly with their customers to address capability gaps. These capability gaps in many ways are just the beginning. Additional detail about their requirements must be gathered to enable the cost-effective and efficient development of a technology or product. In order to achieve greater insight into the details that comprise each Capstone IPT, Project-IPTs are created to manage specific project areas within a functional area. While Capstone IPT meetings occur at regular intervals throughout the year, Project-IPTs are created to manage closing capability gaps gathered from the larger Capstone IPT on a daily basis. For example, Border Officer Tools and Safety, and Container Security are Project-IPTs for the Border Security and Cargo Security Capstone IPTs, respectively. Project-IPTs consist of several DHS S&T subject matter experts who are responsible for clarifying the capability gaps derived from the Capstone IPTs and for gathering additional insight into operational requirements with the customers for the overall capability enhancement that is necessary. These requirements assist in decomposing a high-level capability gap into the individual components that may comprise a potential solution. Through this process the grouping of individual technologies into an integrated system creates the overall EHC.

The Project-IPTs work closely with DHS customers to develop a robust understanding of customer needs, through an operational requirements document (C-ORD), to define clearly the specific requirements that must be met in order for a technological solution to address a given problem. Development of detailed C-ORDs further enhances the direction in which technology and product development efforts progress and further reduces duplication of effort across various Project and Capstone IPTs. These subject matter experts are also involved in conducting market surveys, analyses of alternatives, and other functions related to technology and product evaluation, ensuring that developed capabilities are aligned to customers' needs. Additionally, Project-IPTs serve a critical role in integrating developed capabilities into EHCs and fully deployable systems that provide customers with enhanced mission capabilities. All DHS agencies are responsible for integrating and fielding the technology deliverables into operational systems scheduled for delivery to their operating component.

Management—DHS Leadership and DHS S&T

The Capstone IPTs prioritize EHC proposals that respond to customer capability requirements. DHS leadership has a critical role in determining Capstone IPT funding levels and investments once prioritized EHCs are identified. Once approved, budgets are submitted, solicitations may be issued, pre-award technical reviews are conducted, and commercialization efforts are considered. DHS leadership conducts reviews of current EHCs every six months to ensure that EHCs meet cost objectives and that technical development is progressing along milestones. DHS leadership also reviews new EHCs and continually reviews ongoing EHCs in order to make informed decisions regarding continued funding of programs.

The Transition Office manages the process to develop and deliver required technologies/products as defined in the EHCs. Working with its customer requirements, DHS S&T proposes the technology-based solutions in approved EHCs to the Capstone IPTs. By understanding the needs and requirements of its customers, DHS S&T identifies the programs that are ineffective/insufficient in meeting the EHC expectations and offers technical solutions to address the stated requirements. DHS S&T works to conduct market and technology scans to find technology-based solutions that can be developed, matured, and delivered to DHS acquisition programs, commercialized or validated as a standard within a three-year period.

There are several ways products can transition "out of the lab" into fully developed, widely distributed products for the large customer communities. Figure 4.6 identifies possible transition paths to deliver products to customers. DHS S&T may recommend available commercial-off-the-shelf (COTS) products or other non-S&T alternatives in lieu of developing a new DHS S&T solution. DHS S&T also reviews private sector responses to solicitations for capabilities that can be readily addressed with COTS products. Once development plans are approved, DHS S&T engages and involves the customer via technology demonstrations and experimentation to ensure adequate customer feedback throughout the development life cycle. DHS S&T manages costs, schedules, and technical performance of programs under the oversight of the Capstone IPT. The director of transition chairs monthly status meetings that allow technology execution problems to be discussed and resolved in a timely and effective manner.

Technology Transition Agreements

Technology Transition Agreements (TTAs) represent a good-faith contract between the DHS S&T developer and the DHS customer. The

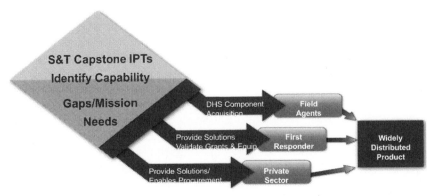

Figiure 4.6.　DHS has three major methods to transition products to end users. DHS field agents are captive end users of the Capstone IPT process while the first-responder community is typically able to select its own solutions. Capabilities are also transitioned to CIKR owners and operators in the private sector. All newly proposed DHS programs must now identify technologies/products already in development in the private sector that are aligned with end user requirements that enable users to make informed purchasing decisions.

TTA is negotiated and signed at the product level by those communities responsible for delivering or advocating a specific product or technology. As a consensus agreement, the TTA is signed by all of the stakeholders responsible for the technology/product in order for continued funding. This good-faith agreement determines the specific exit criteria that must be demonstrated in order for the "hand-off" of the technology/product to the customer. In the case of the Infrastructure Protection IPT, the Office of Infrastructure Protection again serves as the representation to the Capstone IPT process on behalf of CIKR owners and operators.

The TTA provides a detailed description of the deliverable promised by the DHS S&T program managers. The customer program manager certifies that the need for the product or technology is consistent with the needs/requirements as defined by their operating component, and the requirements or acquisition agents state their commitment to integrate the successfully demonstrated technology/product into an identified and funded acquisition program. The TTA ensures that all parties explicitly understand the deliverable is aligned to customer needs and that a funding source is available and aligned with the customer's needs. If any problems are identified by DHS S&T, customer agency, or acquisition offices, all parties are informed and decisions are made regarding continued funding. Once the TTA has been signed, the next step is to move forward with product development and eventual product deployment to the customers.

Using Technology to Give Boots on the Ground a Voice

Traditional communication through e-mail and phone calls has proven insufficient in gathering and compiling input from the sheer number of stakeholders responsible for providing protection to our homeland. There remains room for improvement in gathering requirements from the many different stakeholders across the country. In many ways, the private sector possesses much more reliable information than is seen from DHS's previous, seemingly disjointed, approach. Continued work through the Capstone IPTs and DHS's Requirements Development Initiative training materials will reduce the inefficiency of DHS personnel by providing a common point of entry for end user representatives and perspectives.

Just as needed is deployable technology to create a Community of Practitioners (CoP). The Department of Defense (DoD) has invested in these kinds of technologies to enable reaching not only the millions of first responders nationwide but also other customers and potentially authorized stakeholders (other federal agencies, private sector, venture community, etc). Advanced technologies like the "Semantic Web 3.0" will aid in the communal and open development of capability gaps, C-ORDs, potential available market sizing/applications, and so on, all to the benefit of the American taxpayer, government, and private sector. We are finalizing plans to initiate a pilot program to harness these technologies to engage various user communities to enable broad-based development of widely accepted operational requirements. Figure 4.7 shows graphically the evolving processes used for developing requirements at DHS S&T.

It is clear that DHS S&T needs to lead the development of an easy-to-use technology to generate a CoP for its customer communities. The vast majority of the millions of DHS's stakeholders need to be invited to play an active role in creating, editing, and prioritizing detailed operational requirements to be used by DHS in order to provide (or facilitate through its commercialization efforts) solutions for the stakeholder communities. This approach enables both a bottom-up and top-down view of detailed user requirements—avoiding the age-old discussion of whether a bottom-up or top-down approach is superior. New social networking technologies have opened new opportunities that allow communication to flow and leverage the merit of both approaches.

DHS S&T plans to create a set of detailed operational requirements of a system prototype that, in general:

- Effectively leverages advanced social networking and information sharing (utilizing semantic architecture and TRL management) using genuine DHS scenarios such as developing/editing C-ORDs, to the benefit of taxpayers in an open and transparent way for all to participate easily

Evolution of Change:
DHS Providing Better Information about its Needs

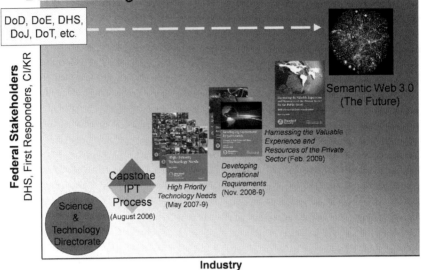

Industry
Business, Venture Capital/Angel Investment, Strategic Partnerships

Figure 4.7.   DHS has progressed in the way that it reaches out to its stakeholders to learn about their needs. Advanced social networking technologies have the potential to greatly enhance communications and understanding of needs.

- Expandable to millions of users in the first-responder, CIKR, and potential solution providers (private sector) communities
- Expandable to include vital interagency partners like DoE, DoD, and National Laboratories for gauging potential users and potential available market sizing
- Expandable to include venture capital, angel investor, and corporate investor communities if desired and/or required

PRODUCT REALIZATION
THROUGH REQUIREMENTS ARTICULATION

We can all point to many examples in both our professional and private lives where the lack of communication or unclear terminology has created misunderstandings, redundancy problems, and myriad other issues. Effective communication is critical to cost-effective and efficient interactions between various parties seeking a mutually beneficial relationship or partnership.

At every step of product development, it is critical to understand and meet user needs. Developing requirements to guide effective product development is not a trivial effort, but with proper planning, dedication, and communication, successful product development can yield measurable positive results and provide DHS operating components, first responders, CIKR owners and operators, and other stakeholders with resources necessary to carry out their mission-critical objectives to protect our nation.

The initial phase of product realization is a mission needs assessment. This assessment should be conducted in relation to the overall mission for an organization. This exercise identifies capabilities needed to perform required functions, highlights deficiencies in functional capability, and documents the results of the analysis. Some of these capabilities may already be addressable with existing products, systems, or services currently accessible by an organization. Analysis may also show that material solutions may not be necessary to solve a problem, as issues may be resolved through resource redistribution, staffing adjustments, standards development, or other actions that do not require the fielding of new technologies. Additionally, a mission needs assessment serves to identify deficiencies in current and projected capabilities. In the event that current products are not able to address a particular capability, a capability gap exists. Briefly, capability gaps are defined by the difference between current operational capabilities and those necessary capabilities needed to perform mission-critical objectives that remain unsatisfied. Capability gaps must be listed in terms of an overall need to perform a specific task and should avoid explaining how that task should be achieved. Capability gaps that are discovered and articulated from a mission needs assessment form the foundation of the Capstone IPT process.

For example, faced with the problem of potential intruders to a sensitive facility, we might define the requirement as "build a wall," whereas the real requirement is "detect, thwart, and capture intruders." Our wall might "thwart" intruders (or might not, if they're adept at tunneling), but it would not detect them or facilitate their capture. In short, the solution would not solve the problem.

The robust capability gap to "detect, thwart, and capture intruders" includes no preconceived solutions and prompts us to analyze alternative conceptual solutions and choose the best. One way to ensure that we are defining a problem, rather than a solution, is to begin the statement of the requirement with the phrase "we need the capability to. . . ." It's nearly impossible to complete this sentence with a solution ("a wall"), and much easier to complete the sentence with a problem ("detect intruders"). Capability gaps and requirements should address what a system should do, rather than how to do it. This approach is sometimes called capability-based planning. It is a very simple yet powerful concept.

Properly defining clear and concise capability gaps is a necessary first step in product realization. This high-level understanding of a problem is a key part in the communication of needs. One may find that capability gaps are oftentimes common for multiple cross-sections of DHS operating components and supporting elements such as the first-responder community and private sector critical infrastructure owner/operators. Discovering these commonalities is a fundamental aspect of the DHS S&T Capstone IPT Process, which seeks to reduce duplication of efforts and expedite product transition.

WHY REQUIREMENTS?

Capstone IPTs generate several outputs that guide the development and fielding of products, services, and systems for DHS operating components, primarily in the form of capability gaps that exist within a particular functional area. These broad descriptions of department-level-identified mission needs that are not met given current products and/or standards catalog opportunities for enhanced mission effectiveness or address deficiencies in national capability. However, capability gaps are just the first step in providing solutions to mission-critical needs. Operational requirements bring detailed information to support the capability gaps and define actionable information through detailed definitions of the problems, which need to be further delineated into technical requirements.

A *requirement* is an attribute of a product, service, or system necessary to produce an outcome(s) that satisfies the needs of a person, group or organization. Requirements therefore define "the problem." In contrast, "the solution" is defined by technical *specifications*.

Defining requirements is the process of determining what to make before making it. Requirements definition creates a method in which appropriate decisions about product or system functionality and performance can be made before investing the time and money to develop it. Understanding requirements early removes a great deal of guesswork in the planning stages and helps to ensure that the end users and product developers are "on the same page."

Requirements provide criteria against which solutions can be tested and evaluated. They offer detailed metrics that can be used to objectively measure a possible solution's effectiveness, ensuring informed purchasing decisions on products, systems, or services that achieve the stated operational goals. A detailed requirements analysis can uncover hidden requirements as well as discover common problems across programs and various DHS operating components. Detailed operational requirements will guide product development so that solutions' specifications actively solve the stated problems.

We could save ourselves a lot of work if we jumped straight to "the solution" without defining "the problem." Why don't we do that? Because if we take that shortcut we are likely to find that our solution may not be the best choice among possible alternatives or, even worse, we're likely to find that our "solution" doesn't even solve the problem!

Defining requirements and adhering to developing solutions to address those needs is often referred to as "requirements-pull." In this situation, user requirements drive product development and guide the path forward as the requirements dictate. This is a powerful circumstance in which fulfilling requirements becomes the central focus of product development and no possible solution is disregarded as long as it facilitates addressing the stated operational requirements.

At the other extreme from the "requirements-pull," or "market-pull," approach is "technology push." Here we start with a solution (perhaps a new technology) and see what problems it might enable us to solve. The danger in this approach is to become enamored of "the solution" and neglect to ensure that it actually solves a problem. With technology push, it is likely that actual user requirements may be modified or even ignored in order to "force-fit" the desired solution. A historical example was the product known as Picture Phone introduced (and discontinued) in the 1960s when the advance of telecommunications technology first made possible the transmission and display of video as well as voice. Picture Phone, which allowed telephone users to see each other during a call, was a technological success but a market disaster. It turned out that callers generally don't want to be seen, as a bit of unbiased market analysis would have disclosed.

Technology push should not be ignored, but if the goal is successful transition to the field with acceptable risk, the technology being pushed must be compared to alternative solutions against a real set of user requirements.

Aside from assuring that the "solution" actually solves the "problem," requirements-driven design has a further advantage in that the requirements provide criteria against which a product's successful development can be measured. Specifically, if the product was developed to address a set of quantified operational requirements, then its success is measured by operational test and evaluation (OT&E) to validate that an end user can use the product and achieve the stated operational goals.

Prior to OT&E, it is common practice to subject products to developmental test and evaluation (DT&E). The purpose of DT&E is to verify that the product meets its technical specifications, which are the engineers' interpretation of the operational requirements. Such DT&E does not obviate the need for OT&E, which validates that the engineers' solution not only is technically successful but also represents a successful interpretation of the end users' needs, satisfying the original operational requirements (not just the technical specifications) when operated by representative users.

Often requirements are stated in terms of "threshold values" and "objective values," where the "objective value" is the desired performance and the "threshold value" is the minimum acceptable performance. This formalism is useful in allowing stretch goals to be asserted without saddling the system development with unacceptable risk.

THE REQUIREMENTS HIERARCHY AND TRACEABILITY

To reiterate the definitions above, the documents that govern product realization include requirements, which define the problem, and specifications, which define the solution. Nevertheless, the hierarchy of requirements and specifications is more complex than that simple dichotomy, as previously discussed and revisited in figure 4.8.

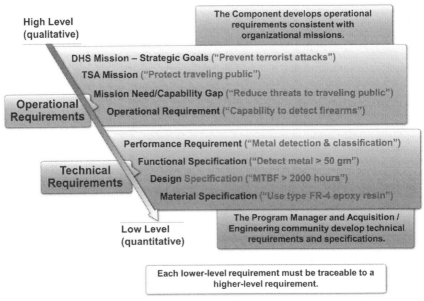

Figure 4.8. The requirements hierarchy drives the traceability of requirements from top to bottom.

The hierarchy is divided into two domains, operational requirements and technical requirements, highlighted in yellow and blue in the figure, representing the "problem space" and the "solution space" respectively. You will remember that the Capstone IPT process begins when S&T works with their customers to define and articulate capability gaps. The DHS stakeholder, representing the end users in the field (the operators), is also responsible for all operational requirements, from the top-level mission requirements to the detailed system-level operational requirements. It is important to articulate these operational requirements in detail to avoid misunderstandings later in the product development life cycle. A system developer is responsible for translating the operational requirements into a system solution, documented in a hierarchy of technical specifications.

The highest-level type of technical "specification" is actually called a performance "requirement." A performance requirement actually represents a bridge from operational requirements to the engineering interpretation of those requirements. Put another way, in the course of developing a new system it is necessary to transform the system operational requirements, which are stated from a given operating component's perspective as required outcomes of system action, into a set of system performance requirements, which are stated in terms of engineering characteristics.

Working through the requirements hierarchy, requirements development is the process of decomposing the problems broadly outlined in the capability gaps gleaned from the mission needs assessment.

The requirements and specifications are described below, first those that define the problem and then those that define the solution:

Problem Definition
- **Mission Needs Statement (MNS)/Capability Gap** is required by the DHS *Acquisition Review Process* (Management Directive 102-01) and is developed by the DHS sponsor (S&T's customer) who represents the end users and is the first step in the Capstone IPT process. The MNS provides a high-level description of the mission need (or, equivalently, capability gap) and is used to justify the initiation of an acquisition program.
- **Operational Requirements Document (ORD)** is also required by the DHS *Acquisition Review Process* and, like the MNS, is developed by the DHS stakeholder. The ORD specifies operational requirements and a concept of operations (CONOPS), written from the point of view of the end user. Note that we place a "C" in front of "ORD" to connote that an ORD is being used in a commercialization model because we believe widely distributed products/services are possible due to market size. The C-ORD is independent of any particular

implementation, should not refer to any specific technologies, and does not commit the developers to a design. A well-written C-ORD states the problem that must be solved along with the necessary capabilities that a system must perform.

Solution Definition

- **Performance Requirements** represent a bridge between the operationally oriented view of the system defined in the C-ORD and an engineering-oriented view required to define the solution. Performance requirements are an interpretation, not a replacement of operational requirements. Performance requirements define the functions that the system *and its subsystems* must perform to achieve the operational objectives and define the performance parameters for each function. These definitions are in engineering rather than operational terms.
- **Functional Specifications** define the system solution functionally, though not physically. Sometimes called the "system specification" or "A-Spec," these specifications define functions at the system, subsystem, and component level including:
  - Configuration, organization, and interfaces between system elements
  - Performance characteristics and compatibility requirements
  - Human engineering
  - Security and safety
  - Reliability, maintainability, and availability
  - Support requirements such as shipping, handling, storage, training, and special facilities
- **Design Specifications** convert the functional specifications of *what* the system is to do into a specification of *how* the required functions are to be implemented in hardware and software. The design specifications therefore govern the materialization of the system components.
- **Material Specifications** are an example of lower-level supporting specifications that support the higher-level specifications. Material specifications define the required properties of materials and parts used to fabricate the system. Other supporting specifications include *process specifications* (defining required properties of fabrication processes such as soldering and welding) and *product specifications* (defining required properties of nondevelopmental items to be procured commercially).

CHARACTERISTICS OF GOOD REQUIREMENTS

Requirements engineering is difficult and time-consuming, but must be done well if the final product or system is to be judged by the end users

Table 4.1.   Attributes of Good Requirements

Necessary	Can the system meet prioritized, real needs without it? If yes, the requirement isn't necessary.
Verifiable	Can one ensure that the requirement is met in the system? If not, the requirement should be removed or revised.
Unambiguous	Can the requirement be interpreted in more than one way? If yes, the requirement should be clarified or removed. Ambiguous or poorly worded requirements can lead to serious misunderstandings and needless rework.
Complete	Are all conditions under which the requirement applies stated? In addition, does the specification include all known requirements?
Consistent	Can the requirement be met without conflicting with any other requirement? If not, the requirement should be revised or removed.
Traceable	Is the origin (source) of the requirement known, and is there a clear path from the requirement back to its origin?
Concise	Is the requirement stated simply and clearly?
Standard constructs	Requirements are stated as imperative needs using "shall." Statements indicating "goals" or using the words "will" or "should" are not imperatives.

as successful. From the International Council of Systems Engineers (IN-COSE) Requirements Working Group,[1] Table 4.1 presents eight attributes of good requirements.

DEVELOPING COMMERCIALIZATION-BASED OPERATIONAL REQUIREMENTS (C-ORDS): CUSTOMER INPUT

So far, we've discussed operational requirements but have not provided any insight into how to develop them. In an effort to provide a basic framework for the articulation and documentation of operational requirements when there are large potential markets present, the operational requirements document (C-ORD) was created. C-ORDs provide a clear definition and articulation of a given problem, providing several layers of information that comprise the overall problem. Using resources such as this book and the accompanying template, we have tried to simplify and streamline the process of communicating requirements. C-ORDs can also be used in acquisition, procurement, internal development, commercialization, and outreach programs—any situation that dictates detailed requirements (e.g., RFQ, BAA, RFP, RFI, etc.). It's clear to see that it's cost-effective and efficient for both DHS and all of its stakeholders to communicate needs clearly and effectively.

C-OPERATIONAL REQUIREMENTS DOCUMENT

1.0 General Description of Operational Capability
    1.1. Capability Gap
    1.2. Overall Mission Area Description
    1.3. Description of the Proposed System
    1.4. Supporting Analysis
    1.5. Mission the Proposed System Will Accomplish
    1.6. Operational and Support Concept
        1.6.1. Concept of Operations
        1.6.2. Support Concept
2.0. Threat
3.0. Existing System Shortfalls
4.0. Capabilities Required
    4.1. Operational Performance Parameters
    4.2. Key Performance Parameters (KPPs)
    4.3. System Performance
        4.3.1. Mission Scenarios
        4.3.2. System Performance Parameters
        4.3.3. Interoperability
        4.3.4. Human Interface Requirements
        4.3.5. Logistics and Readiness
        4.3.6. Other System Characteristics
5.0. System Support
    5.1. Maintenance
    5.2. Supply
    5.3. Support Equipment
    5.4. Training
    5.5. Transportation and Facilities
6.0. Force Structure
7.0. Schedule
8.0. System Affordability

Figure 4.9. The Contents of a C-Operational Requirements Document

Let's first look at the contents of a typical Commercialization-based Operational Requirements Document (C-ORD) shown in figure 4.9.

The complexity of the intended system and its operational context will govern the required level of detail in the C-ORD. The most difficult sections to develop are typically Section 4.0, which describes the capabilities required of the system to be developed, and Section 1.6, which describes the operational and support concepts.

There is no "silver bullet" to solve the potential challenges in developing a C-ORD, but since the issues are universal, there is a wealth of literature that offers approaches to requirements development. As an example, here are nine requirements-elicitation techniques described in the *Business Analyst Body of Knowledge* (from the International Institute of Business Analysis).[2]

1. Brainstorming
   - Purpose
     - An excellent way of eliciting many creative ideas for an area of interest. Structured brainstorming produces numerous creative ideas.
   - Strengths
     - Able to elicit many ideas in a short time period.
     - Nonjudgmental environment enables outside-the-box thinking.
   - Weaknesses
     - Dependent on participants' creativity.
2. Document Analysis
   - Purpose
     - Used if the objective is to gather details of the "as-is" environment such as existing standard procedures or attributes that need to be included in a new system.
   - Strengths
     - Not starting from a blank page.
     - Leveraging existing materials to discover and/or confirm requirements.
     - A means to crosscheck requirements from other elicitation techniques such as interviews, job shadowing, surveys, or focus groups.
   - Weaknesses
     - Limited to "as-is" perspective.
     - Existing documentation may not be up-to-date or valid.
     - Can be a time-consuming and even tedious process to locate the relevant information.
3. Focus Group
   - Purpose
     - A means to elicit ideas and attitudes about a specific product, service, or opportunity in an interactive group environment. The participants share their impressions, preferences, and needs, guided by a moderator.
   - Strengths
     - Ability to elicit data from a group of people in a single session saves time and costs as compared to conducting individual interviews with the same number of people.
     - Effective for learning people's attitudes, experiences, and desires.

      o Active discussion and the ability to ask others questions creates an environment where participants can consider their personal view in relation to other perspectives.
- Weaknesses
  - In the group setting, participants may be concerned about issues of trust, or may be unwilling to discuss sensitive or personal topics.
  - Data collected (what people say) may not be consistent with how people actually behave.
  - If the group is too homogenous, the group's responses may not represent the complete set of requirements.
  - A skilled moderator is needed to manage the group interactions and discussions.
  - It may be difficult to schedule the group for the same date and time.

4. Interface Analysis
- Purpose
  - An interface is a connection between two components. Most systems require one or more interfaces with external parties, systems, or devices. Interface analysis is initiated by project managers and analysts to reach agreement with the stakeholders on what interfaces are needed. Subsequent analysis uncovers the detailed requirements for each interface.
- Strengths
  - The elicitation of the interfaces' functional requirements early in the system life cycle provides valuable details for project management:
    - Impact on delivery date. Knowing what interfaces are needed, their complexity and testing needs enables more accurate project planning and potential savings in time and cost.
    - Collaboration with other systems or projects. If the interface to an existing system, product, or device and the interface already exist, it may not be easily changed. If the interface is new, then the ownership, development, and testing of the interface needs to be addressed and coordinated in both projects' plan. In either case, eliciting the interface requirements will require negotiation and cooperation between the owning systems.
- Weaknesses
  - Does not provide an understanding of the total system or operational concept since this technique only exposes the inputs, outputs, and key data elements related to the interfaces.

5. Interview
   - Purpose
     - A systematic approach to elicit information from a person or group of people in an informal or formal setting by asking relevant questions and documenting the responses.
   - Strengths
     - Encourages participation and establishes rapport with the stakeholder.
     - Simple, direct technique that can be used in varying situations.
     - Allows the interviewer and participant to have full discussions and explanations of the questions and answers.
     - Enables observations of nonverbal behavior.
     - The interviewer can ask follow-up and probing questions to confirm own understanding.
     - Maintains focus using clear objectives for the interview that are agreed upon by all participants and can be met in the time allotted.
   - Weaknesses
     - Interviews are not an ideal means of reaching consensus across a group of stakeholders.
     - Requires considerable commitment and involvement of the participants.
     - Training is required to conduct good interviews. Unstructured interviews, especially, require special skills. Facilitation/virtual facilitation and active listening are a few of them.
     - Depth of follow-up questions may be dependent on the interviewer's knowledge of the operational domain.
     - Transcription and analysis of interview data can be complex and expensive.
     - Resulting documentation is subject to interviewer's interpretation.
6. Observation
   - Purpose
     - A means to elicit requirements by assessing the operational environment. This technique is appropriate when documenting details about current operations or if the project intends to enhance or change a current operational concept.
   - Strengths
     - Provides a realistic and practical insight into field operations by getting a hands-on feel for current operations.
     - Elicits details of informal communication and ways people actually work around the system that may not be documented anywhere.

- Weaknesses
  - ○ Only possible for existing operations.
  - ○ Could be time-consuming.
  - ○ May be disruptive to the person being shadowed.
  - ○ Unusual exceptions and critical situations that happen infrequently may not occur during the observation.
  - ○ May not well work if current operations involve a lot of intellectual work or other work that is not easily observable.
7. Prototyping
   - Purpose
     - ○ Prototyping, when used as an elicitation technique, aims to uncover and visualize user requirements before the system is designed or developed.
   - Strengths
     - ○ Supports users who are more comfortable and effective at articulating their needs by using pictures or hands-on prototypes, as prototyping lets them "see" the future system's interface.
     - ○ A prototype allows for early user interaction and feedback.
     - ○ A throwaway prototype is an inexpensive means to quickly uncover and confirm user interface requirements.
     - ○ A revolutionary prototype can demonstrate what is feasible with existing technology, and where there may be technical gaps.
     - ○ An evolutionary prototype provides a vehicle for designers and developers to learn about the users' interface needs and to evolve system requirements.
   - Weaknesses
     - ○ Depending on the complexity of the target system, using prototyping to elicit requirements can take considerable time if the process is bogged down by the "hows" rather than "whats."
     - ○ Assumptions about the underlying technology may need to be made in order to present a starting prototype.
     - ○ A prototype may lead users to set unrealistic expectations of the delivered system's performance, reliability, and usability characteristics.
8. Requirements Workshop
   - Purpose
     - ○ A requirements workshop is a structured way to capture requirements. A workshop may be used to scope, discover, define, prioritize, and reach closure on requirements for the target system. Well-run workshops are considered one of the most effective ways to deliver high-quality requirements quickly. They promote trust, mutual understanding, and strong communications among the project stakeholders and

project team, produce deliverables that structure, and guide future analysis.

- Strengths
  - ○ A workshop can be a means to elicit detailed requirements in a relatively short period of time.
  - ○ A workshop provides a means for stakeholders to collaborate, make decisions, and gain a mutual understanding of the requirements.
  - ○ Workshop costs are often lower than the cost of performing multiple interviews.
  - ○ A requirements workshop enables the participants to work together to reach consensus, which is typically a cheaper and faster approach than doing serial interviews, as interviews may yield conflicting requirements and the effort needed to resolve those conflicts across all interviewees can be very costly.
  - ○ Feedback is immediate if the facilitator's interpretation of requirements is fed back immediately to the stakeholders and confirmed.
- Weaknesses
  - ○ Due to stakeholders' availability it may be difficult to schedule the workshop.
  - ○ The success of the workshop is highly dependent on the expertise of the facilitator and knowledge of the participants.
  - ○ Requirements workshops that involve too many participants can slow down the workshop process, thus negatively affecting the schedule. Conversely, collecting input from too few participants can lead to overlooking requirements that are important to users or to specifying requirements that do not represent the needs of the majority of the users.

9. Survey/Questionnaire
   - Purpose
     - ○ A means of eliciting information from many people, anonymously, in a relatively short time. A survey can collect information about customers, products, operational practices, and attitudes. A survey is often referred to as a questionnaire.
   - Strengths
     - ○ When using "closed-ended" questions, effective in obtaining quantitative data for use in statistical analysis.
     - ○ When using open-ended questions, the survey results may yield insights and opinions not easily obtainable through other elicitation techniques.
     - ○ Does not typically require significant time from the responders.

- ○ Effective and efficient when stakeholders are not located at one place.
  - ○ May result in large number of responses.
  - ○ Quick and relatively inexpensive to administer.
- Weaknesses
  - ○ Use of open-ended questions requires more analysis.
  - ○ To achieve unbiased results, specialized skills in statistical sampling methods are needed when the decision has been made to survey a sample subset.
  - ○ Some questions may be left unanswered or answered incorrectly due to their ambiguous nature.
  - ○ May require follow-up questions or more survey iterations depending on the answers provided.
  - ○ Not well suited for collecting information on actual behaviors.

ADDRESSING REQUIREMENTS VERSUS PROPOSING SOLUTIONS

When employing efforts to elicit and explain requirements using any of these methods, it is imperative to steadfastly *avoid requirements that define potential solutions or otherwise restrict the potential solution space.* Again, requirements only deal with the problem at hand and do not discuss the preferred or desired tool or way to go about solving the problem. Any standards or limitations that a system must address within a given scenario are important to mention within a C-ORD, but entire solution sets may not be discounted, as potential scientific advances may make certain technologies feasible. While it is necessary and useful to understand the current state of the art within a given technology space and knowledge about potential solutions that may already be in development, *requirements are meant to simply define problems.* Properly drafted requirements allow for a variety of solutions, each with their own advantages and disadvantages, for consideration as potential ways to address a problem. *Solution-agnostic requirements prevent limiting and defining the outcome of product realization.* Within the context of the Operational Requirements Document template described in detail below, the solution definition aspect of the requirements hierarchy is purposefully not addressed. This is useful given that an open and honest review of one's needs might show that a preconceived notion about a desired solution may turn out not to be the best solution, or that modifications to existing products or services may be necessary and useful to end users.

The following insert provides the C-Operational Requirements Document template. This template guides you through drafting a new C-ORD by describing the information that should be captured in each section of the document. This template is useful in organizing and delineating the problem to be solved. Several important topics are covered by the template, and it assists in presenting many questions that must be addressed in order to articulate fully and clearly the desired outcome from deploying a system to address a problem. See chapter 11 for actual examples of C-ORDs.

COMMERCIALIZATION-BASED OPERATIONAL REQUIREMENTS DOCUMENT TEMPLATE

1. General Description of Operational Capability
In this section, summarize the capability gap that the product or system is intended to address, describe the overall mission area, describe the proposed system solution, and provide a summary of any supporting analyses. Additionally, briefly describe the operational and support concepts.

   1.1. Capability Gap
Describe the analysis and rationale for acquiring a new product or system, and identify the DHS component that contains or represents the end users. Also, name the Capstone IPT, if any, that identified the capability gap.

   1.2. Overall Mission Area Description
Define and describe the overall mission area to which the capability gap pertains, including its users and its scope.

   1.3. Description of the Proposed System
Describe the proposed product or system. Describe how the product or system will provide the capabilities and functional improvements needed to address the capability gap. Do not describe a specific technology or system solution. Instead, describe a conceptual solution for illustrative purposes.

   1.4. Supporting Analysis
Describe the analysis that supports the proposed system. If a formal study was performed, identify the study and briefly provide a summary of results.

   1.5. Mission the Proposed System Will Accomplish
Define the missions that the proposed system will be tasked to accomplish.

   1.6. Operational and Support Concept

      1.6.1. Concept of Operations
Briefly describe the concept of operations for the system. How will the system be used, and what is its organizational setting? It is appropriate to include a graphic that depicts the system and its operation. Also, describe the system's interoperability requirements with other systems.

      1.6.2. Support Concept
Briefly describe the support concept for the system. How will the system (hardware and software) be maintained? Who will maintain it? How, where, and by whom will spare parts be provisioned? How, where, and by whom will operators be trained?

2. Threat

If the system is intended as a countermeasure to a threat, summarize the threat to be countered and the projected threat environment.

3. Existing System Shortfalls

Describe why existing systems cannot meet current or projected requirements. Describe what new capabilities are needed to address the gap between current capabilities and required capabilities.

4. Capabilities Required

4.1. Operational Performance Parameters

Identify operational performance parameters (capabilities and characteristics) required for the proposed system. Articulate the requirements in output-oriented and measurable terms. Use Threshold/Objective format and provide criteria and rationale for each requirement.

4.2. Key Performance Parameters (KPPs)

The KPPs are those attributes or characteristics of a system that are considered critical or essential. Failure to meet a KPP threshold value could be the basis to reject a system solution.

4.3 System Performance.

4.3.1 Mission Scenarios

Describe mission scenarios in terms of mission profiles, employment tactics, and environmental conditions.

4.3.2 System Performance Parameters

Identify system performance parameters. Identify KPPs by placing an asterisk in front of the parameter description.

4.3.3 Interoperability

Identify all requirements for the system to provide data, information, materiel, and services to, and accept the same from, other systems, and to use the data, information, materiel, and services so exchanged to enable them to operate effectively together.

4.3.4 Human Interface Requirements

Discuss broad cognitive, physical, and sensory requirements for the operators, maintainers, or support personnel that contribute to, or constrain, total system performance. Provide broad staffing constraints for operators, maintainers, and support personnel.

4.3.5 Logistics and Readiness

Describe the requirements for the system to be supportable and available for operations. Provide performance parameters for availability, reliability, system maintainability, and software maintainability.

4.3.6 Other System Characteristics

Characteristics that tend to be design, cost, and risk drivers.

5. System Support

Establish support objectives for initial and full operational capability. Discuss interfacing systems, transportation and facilities, and standardization and interoperability. Describe the support approach including configuration man-

agement, repair, scheduled maintenance, support operations, software support, and user support (such as training and help desk).

5.1 Maintenance

Identify the types of maintenance to be performed and who will perform the maintenance. Describe methods for upgrades and technology insertions. Also, address post-development software support requirements.

5.2 Supply

Describe the approach to supplying field operators and maintenance technicians with necessary tools, spares, diagnostic equipment, and manuals.

5.3 Support Equipment

Define the standard support equipment to be used by the system. Discuss any need for special test equipment or software development environment

5.4 Training

Describe how the training will ensure that users are certified as capable of operating and using the proposed system.

5.5 Transportation and Facilities

Describe how the system will be transported to the field, identifying any lift constraints. Identify facilities needed for staging and training.

6. Force Structure

Estimate the number of systems or subsystems needed, including spares and training units. Identify organizations and units that will employ the systems being developed and procured, estimating the number of users in each organization or unit.

7. Schedule

To the degree that schedule is a requirement, define target dates for system availability. If a distinction is made between Initial Capability and Full Operational Capability, clarify the difference between the two in terms of system capability and/or numbers of fielded systems.

8. System Affordability

Identify a threshold/objective target price to the user at full-rate production. If price is a KPP, include it in the section on KPPs above.

NOTES

1. Pradip Kar and Michelle Bailey, *Characteristics of Good Requirements*. International Council of Systems Engineers, Requirements Working Group (INCOSE Symposium, 1996), www.afis.fr/nav/gt/ie/doc/Articles/CHARACTE.HTM.

2. International Institute of Business Analysis, *A Guide to the Business Analyst Body of Knowledge*, Release 1.6. 2006, www.theiiba.org/Content/NavigationMenu/Learning/BodyofKnowledge/Version16/BOKV1_6.pdf.

Chapter 5

Public-Private Partnerships

Public-private partnerships, as defined by the National Council for Public-Private Partnership (NCPPP) are "a contractual agreement between a public agency (federal, state, or local) and a private sector entity. Through this agreement, the skills and assets of each sector (public and private) are shared in delivering a service or facility for the use of the general public. In addition to the sharing of resources, each party shares in the risks and rewards potential in the delivery of the service and/or facility." Typically, public sectors are government infrastructures: programs that run on taxpayer capital. The private sector comprises businesses that are owned by private individuals or shareholders, and not by the government.

Some major benefits of having public-private partnerships are that they: (1) provide a greater efficiency of getting tasks and requirements completed; (2) reduce the spending of taxpayer money; (3) provide improved compliance with government regulations, needs, and requirements in regards to the environment and workplace; and (4) improve the quality of services and products.

A HISTORICAL PERSPECTIVE
ON PUBLIC-PRIVATE PARTNERSHIPS

Colonial Period

Public-private partnerships are nothing new to the United States. In fact, public-private partnerships occurred in North America before the Revolutionary War. One of the first people to implement this idea in the New World was John Winthrop Jr. Born in 1605, Winthrop was the eldest son of the first governor of the Massachusetts Bay Colony. Winthrop and his wife sailed to Boston in 1631, where he obtained political power and influence in both the Massachusetts and Connecticut colonies. In the New World, he was known for being a chemist and scientist, and he conducted experiments in obtaining salt from sea water. He was famous for starting one of the first ironworks in Massachusetts colony and for establishing "druggist shops" and chemistry laboratories in order to meet the demands for medicine. These pharmacies were considered one of the first science-based enterprises in North America. While Winthrop did not create a public-private partnership, he helped start the idea that the government and political leaders should use and support private businesses in order to progress scientific advancement for the benefit of society.

Elsewhere in the world, the United Kingdom passed the Longitude Act of 1714, where a monetary prize would be offered for a practical solution for sailing ships to determine longitude. Without the ability to accurately find their location, ships would sail off course and often end in tragedy. The British government created a competition among its citizens, where firms and people competed to be the first to find the best way to calculate longitude. With a financial reward at stake, it was the private sector that eagerly answered the demand.

One of the first instances of a public-private partnership in the New World occurred in 1742 when Benjamin Franklin established the American Philosophical Society of Philadelphia. This society, along with the Pennsylvania House of Representatives, sponsored the University of Pennsylvania, the first medical school in the English colonies with the purpose of making available to all citizens the advancements in agriculture, science, and medicine. This showed that public and private sectors could work together harmoniously in advancing the sciences for the common good.

After the American Revolutionary War, the 1787 Constitutional Convention discussed the possibility of creating national universities to promote the sciences. This topic was inspired by the influence that both the American Philosophical Society of Philadelphia and the Boston Philosophical Society had in the progression of scientific research. The Constitutional Convention felt that the national government should not be in direct control over the nation's educational and scientific activities; instead, the government should be influential to the universities and research societies through indirect means. One of these indirect means was through public-private partnerships.

1800s

In 1803, President Thomas Jefferson bought 828,800 square miles of land from France, known as the Louisiana Purchase. This more than doubled the size of the United States at the time, and the purchased land now comprises more than 20 percent of the present United States. For $2,500, President Jefferson hired the expedition team of Meriwether Lewis and William Clark to explore the new land along the Mississippi and Missouri Rivers. With thirty-three members in their party, Lewis and Clark began their journey from the Ohio River to the Pacific Ocean. As well as exploring and mapping a water passage to the Pacific Ocean, they collected and sent back 68 mineral specimens and 108 biological specimens to President Jefferson, one of them being a living prairie dog, which had never been seen in the east. This was another example of a private-public partnership funded by the federal government. President Jefferson's hiring of a private team of explorers to increase scientific knowledge of the western part of the country helped increase the country's westward expansion because of the maps that were made possible as well as the discovery of a faster method of travel to the Pacific Ocean, which President Jefferson hoped would increase trade and settlement.

Starting in the early 1800s, states began creating science and technology universities. In 1799, Connecticut founded the first State Academy of the Arts and Sciences, and the United States Military Academy at West Point, New York, was established three years later. Starting in 1824, many more states began establishing academies. The Enlightenment Era, during which the scientific method of research was emphasized, saw many more states begin to establish their own universities. The purpose was for citizens of the United States to greatly benefit from the increasing scientific knowledge in the country.

In the 1820s, the federal government funded a project of the Franklin Institute in Philadelphia to find the cause of a cholera epidemic that was sweeping the country. This is a prime example of how a public need created the motivation to find new technological knowledge provided by the private sector.

Samuel Morse was the inventor of the telegraph and its language, Morse code. In 1843, Congress funded Morse $30,000 to install an experimental telegraph line from Baltimore, Maryland, to Washington, D.C., along the Baltimore and Ohio Railroad (roughly thirty-eight miles in length). This was the first instance in which the federal government funded the private sector for an experimental product that the government wanted in widespread use. Soon after, the telegraph became a major form of long-distance communication.

The Morrill Act of 1862 was passed by Congress, which stated that at least one college of agricultural and mechanical sciences would be established by every state. Each state was given 3,000 acres of land per senator and representative the state had in order to build these colleges. Like

Winthrop, the government started private businesses so that research by those private sectors would benefit the country.

World War I

By the time World War I erupted in Europe, many of the research bases for American companies could be found located in Europe, as many scientists lived and taught in European universities. The war proved to be a hindrance to American companies, which now had limited access to the research conducted abroad. In response to this, President Woodrow Wilson established the Council of National Defense in 1916 in order to identify domestic research facilities of scientific technological excellence. It was composed of the secretary of war, the secretary of the Navy, the secretary of the interior, the secretary of agriculture, the secretary of commerce, and the secretary of labor. Because World War I was a war of technology with the introduction of the tank, machine gun, fighter plane, zeppelin bombers, and gas warfare, President Wilson knew that the only way to win the war would be through scientific and technological advancements of weaponry. The mission of the council was to coordinate the placement of resources and industrial goods in case the United States entered the war.

The Great Depression and World War II

During the Great Depression in the 1930s, the Science Committee of the National Resources Committee created the report, "Research: A National Resource" which stated that "there are certain fields of science and technology which the government has a Constitutional responsibility to support. These fields include defense, determination of standards, and certain regulatory functions." This report explicitly stated that one of the duties the federal government had to the American people was to support research.

In June 1941, just before the United States entered World War II, President Franklin Delano Roosevelt created the National Defense Research Committee, which was headed by the president of the Carnegie Institution, Vannevar Bush. The committee was later changed to the Office of Scientific Research and Development (OSRD), still headed by Vannevar Bush. The OSRD did not conduct any research itself, but instead realized that it could harness many different industries and give them all a specific goal. The OSRD funded the Massachusetts Institute of Technology and the University of California, who helped create radar, and funded hundreds of industrial sites, which resulted in the creation of the DUKW (an amphibious vehicle used in warfare), the proximity fuse, and research that would later be used in the Manhattan Project.

When the end of World War II was in sight, President Roosevelt said that the OSRD "should be used in the days of peace ahead for the improvement of the national health, the creation of new enterprises bringing new jobs, and the betterment of the national standard of living." Following this, Bush submitted a report called "Science: The Endless Frontier" to President Roosevelt. In his report, Bush stated that "a nation [that] depends upon others for its new basic scientific knowledge will be slow in its industrial progress and weak in its competitive position in world trade, regardless of its mechanical skill" and that "the Government should accept new responsibilities for promoting the flow of new scientific knowledge and the development of scientific talent in [the] youth."

The chairman of the President's Scientific Research Board at that time was John Steelman, who wrote a report entitled "Science and Public Policy" for then president Harry S. Truman. The report contained a list of recommendations on what the federal government should do in order to benefit the country with regard to scientific research. The recommendations were:

1. *Need for Basic Research.* Much of the world is in chaos. We can no longer rely as we once did upon the basic discoveries of Europe. At the same time, our stockpile of unexploited fundamental knowledge is virtually exhausted in crucial areas.
2. *Prosperity.* This Nation is committed to a policy of maintaining full employment and full production. Most of our frontiers have disappeared and our economy can expand only with more intensive development of our present resources. Such expansion is unattainable without a stimulated and growing research and development program.
3. *International Progress.* The economic health of the world—and the political health of the world—are both intimately associated with our own economic health. By strengthening our economy through research and development we increase the chances for international economic wellbeing.
4. *Increasing Cost of Discovery.* The frontiers of scientific knowledge have been swept so far back that the mere continuation of pre-war growth, even in stable dollars, could not possibly permit adequate exploration. This requires more time, more men, more equipment than ever before in industry.
5. *National Security.* The unsettled international situation requires that our military research and development expenditures be maintained at a high level for the immediate future. Such expenditures may be expected to decrease in time, but they will have to remain large for several years, at least.

The Cold War Years

In 1957, the Soviet Union launched the first manmade satellite, Sputnik I, into orbit. In response, President Dwight D. Eisenhower gave $1 billion of federal money for support of science, mathematics, and technology graduate education. Eisenhower's successor, President John F. Kennedy, partnered with the necessary private sector organizations in order to complete a moon landing before the end of the 1960s.

President Richard Nixon also gave federal funding to the private sector for research; this time it was to fund his War on Cancer. This was another example where the federal government gave money to private institutions so that the private businesses would use their influence to better the country.

President Jimmy Carter created research programs that worked on the development of alternative renewable energy sources, such as solar energy and fission.

Current Examples of Public-Private Partnerships

Public-private partnerships can still be found in abundance around the globe. Many local governments use public-private partnerships for the construction of their water management and cleaning facilities. These facilities are built so that they meet the requirements of the Safe Water Drinking Act and the Clean Water Act while holding down costs to the taxpayers.

The Milwaukee Metropolitan Sewage District signed a ten-year contract with United Water in order to reduce taxpayer costs as well as improve the city's sewage system and wastewater management. The partnerships worked so well, it was placed in the top ten best-performing wastewater and sewage facilities in the nation. The facility also received the AMSA Platinum and Gold Awards for the improved operating standards and decline in waste matter discharges, as well as there being a 30 percent reduction of production costs.

Another common example of public-private partnerships found today is the construction of transportation infrastructure such as roads and highways. The state and local governments of California, Virginia, and Texas work with private sector companies to build and maintain this infrastructure with limited impacts on taxes. One method to this approach is to create transportation-oriented development. This includes the construction of train stations, metro stations, tram stops, and bus stops. This increase in public transportation reduces the amount of roads that need to be made or extended, as well as facilitates the better distribution of urban density. More people are able to commute outside of the urban communities they work in because of the public transportation that reaches out to where they live.

Other nations, like Ireland, utilize public-private partnerships. The reason for the introduction of public-private partnerships in Ireland was due to government frustration with the slow delivery, inefficient development, and overrunning costs that would occur when developing projects in the public-sector. They also found that through public-private partnerships, the public infrastructure's needs would be addressed quicker than if it was to be achieved by traditional means. The Irish government found that it was more cost-effective and less time-consuming to seek help from the private sector than it was for them to use their own public research and development sectors.

PUBLIC-PRIVATE PARTNERSHIPS AND THE FREE MARKET SYSTEM

As previously stated, a public-private partnership is an agreement between a public agency and a private sector entity that combines skills and resources to develop a technology, product and/or service that improves the quality of life for the general public. The private sector has been called upon numerous times to use its resources, skills, and expertise to perform specific tasks for the public sector. Historically, the public sector has frequently taken an active role in spurring technological advances by directly funding the private sector to fulfill a specialized need that cannot be completed by the public sector itself.

The public sector has been motivated to take this active role to promote the development of a given technology or capability because the business case for the private sector's involvement in a certain area is not apparent. In these cases, the public sector relied on the private sector to develop needed capabilities, but had to pay the private sector to divert its valuable (and limited) resources to an area that did not necessarily show a strong potential to provide an acceptable return on investment (ROI) for a company. This could be caused by a number of issues ranging from a high cost to perform the research and development (R&D) to a limited potential available market (PAM) that may have prevented the company from making sufficient profit and returns to the company and its shareholders.

Increasingly, however, users in the public sector are now viewed as stable markets—that is, a sizable customer base for the private sector to warrant investments of time and money. A commercialization-based public-private partnership has the same goal as more traditional public-private partnerships, but the method is inspired to leverage positive attributes of the free-market system. The introduction of a commercialization-based public-private partnership, developed and implemented at the U.S. Department of Homeland Security (DHS), provides benefits for three constituents of the Homeland Security Enterprise (HSE): the private sector, the public sector, and the taxpayer. This is a desirable scenario where there is a "win-win-win" environment created in which all participants are in a position to benefit.

In the free-market system, private sector companies and businesses must sell commercial products consumers want to purchase. Commercialization is defined as the process of developing markets and producing and delivering products and/or services to address the needs of those targeted markets. The development and understanding of markets is a critical undertaking for many companies seeking to gain share of a market, with companies directing significant amounts of money and resources to these activities in addition to their product development efforts. Sometimes a company does not understand the correct needs or demand data of a market or market segment and their product(s) does not sell well. The company's investment in designing, manufacturing, and advertising the product can be, and is in many cases, a waste of time and money if the company "misses the mark."

What a commercialization-based public-private partnership offers to the private sector is detailed information and opportunity. The public sector has turned into the "consumer" in this free-market scenario, who literally gives the private sector a detailed description of what they need, as well as insight into which agencies would be interested in potentially purchasing a product/service that fulfills these requirements. While it remains prudent business to verify this kind of information, there is considerable value for the private sector to obtain this information because four things are provided to the private sector that would not be available in normal market dynamics: (1) decreases in resources spent researching the market; (2) increases in time and money focused on product design and manufacturing; (3) reduced risk of the research data being incorrect, and (4) an estimate as to how large the potential market can be.

The development and communication of detailed requirements or needs is the cornerstone to the success of these public-private partnerships. The public sector's ability to collect the needs of its stakeholders will catalyze and support the future actions of the partnership. Requirements definition creates a method in which appropriate decisions about product or system functionality and performance can be made before investing the time and money to develop it. Effective communication with and access to the stakeholders of a given agency will bring greater clarity and understanding to the challenges that they face. Understanding requirements early in the search for solutions removes a great deal of guesswork in the planning stages and helps to ensure that the end users and product developers are "on the same page." The requirements hierarchy (figure 5.1) shows how the definition of requirements must remain

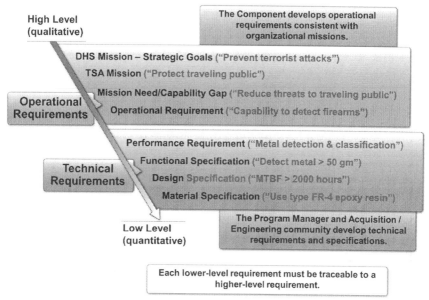

High Level (qualitative)

The Component develops operational requirements consistent with organizational missions.

Operational Requirements

DHS Mission – Strategic Goals ("Prevent terrorist attacks")

TSA Mission ("Protect traveling public")

Mission Need/Capability Gap ("Reduce threats to traveling public")

Operational Requirement ("Capability to detect firearms")

Technical Requirements

Performance Requirement ("Metal detection & classification")

Functional Specification ("Detect metal > 50 gm")

Design Specification ("MTBF > 2000 hours")

Material Specification ("Use type FR-4 epoxy resin")

Low Level (quantitative)

The Program Manager and Acquisition / Engineering community develop technical requirements and specifications.

Each lower-level requirement must be traceable to a higher-level requirement.

Figure 5.1. The "requirements hierarchy" shows the development of lower ("Mission") to higher ("Technical") resolution requirements or needs

traceable to the overall mission to be accomplished, helping ideas stay on track and working toward a common goal.

In this partnership model, the proactive articulation and sharing of requirements and needs provides the necessary starting point to begin effective communication with private sector partners. Openly publishing the needs or requirements of public sector stakeholders has a number of ancillary benefits for those involved. A common challenge for solution developers has been a general lack of insight into the exact needs of public sector stakeholders. Instead, the private sector attempts to develop solutions that may not exist and tries to sell products based on the merit of their capabilities and features rather than their ability to solve the specific problem of the users. This is a situation where "a solution defines a problem" that it can solve, rather than the problem guiding the development of a solution to close a "capability gap."

Requirements provide criteria against which solutions can be tested and evaluated. They offer detailed metrics that can be used to objectively measure a possible solution's effectiveness. Detailed operational requirements will guide product development so that solutions' specifications actively solve the stated problem(s). The effective articulation of the requirements creates the mindset in which fulfilling requirements becomes the focus of product development. This requirements-led method places the users' need at the center of all future actions so that solutions are developed and delivered quickly and efficiently.

With more knowledge about the needs and requirements of their potential customers, the private sector is in a better position to consider how their current technology offerings align to needed capabilities. The next thing that must be considered is how many potential users are in a given market in order to determine if investment of additional resources to develop the solution will provide the necessary returns. In many cases, the market for a commercialization-based public-private partnership is substantial, composed of millions of potentially funded users. In addition, many government agencies across federal, state, and local government levels may have similar requirements for products and services (if the ability to modify and add or take away options is available). Furthermore, the products developed for the government can often be sold in civilian markets such as critical infrastructure and key resources owners and operators. Even if the government does not purchase a specific company's product, in many cases the product can still be useful and have value for nongovernmental applications.

Innovative ideas flow freely in the private sector, most especially from small businesses. There is a demand for these innovative technologies as other private sector companies begin to position themselves to address these newly emerging commercial markets found in the private sector. Mergers and acquisitions continue to take place in the private sector as larger companies and investors seek to build their enterprises. Discovering the potential benefits of partnering with the public sector has demonstrated its attractiveness to investor communities like venture capitalists and angel investors. This investment has created more opportunities for those innovative ideas to grow and develop into fully deployable products. Sharing information like needs and requirements provides a defined target that allows those private sector partnerships to take hold. These strategic partnerships are becoming more common, and it is now a regular event for these strategic partners to pursue the public sector together to engage and demonstrate new technology offerings.

A commercialization-based public-private partnership benefits the public sector because the private sector competes in an open and transparent way for the public sector's purchase potential and business. Since companies and businesses openly receive information about the requirements or needs of an identified market, multiple companies may competitively make products/services that meet requirements at the lowest cost to the potential buyer. The end user benefits by being able to purchase the best product at the lowest price.

The taxpayers win in a commercialization-based public-private partnership because their tax money is not spent on research and development

Table 5.1. Benefit Analysis—"Win-Win-Win"

Taxpayers	Public Sector	Private Sector
1. Citizens are better protected by DHS personnel using mission-critical products	1. Improved understanding and communication of needs	1. Save significant time and money on market and business development activities
2. Tax savings realized through private sector investment in DHS	2. Cost-effective and rapid product development process saves resources	2. Firms can genuinely contribute to the security of the nation
3. Positive economic growth for American economy	3. Monies can be allocated to perform greater number of essential tasks	3. Successful products share in the "imprimatur of DHS"; providing assurance that products really work
4. Possible product " spin-offs" can aid other commercial markets	4. End users receive products aligned to specific needs	4. Significant business opportunities with sizable DHS and DHS ancillary markets
5. Customers ultimately benefit from COTS produced within the free-market system—more cost-effective and efficient product development	5. End users can make informed purchasing decisions with tight budgets	5. Commercialization opportunities for small, medium, and large business

The benefits of commercialization-based public-private partnerships are evident for all participants.

for the private sector. Normally the government pays a company for research and development, yet many products/services are *not* developed. All of this is funded by taxpayers' money, often without much benefit to society. In a commercialization-based public-private partnership, the research and development of the product is *not* paid by government. It is the private-sector that spends money on research and development, and then sells the product to the government at the lowest price. This results in saving the taxpayer money as well and, in fact, expands the net realizable budgets of the public sector. Table 5.1 outlines the various benefits of commercialization-based public-private partnerships for all parties:

DEPARTMENT OF HOMELAND SECURITY
LEVERAGES PUBLIC-PRIVATE PARTNERSHIPS

Given the current economic situation facing our country, it becomes increasingly important for the public sector to make wise investments of its time, money and resources. Most government agencies do not have the budgets necessary to complete every research and development project that they would like to undertake. The effective prioritization of programs is critical to managing the limited resources available to various agencies. Rigorously developed requirements for each project facilitate these prioritization efforts and increase the ability to perform critical analyses of alternatives (AoAs) used in determining the best course of action to solve a problem. An analysis of alternatives will uncover a great deal of information on potential solutions that may already exist and is a necessary consideration before pursuing a commercialization public-private partnership. When successful, the option to utilize commercialization public-private partnerships to solve a problem frees resources for those projects that require significant government involvement and expenditure of resources.

The Department of Homeland Security (DHS) through the Science & Technology Directorate (S&T) initiated an innovative commercialization-based public-private partnership called the System Efficacy through Commercialization, Utilization, Relevance and Evaluation (SECURE) Program. The SECURE Program leverages the resources, experience, and expertise to develop and deliver fully deployable solutions aligned to the detailed operational requirements of DHS's many stakeholders. The SECURE Program covers the needs of all of the DHS stakeholders including the operating components (FEMA, TSA, CBP, Secret Service, ICE, USCIS, and Coast Guard) but most especially first responders (local police and fire department, hospitals, rescue teams) and critical infrastructure/key resources (CIKR) owners and operators, representing a large market for potential private sector partners. It is the role of DHS to ensure that these stakeholders are provided with the mission-critical capabilities that they need in order to perform their jobs well.

The SECURE Program was developed as a way to address requests for assistance from DHS stakeholders to find better solutions to their problems. These stakeholders were used to a culture where vendors present "solutions looking for problems" and wanted to find a better way to not only have solutions developed to address their needs, but also to have some assurance that the products being sold to them have been thoroughly tested and evaluated in real operational environments. The requirements of these stakeholders are gathered and articulated in a Commercialization-based Operational Requirements Document (C-ORD). When appropriate, approved C-ORDs are posted online so that potential solution providers or vendors with capability offerings may apply for participation in the SECURE Program. In an open and freely competitive way, multiple vendors are able to offer potential solutions to provide the required capabilities outlined in a given C-ORD.

It is important to stress the relationship that DHS has with its nonfederal stakeholders in the first-responder and CIKR communities. DHS has direct authority over its operating components and can directly influence acquisition activities. This same relationship does not extend to its nonfederal stakeholders, who are responsible for managing their own budgets and purchasing decisions. Because the SECURE Program is not a procurement activity, DHS is able to share valuable information about its nonfederal stakeholders to the private sector and gain knowledge about potential solutions without the need for contracts or monetary exchanges. First responders and nonfederal stakeholders now have a unified voice to convey their needs or requirements and gain from the collective size as potential available markets.

The SECURE Program, in addition to leveraging cooperative public-private partnerships, incorporates a rigorous review process based on rigorous operational test and evaluation (OT&E) to ensure that the operational performance of a system is directly aligned to stated stakeholder requirements but also that the system meets or exceeds the stated performance of the private sector vendor or supplier. This review process analyzes capability requirements in addition to an evaluation of the system's safety record, quality assurance criteria, performance limitations, and other considerations to ensure that when a system is deployed in the field it is both effective and safe.

Through the SECURE Program, the department provides potential solution providers detailed operational requirements and a conservative estimate of the potential available market(s) offered by DHS stakeholders. In exchange for this valuable information, the private sector (eventually, if not having already developed) offers deployable products and services (along with recognized third-party test and evaluation data) that meet these stated requirements in an open and free way that creates an ergonomic "clearinghouse of solutions" available to DHS's stakeholders. Because of the success and "win-win-win" nature of this program in that it provides benefits for the American taxpayer, the private sector, and DHS, DHS-S&T recently introduced the FutureTECH Program, which describes the long-term capabilities/technologies required by DHS stakeholders (see figure 5.2).

FutureTECH identifies and focuses on the future needs of the department as fully deployable technologies and capabilities, which in some cases are not readily available in the private sector or federal government space. While the SECURE Program is valuable to all DHS operating components, organizational elements, and DHS stakeholders, FutureTECH is intended for DHS S&T use only, particularly in the fields/portfolios related to research and innovation.

After providing independent third-party testing and evaluation of potential products, services, or technologies to show they do in fact meet or

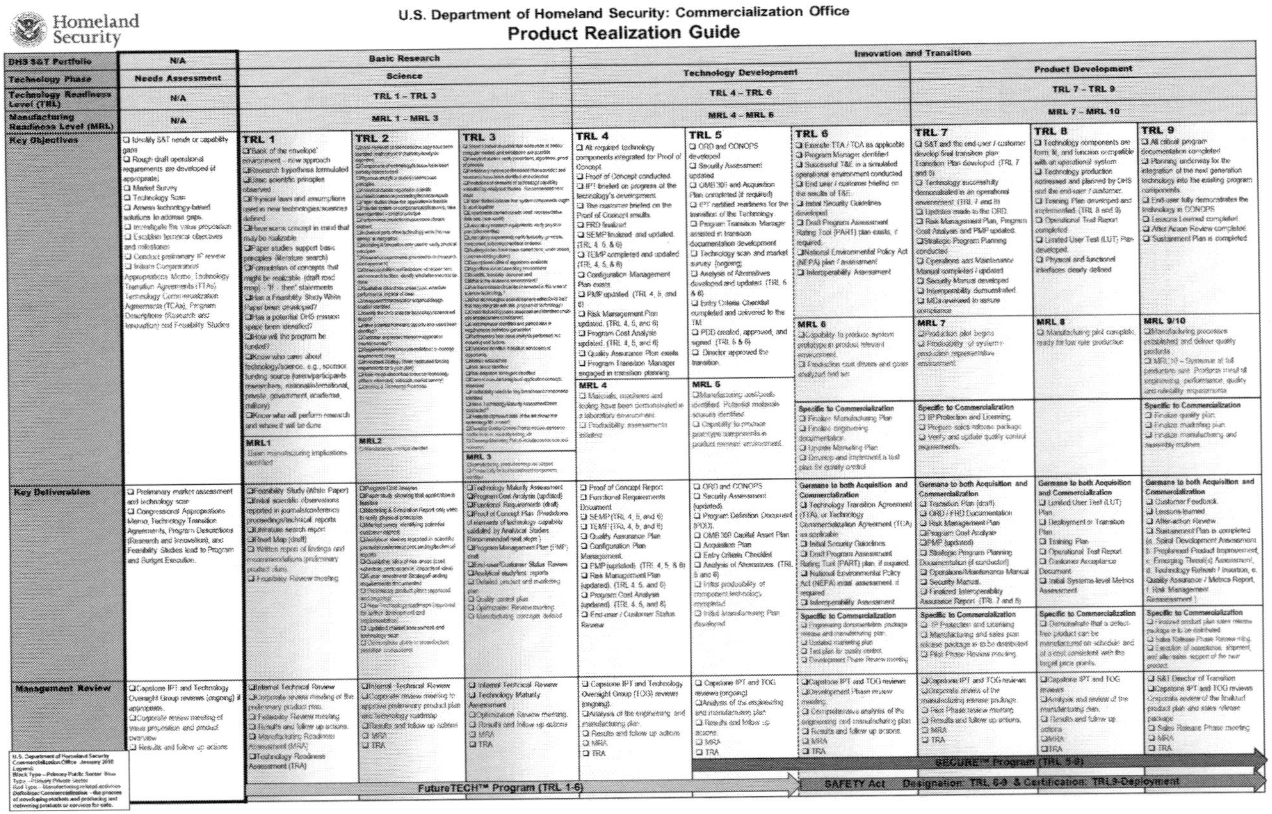

U.S. Department of Homeland Security: Commercialization Office
Product Realization Guide

DHS S&T Portfolio	N/A	Basic Research		Innovation and Transition	
Technology Phase	Needs Assessment	Science	Technology Development	Product Development	
Technology Readiness (TRL)	N/A	TRL 1 - TRL 3	TRL 4 - TRL 6	TRL 7 - TRL 9	
Manufacturing Readiness Level (MRL)	N/A	MRL 1 - MRL 3	MRL 4 - MRL 6	MRL 7 - MRL 10	

Column headings: TRL 1 | TRL 2 | TRL 3 | TRL 4 | TRL 5 | TRL 6 | TRL 7 | TRL 8 | TRL 9

Row headings: Key Objectives | Key Deliverables | Management Reviews

Program bands: FutureTECH™ Program (TRL 1-6) | SECURE™ Program (TRL 5-9)

SAFETY Act — Designation: TRL 6-9 & Certification: TRL3-Deployment

Figure 5.2. The Product Realization Guide outlines the necessary steps (and additional information [5.2a]) for product development along the Technology Readiness Level (TRL) and Manufacturing Readiness Level (MRL) backbone.

- This guide is designed as a resource to assist in project execution relative to technology development. This systematic approach facilitates efficient and effective product development by reducing the risk of unidentified errors and product development shortfalls. It is intended that this guide be incorporated as an easy-to-use resource to ensure due diligence throughout the product development life cycle. Please note that this guide presents a general framework for product realization and that individual projects may require a tailored product realization path.

- Additional information on TRLs, MRLs and other product development related resources can be found at the following links:

  - Technology Readiness Assessment (TRA) Deskbook, July 2009 - https://acc.dau.mil/CommunityBrowser.aspx?id=18545
  - Definition of Technology Readiness Levels - http://esto.nasa.gov/files/TRL_definitions.pdf
  - Technology Readiness Levels NASA white paper, April 1995 - http://www.hq.nasa.gov/office/codeq/trl/trl.pdf
  - Using the Technology Readiness Levels Scale to Support Technology Management in the DoD's ATD/STO Environments, September 2002 - http://www.sei.cmu.edu/reports/02sr027.pdf
  - DHS S&T Technology Readiness Level Calculator (ver 1.1.) - http://www.homelandsecurity.org/hsireports/DHS_ST_RL_Calculator_report20091020.pdf
  - DAU TRL Calculator - https://acc.dau.mil/CommunityBrowser.aspx?id=25811
  - Manufacturing Readiness Assessment (MRA) Deskbook. May 2009 - https://acc.dau.mil/CommunityBrowser.aspx?id=182129
  - Assessing Manufacturing Risk - https://acc.dau.mil/CommunityBrowser.aspx?id=18231
  - GAO Report – Defense Acquisitions: Assessment of Selected Major Weapons Programs - http://www.gao.gov/new.items/d06391.pdf
  - About Manufacturing Readiness Assessments - http://www.wpafb.af.mil/library/factsheets/factsheet.asp?id=9757

Figure 5.2a.

exceed the requirements listed in the detailed operational requirements, private sector entities can potentially enter into a partnership with the department in order to deliver commercial-off-the-shelf (COTS) products to the department's stakeholders. In addition to providing products to DHS and its stakeholders, these partnership programs, SECURE[1] and FutureTECH,[2] give much-needed assurance to the first-responder and CIKR communities that a certified product or service works as specified and is aligned to a requirements document.

The products that are developed through this partnership (even the ones that were not purchased by DHS) can be offered to other private sector entities, such as airport security, school and university security, and security for professional sports and concerts, many of whom support the defense of critical infrastructure and key resources nationwide. There is then an increase in public safety and security, all while the private sector, public sector, and taxpayer benefit from the partnership.

Execution and Action

The success of the SECURE and FutureTECH pilot programs was the result of effective communication, fostering cooperative relationships, and sticking to the plan. The Commercialization Office learned a great deal from the execution of the pilots and from listening with an open mind to the suggestions and recommendations received from partners, colleagues, and leadership. Based on this valuable feedback, the Commercialization Office created a detailed flow process and documented the roles and responsibilities for those involved with the program. This is shared in an open and free way and provides a roadmap to potential certification. The processes were developed with the mindset of "keeping it simple and making it easy" for all participants to understand their roles and what is expected of them and when.

This detailed process describes the necessary actions for the successful execution of the SECURE and FutureTECH programs at full participation and buy-in from the department. As discussed previously, both programs begin with a detailed analysis of the needs and requirements for specific problems facing groups of stakeholders. After an analysis of the needs and requirements, the department conducts extensive internal evaluations to prioritize potential programs and determine the alignment of these needs to the overall mission of the department. A number of resources have been created at DHS for the relative prioritization of programs using value-based metrics to quantify the value gained from pursuing a given program.

The department then publishes approved documents and PAMs. It is at this time that the private sector is able to take advantage of the open and cooperative relationship to develop potential solutions and consider entering into a partnership with the department. These partnerships are formalized utilizing Cooperative Research and Development Agreements (CRADAs) that describe in detail the relationship, roles and responsibilities, and deliverables for each party. Through the CRADA, the private sector partner will be able to submit third-party, recognized, independent operational testing and evaluation (IOT&E) for review by the Department and its subject matter experts (SMEs). Certification will be granted to those technologies, products, and/or services that meet or exceed the operational performance claimed by the private sector partner and are aligned to the needs/requirements contained in the posted 5W or C-ORD documents. The following pages lay out this straightforward process.

CRADAs: An Overview

In the United States today, many public-private partnerships are based on cooperative research and development agreements (CRADAs). These agreements are executed between federal government agencies and private sector participants, where both parties work on a mutually beneficial project. Each group applies the resource that they agreed to use, such as personnel, equipment, services, and/or facilities. Though the private sector participant may fund portions of the effort, the government agency cannot use federal funds (i.e., cash) to support the private sector directly. The partners are able to share information and leverage each other's technical expertise, ideas, and information in a protected environment.

The benefits of having a CRADA are: (1) the private sector participants are able to take advantage of the government agencies' analytical capabilities; (2) the government agency and the private sector participants can negotiate on intellectual property disposition, such as rights to patents, the protection of information, and exclusive or nonexclusive licensing of inventions or other intellectual properties developed that are made through the agreement; (3) the government agencies and the private sector participants have the opportunity to develop work and business relationships.

Agency and private participants define a project that would benefit both sectors. If the needed resources are available to perform the discussed project, the representative (usually a program manager) of the public sector makes the final decision about whether they will pursue a CRADA opportunity. Funds are not transferred from the government agency to the private sector participant, so most regulations limiting federal procurement do *not* apply. As a result, the CRADA can be put into practice quickly and with little difficulty.

SECURE™: System Efficacy through Commercialization Utilization Relevance and Evaluation

The SECURE™ Program is an innovative public-private partnership designed to leverage the experience, expertise and resources of the private sector to develop required capabilities for Department stakeholders efficiently, cost-effectively and with an emphasis on speed of execution. The SECURE Program's primary focus is on the non-federal first responders and critical infrastructure/key resources (CIKR) owners and operators. The Commercialization Office is responsible for the management and oversight of the program and will work closely with all participants in the process.

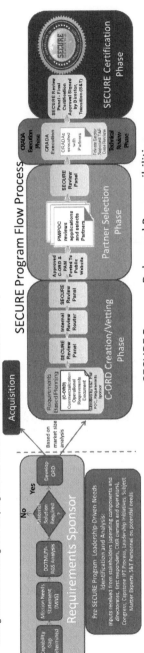

SECURE Program Flow Process

Commercialization Office Resource Library
- Product Realization Guide (TRA/MRA Guidelines)
- TSD's TRL Guide
- Program Prioritization Index (PPI) Model
- C-ORD Template
- CRADA Template
- Due Diligence Questions for Potential Partners
- Nationally Recognized Testing Laboratories (NRTLs) List
- SECURE Overview and Concept of Operations
- External and Internal SECURE Application Forms
- SECURE Certification Document (Under OGC Review)
- Market Analysis Templates (PAMs)
- SECURE Program Flow Process Brief
- SECURE Program Swim Lane Chart
- DHS S&T RL Calculator and User's Manual, Ver. 1.1

SECURE Program Roles and Responsibilities

Requirements Sponsor: A Requirements Sponsor represents the operational needs of the cognizant organizational element and ultimately the end-users of the required system. The Sponsor conducts mission analysis, identifies capability gaps, conducts requirements analysis, and participates in long range planning process and the prioritization of needs. The Sponsor's final requirements are formally documented in an Operational Requirements Document. The Sponsor participates in all phases of the development to ensure that the item or system being developed meets operational requirements. In many contexts, the word "Sponsor" refers to the sponsoring organization, and the term "Sponsor's representative" is the person empowered to represent the Sponsor for a given investment.

Program Manager (PM)/Point of Contact (POC): The PM/POC will be the S&T representative responsible for managing the execution of the SECURE Program Flow Process. The PM/POC will coordinate with the requirements sponsor to determine the capability gaps and requirements of the stakeholder community. PM/POC will also conduct DOTMLPF analysis to ensure that a material need exists and that the SECURE program is a viable option to realize product development. PM/POC will be responsible for creating and maintaining the certification package over the course of executing the Program. The PM/POC will provide necessary briefs to SECURE Review Panel, manage interactions with the private sector and serve as the central point of contact for questions relating a particular C-ORD. The PM/POC will provide recommendation on certification to the Director—S&T Transition.

SECURE Review Panel: The Panel is a group familiar with the strategic goals and mission of the Department are its stakeholders. The Panel is responsible for accepting C-ORDs for inclusion in the SECURE Program based on C-ORD alignment of overall mission needs and priorities. The Panel also determines whether a material solution is best to address a capability gap and that the SECURE Program is a viable option for the development of new products and C-ORD /or services for Department stakeholders. The Panel also participates in the review of CRADAs and T&E reports and will advise the Director—S&T Transition with recommendations for certification.

Internal Review Router: The Internal Review Router will review C-ORDs accepted into the SECURE Program by the SECURE Review Panel. The Internal Review Router members will provide technical feedback and recommended changes to the SECURE Review Panel and PM/POC. Members will review C-ORDs to ensure that the requirements are specific, achievable, testable, measurable, feasible and are solution agnostic. (Note: individual members of the Internal Review Router may have additional roles and responsibilities within the SECURE Program process. For example, the T&E representative and subject matter experts are critical in the review of.)

Third Party Independent T&E Team: The Third Party Independent T&E Team will provide subject matter expertise on the necessary test and evaluation considerations related to the SECURE Program. The T&E Team, as a member of the Internal Review Router, reviews C-ORDs for technical merit and ensure compliance or conformity to any relevant standards and regulations. The T&E Team will also confer with the SECURE Review Panel for the preliminary discussions on operational test and evaluation considerations. The T&E Team is responsible to review and modify the detailed test plan, developed by the PM/POC and selected private sector partners. A T&E representative may elect to observe/oversee the conduct of operational testing and evaluation as warranted by the type of testing required. The T&E Team also contributes to the paper review of T&E data submitted by the private sector and ensures that all testing was performed in accordance with the written detailed test plan and that the data contained in the T&E results demonstrate that the operational performance of a system meets or exceeds the stated specifications of a potential private sector partner and provides an assessment of whether C-ORD requirements are met.

Commercialization Office: The Commercialization Office is responsible for the overall execution of the SECURE Program. The Commercialization Office will assist during all phases of the SECURE Program to ensure uniform guidelines and resources are available to facilitate the completion of all phases. The Commercialization Office will work closely will all participants of the SECURE Program and address any questions that may arise. The Commercialization Office is also responsible for the continued private sector outreach to promote and enhance the engagement of the private sector in the SECURE Program. The Commercialization Office will also assist the PM/POC in conducting market analyses and evaluating potential private sector partners. The Chief Commercialization Officer (CCO) is also a member of the SECURE Review Panel.

Figure 5.3. SECURE Program Process Overview.

SECURE™ Program: Public-Private Product Certification Process

6/3/2010

	C-ORD Creation/Vetting Phase	Partners Selection Phase	CRADA Development and Execution Phase	Technical Review Phase	SECURE Certification Phase
	Objective: Develop detailed operational requirements (with concepts of operations) for new material capabilities needed by DHS stakeholders **Inputs:** Mission Needs Statement/Capability Gap/Enhanced Homeland Capability (EHC), DOTMLPF-RGS analysis, requirements elicitation from broad range of DHS stakeholders **Output:** Representative and well-vetted Commercialization - Operational Requirements Document (C-ORD)	**Objective:** Identify potential private sector partners capable of delivering required capabilities which can be validated **Inputs:** Applications from private sector entities seeking to provide solutions to a C-ORD **Output:** Detailed analysis of a given company's capabilities, technology/manufacturing maturity and commercialization capabilities and experience	**Objective:** Outline roles and responsibilities for DHS and private sector partners **Inputs:** Discussions with Private Sector Partners to develop CRADA and supporting documents **Output:** Binding CRADA agreement between DHS and private sector partner includes: SOW, Detailed Test Plan, Milestones & Deliverables	**Objective:** Determine ability of proposed solutions to meet stated requirements and performance specifications **Inputs:** T&E data from operational tests conducted by recognized third party T&E entity or DHS sponsored test facility **Output:** Detailed report of T&E data review for operational performance alignment to requirements and performance specifications	**Objective:** Provide SECURE Certification, if appropriate **Inputs:** Detailed report on certification package containing T&E data review, vetted ORD, PAM, MNS, AOA, DOTMLPF analysis **Output:** Determination on granting certification for a potential solution
Requirements Sponsor (e.g. First Responder, CIKR stakeholder, etc.)	• Elicit needs and requirements from stakeholders (approx. 2-4 months) • Communicate with national user associations/organizations • Develop Mission Needs Statement (MNS) • Conduct DOTMLPF-RGS analysis • Ensure requirements are representative of user community • Represent user community as necessary • Grants development with DHS customer/stakeholder, if required		• Provide input on operational considerations necessary to conduct effective operational testing and evaluation (IOT&E)	• Assist PM/POC as necessary to evaluate efficacy and alignment of operational performance data to meet/exceed stated C-ORD requirements	• End users/customers notified of Certified products
Commercialization Office	• Assist in C-ORD drafting by offering requirements development materials • Assist in analyzing potential available market (PAM) and program prioritization index model (PPI) • Assist in analysis of alternatives, technology scans and market scans • Continue outreach on "How to do Business with DHS" with private sector • Engaged internal and/or external subject matter expert(s)/FFRDC/Non-S&T organization(s) to assist in review of C-ORD, detailed test plan and T&E data • Post approved C-ORD and PAM to SECURE Program website, if/when approved by SECURE Review Panel and Internal Review Router	• Provide resources to assist in technology/manufacturing maturity assessments and business analysis • Manage incoming applications to posted C-ORDs • Assist with business analysis of potential partners: experience in commercializing products, business history, likeliness to achieve TRL-9 etc. (approx. 1 week per company) • Notify private sector partners of selection or non-selection within one week after decisions are made	• Assist PM/POC to develop CRADA and necessary documentation (e.g. SOW, detailed test plan, milestones and deliverables)	• Provide resources and materials to develop the criteria necessary for thorough review of IOT&E data. • Provide recommendation on certification	• Assist PM/POC in preparation of certification package • New COTS SECURE Certified product marketed by private sector with DHS support, and oversight of Certification mark usage
PM/POC*	• Collect and support requirements data/information/documentation articulation from Requirements Sponsor • Determine alignment to mission needs/capability gaps • Conduct an analysis of alternatives (AOA) and research similar efforts • Conduct feasibility study with support from subject matter expert(s), if necessary • Identify external sources of information (e.g. subject matter expert(s) • Prepare C-ORD and potential available market (PAM) documents for review by SECURE Review Panel and Internal Review Router • Ensure conformance/inclusion of any necessary regulation(s) or standard(s)	• Establish timeline for application acceptance cycles • Conduct due diligence review of potential partners with assistance of Commercialization Office ❑ Verify current TRL/MRL of potential solution ❑ Analyze likelihood of potential solution to provide desired capability and capability alignment to C-ORD • Recommend future action with potential partners to SECURE Review Panel (to be completed within one month of acceptance cycle closing)	• Draft CRADA with OGC, Tech Transfer Manager and Commercialization Office (approx. 2-3 weeks) ❑ Work with private sector partner to determine milestones and deliverables ❑ Develop Statement of Work ❑ Develop detailed test plan with private sector partner with input from T&E representative • Verify TRL-9 maturity is achieved prior to operational test, based on requirements for certification	• Provide analysis of capability alignment to stated requirements • Evaluate efficacy and alignment of operational performance data to meet/exceed stated C-ORD requirements • Communicate questions/comments or clarification needs to private sector partner • Provide recommendation on certification	• Prepare and present to SECURE Review Panel the supporting documentation in certification package and provide recommendation for certification, if appropriate
SECURE Review Panel**	• Ensure requirements alignment and priority to overall mission objectives based on MNS, EHC, Capstone IPT Capability Gap • Review DOTMLPF-RGS analysis and AOA • Accept or decline initial package from PM/POC into SECURE Program prior to reviews by Internal Review Router	• Confirm PM/POC analysis of potential private sector partner • Approve/Recommend course of action with potential partner(s) to PM/POC	• Review documentation and provide approval on CRADA and appendices • Authorize final approval of CRADA • Approved CRADA signed by Director – S&T Transition and partner	• Review analysis from PM/POC and T&E Team to ensure that all data verifies TRL 9/MRL 10 compliance, alignment to ORD and that operational performance meets or exceeds published vendor specifications	• Review certification package and recommendation from PM/POC • Make final decision on certification of a given product/service
Internal Review Router*	• Review technical merit of C-ORD accepted by SECURE Review Panel: Are requirements testable, measurable, specific, achievable and solution agnostic? • Express opinions with recommendations to SECURE Review Panel • Ensure requirements alignment and priority to overall DHS stakeholder mission				
Subject Matter Expert(s)*	• Review technical merits of C-ORD accepted by SECURE Review Panel: Are requirements testable, measurable, specific, achievable and solution agnostic? • Ensure requirements are representative of user community • Provide insight into any similar efforts and leverage existing information/research		• Provide input on operational considerations necessary to conduct effective IOT&E	• Provide analysis of capability alignment to stated requirements	
Third Party Independent T&E Team*	• Review technical merit of C-ORD: Are the requirements testable, measurable, specific, achievable, feasible and solution agnostic?		• Assist in reviewing detailed test plan to include measures of reliability, safety, and quality assurance • Provide input on technical considerations necessary to conduct effective product testing • Provide recommendation on necessary DHS participation during IOT&E • Review and modify detailed test plan as required prior to inclusion in CRADA	• Validate operational performance data meets/exceeds stated specifications • Ensure test results and procedures followed detailed test plan • Pose questions/comments to PM/POC to relay to partner • Provide assessment of whether C-ORD requirements are met	
Deliverables	Deliverables: (Typical Time Frame: 4-6 months) 1. Written report/brief by PM/POC justifying participation in SECURE program including MNS, DOTMLPF-RGS analysis, PAM, AOA and C-ORD to be distributed and reviewed by SECURE Review Panel (approx. 3-6 months) 2. C-ORD review and feedback loop to confirm accuracy, feasibility and level of detail of requirements performed by SECURE Review Panel and Internal Review Router (approx. 3-4 weeks for initial reviews) 3. Preliminary operational testing procedures and potential performers considered 4. Approved C-ORDs will be posted online to the SECURE Program website by the Commercialization Office 5. Results/Follow up actions will be communicated/coordinated by the PM/POC	Deliverables: (Typical Time Frame: 2 Months) 1. Management of interest and questions from potential private sector partners offering their solutions to the stated requirements by Commercialization Office and PM/POC. 2. Conduct detailed analysis of potential solution technology and manufacturing maturity levels and review business standing of potential partners 3. Select private sector partners that demonstrate ability to deliver required capabilities timely and effectively 4. Results/Follow up actions will be communicated/coordinated by the PM/POC	Deliverables: (Typical Time Frame: 1-2 Months) 1. Work in close collaboration with selected private sector partners to develop CRADA, SOW, detailed test plan based on proposed solution 2. Formalize Detailed Test Plan and determine IOT&E sponsorship and responsibilities 3. PM/POC to oversee and monitor progress of private sector partners to achieve milestones and deliverables 4. PM/POC and T&E Team to observe/oversee IOT&E as necessary 5. Results/Follow up actions will be communicated/coordinated by the PM/POC.	Deliverables: (Typical Time Frame: 3-4 weeks) 1. The results of performed IOT&E are to be distributed to the PM/POC, T&E team and Subject Matter Expert(s) as necessary for detailed review and report on findings of IOT&E data. 2. Whenever possible, a paper review of IOT&E data will be used to analyze whether operational performance to address requirements and meet/exceed stated specifications 3. SECURE Review Panel will review reports written by PM/POC and T&E Team to evaluate conformance of operational performance 4. Results/Follow up actions will be communicated/coordinated by the PM/POC.	Deliverables: (Typical Time Frame: 2-3 Months) 1. The finalized certification package and recommendation for certification prepared by PM/POC to be reviewed by SECURE Review Panel 2. Director – S&T Transition analyzes recommendations of SECURE Review Panel signs certification, if appropriate 3. Prepare disclaimers/waivers to be signed by private sector partner if certified 4. Publish certification notice on public websites and approved lists, as appropriate.

* **Internal Review Router** consists of: PM/POC, S&T Portfolio Manager, S&T Division Director, Third Party Independent T&E Team, and Subject Matter Expert(s)

** **SECURE Review Panel** consists of: Director - APMD; Director – S&T Transition; Director – S&T Innovation; Technology Transfer Manager; OGC representative (S&T); Chief Commercialization Officer, and Director – S&T Transition (Final sign-off)

Acronym Legend:

DOTMLPF-RGS: Doctrine, Organization, Training, Materiel, Leadership, Personnel, Facilities – Regulations, Grants, Standards
AOA: Analysis of Alternatives
MNS: Mission Needs Statement
IOT&E: Independent Operational Testing and Evaluation
EHC: Enabling Homeland Capability
PAM: Potential Available Market
C-ORD: Commercialization – Operational Requirements Document
PM/POC: Program Manager/Point of Contact
TRL/MRL: Technology Readiness Level/Manufacturing Readiness Level
SOW: Statement of Work
CRADA: Cooperative Research and Development Agreement
CIKR: Critical Infrastructure & Key Resources
PPI: Program Prioritization Index

Figure 5.4. SECURE Program Roles and Responsibilities.

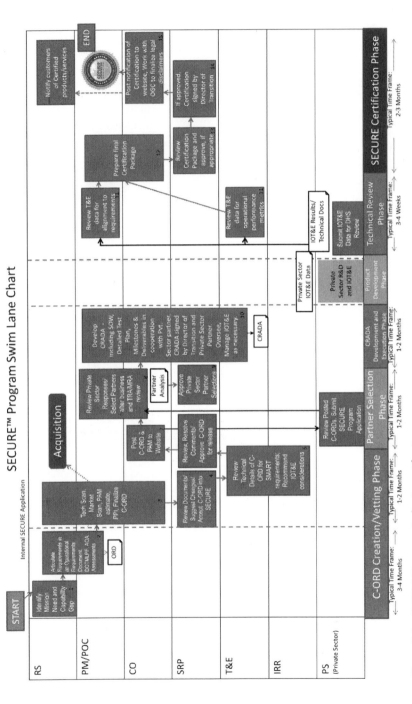

Figure 5.5   SECURE Program Swim Lane Chart.

FutureTECH

The FutureTECH Program is an innovative public-private partnership designed to leverage the experience, expertise and resources of the private sector to develop required technologies/capabilities for Department stakeholders efficiently, cost-effectively and with an emphasis on speed of execution. The FutureTECH Program's primary focus is on the non-federal first responders and critical infrastructure/key resources (CIKR) owners and operators. The FutureTECH Program is reserved for those research/innovation focus areas that could be inserted eventually into DHS acquisition or commercialization programs when development reaches TRL-6, which is described as a representative model or prototype system or subsystem that is tested in a relevant environment. The S&T Commercialization Office is responsible for the management and oversight of the program and will work closely with all participants in the process.

Pre-FutureTECH Program Leadership-Driven Needs Identification and Analysis:

Inputs received from stakeholders (operating components and directorates, first responders, CIKR owners and operators), Congress, Capstone IPT Process, Leadership Initiatives, Subject Matter Experts, S&T Personnel on potential needs. Entry criteria for FutureTECH Program are based on the potential market size and the opportunity for promising advances in technology/capability.

Commercialization Office Resource Library
- Product Realization Guide (TRA/MRA Guidelines)
- TSD's TRL Guide
- MD on TRAs at DHS S&T
- MD for CRADAS at DHS S&T
- Program Prioritization Index (PPI) Model
- Research/Innovation Focus Area Template
- CRADA Template
- Due Diligence Questions for Potential Partners
- Nationally Recognized Testing Laboratories (NRTLs) List
- FutureTECH Overview and Concept of Operations
- External and Internal FutureTECH Application Forms
- FutureTECH Certification Document (Under OGC Review)
- FutureTECH Program Flow Process Brief
- FutureTECH Program Swim Lane Chart

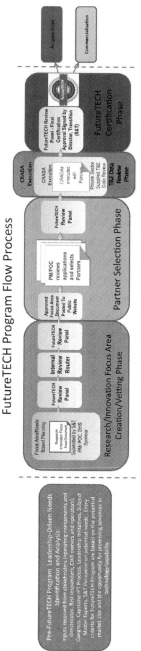

FutureTECH Program Flow Process

FutureTECH Program Roles and Responsibilities

Figure 5.6. FutureTECH Program Process Overview.

FutureTECH Program: Public-Private Technology Certification Process

	Research/Innovation Focus Area Creation/Vetting Phase	Partners Selection Phase	CRADA Execution and Technology Development Phase	T&E Data Review Phase	FutureTECH Certification Phase
	Objective: Develop research/innovation focus areas/needs for potential materiel capabilities needed by DHS stakeholders **Inputs:** Mission Needs Statement/Capability Gap/Enhanced Homeland Capability (EHC), DOTMLPF-RGS analysis, preliminary requirements elicitation from broad range of DHS stakeholders **Output:** Representative and well-vetted research/innovation focus area documents	**Objective:** Identify potential private sector partners capable of delivering required capabilities which can be validated **Inputs:** Applications from private sector entities seeking to provide capabilities/technologies to a research/innovation focus area/need **Output:** Detailed analysis of a given company's capabilities, technology/manufacturing maturity, capabilities and experience	**Objective:** Outline roles and responsibilities for DHS and private sector partners **Inputs:** Discussions with Private Sector Partners to develop CRADA and supporting documents **Output:** Binding CRADA agreement between DHS and private sector partner includes: SOW, developmental test plan/TRA, Milestones & Deliverables	**Objective:** Determine ability of proposed technologies to meet stated research/innovation focus areas /needs and performance specifications **Inputs:** T&E data from developmental test plan/TRA conducted by recognized third party T&E entity or DHS sponsored test facility **Output:** Detailed report of T&E data review for performance alignment to research/innovation focus areas /need and performance specifications	**Objective:** Provide FutureTECH Certification, if appropriate **Inputs:** Detailed report on certification package containing T&E data review, vetted research/innovation, focus area document, MNS, AOA, DOTMLPF analysis **Output:** Determination on granting certification for a potential technology
DHS Sponsor (e.g. First Responder, CIKR stakeholder, etc.)	• Elicit needs and preliminary requirements from stakeholders (approx. 2-4 months) • Communicate with national user associations/organizations • Develop Mission Needs Statement (MNS) • Conduct DOTMLPF-RGS analysis • Ensure preliminary requirements are representative of user community • Represent user community as necessary • Grants development with DHS customer/stakeholder, if required		• Provide input on developmental considerations necessary to conduct effective developmental test plan/TRA	• Assist PM/POC as necessary to evaluate efficacy and alignment of performance data to meet/exceed stated research/innovation focus areas/needs	• End users/customers notified of Certified technologies/capabilities
Commercialization Office	• Assist in research/innovation focus area drafting by offering requirements development materials • Assist in analyzing program prioritization index model (PPI) • Assist in analysis of alternatives, technology scans and market scans • Continue outreach on "how to do Business with DHS" with private sector • Engaged internal and/or external subject matter expert(s)/FFRDC/Non-S&T organization(s) to assist in review of research/innovation focus area document, developmental test plan/technology readiness assessment (TRA) and T&E data • Post approved research/innovation focus area document to FutureTECH Program website, if/when approved by FutureTECH Review Panel and Internal Review Router	• Provide resources to assist in technology/manufacturing maturity assessments and business analysis • Manage incoming applications to posted research/innovation focus area documents • Assist with business analysis of potential partners: experience in technology development, business history, likeliness to achieve TRL-6 etc. (approx. 1 week per company) • Notify private sector partners of selection or non-selection within one week after decisions are made	• Assist PM/POC to develop CRADA and necessary documentation (e.g. SOW, developmental test plan/TRA milestones and deliverables)	• Provide resources and materials to develop the criteria necessary for thorough review of developmental test data/TRA • Provide recommendation on certification	• Assist PM/POC in preparation of certification package • New FutureTECH Certified technology/capability marketed by private sector with DHS support, and oversight of Certification mark usage, if approved
PM/POC	• Collect and support preliminary requirements data/information/documentation articulation from DHS Sponsor • Determine alignment to mission needs/capability gaps • Conduct an analysis of alternatives (AOA) and research similar efforts • Conduct feasibility study with support from subject matter expert(s), if necessary • Identify external sources of information (e.g. subject matter expert(s)) • Prepare research/innovation focus area document for review by FutureTECH Review Panel and Internal Review Router • Ensure conformance/inclusion of any necessary regulation(s) or standard(s)	• Establish timeline for application acceptance cycles • Conduct due diligence review of potential partners with assistance of Commercialization Office ❑ Verify current TRL/TRA/MRL of potential technology ❑ Analyze likelihood of potential technology to provide desired capability and capability alignment to research/innovation focus area document • Recommend future action with potential partners to FutureTECH Review Panel (to be completed within one month of acceptance cycle closing)	• Draft CRADA with OGC, Tech Transfer Manager and Commercialization Office (approx. 2-3 weeks) ❑ Work with private sector partner to determine milestones and deliverables ❑ Develop Statement of Work ❑ Develop developmental test plan/TRA with private sector partner with input from T&E team • Verify TRL-6 maturity is achieved prior to developmental test plan/TRA based on requirements for certification	• Provide analysis of capability alignment to stated research/innovation focus area/need • Evaluate efficacy and alignment of performance data to meet/exceed stated research/innovation focus areas /needs • Communicate questions/comments or clarification needs to private sector partner • Provide recommendation on certification	• Prepare and present to FutureTECH Review Panel the supporting documentation in certification package and provide recommendation for certification, if appropriate
FutureTECH Review Panel*	• Ensure preliminary requirements alignment and priority to overall mission objectives based on MNS, EHC, Capstone IPT Capability Gap • Review DOTMLPF-RGS analysis and AOA • Accept or decline initial package from PM/POC into FutureTECH Program prior to reviews by Internal Review Router	• Confirm PM/POC analysis of potential private sector partner • Approve/Recommend course of action with potential partner(s) to PM/POC	• Review documentation and provide approval on CRADA and appendices • Authorize final approval of CRADA • Approved CRADA signed by Director – S&T Transition and private sector partner	• Review analysis from PM/POC and T&E team to ensure that all data verifies TRL 6/MRL 7 compliance, alignment to research/innovation focus area document and that performance meets or exceeds published vendor specifications	• Review certification package and recommendation from PM/POC • Make final decision on certification of a given technology/capability
Internal Review Router**	• Review technical merit of research/innovation focus area document accepted by FutureTECH Review Panel: Are preliminary requirements testable, measurable, specific achievable and solution agnostic? • Express opinions with recommendations to FutureTECH Review Panel • Ensure preliminary requirements alignment and priority to overall DHS stakeholder mission				
Subject Matter Expert(s)	• Review technical merits of research/innovation focus area document accepted by FutureTECH Review Panel: Are preliminary requirements testable, measurable, specific, achievable and solution agnostic? • Ensure preliminary requirements are representative of user community • Provide insight into any similar efforts and leverage existing information/research		• Provide input on developmental considerations necessary to conduct effective developmental test plan/TRA	• Provide analysis of capability alignment to stated research/innovation focus areas/needs	
Third Party Independent T&E Team	• Review technical merit of research/innovation focus area document: Are the preliminary requirements testable, measurable, specific, achievable, feasible and solution agnostic?		• Assist in reviewing developmental test plan/TRA to include measures of reliability, safety, and quality assurance • Provide input on technical considerations necessary to conduct effective capability testing • Provide recommendation on necessary DHS participation during developmental test plan/TRA • Review and modify developmental test plan/TRA as required prior to inclusion in CRADA	• Validate T&E performance data meets/exceed stated specifications • Ensure test results and procedures followed developmental test plan/TRA • Pose questions/comments to PM/POC to relay to partner • Provide assessment of whether research/innovation focus areas/needs are met	
Deliverables	Deliverables: (Typical Time Frame: 4-6 months) 1. Written report/brief by PM/POC justifying participation in FutureTECH program including MNS, DOTMLPF-RGS analysis, AOA and research/innovation focus area document is to be distributed and reviewed by FutureTECH Review Panel (approx 3-6 months) 2. Research/innovation focus area document review and feedback loop to confirm accuracy, feasibility and level of detail of preliminary requirements performed by FutureTECH Review Panel and Internal Review Router (approx 3-4 weeks for initial reviews) 3. Preliminary developmental test plan/TRA procedures and potential performers considered 4. Approved research/innovation focus area documents will be posted online to the FutureTECH Program website by the Commercialization Office 5. Results/Follow up actions will be communicated/coordinated by the PM/POC	Deliverables: (Typical Time Frame: 2 Months) 1. Management of interest and questions from potential private sector partners offering their capabilities to the stated focus areas/needs by Commercialization Office and PM/POC 2. Conduct detailed analysis of potential technology and manufacturing maturity levels and critical business standing of potential partners 3. Select private sector partners that demonstrate ability to deliver required capabilities timely and effectively 4. Results/Follow up actions will be communicated/coordinated by the PM/POC	Deliverables: (Typical Time Frame: 1-2 Months) 1. Work in close collaboration with selected private sector partners to develop CRADA, SOW, developmental test plan based on proposed technology 2. Formalize developmental test plan/TRA and determine T&E sponsorship and responsibilities 3. PM/POC to oversee and monitor progress of private sector partners to achieve milestones and deliverables 4. PM/POC and Independent T&E team to observe/oversee T&E as necessary 5. Results/Follow up actions will be communicated/coordinated by the PM/POC	Deliverables: (Typical Time Frame: 3-4 weeks) 1. The results of performed T&E are to be distributed to the PM/POC, Independent T&E team and Subject Matter Expert(s) as necessary for detailed review and report on findings of T&E data. 2. Whenever possible, a [illegible] review of T&E data will be used to analyze whether performance to address requirements and meets/exceed stated specifications. 3. FutureTECH Review Panel will review reports written by PM/POC and Independent T&E team to evaluate conformance of performance. 4. Results/Follow up actions will be communicated/coordinated by the PM/POC	Deliverables: (Typical Time Frame: 2-3 Months) 1. The finalized certification package and recommendation for certification prepared by PM/POC to be reviewed by FutureTECH Review Panel 2. Director – S&T Transition analyzes recommendations of FutureTECH Review Panel signs certification, if appropriate 3. Prepare disclaimers/waivers to be signed by private sector partner if certified 4. Publish certification notice on public websites and [illegible] lists, as appropriate

* **Internal Review Router** consists of: PM/POC, S&T Portfolio Manager, S&T Division Director, Independent T&E team, Subject Matter Expert(s), and Director – S&T Transition (Final sign-off)

** **FutureTECH Review Panel** consists of: Director - APMD; Director – S&T Transition; Director – S&T Innovation; Director – S&T Basic Research, Technology Transfer Manager; OGC representative (S&T); Chief Commercialization Officer

Acronym Legend:
DOTMLPF-RGS: Doctrine, Organization, Training, Materiel, Leadership, Personnel, Facilities – Regulations, Grants, Standards
AOA: Analysis of Alternatives
MNS: Mission Needs Statement
OT&E: Operational Testing and Evaluation
EHC: Enabling Homeland Capability
PM/POC: Program Manager/Point of Contact
TRL/MRL: Technology Readiness Level/Manufacturing Readiness Level
SOW: Statement of Work
CRADA: Cooperative Research and Development Agreement
CIKR: Critical Infrastructure & Key Resources
PPI: Program Prioritization Index

Figure 5.7. FutureTECH Program Roles and Responsibilities.

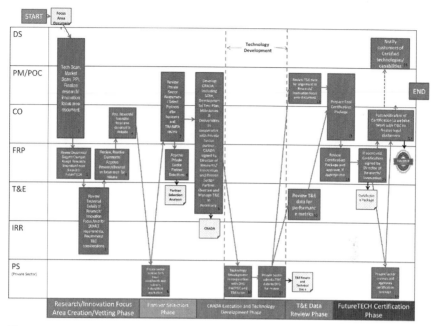

Figure 5.8. FutureTECH Program Swim Lane Chart.

A CRADA is an extremely useful tool to both the public and private sectors. The private sector can receive property and patent rights for an invention, while the public sector benefits because it does not use any taxpayer money to fund the project and may use information gathered by the agreement.

TRANSFORMATIONAL CHANGE BEYOND DHS

While it is gratifying that our commercialization process and private sector outreach programs are being incorporated and mandated by the department in the forthcoming and updated Acquisition Management Directive (MD 102-01), it is worth noting that our model can be readily extended to and adopted by other agencies in the federal government. Examination of figure 5.9 clearly shows how the incorporation of commercialization adds a "valuable tool to an agency's toolbox" in providing increased speed of execution in deploying technologies/products/services to solve problems, as well as provides an increase in the net realizable budget of an agency. In addition, as evidenced by figure 5.10, the potential return-on-investment (ROI) of these commercialization-based public-private partnerships can yield impressive results.

Why a Commercialization Office?: Creating and Demonstrating Value

S&T Commercialization Office -- Four Major Activities

Parameter	Requirements Development Initiative	Commercialization Process	SECURE Program	S&T Private Sector Outreach
1) Increases speed-of-execution of DHS programs/projects	✓	✓	✓	✓
2) DHS and its stakeholders receive products more closely aligned to specific requirements/needs	✓	✓	✓	✓
3) Increases effective and efficient communication	✓	✓	✓	✓
4) End users can make informed purchasing decisions	✓	✓	✓	✓
5) Large savings of cost and time for DHS and its stakeholders	✓	✓	✓	✓
6) Increases goodwill between taxpayers, private sector and DHS	✓	✓	✓	✓
7) Fosters more opportunities for small, medium and large businesses	✓	✓	✓	✓
8) Large taxpayer savings	✓	✓	✓	✓
9) Possible product "spin-offs" can aid other commercial markets	✓	✓	✓	✓
10) Promotes open and fair competition	✓	✓	✓	✓

Return-on-DHS Investment is LARGE!

Figure 5.9. The major activities of the Commercialization Office demonstrate positive results for taxpayers, the private sector, and DHS.

Commercialization Office – Return on Investment (ROI)

SECURE Program – C-ORD	Market Size	ROI
Blast Resistant Autonomous Video Equipment (BRAVE) C-ORD Requirements for a forensic camera deployed in public transportation vehicles to assist in incident cause analysis.	Over 1.5 million units	290
National Emergency Response Interoperability Framework and Resilient Communication System of Systems C-ORD Requirements for a system to provide interoperable communications on a national framework for remote use by first responders.	Over 2,000 units	525
Interoperable Communications Switch C-ORD Requirements for an interoperability switch-based communications system that provides networked communications between any number of agencies and personnel.	Over 230 units	525
Crisis Decision-Support Software C-ORD Requirements for a system with a user-centric approach matched with an expansive database of past decisions and a proven method to quickly reach critical decisions in high pressure environments for wide operational use.	Approx. 50,000 units	1023
Blast Mitigation of Fuel Tank Explosions C-ORD Requirements for an explosion suppression system to protect fuel containers. A "fuel container" ranges from fuel tanks found in vehicles, boats or trains to fuel storage tanks at airports, seaports and the neighborhood gas station.	Over 1 million units	727
Integrated Intrusion Protection C-ORD Requirements for an adaptable, scalable surveillance capability that provides automated, real-time protection for a wide range of operational scenarios.	Over 41,000 units	290
Predictive Modeling for Counter-Improvised Explosive Devices (IED) C-ORD Requirements for a system to predict the threat of an IED attack and further data fusion from law enforcement, intelligence partners and other sources to support the common operating picture.	Over 250,000 seats in US alone	870

Assumptions for Conservative ROI Projections:

➤ *Return on Investment* – (Gain on Investment/Cost Savings – Cost of Investment) / Cost of Investment

➤ *Gain on Investment/Cost Savings* – conservative estimate of potential savings of nominally expended R&D dollars at S&T; in general, estimated savings is 75% of given/related FY09 enabling homeland capability (EHC), which is identified through Capstone IPT process

➤ *SECURE Program – Cost of Investment* – 20% of Commercialization Office personnel salary + (10% Other expenses such as OGC, OPA, CCD, etc.); divided by 20 commercialization operational requirements documents (C-ORDs) completed and publically released in given year

➤ *R&D Funds at DHS S&T* – R&D funds do not include labor or overhead (not fully burdened cost of managing program/projects/EHCs)

Note: Return on DHS Investment is LARGE when compared to Angel Investors (4x to 7x) and Venture Capitalists (5x to 20x)

Figure 5.10. The use of commercialization has the potential to realize significant return-on-investment (ROI) values as evidenced by the SECURE pilot program at DHS.

We have shown through the SECURE and FutureTECH programs that the federal government can engage and influence—in a positive way— the private sector by offering detailed requirements and conservative estimates of market potential. The reason that these partnerships are successful is simple and straightforward. Firms spend significant resources in trying to understand market needs and market potential through their business and market development efforts. By offering this open and transparent information, government saves the private sector both time and money while demonstrating its genuine desire to work cooperatively to develop technologies and products to meet DHS stakeholders' needs in a cost-effective and efficient way that benefits the private and public sectors—but also, most importantly, the American taxpayers.

Because of its obvious benefits, it is reasonable to examine the possibility of extending the concepts developed at DHS to other federal agencies. Logic dictates that in cases where operational requirements can be developed across agencies, the size of a given potential available market would increase. It is also certainly conceivable that various agencies across the federal government share similar requirements for products and services. Just as business experts discuss "technology platform" strategies and models, one can envision a detailed requirements document delineating core requirements with additional agency-driven "options"—analogous to the variety of options offered on automobiles. Just as consumer products are developed with a variety of options (at varying price points), a

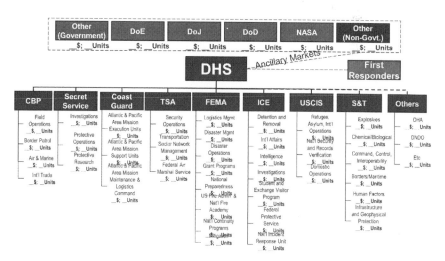

Figure 5.11. The market potential template for DHS outlines potential user communities within DHS markets but also to "ancillary markets" represented by other federal government agencies.

detailed requirements document could outline all the options required by agencies through a "requirements platform." Figure 5.11 shows how an agency like DHS is related to other government and nongovernment ancillary markets. Figures 5.12 and 5.13 delineate the diversity of the other DHS stakeholders in the first-responder community and CIKR owners and operators, respectively.

Communities of Practitioners and Dual-Use Technologies

The prevalence of national associations for various homeland security stakeholder communities drives the creation of a significant amount of information relative to the challenges, needs, and requirements of their representative membership. Government can play a vital role in communication with these associations to gather this critical information. Sharing this with larger audiences and creating a nationwide understanding of the problems has increased the awareness and identification of similar requirements in a number of user communities. The more cross-cutting a set of requirements becomes, the more opportunities exist to save taxpayers' resources. How could this be accomplished in a practical way? The answer is simple: It has already begun. DHS Science & Technology Directorate is planning to utilize deployable technology to create a community of practitioners (CoP) in order to gather and communicate requirements across such a large-scale community of users.

DoD, for example, has invested in these kinds of technologies. Technology will enable users to reach not only the millions of first responders but also other potentially authorized stakeholders and members of the Homeland Security Enterprise (HSE) (other federal agencies, private sector, venture community, etc.). Advanced technologies like the Semantic Web 3.0 will aid in the communal and open development of detailed operational requirements, potential available market sizing/applications, and so on. We are finalizing plans to initiate a pilot program to harness these technologies to engage various user communities to enable broad-based development of widely accepted operational requirements. Figure 5.14 shows graphically the evolution of developing detailed requirements culminating in the establishment of CoPs. As cooperative partnerships increase between the public and private sector, sharing information becomes the most important tool to improve the effectiveness of the relationship.

CoPs can be developed at a number of levels to gather information from all government stakeholders at the federal, state, local, and tribal levels. Open communication can gather information from stakeholders regionally as well as capturing the unique needs of localities that may be large urban centers, widespread townships, or coastal cities, for example.

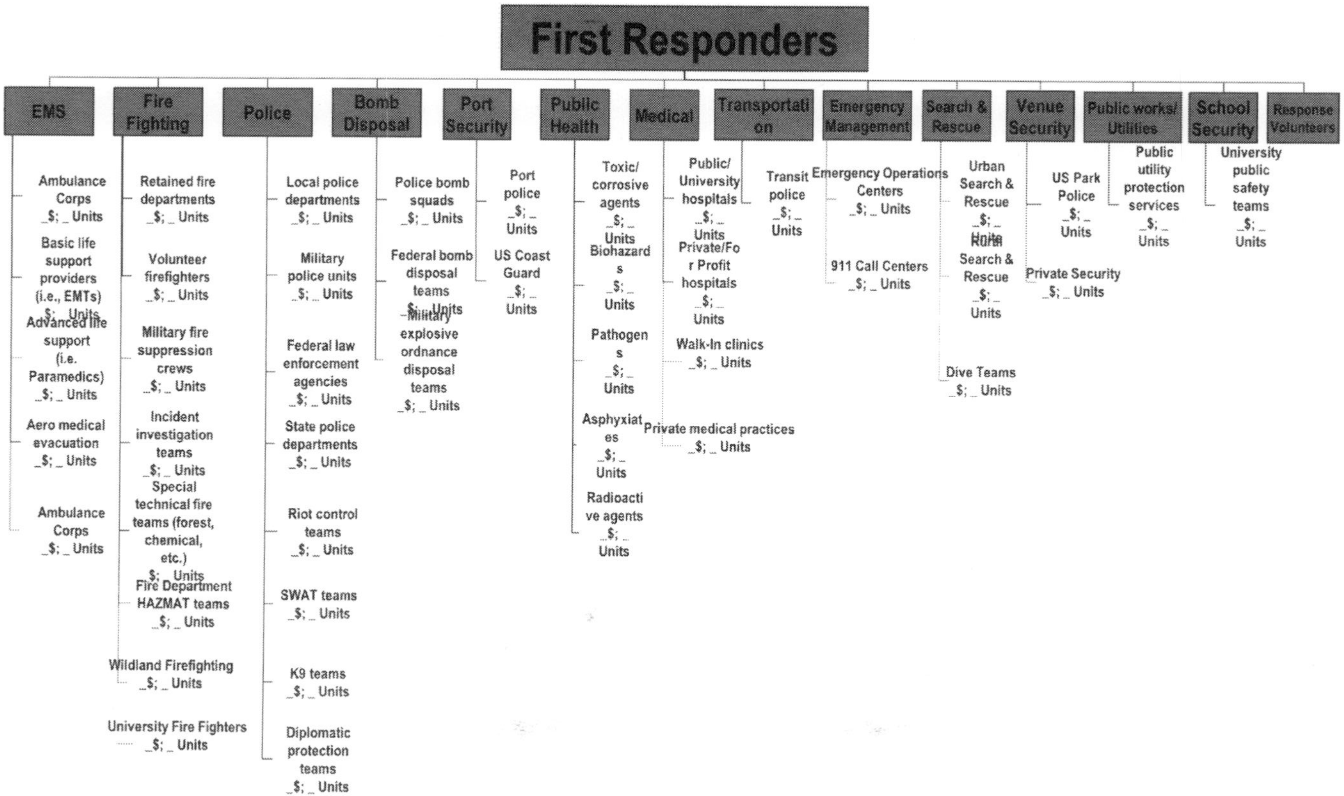

Figure 5.12. Market potential template for the first-responder market.

Critical Infrastructure Key Resources (CIKR)

Agriculture and Food
- Food Retail $:_ Units
- Farm Equipment $:_ Units
- Meat/Poultry Processing $:_ Units
- Food Processing $:_ Units
- Dairy $:_ Units
- Dairy Farms $:_ Units
- Ranching $:_ Units
- Organic Farming/Sustainable Agriculture $:_ Units
- Traditional Planting $:_ Units
- Commercial fishing $:_ Units

Defense Industrial Base
- Defense Contractors $:_ Units
- Industry analysts $:_ Units
- Think tanks/research institutions $:_ Units
- University partnership programs $:_ Units
- National laboratories $:_ Units

Public Health and Healthcare
- Public/University hospitals $:_ Units
- Private/For Profit hospitals $:_ Units
- Clinics $:_ Units
- Private medical practices $:_ Units
- Medical laboratories $:_ Units
- Pharmaceutical $:_ Units
- Health insurance $:_ Units
- Medical equipment manufacturers $:_ Units
- Medical technology manufacturers $:_ Units
- Biotechnology $:_ Units

Energy
- Coal mining operations $:_ Units
- Coal power plants $:_ Units
- Coal equipment manufacturers $:_ Units
- Hydroelectric $:_ Units
- Dam operators $:_ Units
- Wind power $:_ Units
- Solar power $:_ Units
- Public utilities companies $:_ Units
- Oil companies $:_ Units

National Monuments and Icons
- Guided tour services $:_ Units
- Travel services $:_ Units
- Lodging/Motel $:_ Units
- Guest services/tourism hospitality $:_ Units
- People moving services $:_ Units
- Queuing equipment makers $:_ Units
- Private security $:_ Units

Banking and Finance
- Credit lending institutions $:_ Units
- Commercial banking $:_ Units
- Private equity $:_ Units
- Consumer banking $:_ Units
- Building societies/Private banks $:_ Units
- Merchant banks $:_ Units
- Global financial services firms $:_ Units
- Community development institutions $:_ Units
- Community banks $:_ Units
- Savings and Loans $:_ Units
- Credit unions $:_ Units
- Insurance companies $:_ Units
- Insurance brokerages $:_ Units
- Reinsurance companies $:_ Units
- Stock brokerages $:_ Units
- Capital market banks $:_ Units
- Custody services $:_ Units
- Angel investment $:_ Units
- Venture capital $:_ Units

Water
- Public utilities $:_ Units
- Desalinization plants $:_ Units
- Treatment plants $:_ Units
- Equipment manufacturers $:_ Units
- Pipe and water control device manufacturers $:_ Units

Chemical
- Inorganic chemical production $:_ Units
- Organic industrial production $:_ Units
- Ceramics $:_ Units
- Petrochemicals $:_ Units
- Agrochemical $:_ Units
- Polymers $:_ Units
- Elastomer production $:_ Units
- Oleochemical $:_ Units
- Explosives $:_ Units
- Fragrance production $:_ Units
- Chemical wholesale $:_ Units
- Exotic chemicals $:_ Units

Commercial Facilities
- Hotels $:_ Units
- Shopping centers $:_ Units
- Stadiums and sport arenas $:_ Units
- Schools $:_ Units
- Commercial office buildings $:_ Units
- Museums $:_ Units
- Zoos and Aquariums $:_ Units
- Public Libraries $:_ Units
- Amusement parks $:_ Units

Emergency Services
- Fire Departments $:_ Units
- Law enforcement agencies $:_ Units
- Search and rescue teams $:_ Units
- Ambulance companies $:_ Units
- Mine rescue teams $:_ Units
- technical rescue teams $:_ Units
- Bomb disposal units $:_ Units
- Blood/Organ transplant supply $:_ Units
- emergency comms $:_ Units
- Public utility protection providers $:_ Units
- Emergency Social services $:_ Units
- Community emergency response teams $:_ Units
- Disaster relief $:_ Units
- Famine relief teams $:_ Units
- Poison Control units $:_ Units
- Animal control teams $:_ Units
- Wildlife services $:_ Units

Materials Reactors and...
- Electric utilities $:_ Units
- Reactor and associated materials $:_ Units
- University and educational institutions $:_ Units
- Control systems $:_ Units
- Nuclear safety systems $:_ Units
- Waste disposal services $:_ Units
- Uranium processors $:_ Units
- Protective garment manufacturing $:_ Units

Telecommunications
- Telephone/Cellular services $:_ Units
- Satellite data transmission providers $:_ Units
- Broadcasting $:_ Units
- Broadcast equipment manufacturing $:_ Units
- Radio equipment manufacturing $:_ Units
- equipment manufacturing $:_ Units
- High speed data transmission $:_ Units
- Internet service providers $:_ Units
- Print media $:_ Units
- Internet technology providers $:_ Units

Critical Manufacturing
- Iron and Steel mills $:_ Units
- Aluminum production and processing $:_ Units
- Nonferrous metal production and processing $:_ Units
- Engine Turbine and Power transmission $:_ Units
- Electrical Equipment manufacturing $:_ Units
- Motor Vehicle manufacturing $:_ Units
- Aerospace product & parts $:_ Units
- Railroad rolling stock $:_ Units
- Other Transportation equipment $:_ Units

Postal and Shipping
- United States Postal Service $:_ Units
- High volume document and parcel shipping $:_ Units
- Container shipping services $:_ Units
- Marine shipping $:_ Units
- Trucking industry $:_ Units
- Airborne shipping $:_ Units
- Distribution services $:_ Units

Transportation
- AMTRAK $:_ Units
- Commuter rail $:_ Units
- Intracity rail services $:_ Units
- Commercial airline $:_ Units
- Private air services $:_ Units
- Cruise lines $:_ Units
- Subway systems $:_ Units
- Long-haul maritime shipping $:_ Units
- Bus services $:_ Units
- Freight rail service $:_ Units
- Automobile travel $:_ Units
- Roads, Highways, bridges and tunnels $:_ Units

Information Technology
- Hardware providers $:_ Units
- IT Conglomerates $:_ Units
- Semiconductor production $:_ Units
- Electronics manufacture $:_ Units
- IT services $:_ Units
- Server and network hardware $:_ Units
- Display/digital TV $:_ Units
- Software production $:_ Units
- Gaming $:_ Units
- Information security $:_ Units
- Semiconductor equipment $:_ Units

Figure 5.13.
Market potential template for the CIKR market.

Evolution of Change:
DHS Providing Better Information about its Needs

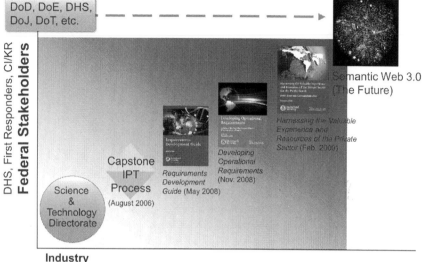

DoD, DoE, DHS, DoJ, DoT, etc.

DHS, First Responders, CI/KR
Federal Stakeholders

Semantic Web 3.0 (The Future)

Harnessing the Valuable Experience and Resources of the Private Sector (Feb. 2009)

Developing Operational Requirements (Nov. 2008)

Capstone IPT Process *(August 2006)*

Science & Technology Directorate

Requirements Development Guide (May 2008)

Industry
Business, Venture Capital/Angel Investment, Strategic Partnerships

Figure 5.14. DHS is transforming the way that it reaches out to its stakeholders to learn about their needs. Advanced social networking technologies have the potential to greatly enhance communications and the understanding of needs to allow open and free competition to provide the best solutions at the best price for government.

CoPs will enhance connections between personnel in a number of mission spaces who may find similarities in capability gaps or share information on best practices and possible standards that can facilitate coordinated responses to incidents involving users from a number of jurisdictions.

Uncovering common requirements across stakeholder communities highlights the connections between ancillary markets and the possibility for a technology to work in varied applications. Dual-use technologies provide useful capabilities to a larger market of potential users. It follows that addressing additional markets increases the potential benefits to solution providers who can distribute their company's capabilities to a wider audience, increasing sales volumes and driving prices down for consumers as economies of scale are improved.

Commercialization and partnerships are tools that have genuine value well beyond DHS. In fact, these efforts can offer more and more opportunities to increase the speed of execution of government programs and increase the net realizable budget of the government—all to the benefit of taxpayers the more the models are used both across and within government.

CREATING AN INTEGRATED APPROACH: BLENDING AND COORDINATING EFFORTS AT DHS

Despite the numerous benefits offered through commercialization-based public-private partnerships, there are instances in which it is not the best method and traditional public-private partnerships are more appropriate. DHS has a number of organizations charged with working directly with the private sector to provide funding, when necessary, to spur the development of new technologies, products, and services. These organizations and efforts are located throughout DHS and the federal government as a whole to allow private sector vendors greater access to opportunities throughout the public sector. The cooperative and complementary nature of these organizations ensures that the right technology, product, or service is reviewed by the right people in an efficient manner. The organizations and opportunities listed below cover a wide range of possible means to engage with the public sector, including those with grant and funding opportunities as well as other partnership and mentoring programs for small businesses to engage more easily with larger companies looking for strategic partnerships.

The SAFETY Act: Liability Protection for Anti-Terrorism Technologies

The Supporting Anti-Terrorism by Fostering Effective Technologies Act (SAFETY Act) is intended to provide critical incentives for the development and deployment of antiterrorism technologies by providing liability protections for sellers of "qualified antiterrorism technologies." The goal of the SAFETY Act is to ensure the possessors of such antiterrorism technologies are not deterred by the threat of liability from developing and commercializing products and technologies that could save lives in the event of a terrorist attack.

As part of the Homeland Security Act of 2002, Public Law 107-296, Congress enacted several liability protections for providers of antiterrorism technologies. The SAFETY Act provides incentives for the development and deployment of antiterrorism technologies by creating a system of "risk management" and a system of "litigation management." The Act creates certain liability limitations for "claims arising out of, relating to, or resulting from an act of terrorism" where qualified antiterrorism technologies have been deployed.

Table 5.2.   U.S. Department of Homeland Security and Other Federal Contact Information

DHS and/or Federal Contact	Description	Contact Information
Private Sector Office	Part of the DHS Office of Policy, the Private Sector Office engages individual businesses, trade associations, and other nongovernmental organizations to foster dialogue with the department. It also advises the secretary on prospective policies and regulations and in many cases on their economic impact. The Private Sector Office promotes public-private partnerships and best practices to improve the nation's homeland security, and promotes department policies to the private sector.	www.dhs .gov/xabout/ structure /gc_11662 20191042 .shtm
Federal Business Opportunities (Fed Biz Opps)	"Virtual marketplace" that captures the official federal government procurement opportunities, allowing contractors to retrieve services posted by government buyers.	www.fbo .gov/
Small Business Innovation Research (SBIR)	SBIR is a set-aside program (2.5% of an agency's extramural budget) for domestic small business concerns to engage in research/ research and development (R/R&D) that has the potential for commercialization.	www.sbir. dhs.gov/
Small Business Assistance	Provides numerous resources, links, and contacts to ensure that small companies have a fair opportunity to compete and be selected for Department of Homeland Security contracts.	www.dhs .gov/ xopnbiz/ small business/
Mentor-Protégé Program	Designed to motivate and encourage large business prime contractor firms to provide mutually beneficial developmental assistance to small business, veteran-owned small business, service-disabled veteran-owned small business, HUBZone small business, small disadvantaged business, and women-owned small business concerns.	www.dhs .gov/xopn biz/small business/ editorial_ 0716.shtm
FEMA Industry Liaison Program	Designed to establish strategic relationships with industry partners and stakeholders with access to vendors/contractors; serving as an industry advocate; and acting as the liaison between vendors and the program offices. The IL Program is the portal for all vendors seeking to do business with FEMA. Additionally, small business vendors are routed to the FEMA Small Business Analyst for notification, support, and processing. During a disaster, the IL Program has created a process to ensure that information about your company's products or services is routed as supplemental market research to the appropriate FEMA contracting and acquisition professionals.	www.fema .gov/ business/ contractor .shtm
EAGLE and EAGLE II Programs	Department-wide contracts for Information Technology (IT) services and commodities. These procurements are being conducted by the Office of Procurement Operations (OPO) in cooperation with the chief information officer (CIO) and the component IT and procurement communities.	www.dhs .gov/xopn biz/ opportunities /editorial_ 0700.shtm

Table 5.3. S&T Directorate—Homeland Security

DHS and/or Federal Contact	Description	Contact Information
TechSolutions Program	Established to provide information, resources, and technology solutions that address mission capability gaps identified by the emergency response community. The goal of TechSolutions is to field technologies that meet 80% of the operational requirement, in a twelve- to fifteen-month time frame, at a cost commensurate with the proposal but less than $1 million per project.	http://www .dhs.gov/ xfrstresp/ training/gc_ 117405742 9200.shtm
SBIR	Please refer to table 5.2.	https://www .sbir.dhs.gov/
SAFETY (Support Anti-terrorism by Fostering Effective Technologies) Act	Part of the Homeland Security Act of 2002, the SAFETY Act encourages the development and deployment of antiterrorism technologies to protect the nation and provide "risk management" and "litigation management" protections for sellers of qualified antiterrorism technologies and others in the supply and distribution chain.	https://www .safetyact .gov/
Homeland Security Advanced Research Projects Agency (HSARPA)	Manages a broad portfolio of solicitations and proposals for the development of homeland security technology. HSARPA performs this function in part by awarding procurement contracts, grants, cooperative agreements, or other transactions for research or prototypes to public or private entities, businesses, federally funded research and development centers, and universities.	https://baa .st.dhs.gov/
Unsolicited Proposals	Composed of several component agencies that handle different types of acquisitions. This department has several resources, links, and contacts if a given small company has products or services that may be of interest to one or more DHS component agencies.	http://www .dhs.gov/ xopnbiz/ opportunities/ editorial_ 0617.shtm
University Programs	Office of University Programs engages the academic community to conduct research and analysis and provide education and training to enhance the department's homeland security capabilities. University Programs' three thrust areas include: Centers for Excellence; Education Programs; Minority Serving Institutions (MSI) Programs	http://www .dhs.gov/ xabout/ structure/ editorial_ 0555.shtm

The department recognizes that the universe of technologies that can be deployed against terrorism includes far more than physical products. Therefore, the defense of the homeland will require deployment of a broad range of technologies that includes services, software, and other forms of intellectual property. Qualified antiterrorism technologies have been very broadly defined to include "any qualifying product, equipment, service (including support services), device, or technology (including information technology)" that the secretary, as an exercise of discretion and judgment, determines to merit designation under the statutory criteria.

CONCLUSION

As history shows, public-private partnerships have been integral to the advancement of science and technology for the common good through the efficient completion of tasks and requirements, a decrease in the amount of taxpayer money spent, and the enhancement of the quality of products and services. These prevalent agreements between public and private sector entities have historically involved the public sector funding the private sector to divert its time and resources to address an area without the potential of acceptable return on investment.

The Department of Homeland Security's Commercialization Office has built upon this traditional public-private partnership model to leverage the free-market system in order to create commercialization-based public-private partnerships. These partnerships center on the basis that the public sector often represents sizable customer bases for the private sector to warrant investments of time and money. By providing the private sector with detailed, articulated requirements and a conservative estimate of the potential available market, the public sector becomes the "consumer" in this free-market scenario.

The SECURE and FutureTECH programs of the Commercialization Office utilize this commercialization-based public-private partnership. SECURE leverages the resources, experience, and expertise of the private sector to develop and deliver fully deployable solutions aligned to the detailed operational requirements of DHS's stakeholders. FutureTECH focuses on the long-term needs of the department itself that require the development of new technology. These two programs provide great opportunities for the private sector to "do business" with DHS and to create a "win-win-win" scenario for all participants. With the knowledge of needs and requirements from the public sector, the private sector is better positioned to align their technology offerings to needed capabilities within the department and its stakeholders. The public sector benefits from this partnership through the formation of a clearinghouse where the private sector can compete in an open and transparent way for the business of the public sector, which ultimately lowers costs and increases the quality of products and services available for purchase. The taxpayer "wins" because the private sector spends its own money, time, and resources on the research and development of technology and products and then sells those products to the government at a competitively low price not only saving the money of the taxpayer but also expanding the net realizable budget of the public sector.

The obvious benefits available to the public sector, private sector, and taxpayer allow for the commercialization-based public-private partnership model through the SECURE and FutureTECH programs to be a useful "tool in the toolbox" not only for DHS but across all federal government agencies to meet the needs and capability gaps of stakeholders in order to protect and secure the homeland of the United States of America.

NOTES

1. Thomas A. Cellucci, "Commercialization Office: Offering Transformational Change beyond DHS," June 2009.
2. Thomas A. Cellucci, "FutureTECH: Guidance to Understanding Future DHS S&T Critical Research/Innovation Focus Areas," April 2009.

REFERENCES

Many references were used to develop this chapter. See, for example:

Hearne, Rory. "Origins, Development and Outcomes of Public Private Partnerships in Ireland: The Case of PPPs in Social Housing Regeneration." *Combat Poverty Agency* 09/07 (2009). Web.
"John Winthrop, Jr." *Connecticut State Library*. Connecticut State Library. Web. 25 May 2010. www.cslib.org/gov/winthropj.htm.
Link, Albert N. "The History of Public/Private Partnerships." *Public/private Partnerships: Innovation Strategies and Policy Alternatives*. New York: Springer, 2006. 7-22. Print.
Medalye, Jacqueline. "Support and Opposition of Public-private Partnerships." *Encyclopedia of Earth*. 21 Nov. 2006. Web. 25 May 2010. www.eoearth.org/article/Support_and_opposition_of_public-private_partnerships.
The National Council for Public-Private Partnerships. Web. 25 May 2010. http://ncppp.org/.
"NETL: Cooperative Research and Development Agreement." *DOE - National Energy Technology Laboratory: Home Page*. Web. 25 May 2010. www.netl.doe.gov/business/crada/crada.html.
"What Is a CRADA? Technology Transfer, Bureau of Reclamation, U.S. Department of the Interior." *Bureau of Reclamation Homepage*. 6 Nov. 2009. Web. 25 May 2010. www.usbr.gov/research/tech-transfer/crada/whatcrada.html.

Chapter 6

Creating Opportunities for the Private Sector

Simply put, the mission of the Department of Homeland Security (DHS) is to protect our nation's most valuable asset—our people. There is no more important need than to provide the DHS and its stakeholders with the necessary resources and capabilities that enable them to ensure mission success. Addressing the needs and requirements of these groups continues to be a challenge requiring new ideas to gather resources and innovative technologies and products effective at combating the numerous threats facing our nation.

DHS experienced several challenges merging twenty-two disparate organizations, along with taking responsibility for the millions of our nation's first responders and CIKR owners and operators into a cohesive organization with a unified mission and culture. Those familiar with merger and acquisition (M&A) activities realize that while integration of organizations poses difficulties, it also represents opportunities to infuse new processes and values into the newly created organization. Through both top-down and bottom-up approaches, DHS has been successful in developing, socializing, and now implementing an innovative commercialization framework that has started to gain traction throughout the agency.

Many situations arise within the department, first-responder community, and private sector where there is a need for widely distributed products. Recognizing this fact, the department recently began fostering a "commercialization mindset"[1] in order to leverage the vast capability and resources of the private sector through innovative win-win public-private partnerships stressing the need for detailed requirements. Commercialization represents another "tool in the toolbox" that can be used to provide much-needed products and services to the DHS stakeholders. While the development of highly specialized products using traditional acquisition channels is still relevant to the department, the fact that DHS is a conduit to large markets is highly advantageous for its stakeholders. The process of partnering with the private sector solution providers to work cooperatively on many of the steps in the system engineering life cycle will allow more groups to be involved in developing competing solutions to DHS's customer needs when low-unit-volume custom systems are not required. Not only is this a new way of thinking about developing and procuring products, it necessitates clear and precise communications between the public and private sectors.

In order for solution providers to invest their valuable time, money, and resources to develop products and services for use by DHS operating components, first-responder communities, CIKR owners and operators, and other stakeholders, the DHS commercialization process relies on providing them with two key pieces of information:

1. A clear and detailed delineation and explanation of the operational requirements
2. A conservative estimate of the potential available market for a potential commercialization partner to offer potential solution(s).

Resources like this guide are useful aides in addressing the first piece of developing cooperative partnerships.

COMMERCIALIZATION OFFICE INITIATIVES AT DHS

As a natural extension of the Capstone IPT process, the department's Commercialization Office has taken the lead in developing innovative programs and processes that actively seek to foster public-private partnerships to develop and deploy much-needed capabilities with the speed of execution and efficiency needed to match the demands of DHS's stakeholders. The Commercialization Office focuses on bringing improved clarity and communication of stakeholders' needs across the department and to private sector partners who have resources to assist in product and technology development. Working in a constructive way in which all the participants, including the private sector, public sector, and taxpayer, benefit enables the high probability of expediting the cost-effective and efficient development of products and services to meet the unsatisfied needs and wants of the department, its operating components, first responders, and the CIKR owners and operators.

The Commercialization Office, found within S&T's Office of Transition, is responsible for accelerating the delivery of enhanced technological capabilities to meet the requirements and close the capability gaps to support DHS agencies and its stakeholders in accomplishing their missions. The major activities that enable the accomplishment of the goals of the Commercialization Office are the requirements development initiative, commercialization process, creation of public-private partnerships, and outreach to the private sector.

To facilitate the development of new products and technologies a clear understanding is necessary so that efforts are well coordinated and move with a common purpose. To build upon the capability gaps that are outputs of the Capstone IPT process, DHS recognized the importance in developing operational requirements at an early stage in product development. As previously stated, this discipline enables DHS personnel to articulate, in detail, a given problem and its associated requirements. Stakeholders can communicate those needs to both internal and external audiences. This effort addresses a long-standing need for DHS to fully articulate its requirements and explain in detail the capabilities necessary for mission success. Once again, the requirements hierarchy shows how a Commercialization-based Operational Requirement Document (C-ORD) takes a capability gap to "much higher resolution," a necessary step required for product developers to assist DHS in its goal of expediting the deployment of cost-effective and efficient widely distributed products.

Through the publication of a number of books, including the *Requirements Development Guide* and *Developing Operational Requirements*, the Commercialization Office provides resources for understanding the importance of requirements guidelines and templates for creating C-ORDs. The clear communication of requirements ensures that all parties involved are "on the same page" and that product and technology development moves along clearly defined paths.

MARKET POTENTIAL IS CATALYST
FOR RAPID NEW PRODUCT DEVELOPMENT

It is important to understand not only the detailed operational requirements necessary to provide DHS stakeholders with mission-critical capabilities, but also the volume of potential users of these solutions. DHS itself can represent a substantial potential available market, in many instances requiring hundreds, if not thousands of product or service units to address unsatisfied needs. Couple to this the fact that DHS is responsible for so many ancillary markets (e.g., first responders, critical infrastructure and key resource owners and operators, etc.) representing large potential available markets, it is evident that substantial business opportunities exist for the private sector, as these large pools of potential customers and users represent the "lifeblood" for businesses (see figure 6.1).

In order to provide opportunities for a greater number of private sector entities to get involved in addressing the needs of these markets, it is hoped that the market analysis and proper articulation of requirements encourages innovative thinking on the part of the private sector to market valuable solutions, given that many needs may be shared across both public and private sector communities.

The DHS commercialization process is based upon the simple premise that the private sector is willing and able to use its own money, resources, expertise, and experience to develop and produce fully developed products and services for DHS if significant market potential exists. The private sector has shown remarkable interest in devoting its time and resources to such activities if and when an attractive business case can be made related to large revenue/profit opportunities. Market analyses clearly demonstrate that large potential available markets exist for DHS and its ancillary markets. In order to actively engage with the private sector, DHS must share two pieces of critical information: (1) detailed operational requirement(s) and (2) a conservative estimate of the potential available market(s). This information can then be used to generate a business case for possible private sector participation in the program.

In its new commercialization model, S&T acts as a facilitator between its customers—DHS's operating components and ancillary markets— and the private sector entities who may potentially develop products for use by DHS's stakeholders. S&T must work with its valued customers in the creation of C-ORDs that accurately reflect their mission-critical operational requirements through active participation in the requirements development initiatives. S&T also conducts market surveys and technology scans to ensure that needed technical capabilities and/ or products can be made accessible in response to the requirements of generated C-ORDs. This analysis also leads to understandings of the number of potential users and applications for potential solutions. This allows the private sector to understand in a clear and transparent way what the department and its customers need in order to use their time, money, and resources to create products, services, or technologies where market potential is large. Oftentimes, private sector entities have products in development that are closely aligned with current homeland security capability gaps and can be transitioned to the field rapidly and cost effectively.

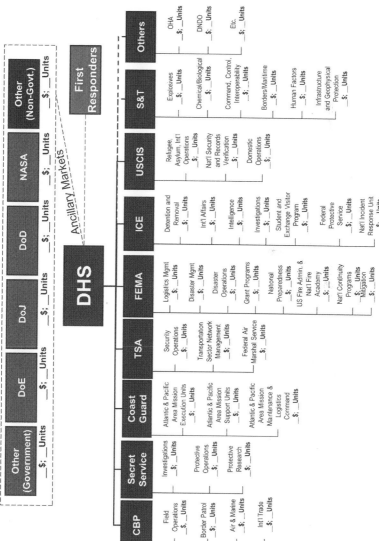

Figure 6.1. While the development of highly specialized products using traditional acquisition channels is still relevant to the department, the fact that DHS is a conduit to such large markets is highly advantageous for its stakeholders.

SECURE AND FutureTECH: A SUMMARY

The Commercialization Office created two innovative public-private partnership programs to engage the private sector for cooperative product development efforts. The SECURE (System Efficacy through Commercialization Utilization Relevance and Evaluation) Program seeks to find highly developed (TRL 5–9) private sector product offerings aligned to DHS-generated and -vetted C-ORDs posted on the DHS website. Its sister program, FutureTECH, focuses on the long-term needs of the department that require the development of new technologies (TRL 1–6) to address future capability gaps. We have demonstrated through the SECURE and FutureTECH programs that the federal government can engage and influence—in a positive way—the private sector by offering detailed requirements and conservative estimates of market potential. The reason that these partnerships are successful is simple and straightforward. Firms spend significant resources in trying to understand market needs and potential through their business and market development efforts. By offering this information, government saves the private sector both time and money while demonstrating its genuine desire to work cooperatively to develop technologies and products to meet DHS stakeholders' needs in a cost-effective and efficient way that benefits the private and public sectors—but also, most importantly, the American taxpayers.

Through the SECURE Program, the department provides to potential solution providers detailed operational requirements and a conservative estimate of the potential available market(s) offered by DHS stakeholders. In exchange for this valuable information, the private sector offers deployable products and services (along with recognized third-party test and evaluation data) that meet these stated requirements in an open and free way that creates an ergonomic "clearinghouse of solutions" available to DHS's stakeholders. Because of the success and "win-win-win" nature of this program in that it provides benefits for the American taxpayer, the private sector and DHS, DHS-S&T recently introduced the FutureTECH Program, which describes the long-term capabilities/technologies required by DHS stakeholders.

FutureTECH identifies and focuses on the future needs of the department as fully deployable technologies and capabilities, in some cases, are not readily available in the private sector or federal government space. While the SECURE Program is valuable to all DHS operating components, organizational elements, and DHS stakeholders, FutureTECH is intended for DHS S&T use only, particularly in the fields/portfolios related to research and innovation.

After providing independent third-party testing and evaluation of potential products, services, or technologies to show they do in fact meet or exceed the specifications listed in the detailed operational requirements, private sector entities can potentially enter into a partnership with the department in order to deliver commercial-off-the-shelf products to the department's stakeholders. In addition to providing products to DHS and its stakeholders, these partnership programs, SECURE[2] and FutureTECH,[3] give much-needed assurance to the first-responder and CIKR communities that a certified product or service works as specified and is aligned to the requirements document.

OUTREACH TO THE PRIVATE SECTOR

In order for these programs to be successful in providing needed products, services, and technologies to DHS and its stakeholders, partnerships with the private sector are imperative. The private sector outreach efforts of the Commercialization Office are designed to provide information to the public on "How to Do Business with DHS." Efforts demonstrate the value of engaging in mutually beneficial relationships to provide business opportunities to produce products/services to DHS components and ancillary markets. The private sector outreach efforts of the Commercialization Office center on notifying the private sector about opportunities that exist for partnership and business development to address the needs of the Department.

Through websites,[4] speeches, conferences, seminars, and publications the Commercialization Office is able to provide to the private sector information on partnership opportunities and helpful resources and contacts to foster a public-private partnership. A "full response package" can be requested that includes more background on the SECURE and FutureTECH programs as well as a template company overview that can be submitted and entered into our repository that is available for the whole department to review.

Doing business with DHS creates a number of ancillary benefits for the private sector. The communication of detailed requirements and conservative estimates of potential available markets helps guide businesses as they continue to pursue new opportunities. The involvement of the venture capital and angel investor communities is a critical function in assisting small businesses and start-up companies with innovative new technologies for the homeland security market place. These groups are traditionally entrepreneurial, seeking opportunities to advance cutting-edge technology with a primary focus on speed of execution. Partnerships within the private sector itself are fostered regularly to bring fully deployable solutions to these new markets. Companies are enabled to approach potential partnerships with a stronger business case based on a credible understanding of the needs of their potential customers that show true business opportunities. Funding new and innovative technologies that have the potential to address numerous large markets is an attractive opportunity for venture capitalists and angel investors. In addition, there has been a marked increase in the number of strategic partnerships between small businesses and large companies as each has something to offer.

Small businesses are the "engines of innovation."[5] These small businesses are creative entities, offering new solutions and ideas to solve many complex challenges. However, many small businesses lack the resources for proper business development and sales development practices. In these cases strategic partnerships offer opportunities to grow sales and market channels that can bring their innovative technologies to the field where they can be of the greatest benefit. Table 6.1 below is a benefit analysis demonstrating how all participants receive positive outcomes as a result of fostering public-private partnerships.

Table 6.1.   Benefit Analysis—"Win-Win-Win"

Taxpayers	Public Sector	Private Sector
1. Citizens are better protected by DHS personnel using mission critical products	1. Improved understanding and communication of needs	1. Save significant time and money on market and business development activities
2. Tax savings realized through Private Sector investment in DHS	2. Cost-effective and rapid product development process saves resources	2. Firms can genuinely contribute to the security of the nation
3. Positive economic growth for American economy through creation of jobs and business opportunities	3. Monies can be allocated to perform greater number of essential tasks	3. Successful products share in the "imprimatur of DHS"; providing assurance that products really work
4. Possible product "spin-offs" can aid other commercial markets	4. End users receive products aligned to specific needs	4. Significant business opportunities with sizable DHS and ancillary markets
5. Customers ultimately benefit from COTS produced within the Free Market System—more cost-effective and efficient product development	5. End users can make informed purchasing decisions with tight budgets	5. Potential strategic partnership and commercialization opportunities between small, medium, and large businesses result

The Commercialization Office's public-private partnerships are viewed positively by DHS stakeholders. The success of the program lies in the fact that all participants receive significant benefits.

For many private sector solution providers the potential to do business with DHS has never been greater. New programs have opened significant business opportunities to work in cooperative public-private partnerships. The private sector can now play a critical role in developing needed capabilities for DHS's stakeholders in a freely competitive way that shows demonstrable benefits for many different groups. New collaborative business practices will enable DHS to field fully developed products with a speed of execution not seen before in many government programs. Continued participation and engagement through these partnership programs will only increase as more requirements are gathered and shared, creating the opportunities necessary for businesses to get involved. The private sector shows every day its willingness to be an active partner through genuine interest in ensuring that DHS's stakeholders are better able to carry out their mission and protect the people of the United States. DHS will continue to enable these relationships with the goal of facing the many challenges that lay ahead.

NOTES

1. See, for example, *Developing Operational Requirements, Version 2*, "Product Realization Chart," "DHS Implements a Commercialization Process," and other valuable resources online at www.dhs.gov/xres/programs/gc_1211996620526.shtm.

2. Thomas A. Cellucci, "Commercialization Office: Offering Transformational Change Beyond DHS," June 2009.

3. Thomas A. Cellucci, "FutureTECH: Guidance to Understanding Future DHS S&T Critical Research/Innovation Focus Areas," April 2009.

4. See Commercialization Office websites at www.DHS.gov. Homepage found at www.dhs.gov/xabout/structure/gc_1234194479267.shtm.

5. Thomas A. Cellucci, "Focus on Small Business: Opportunities Abound for the Engines of Innovation," March 2009.

Chapter 7

Offering Transformational Change beyond DHS

The U.S. Department of Homeland Security, through the Science & Technology Directorate (S&T) initiated an innovative commercialization-based public-private partnership called the SECURE Program. As previously mentioned, the department—through this program—provides to potential solution providers detailed operational requirements and a conservative estimate of the potential available market(s) offered by DHS stakeholders, such as DHS operating components (FEMA, TSA, CBP, Secret Service, ICE, USCIS, and Coast Guard), first responders, and critical infrastructure/key resources (CIKR) owners and operators. In exchange for this valuable information, the private sector offers deployable products and services (along with recognized third-party operational test and evaluation data) that meet these stated requirements in an open and free way that creates an ergonomic "clearinghouse of solutions" available to DHS stakeholders. Because of the success and "win-win-win" nature of this program in that it provides benefits for the American taxpayer, the private sector, and DHS, DHS S&T recently introduced the FutureTECH Program that describes the long-term capabilities/technologies required by DHS stakeholders. Please see www.dhs.gov/xres/programs/gc_1211996620526.shtm and www.dhs.gov/xres/programs/gc_1242058794349.shtm to review these programs.

While it is gratifying that our commercialization process and private sector outreach programs are being incorporated and mandated by the department in a forthcoming and updated Acquisition Management Directive (MD 102-01), it is worth noting that our model can be readily extended to and adopted by other agencies in the federal government. Examination of table 7.1 clearly shows how the incorporation of

Why a Commercialization Office?: Creating and Demonstrating Value

S&T Commercialization Office -- Four Major Activities

Parameter	Requirements Development Initiative	Commercialization Process	SECURE Program	S&T Private Sector Outreach
1) Increases speed-of-execution of DHS programs/projects	✓	✓	✓	✓
2) DHS and its stakeholders receive products more closely aligned to specific requirements/needs	✓	✓	✓	✓
3) Increases effective and efficient communication	✓	✓	✓	✓
4) End users can make informed purchasing decisions	✓	✓	✓	✓
5) Large savings of cost and time for DHS and its stakeholders	✓	✓	✓	✓
6) Increases goodwill between taxpayers, private sector and DHS	✓	✓	✓	✓
7) Fosters more opportunities for small, medium and large businesses	✓	✓	✓	✓
8) Large taxpayer savings	✓	✓	✓	✓
9) Possible product "spin-offs" can aid other commercial markets	✓	✓	✓	✓
10) Promotes open and fair competition	✓	✓	✓	✓

Return-on-DHS Investment is LARGE!

Table 7.1. The major activities of the Commercialization Office demonstrate positive results for the American taxpayer, private sector, and DHS.

commercialization adds a "valuable tool to an agency's toolbox" in providing increased speed of execution of deploying technologies/products/services to solve problems as well as provide an increase in the net realizable budget of an agency. In addition, as evidenced by figure 7.2, the potential return-on-investment (ROI) of these commercialization-based public-private partnerships can yield impressive results.

The reason that these partnerships are successful is simple and straightforward. Firms spend significant resources in trying to understand market needs and market potential through their business and market development efforts. By offering this information, government saves the private sector both time and money while demonstrating its genuine desire to work cooperatively to develop technologies and products to meet DHS stakeholders' needs in a cost-effective and efficient way that benefits the private and public sectors, and also, most importantly, the American taxpayer.

Because of its obvious benefits, it is reasonable to examine the possibility of extending the concepts developed at DHS to other federal agencies. Logic dictates that in cases where operational requirements can be developed across agencies, the size of a given potential available market would

Assumptions for Conservative ROI Projections:

➢ *Return on Investment* – (Gain on Investment/Cost Savings – Cost of Investment) / Cost of Investment

➢ *Gain on Investment/Cost Savings* – conservative estimate of potential savings of nominally expended R&D dollars at S&T; in general, estimated savings is 75% of given/related FY09 enabling homeland capability (EHC), which is identified through Capstone IPT process

➢ *SECURE Program – Cost of Investment* – 20% of Commercialization Office personnel salary + (10% Other expenses such as OGC, OPA, CCD, etc.); divided by 20 operational requirements documents (ORDs) completed and publically released in given year

➢ *R&D Funds at DHS S&T* – R&D funds do not include labor or overhead (not fully burdened cost of managing program/projects/EHCs)

SECURE Program – ORD	ROI
Blast Resistant Autonomous Video Equipment (BRAVE) ORD Requirements for a forensic camera deployed in public transportation vehicles to assist in incident cause analysis.	290x
National Emergency Response Interoperability Framework and Resilient Communication System of Systems ORD Requirements for a system to provide interoperable communications on a national framework for remote use by first responders.	525x
Interoperable Communications Switch ORD Requirements for an interoperability switch-based communications system that provides networked communications between any number of agencies and personnel.	525x
Crisis Decision-Support Software ORD Requirements for a system with a user-centric approach matched with an expansive database of past decisions and a proven method to quickly reach critical decisions in high pressure environments for wide operational use.	1023x
Blast Mitigation of Fuel Tank Explosions ORD Requirements for an explosion suppression system to protect fuel containers. A "fuel container" ranges from fuel tanks found in vehicles, boats or trains to fuel storage tanks at airports, seaports and the neighborhood gas station.	727x
Integrated Intrusion Protection ORD Requirements for an adaptable, scalable surveillance capability that provides automated, real-time protection for a wide range of operational scenarios.	290x
Predictive Modeling for Counter-Improvised Explosive Devices (IED) ORD Requirements for a system to predict the threat of an IED attack and further data fusion from law enforcement, intelligence partners and other sources to support the common operating picture.	870x

Figure 7.2. The use of Commercialization has the potential to realize significant return-on-investment (ROI) values as evidenced by the SECURE pilot program at DHS.

increase. It is also certainly conceivable that various agencies across the federal government share similar requirements for products and services. Just as business experts discuss "technology platform" strategies and models, one can envision a detailed requirements document delineating core requirements with additional agency-driven "options"—analogous to the variety of options offered on automobiles. Just as consumer products are developed with a variety of options (at varying price points), a detailed requirements document could outline all the options required by agencies through a "requirements platform." Figure 7.3 shows how an agency like DHS is related to other government and nongovernment ancillary markets.

The more cross-cutting a set of requirements becomes, the more opportunities exist to save taxpayers' resources. How could this be accomplished in a practical way? The answer is simple: It has already begun. The DHS Science & Technology Directorate is planning to utilize the semantic web (also known as Web 3.0). In order to gather and communicate requirements across such a large-scale community of users, there is a need to use deployable technology to create a community of practitioners (CoP). DoD, for example, has invested in these kinds of technologies. Technology will enable the ability to reach not only the millions of first

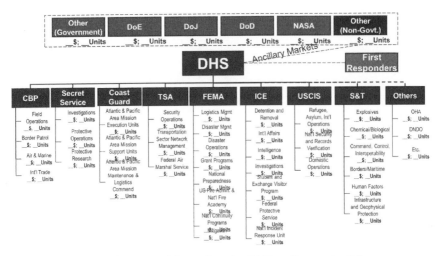

Figure 7.3. The market potential template for DHS outlines potential user communities within DHS markets but also "ancillary markets" represented by other federal government agencies.

responders but also other potentially authorized stakeholders (other federal agencies, private sector, venture community, etc.). Advanced technologies like the Semantic Web 3.0 will aid in the communal and open development of detailed operational requirements, potential available market sizing/applications, and so on, all to the benefit of the American taxpayer, government, and private sector. We are finalizing plans to initiate a pilot program to harness these technologies to engage various user communities to enable broad-based development of widely accepted operational requirements. Figure 7.4 shows graphically the evolution of developing detailed requirements culminating in the establishment of CoPs.

PROGRAM PRIORITIZATION INDEX (PPI)

The U.S. Department of Homeland Security (DHS) was created through the merging of twenty-two separate federal government agencies under a central department with, most notably, seven operating components (Federal Emergency Management Agency, Transportation and Security Administration, U.S. Customs and Border Patrol, U.S. Immigration and Customs Enforcement, U.S. Secret Service, U.S. Coast Guard, and U.S. Citizen and Immigration Services). These agencies represent mission-critical activities that are collectively far-reaching and all-encompassing efforts and initiatives necessary for securing our nation. There exist significant management challenges to understand,

Evolution of Change:
DHS Providing Better Information about its Needs

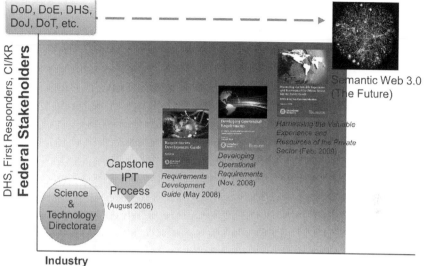

Figure 7.4. DHS is transforming the way that it reaches out to its stakeholders to learn about their needs. Advanced social networking technologies have the potential to greatly enhance communications and the understanding of needs to allow open and free competition to provide the best solutions at the best price for government.

articulate, and address the needs, unique and common, of each of the agencies that comprise DHS.

With so many needs and requirements generated from DHS stakeholders, an effective and efficient means of prioritizing programs and projects is essential for generating the highest yield per DHS investment dollar. The DHS limited budgets, personnel, and time to address all requirements make efforts to rank and prioritize projects and programs a necessity. A simple, yet effective, method to evaluate the benefits of pursuing certain proposed programs or projects relative to others across the department is essential.

The DHS's Science and Technology Directorate developed a Program/Project Prioritization Index (PPI) that is arranged as a value-based model to capture the relative utility of one program/project over another. The PPI described below provides DHS managers a means to make rational rankings based on sound and useful parameters provided by a given program/project. The PPI is calculated using a combination of objective and subjective metrics of practical considerations for the open analysis of various factors.

The PPI is a first-pass simple index to use as a guide for discussions related to program/project prioritization and justification. It incorporates a utilitarian approach to provide the most good for the most amount of people and property, while recognizing political sensitivity, risk and cost-saving factors. It should be noted that the PPI is a figure of merit to be utilized as only one tool in making a DHS investment decision, in the same way personnel assessment tools can "red-flag" potential issues in a hiring decision. The PPI is not intended to be used as the single decision-making tool, as we operate in a dynamic environment.

This resource is to be used in the same vein as a quote by General Eisenhower during World War II, "The plan is not important, but planning means everything." The PPI is a tool to spark discussion and critical thinking about the management of resources, expected outcomes, and the overall impact of a program.

The Program/Project Prioritization Index is based upon:

1. *People Protected* from potential threat (typical occurrence): Attach the following points for number of people potentially protected: assign 0 for zero people; 1 for 1–10 people; 2 for 11–100; 3 for 101–500 people; 4 for 501–1,000 people; 5 for 1,001–100,000 people, and an additional point for each additional 20,000 people potentially protected. (If desired, a threat potential from 0.0–1.0 can be multiplied to calculate a threat expectation value.)

2. *Property Protected* from potential threat: assign a point for each $50,000,000 of property protected. (If desired, a threat potential from 0.0–1.0 can be multiplied to calculate a threat expectation value.)

3. *Positive Political Impact Generated* (*Societal Perception*) as a result of a program/project's implementation: assign 0 points for "low"; 5 points for "medium"; and 10 points for "high."

4. *Cost Savings Realized by DHS* upon full implementation: assign 1 point for each $1,000,000 saved (includes personnel plus resources).

5. *Dollars Requested/Spent by DHS* on the program/project: assign 1 point for each $1,000,000.

6. *PPI Calculation*: Add items 1–4 and divide by item 5 to obtain the PPI. The higher the PPI value, the more value it potentially returns for a given DHS investment.

7. *Risk Adjusted PPI*: Multiply item 6 by the "probability of success" of the program/project (i.e., obtain all stated objective(s)/specification(s) expressed in a fraction ranging from zero percent probability of success (0.0) to 100 percent probability (1.0). For example, 0.5 would relate to a 50 percent probability of success.

The master equation is then:

$$PPI = \frac{(People\ Protected\ Points + Property\ Protected\ Points +\ Societal\ Perception\ Points + Cost\ Savings\ by\ DHS)}{Dollars\ Requested/Spent\ by\ DHS}$$

For example, table 7.1 gives an analysis of three hypothetical projects. Definition of values:

People Protected (typical occurrence): This value represents the number of people affected by a single incident.

Property Protected (typical occurrence): This value represents the value in dollars of the property affected by a single incident. This value can include surrounding infrastructure that may be affected by collateral damage.

Societal Perception: This value represents the impact that a program/project will have on the way society perceives the department and its use of the program/project to provide protection. For example, intrusive inspection technologies may be poorly perceived by the public, while stream-lined unobtrusive techniques may be favorably perceived. The assigned value can be ranked on a scale of 0–100.

Cost Savings Realized by DHS: What would be the savings of DHS resources (materials, personnel, opportunity costs) if the program prevented an incident? What are the cost savings from improved efficiencies or capabilities that improve the way a particular task is

Table 7.1.   PPI Analysis of Three Hypothetical Projects

PPI Metric	Project A	Project B	Project C
People Protected	75	250	100,000
(1) People Protected Points	2	3	5
Probability of Occurrence (Value)	0.5 (1)	0.4 (1.2)	0.25 (1.25)
Property Protected	$5,000,000	$15,000,000	$1,000,000,000
(2) Property Protected Points	0.1	0.3	20
Probability of Occurrence (Value)	0.7 (.07)	0.4 (0.12)	0.25 (5)
Societal Perception	Medium	Medium	High
(3) Societal Perception Points	5	5	10
Cost Savings	$5,000,000	$1,500,000	$10,000,000
(4) Cost Savings Points	5	1.5	10
Dollars Requested/Spent	$2,000,000	$6,000,000	$15,000,000
(5) Dollars Requested/Spent Points	2	6	15
Total (1+2+3+4)	11.07	7.712	31.25
(6) PPI Calculation	**5.535**	**1.285**	**2.083**
"Probability of Success"	0.7	0.7	0.8
(7) Risk Adjusted PPI	**3.8745**	**0.899**	**1.664**

conducted? To what extent can partnerships reduce the cost of developing/deploying/using the output of a program?

Dollars Requested/Spent by DHS: What is the requested amount necessary for DHS to execute the proposed program/project in terms of development and transition dollars?

Threat Potential/Probability of Occurrence: How likely is the typical occurrence for which the program/project is designed to address expected to happen? This value is based on a percentage from 0.0 to 1.0 and is multiplied against the people and property protected. For example, 0.5 would relate to a 50 percent probability of success.

Probability of Success: What is the expected impact of the fully developed system? How likely is it that a system will be developed to provide 100 percent of the desired capability when used in the field? This value is based on a percentage from 0.0 to 1.0 and is multiplied against the people and property protected. For example, 0.5 would relate to a 50 percent probability of success.

In summary, the PPI is a useful figure of merit to induce meaningful discussion among Homeland Security Enterprise members to effectively and efficiently develop technology products/services/processes to meet the ever-increasing challenges faced in securing the homeland. This value-based decision model can easily be modified in the future to accommodate new potential variables and parameters in program management decision making.

To conclude, commercialization is a tool that has genuine value well beyond DHS. In fact, commercialization can offer more and more opportunities to increase the speed of execution of government programs and increase the net realizable budget of the government—all to the benefit of taxpayers—the more the model is used across and within government.

Chapter 8

Conservative Estimates of Potential Available Markets

While volumes have been written on effective market sizing and segmentation, the SECURE Program provides a conservative estimate of the potential available market (PAM) for a given system (product or service), which needs to be verified through independent research by a potential commercialization partner.

The DHS commercialization process relies on providing two key pieces of information to potential solution providers in order for them to devote their valuable time, money, and resources to develop products and services for use by DHS operating components, first-responder communities, critical infrastructure and key resources (CIKR) owner/operators, and other stakeholders: (1) a clear and detailed delineation and explanation of the operational requirements, and (2) a conservative estimate of the potential available market for a potential commercialization partner to offer potential solution(s). We have forged the development of Commercialization-based Operational Requirements Documents (C-ORDs) through the publication of several books, training materials, and articles to address the first piece of information. Figure 8.1 shows a comprehensive market potential template that addresses the second piece.

It is important to understand not only the detailed requirements necessary to provide DHS stakeholders with mission-critical capabilities, but also the volume of potential users of these solutions. DHS itself can represent a substantial potential available market; in many instances requiring hundreds if not thousands of product or service units to address unsatisfied needs. Couple to this the fact that DHS has responsibility for so many ancillary markets (e.g., first responders, critical infrastructure and key resources, etc.) representing large potential available markets, it is evident

119

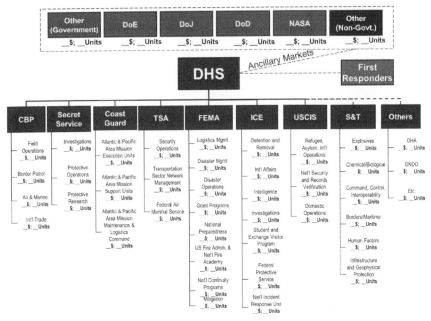

Figure 8.1.   The market potential template maps out many potential available markets to which DHS has direct control and responsibility or acts as a conduit.

that substantial business opportunities exist for the private sector as these large pools of potential customers and users represent the "lifeblood" for businesses (see figure 8.1). We outline the top level of key players in the public and private sectors. In turn, each "branch" of the template has been further segmented to home in on detailed opportunities.

As an example, in figure 8.2 we're interested in demonstrating the number and scope of various firefighting sub-segments or applications within the firefighting market segment. While these groups confront the same basic threat, each sub-segment represents and responds to specific threat profiles requiring different tactics. Similarly, another part of this market revolves around special technical fire teams, which encounter very unique challenges that most fire departments are not expected or are ill-equipped to confront, such as widespread forest fires. HAZMAT-capable fire teams may deal with material disposal; incident investigators might not require the same heavy-duty tools that fire crews need; and military fire suppression crews frequently have to battle an inferno that is driven by special propellants (e.g., jet fuel).

The wide variety of requirements within the fire protection and suppression market shows the keen observer just how potentially large this market may be for a given product or service, or demonstrates potential

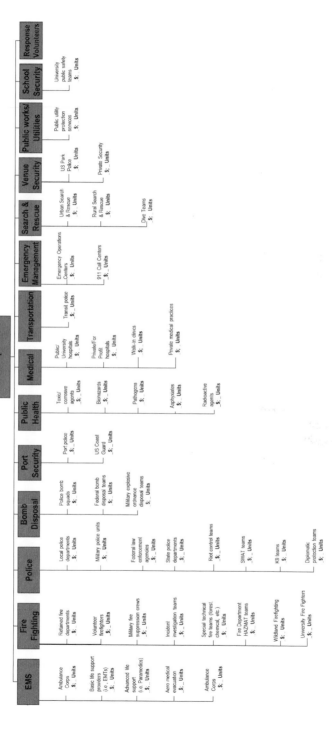

Figure 8.2. The chart maps various fire fighting segments.

new unsatisfied needs/wants. In addition, rather than limiting a solution provider to offering a given solution to a very specific sub-segment of a given market, this comprehensive template demonstrates the wide variety of market users of a requirements-driven firefighting solution *platform* that can be potentially tailored to meet the individual and unique needs among the various firefighting sub-segments. Instead of limiting the solution provider, we hope that our market analysis encourages innovative thinking on the part of the private sector to market a valuable solution because a given need may be shared across both public and private sector communities.

Chapter 9

Bridging the "Communications Gap" between the Public and Private Sectors
Making It Easier to Do Business with DHS

The U.S. Department of Homeland Security's commercialization outreach efforts center on notifying the private sector about opportunities that exist for partnership and business development to address the needs of the department. As in any worthwhile pursuit, effective communication is critical in the cost-effective and efficient interactions between the various parties. DHS is putting into practice the necessary rigor to improve communication that will allow the public and private sectors to work jointly to meet the unsatisfied needs of the DHS in order to protect the nation.

To this end, the DHS Commercialization Office has developed a number of processes, programs, and tools to facilitate the clear articulation of DHS needs (see figure 9.1). In that same spirit of working together with the private sector, the office developed a "Product Realization Guide" (see https://dhsonline.dhs.gov/portal/jhtml/dc/sf.jhtml?doid=116836) that is a useful guide to relate concepts and correlate terminology used by both the public and private sectors to clearly delineate how science, technology development, and product development (terms used in the private sector) are related to basic research, innovation, and transition using a Technology Readiness Level[1] (TRL) "backbone" (terms used commonly in the public sector).

Further examination of the "Product Realization Guide" (see appendix C) shows that this resource also provides a stage-gated approach for cost-effective and efficient product development to provide a "discussion framework" useful in private-public sector discussions as well as a template for utilization to develop and communicate agreements. The chart describes the objectives, deliverables, and the type of management review necessary to develop and deliver technologies/products/services that

123

meet the specific requirements of the DHS's operating components (U.S. Coast Guard, FEMA, TSA, CBP, USCIS, U.S. Secret Service, and ICE) and its end users such as first responders.

STAGE ONE: NEEDS ASSESSMENT

Needs assessment is the critical first stage of product realization (accomplished via acquisition or commercialization processes) that enables DHS to identify capability gaps and investigate new product/technology/service capabilities. By understanding the specific and detailed requirements of its customers, the DHS Science & Technology Directorate (DHS S&T) conducts market research and technology scans to find and assess technology-based solutions that could potentially be developed, matured, and delivered to DHS end users.

Please note that management reviews for both the public and private sector are required to ensure that exit criteria and deliverables are met when discussing public-private programs like the SECURE Program.

The remainder of the chart shows the various key objectives and deliverables for each major phase of product realization. Entrance at any point of the chart is possible, and certainly the overall objective of many

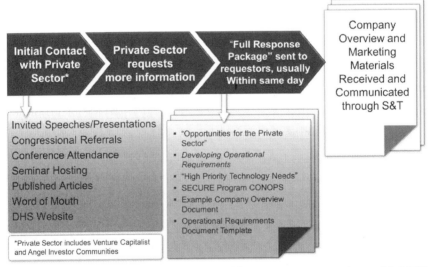

Figure 9.1.   Outreach efforts to inform the public on "How to Do Business with DHS" is receiving positive feedback from the private sector and media. See the following website for additional information: https://dhsonline.dhs.gov/portal/jhtml/community .jhtml?index=15&community=S%26T&id=2041380003.

projects currently underway at DHS is to obtain widely distributed products or services (where commercialization is key). DHS also sometimes has unique "custom-like" requirements with lower unit-volume potential (normally using the acquisition model as shown in figure 9.2). It also should be noted that in a basic research program, it may certainly not be possible to generate a C-ORD, as the objective may be the "exploring uncharted territory" rather than the development of products or services for sale to a particular market. For this reason, a dark box is drawn around Stage 1 to indicate that the Product Realization Chart is a multiple-use chart, rather than a concrete process, because it simply offers a framework to visualize several processes, some of which (developing custom or widely distributed products/services) require a needs assessment.

STAGE TWO: SCIENCE

At the beginning of the second stage, basic principles are observed and reported, and scientific research begins to be translated into applied research and development (R&D). At this stage, a program sponsor and end user/customer have been identified, and the mission needs statement, feasibility study, and program management vision have been developed.

Once basic principles are observed, practical applications can be invented. Applications are speculative, and there may be no proof or detailed analysis to support the assumptions. In the case of developing products/services, operational requirements analysis has been conducted, and operational requirements are applied to functional requirements. A risk management plan has been developed, a program cost analysis has been completed, and a preliminary security assessment has been conducted.

As the technology concept and/or application is formulated, active R&D is initiated that results in an analytical and experimental critical function and/or characteristic proof of concept. This includes analytical studies to physically validate the analytical predictions of separate elements of the technology. A Systems Engineering Management Plan (SEMP), Program Management Plan (PMP), and proof-of-concept plan are key deliverables and serve as exit criteria for the next stage of product realization.

During the second stage, the private sector normally produces a complete product plan during commercialization that addresses marketing opportunities, financial considerations, design concept, and many additional analyses. Sales/marketing team performs a SWOT (strengths, weaknesses, opportunities, and threats), a scenario analysis, and a sales forecast estimate. Research assembles the key IP disclosure submissions. Quality Assurance (QA) generates all safety/standards compliance items, calibration requirements, and other quality-control specifications.

Management reviews for both the public and private sector are required (in partnership projects or programs) to ensure that exit criteria and deliverables are met.

STAGE THREE: TECHNOLOGY DEVELOPMENT

The third stage of product realization ensues when basic technological components are integrated to establish that they will work together, which is a relatively "low-fidelity" analysis when compared with the eventual system. The proof-of-concept report and functional requirements document have been finalized. The SEMP, Test and Evaluation Master Plan (TEMP), quality-assurance plan and other deliverables are revised and updated on a continuous basis.

The basic technological components are then integrated with reasonably realistic supporting elements so they can be tested in a simulated environment. The fidelity of the breadboard technology increases significantly in this case. The Operational Requirements Document (ORD) and CONOPS are better developed. The technology scan and market survey are ongoing during the third stage, and an analysis of alternatives is provided.

Once the component is validated in a relevant environment, the system/subsystem model or prototype is demonstrated in a relevant environment. After successful T&E in a simulated operational environment, a preliminary Technology Transition Agreement (TTA) or a Technology Commercialization Agreement (TCA) is executed as applicable. A program manager is identified, and an interoperability assessment is performed.

During this stage, the private sector uses its product plan to conduct a beta design review, produce a detailed supplier list and supplier benchmark, begin writing the user's manual, develop a service strategy, confirm the risk analysis, and review engineering change orders. Manufacturing creates a preliminary manufacturing plan and works with Marketing/Sales to finalize product packaging. Quality Assurance defines regulatory requirements, prepares a preliminary quality plan and procedure for first prototype testing, and designs the inspection tooling.

Management reviews for both the public and private sector are required to ensure that exit criteria and deliverables are met.

ACQUISITION VERSUS COMMERCIALIZATION

Once a representative model or prototype system beyond TRL-5 is tested in a relevant environment, the product realization process splits into two paths that are extraordinarily different as evidenced in figure 9.2. Acquisition occurs when a government contractor executes design, development, and production driven by DHS requirements; using DHS funding; and being under contract to DHS. In this case, the product is then deployed to captive users and the product unit price is determined by cost-based pricing. The contractor's customer is DHS and not the end user community.

Commercialization, on the other hand, is a private-sector-driven activity enterprise that executes design, development, and production driven by market requirements using private funding and perhaps assisted by DHS technology licenses, standards, and grants. The product is then sold as commercial-off-the-shelf (COTS) directly to end users and the product unit price is determined by market-based pricing. The vendor's major customer is the end user community (e.g., first responders) as well as various private sector markets.

Why is there a need for commercialization? As previously mentioned, DHS requirements, in most instances, are characterized by the need for widely distributed COTS products. Oftentimes, the need is for thousands, if not millions of products for DHS's seven operating components and the fragmented, yet substantial first responder end user market. Figure 9.2 shows the major differences between a "pure" acquisition versus "pure" commercialization processes, along with the recently developed and implemented DHS "hybrid" commercialization process.

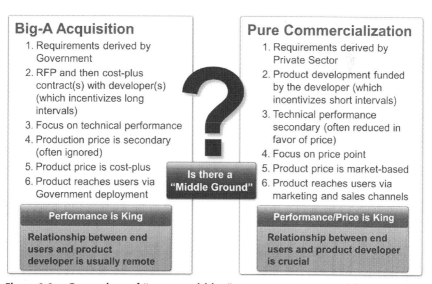

Figure 9.2. Comparison of "pure acquisition" versus "pure commercialization" models for product/system development and the resultant hybrid model implemented by DHS.

Figure 9.3 delineates the overall description of DHS's commercialization model and its first private sector outreach program called the SECURE (System Efficacy through Commercialization, Utilization, Relevance and Evaluation) Program to develop products and services in a private-public "win-win" partnership, approved in June 2008 by DHS and described in detail at www.dhs.gov/xres/programs/gc_1211996620526.shtm. Briefly, the SECURE Program is based on the premise that the private sector has shown that it is willing and able to use its own money, resources, expertise, and commercialization experience to develop and produce fully developed products and services for DHS if significant market potential exists. The private sector has shown remarkable interest in devoting its time and money to such activities if and when an attractive business case can be made related to large revenue/profit opportunities that certainly exist at DHS and its ancillary markets to participate in the advancement of DHS commercialization efforts. The private sector requires two things from DHS: (1) detailed operational requirements, and (2) a conservative estimate of the potential available market(s). Once this information is

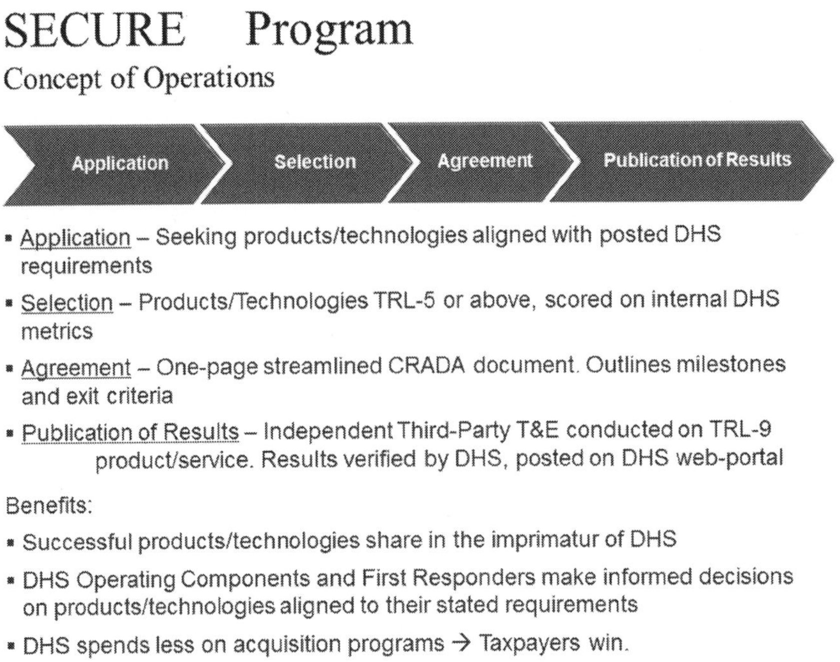
SECURE Program
Concept of Operations
Application
Selection
Agreement
Publication of Results
▪ Application – Seeking products/technologies aligned with posted DHS requirements
▪ Selection – Products/Technologies TRL-5 or above, scored on internal DHS metrics
▪ Agreement – One-page streamlined CRADA document. Outlines milestones and exit criteria
▪ Publication of Results – Independent Third-Party T&E conducted on TRL-9 product/service. Results verified by DHS, posted on DHS web-portal
Benefits:
▪ Successful products/technologies share in the imprimatur of DHS
▪ DHS Operating Components and First Responders make informed decisions on products/technologies aligned to their stated requirements
▪ DHS spends less on acquisition programs → Taxpayers win.

Figure 9.3. Step-by-step guide to the commercialization process developed and adopted by DHS with a brief summary of the popular SECURE Program.

posted to the SECURE Program website, small, medium, and large companies are open to generate their own business cases and pursue possible participation in the program.

The SECURE program provides a vehicle by which private sector entities can offer products and/or conduct product development geared specifically toward meeting specific needs. Private sector entities currently possessing a technology/product/system rated at a Technology Readiness Level TRL-5 (i.e., applied or advanced R&D) or above that potentially closes a defined DHS capability gap by addressing detailed operational requirements supplied by DHS S&T on the SECURE Program website will have the opportunity enter into a CRADA-like agreement to continue development of their technology/product/system to TRL-9 (i.e., fully field-deployable product) at their expense. The CRADA-like agreement also provides private sector entities with the assurance that DHS S&T will verify their recognized independent third-party test(s) of a given technology/product/system. A Cooperative Research and Development Agreement (CRADA) is a written agreement between a private company and a government agency to work together on a project.[2]

STAGE FOUR: PRODUCT DEVELOPMENT

After DHS determines whether the acquisition or the commercialization process is appropriate, the fourth stage commences and the system prototype is demonstrated in an operational environment. S&T and the end user/customer have begun to develop a final transition plan and updates have been made to the operational and/or functional requirements document. Interoperability has been demonstrated, and management directives (MD) have been reviewed to assure compliance. An operations and maintenance manual has been completed, and a security manual has been developed.

Since the technology has been proven to work in its final form and under expected conditions, TRL-8 represents the end of true system development. Technology components are therefore form, fit, and function compatible with an operational system. The operational test report has been completed, and a Limited User Test (LUT) Plan has been developed. A training plan has also been developed and implemented.

The actual system is then proven through successful mission operations, and the end user fully demonstrates the technology in the CONOPS. All critical documentation has been completed, and planning is underway for the integration of the next generation technology into the existing program components.

MANUFACTURING READINESS LEVELS (MRLs)

Equally important to the development of technologies and products are the manufacturing processes that will facilitate the long-term production of goods. Used in concert with TRLs, Manufacturing Readiness Levels[3] (MRLs) are designed to be measures used to assess the maturity of a given technology, component, or system from a manufacturing prospective. The purpose of MRLs is to provide decision makers (at all levels) with a common understanding of the relative maturity (and attendant risks) associated with manufacturing technologies, products, and processes being considered. Manufacturing risk identification and management must begin at the earliest stages of technology development and continue vigorously throughout each stage of a program's life cycles.

Manufacturing readiness begins before and continues during the development of systems, and it continues even after a system has been in the field for a number of years. The ability to transition technology smoothly and efficiently from the labs onto the factory floor and into the field is a critical enabler for acquisition or deployment. The MRL scale ranges from MRL-1 to MRL-10. These levels directly relate to the nine Technology Readiness Levels that are in use with an additional MRL-10 that is equal to a program in full-rate production. The first three levels are discussed as a single level, which is equal to TRLs 1 through 3.

Considerations for MRLs include manufacturing proofs-of-concept and the actual production of early-stage prototypes and breadboards components. Materials, sourcing, machines, and tooling must be analyzed and matured along with the technology development aspects captured in the TRL. Manufacturing processes must also be able to make the transition from the laboratory into product-relevant environments, where manufacturing costs and goals can be determined as well.

During the last stage, the private sector focuses on the manufacturing plan, and the development effort includes the final design reviews, product prototypes along with documented product test results, and other product development deliverables. Sales/Marketing updates the marketing plan, the sales and distribution plan, and all sales materials. Manufacturing develops assembly and manufacturing procedures and designs and fabricates manufacturing tooling. Quality Assurances updates the Test Q/A plan and creates the quality plan. They also develop testing procedures, create test and fixture designs, perform reliability testing on the prototype, and design and test the shipping container.

The goal of the private sector during the final stage is to demonstrate product manufacturing according to quality assurance standards while remaining within cost/schedule targets. The development effort concludes with a customer-adopted, defect-free product; implemented engineering change orders; and a final user's manual. Applications engineering and technical engineering support are then implemented. Sales/Marketing also provides sales training, creates a promotional plan, and coordinates literature advertising and public relations. Manufacturing establishes the final manufacturing/assembly routines and procedures, the final manufacturing tooling, and the manufacturing document release and acceptance, then undertakes an analysis for future product cost reduction. Quality Assurance does the final QA and test pooling, prepares the final QA/test procedures, and compiles the manufacturing yield data.

Management reviews for both the public and private sector are required to ensure that the final exit criteria and deliverables are met. Since the actual system has been proven through successful mission operations, the product is then deployed to captive users or sold as COTS directly to end users.

CONCLUSION

The Commercialization Office has developed a number of processes, programs, and tools to clearly articulate the needs of DHS. Outreach efforts are also critical and center on notifying the private sector about opportunities that exist for partnership and business development to address the needs of the department. Therefore, we have developed a "Product Realization Chart" that serves as a useful guide to relate and correlate terminology used by both the public and private sector in order to develop and deliver required technologies/products that meet the specific operational requirements of the Department of Homeland Security's operating components and its end users such as first responders.

NOTES

1. The creation of TRLs is credited to NASA during the 1980s. TRLs were then refined by DoD during the 1990s. TRLs remain a common tool used to evaluate the maturity of technology development. For more information, please visit www.hq.nasa.gov/office/codeq/trl/trl.pdf.

2. For more information on CRADAs, please visit http://frwebgate.access.gpo.gov/cgi-bin/getdoc.cgi?dbname=browse_usc&docid=Cite:+15USC3710a and www.usgs.gov/tech-transfer/what-crada.html.

3. MRLs are an evolution of the TRLs and originated as part of a joint DoD/industry working group to focus on measuring scale for manufacturing similar to that used for technology. For more information, please visit https://acc.dau.mil/CommunityBrowser.aspx?id=18231.

Chapter 10

The Capstone
IPT and Beyond

Advances in science and technology continue to spur the development of new and innovative products focused on the homeland security market. As this market place expands, it becomes increasingly important for Homeland Security personnel to assist in guiding product development to match their various needs. Delivering these customer-driven products and technologies is a primary objective for the U.S. Department of Homeland Security (DHS). Among the challenges facing DHS is how to gather and refine the needs or requirements of its various stakeholders, who represent a wide variety of mission spaces and operating environments, in a cost-effective and efficient manner.

The Department was created from the Homeland Security Act of 2002 and became an organization of twenty-two disparate entities combined with a common vision: to enable, support and expedite the mission-critical objectives of DHS's seven operating components in figure 10.1: Transportation Security Administration (TSA); U.S. Customs and Border Protection (CBP); U.S. Secret Service, (USSS); U.S. Citizenship and Immigration Service (USCIS); U.S. Immigration and Customs Enforcement (ICE); Federal Emergency Management Agency (FEMA); and the U.S. Coast Guard (USCG). The seven operating components work closely with, support, and are supported by a large network of first responders at the state, local, and tribal levels. In addition, key collaboration takes place with the eighteen sectors of America's critical infrastructure/key resources (CIKR) that comprise the backbone of the nation's economy.

DHS manages this diverse group of operating components and supporting elements whose missions address a wide variety of terrorist and natural threats to our homeland. Ever-changing threat dynamics often

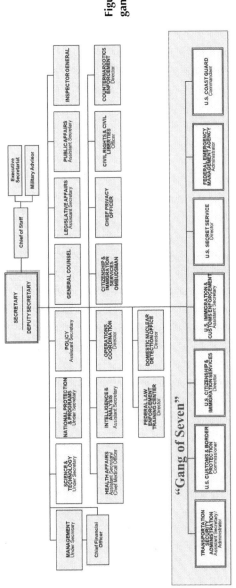

Figure 10.1.   DHS organizational structure.

require new, innovative technology-based solutions in order to prevent or mitigate the potential effects of current and future dangers. The DHS Science and Technology Directorate (DHS S&T) works to understand, document, and offer solutions to current and anticipated threats faced by these stakeholders, our "customers" (DHS operating components and field agents) and our "customers' customers" (first responders and CIKR owners and operators). DHS S&T, through the Capstone Integrated Product Team (IPT) process, ensures that quality, efficacious products are developed in close alignment with detailed customer needs. The Capstone IPT process represents the requirements-driven, output-oriented portion of DHS's technology development investments geared toward providing DHS stakeholders with the necessary tools to protect America's most valuable assets—its people.

CAPSTONE INTEGRATED PRODUCT TEAMS

The Capstone Integrated Product Teams are chartered to ensure that technologies and products are engineered and integrated into systems aligned to the needs of DHS customers. Consistent with the Homeland Security Act of 2002, the Capstone IPT process is the framework used to determine whether developed capabilities meet operational needs, analyze gaps in strategic needs and capabilities, develop operational requirements, and develop programs and projects to close capability gaps and expand mission competencies. This process is a partner-led forum through which the identification of functional capability gaps and the prioritization of these gaps across the department are formalized. The Capstone IPTs enable the proper allocation of resources to the highest priority needs established by DHS operating components and other DHS stakeholders.

Chaired by the DHS S&T partner or customer, Capstone IPTs bring together DHS S&T division heads, management (acquisition or commercialization) partners, and end users (operating components, field agents, and supporting first responders—DHS partners) involved in the research, development, testing, and evaluation (RDT&E) and acquisition or commercialization activities. Working together, the Capstone IPT members identify, evaluate, and prioritize the operational requirements necessary to complete missions successfully. Based on information gained from Capstone IPT meetings, DHS S&T providers assess the technological and system development of products that will ultimately be deployed into the field.

The Capstone IPTs are structured to focus on functional, department-level requirements and deal with programmatic and technology issues within the DHS S&T divisions: currently Explosives, Chemical/Biological,

Command Control and Interoperability, Borders and Maritime Security, Human Factors, and Infrastructure and Geophysical. Currently, Capstone IPTs have been created across thirteen major homeland security core functional areas: Information Sharing/Management, Cyber Security, People Screening, Border Security, Chemical/Biological Defense, Maritime Security, Counter-Improvised Explosive Devices, Transportation Security, Incident Management, Interoperability, Cargo Security, Infrastructure Protection, and First Responders.

Each Capstone IPT is chaired or cochaired by senior leadership from a DHS operating component with corresponding needs within a specific functional area. The chair/cochair, representing the end users of a delivered capability, engage throughout the process to identify, define, and prioritize current and future requirements and ensure that planned technology and/or product transitions and acquisition programs, commercialization efforts, and standards development are optimally suited to their operational requirements. Operating components, field agents, first responders, and other noncaptive end users with an interest in the core functional areas of a Capstone IPT are welcome to participate and contribute throughout the Capstone IPT process. See figure 10.2 for the captive members for each IPT.

Capstone IPTs purposefully cover very broad core functional areas. This broad focus aids in reducing the duplication of efforts geared toward various operating components of DHS. It is often the case that a given capability gap is experienced by numerous operating components and stakeholders simultaneously. Technology development is functionally aligned to allow technologies to be used in support of multiple operating components and customer sets within DHS. The effective management and communication of capability gaps ensures that similar efforts are either combined or developed in concert so that required capabilities are provided to as many stakeholders sharing similar capability gaps, reducing overall technology development costs and accelerating the time-to-market for certain capabilities.

FIRST RESPONDER CAPSTONE IPT

The First Responder IPT, the newest Capstone IPT, was established in FY 2009. This Capstone IPT coordinates the identification and prioritization of the capability gaps and detailed operational requirements of federal, state, local, tribal, and territorial first responders in keeping with DHS S&T's partner-driven process. The IPT was organized to provide a more direct line of communication for first responders to share their unique requirements and needs with DHS S&T. Given the variety and scope of

DHS S&T Capstone IPTs

Gathering Mechanism for Customer Requirements:

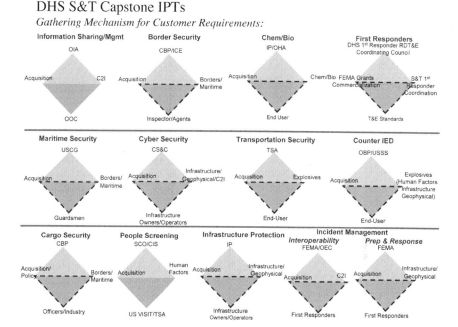

Figure 10.2. This diagram shows the thirteen Capstone IPTs, the DHS operating component, DHS end user(s), the S&T division technical provider, and, when applicable, the acquisition conducted by DHS management.

first-responder duties, the IPT was formed to address the requirements of these first-responder groups in order to respond to all hazards and threats, including preparation for catastrophic natural and man-made crises. Identified technology solutions will be designed, tested, and assessed for effectiveness and reliability before they are produced for the first-responder community.

DHS S&T developed the conceptual framework for the function of the First Responder IPT and the structure for its operation in connection with a large group of knowledgeable persons internal and external to DHS. The First Responder Technology Council was created to identify and prioritize the technology requirements and capability gaps and identify solutions to address those identified gaps. The council will be advised by the First Responder RDT&E Working Group (WG). The WG will comprise first-responder officials representing the fields of emergency management, emergency medical services, fire, and law enforcement. These first-responder officials will represent federal, state, local, and territorial jurisdictions; Native American communities; and key first-responder associations from across the nation. DHS S&T will gain from their involvement, commitment, and expert understating of responder technology gaps to develop solutions to close gaps in a cost-effective, efficient, and timely manner.

CAPABILITY GAPS AND ENABLING HOMELAND CAPABILITIES

Chapter 4 has already described in detail the Capstone IPT process and its applicability to understanding unsatisfied needs and wants for the three major DHS stakeholders. In general, Capstone IPTs generate several outputs that guide the development and fielding of technologies and systems for DHS's stakeholders. The primary role of the IPTs is to conduct strategic needs analysis to determine and prioritize capability gaps. Capability gaps are broad descriptions of identified mission needs that are not met given current products and/or standards. Capability gaps often start with statements that identify needs rather than suggested solutions. See figure 10.3 for the requirements hierarchy diagram.

Capability gaps can come in several forms. Some gaps may appear in the form of modified personnel and resource allocation, training, standards, plans/protocols/procedures, resources, technology, systems, and so on. For those capability gaps requiring technology-based solutions, a grouping of technology components is identified by DHS S&T to ad-

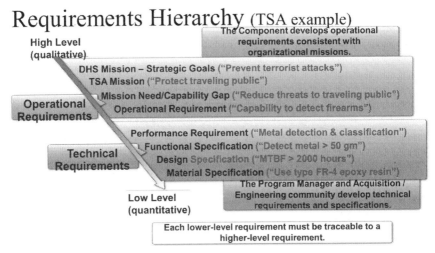

Figure 10.3. This requirements hierarchy shows the evolution of requirements from a high-level macro set of operational requirements to a low-level micro set of technical requirements. Note that each lower-level requirement stems directly from its higher requirement so that all requirements are traceable to the overall DHS mission.

dress the various needs delineated in the capability gaps. These grouped technology solutions, or Enabling Homeland Capabilities (EHCs), collectively deliver new gap-closing capabilities to customers or partners. EHCs enable a focus on discussions related more broadly to overall capability needs rather than discussions simply about potential solutions to problems.

PROJECT-IPTS: MANAGING THE DAY-TO-DAY DEVELOPMENT OF CAPABILITIES

Additional detailed requirements must be developed to enable the development of a technology or product. In order to achieve greater insight into the details that comprise each Capstone IPT, Project-IPTs are created to manage specific project areas within a functional area. Project-IPTs are created to manage closing capability gaps gathered from the larger Capstone IPT on a daily basis. These requirements assist in decomposing a high-level capability gap into the individual components that may comprise a potential solution. Through this process, the grouping of individual technologies into an integrated system creates an overall EHC.

The Project-IPTs work closely with DHS partners to develop a robust understanding of customer needs, through a C-ORD, for example, to define clearly the specific requirements that must be met in order for a technological solution to address a given problem. Development of detailed C-ORDs further enhances the direction in which technology and product development efforts progress.

MANAGEMENT—DHS LEADERSHIP AND DHS S&T

DHS S&T manages the process to develop and deliver required technologies/products as defined in the EHCs. DHS S&T also works to conduct market and technology scans to find technology-based solutions that can be developed, matured, and delivered to DHS acquisition programs and commercialized or validated as a standard within a three-year period.

There are several ways products, services, or technologies can transition into fully developed, widely distributed products for the large customer communities. Figure 10.4 identifies possible transition paths to deliver products to customers. DHS S&T may recommend available commercial-off-the-shelf (COTS) products or other non-S&T alternatives in lieu of developing a new DHS S&T solution.

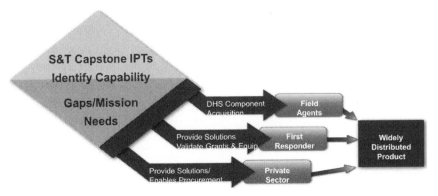

Figure 10.4. DHS has three major methods to transition products to end users. DHS field agents are captive end users of the Capstone IPT process; while the first-responder community is typically able to select its own solutions, all newly proposed DHS programs must now identify technologies/products already in development in the private sector that are aligned with end user requirements for DHS field agents and/or to enable first responders to make informed purchasing decisions.

GIVING USERS A VOICE

It is apparent that there is not an overarching, reliable, and efficient process today for assessing a statistically significant sampling of requirements from the "boots on the ground" of DHS stakeholders—especially the first responders and the CIKR owners and operators.

DHS is exploring the idea of using deployable technology to create a Community of Practitioners (CoP). DoD has invested in these kinds of technologies to enable the ability to reach not only millions of first responders but also other potentially authorized stakeholders (other federal agencies, private sector, venture capital community, etc.). Advanced technologies like the Semantic Web 3.0 will aid in the communal and open development of C-ORDs, potential available market sizing/applications, and so on, all to the benefit of the American taxpayer, government, and private sector.

The millions of DHS stakeholders need to be invited to play an active role in creating, editing, and prioritizing detailed operational requirements to be used by DHS in order to provide (or facilitate through its commercialization efforts) solutions for these stakeholder communities. This approach enables both a bottom-up and top-down view of detailed user requirements. Social networking technologies have enabled new opportunities that allow communication to flow both up and down!

NEXT STEPS

In their outreach efforts with the private sector, DHS S&T realizes that they must work closely with their respective partners to produce detailed operational requirements documents in order to relay effective requirements to the private sector. DHS is forging a new paradigm with far-reaching positive consequences. These benefits are felt by DHS's customers, private sector partners, and the U.S. taxpayers through the rapid, cost-effective, and efficient development and deployment of products and services to protect the homeland of the United States. DHS is creating a "commercialization mindset" utilizing public-private partnerships to expedite the development of products and services to protect the nation. Recently announced commercialization initiatives (like DHS's innovative SECURE and FutureTECH programs) are truly groundbreaking approaches to foster a mutually beneficial relationship between the public and private sectors by creating an open and freely competitive program accessible by small, medium, and large firms. These efforts are a natural extension of the Capstone IPT process.

The future of these initiatives looks bright; we have already experienced an overwhelmingly positive response to the initial private sector outreach initiative. DHS S&T stands at the forefront of innovative thinking within the public sector, and we will continue to monitor and measure the benefits this program will provide.

SUMMARY

The Capstone IPT process is a partner-driven process that requires the participation and input from several DHS stakeholders. This collaborative effort centers on the principle that the customer is "the focus" of this process. The product and technology outputs of the Capstone IPT process are customer requirements driven from start to finish. The customer is involved throughout the process to ensure that they receive products and technologies specifically aligned to their detailed operating requirements. Ultimately, our partners receive quality products that effectively deliver the necessary, mission-critical capabilities to secure our nation.

Chapter 11

It's All about Putting Theory into Practice

Now that we have thoroughly reviewed the theory behind two innovative public-private partnerships—it's time to put what we've articulated into real-world use. This chapter provides two examples of C-ORDs developed and vetted by DHS for each of the three DHS stakeholders: operating components, first responders, and critical infrastructure and key resources owners and operators. Please note that market potential templates, like those discussed in chapter 1, were used to derive conservative estimates of the potential available markets (PAMs). Before we begin, let's review the C-ORD template for reference again, the concept of commercialization, and potential available markets. Let's begin . . .

COMMERCIALIZATION-BASED OPERATIONAL
REQUIREMENTS DOCUMENT TEMPLATE

1. General Description of Operational Capability
In this section, summarize the capability gap that the product or system is intended to address, describe the overall mission area, describe the proposed system solution, and provide a summary of any supporting analyses. Additionally, briefly describe the operational and support concepts.

   1.1. Capability Gap
   Describe the analysis and rationale for acquiring a new product or system, and identify the DHS component that contains or represents the end users. Also, name the Capstone IPT, if any, that identified the capability gap.

1.2. Overall Mission Area Description
Define and describe the overall mission area to which the capability gap pertains, including its users and its scope

1.3. Description of the Proposed System
Describe the proposed product or system. Describe how the product or system will provide the capabilities and functional improvements needed to address the capability gap. Do not describe a specific technology or system solution. Instead, describe a conceptual solution for illustrative purposes.

1.4. Supporting Analysis
Describe the analysis that supports the proposed system. If a formal study was performed, identify the study and briefly provide a summary of results.

1.5. Mission the Proposed System Will Accomplish
Define the missions that the proposed system will be tasked to accomplish.

1.6. Operational and Support Concept

1.6.1. Concept of Operations
Briefly describe the concept of operations for the system. How will the system be used, and what is its organizational setting? It is appropriate to include a graphic that depicts the system and its operation. Also, describe the system's interoperability requirements with other systems.

1.6.2. Support Concept
Briefly describe the support concept for the system. How will the system (hardware and software) be maintained? Who will maintain it? How, where, and by whom will spare parts be provisioned? How, where, and by whom will operators be trained?

2. Threat
If the system is intended as a countermeasure to a threat, summarize the threat to be countered and the projected threat environment.

3. Existing System Shortfalls
Describe why existing systems cannot meet current or projected requirements. Describe what new capabilities are needed to address the gap between current capabilities and required capabilities.

4. Capabilities Required

4.1. Operational Performance Parameters
Identify operational performance parameters (capabilities and characteristics) required for the proposed system. Articulate the requirements in output-oriented and measurable terms. Use Threshold/Objective format and provide criteria and rationale for each requirement.

4.2. Key Performance Parameters (KPPs)
The KPPs are those attributes or characteristics of a system that are considered critical or essential. Failure to meet a KPP threshold value could be the basis to reject a system solution.

4.3 System Performance.

4.3.1 Mission Scenarios

Describe mission scenarios in terms of mission profiles, employment tactics, and environmental conditions.

4.3.2 System Performance Parameters

Identify system performance parameters. Identify KPPs by placing an asterisk in front of the parameter description.

4.3.3 Interoperability

Identify all requirements for the system to provide data, information, materiel, and services to, and accept the same from, other systems, and to use the data, information, materiel, and services so exchanged to enable them to operate effectively together.

4.3.4 Human Interface Requirements

Discuss broad cognitive, physical, and sensory requirements for the operators, maintainers, or support personnel that contribute to, or constrain, total system performance. Provide broad staffing constraints for operators, maintainers, and support personnel.

4.3.5 Logistics and Readiness

Describe the requirements for the system to be supportable and available for operations. Provide performance parameters for availability, reliability, system maintainability, and software maintainability.

4.3.6 Other System Characteristics

Characteristics that tend to be design, cost, and risk drivers.

5. System Support

Establish support objectives for initial and full operational capability. Discuss interfacing systems, transportation and facilities, and standardization and interoperability. Describe the support approach including configuration management, repair, scheduled maintenance, support operations, software support, and user support (such as training and help desk).

5.1 Maintenance

Identify the types of maintenance to be performed and who will perform the maintenance. Describe methods for upgrades and technology insertions. Also, address post-development software support requirements.

5.2 Supply

Describe the approach to supplying field operators and maintenance technicians with necessary tools, spares, diagnostic equipment, and manuals.

5.3 Support Equipment

Define the standard support equipment to be used by the system. Discuss any need for special test equipment or software development environment

5.4 Training

Describe how the training will ensure that users are certified as capable of operating and using the proposed system.

5.5 Transportation and Facilities

Describe how the system will be transported to the field, identifying any lift constraints. Identify facilities needed for staging and training.

6. Force Structure
Estimate the number of systems or subsystems needed, including spares and training units. Identify organizations and units that will employ the systems being developed and procured, estimating the number of users in each organization or unit.
7. Schedule
To the degree that schedule is a requirement, define target dates for system availability. If a distinction is made between Initial Capability and Full Operational Capability, clarify the difference between the two in terms of system capability and/or numbers of fielded systems.
8. System Affordability
Identify a threshold/objective target price to the user at full-rate production. If price is a KPP, include it in the section on KPPs above.

IMPLEMENTING A COMMERCIALIZATION PROCESS

The U.S. Department of Homeland Security (DHS) possesses an "Acquisition mind-set," as do so many government agencies. While the acquisition model has been utilized effectively in developing "custom, one-off" products such as aircraft carriers, it is not particularly germane to a majority of the needs at DHS as well as the first responders (a DHS ancillary market). The timely design, development, and deployment of lower-priced, widely distributed products for both DHS operating components and the first-responder communities represents a critical step in protecting our nation. Recognizing this fact, the department recently started implementing a "commercialization mindset" in order to leverage the vast capabilities and resources of the private sector through an innovative "win-win" private-public partnership called the SECURE (System Efficacy through Commercialization, Utilization, Relevance and Evaluation) Program.

DHS experienced several challenges merging twenty-two disparate organizations into a cohesive organization with a unified mission and culture. Those familiar with merger and acquisition activities realize that while integration of organizations poses difficulties, it also represents opportunities to infuse new processes and values into the newly created organization. Through both top-down and bottom-up approaches, DHS has been successful in developing, socializing, and now implementing an innovative commercialization framework that has started to gain traction throughout the agency. The creation of a "commercialization mindset" has caught the attention of DHS managers and employees and has been embraced by senior management because of its significant benefits to the department's internal and external activities.

Why is there a need for a commercialization mindset in DHS? DHS requirements, in most instances, are characterized by the need for widely distributed COTS (commercial-off-the-shelf) products. Oftentimes, the need is for thousands, if not millions, of products for DHS's seven operating components and the fragmented, yet substantial first-responder and critical infrastructure markets. The DHS commercialization process relies on providing two key pieces of information to potential solution providers in order for them to invest their valuable time, money, and resources to develop products and services for use by DHS operating components, first-responder communities, critical infrastructure and key resources (CIKR) owner/operators and other stakeholders: (1) a clear and detailed delineation and explanation of the operational requirements, and (2) a conservative estimate of the potential available market for a potential commercialization partner to offer potential solution(s). We have forged and promulgated the development of Commercialization-based Operational Requirements Documents (C-ORDs) through the publication of several books, training materials, and articles to address the first half of this equation, and the following pages of a comprehensive market potential template address the latter.

CONSERVATIVE ESTIMATES
OF POTENTIAL AVAILABLE MARKETS

It is important to understand not only the detailed operational requirements necessary to provide DHS stakeholders with mission-critical capabilities, but also understand the volume of potential users of these solutions. DHS itself can represent a substantial potential available market; in many instances requiring hundreds, if not thousands of product or service units to address unsatisfied needs. Couple to this the fact that DHS has responsibility for so many ancillary markets (e.g., first responders, critical infrastructure and key resources, etc.) representing large potential available markets, it is evident that substantial business opportunities exist for the private sector, as these large pools of potential customers and users represent the "lifeblood" for a business (see figure 11.1). We first outline top-level markets. In turn, each "branch" of the template has been further segmented to home in on detailed market opportunities.

Figure 11.2 shows the major differences between a "pure" acquisition versus "pure" commercialization process, along with the recently developed and implemented DHS "hybrid" commercialization process.

Figure 11.3 delineates the overall description of DHS's new commercialization model and its first private sector outreach program, called

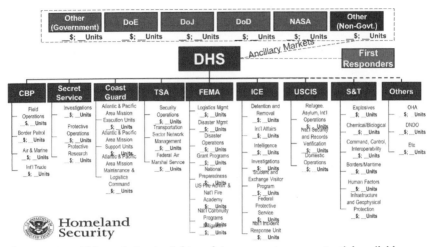

Figure 11.1a.   This market potential template maps out many potential available markets to which DHS has direct control and responsibility or acts as a "conduit."

the SECURE (System Efficacy through Commercialization, Utilization, Relevance and Evaluation) Program to develop products and services in a private-public "win-win" partnership described in detail at www.dhs .gov/xres/programs/gc_1211996620526.shtm. Briefly, the SECURE Program is based on the simple premise that the private sector is willing and able to use its own money, resources, expertise, and experience to develop and produce fully developed products and services for DHS if significant market potential exists. The private sector has shown remarkable interest in devoting its time and resources to such activities if and when an attractive business case can be made related to large revenue/profit opportunities, which certainly exist at DHS and its ancillary markets. As previously stated, the private sector requires two pieces of critical information from DHS: (1) detailed operational requirement(s), and (2) a conservative estimate of the potential available market(s). This information can then be used to generate a business case for possible private sector participation in the program.

Early response from groups within DHS, the private sector, and first responders about this guide and programs like SECURE has been very favorable.[1] The Department plans to regularly update its website with Commercialization-based Operational Requirements Documents (C-ORDs) to continually expand this innovative private-public partnership. In addition, as evidenced in table 11.1, the taxpayers, private sector, and public sector view programs like this as "win-win-win."

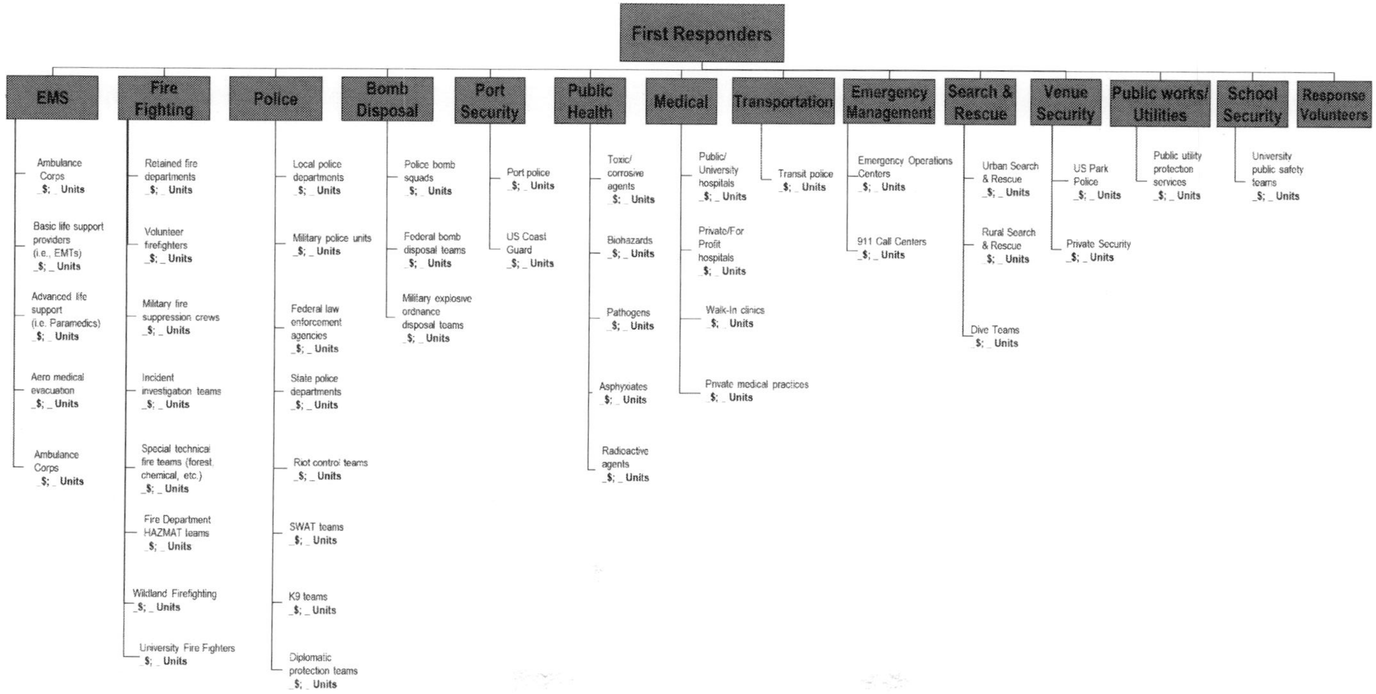

First Responders

- **EMS**
  - Ambulance Corps $:_ Units
  - Basic life support providers (i.e. EMT(s) _$:_ Units
  - Advanced life support (i.e. Paramedics) $:_ Units
  - Aero medical evacuation _$:_ Units
  - Ambulance Corps $:_ Units

- **Fire Fighting**
  - Retained fire departments $:_ Units
  - Volunteer firefighters _$:_ Units
  - Military fire suppression crews $:_ Units
  - Incident investigation teams _$:_ Units
  - Special technical fire teams (forest chemical, etc.) _$:_ Units
  - Fire Department HAZMAT Teams $:_ Units
  - Wildland Firefighting _$:_ Units
  - University Fire Fighters $:_ Units

- **Police**
  - Local police departments $:_ Units
  - Military police units _$:_ Units
  - Federal law enforcement agencies _$:_ Units
  - State police departments _$:_ Units
  - Riot control teams _$:_ Units
  - SWAT teams $:_ Units
  - K9 teams _$:_ Units
  - Diplomatic protection teams $:_ Units

- **Bomb Disposal**
  - Police bomb squads $:_ Units
  - Federal bomb disposal teams $:_ Units
  - Military explosive ordnance disposal teams $:_ Units

- **Port Security**
  - Port police $:_ Units
  - US Coast Guard _$:_ Units

- **Public Health**
  - Toxic/corrosive agents $:_ Units
  - Biohazards _$:_ Units
  - Pathogens $:_ Units
  - Asphyxiates $:_ Units
  - Radioactive agents _$:_ Units

- **Medical**
  - Public/University hospitals $:_ Units
  - Private/For Profit hospitals $:_ Units
  - Walk-in clinics $:_ Units
  - Private medical practices $:_ Units

- **Transportation**
  - Transit police $:_ Units

- **Emergency Management**
  - Emergency Operations Centers _$:_ Units
  - 911 Call Centers _$:_ Units

- **Search & Rescue**
  - Urban Search & Rescue $:_ Units
  - Rural Search & Rescue $:_ Units
  - Dive Teams $:_ Units

- **Venue Security**
  - US Park Police _$:_ Units
  - Private Security $:_ Units

- **Public works/Utilities**
  - Public utility protection services _$:_ Units

- **School Security**
  - University public safety teams $:_ Units

- **Response Volunteers**

Figure 11.1b.   The PAM for the First Responders.

Critical Infrastructure Key Resources (CIKR)

Agriculture and Food
- Food Retail $_ Units
- Farm Equipment $_ Units
- Meat/Poultry Processing $_ Units
- Food Processing $_ Units
- Dairy Processing $_ Units
- Dairy Farms $_ Units
- Ranching $_ Units
- Organic Farming/Sustainable Agriculture $_ Units
- Traditional Planting $_ Units
- Commercial fishing $_ Units

Defense Industrial Base
- Defense Contractors $_ Units
- Industry analysis $_ Units
- Think tanks/research institutions $_ Units
- University partnership programs $_ Units
- National laboratories $_ Units

Energy
- Coal mining operations $_ Units
- Coal power plants $_ Units
- Coal equipment manufacturers $_ Units
- Hydroelectric $_ Units
- Dam operations $_ Units
- Wind power $_ Units
- Solar power $_ Units
- Public utilities companies $_ Units
- Oil companies $_ Units

Public Health and Healthcare
- Public/University hospitals $_ Units
- Private/For Profit hospitals $_ Units
- Clinics $_ Units
- Private medical practitioners $_ Units
- Medical laboratories $_ Units
- Pharmaceutical $_ Units
- Health Insurance $_ Units
- Medical material providers $_ Units
- Medical equipment manufacturers $_ Units
- Medical technology manufacturers $_ Units
- Biotechnology $_ Units

National Monuments and Icons
- Guided tour services $_ Units
- Travel services $_ Units
- Lodging/Hotel/Guest services/tourist hospitality $_ Units
- People moving services $_ Units
- Gaming equipment makers $_ Units
- Private security $_ Units

Banking and Finance
- Credit lending institutions $_ Units
- Commercial banking $_ Units
- Private equity $_ Units
- Consumer banking $_ Units
- Building societies/Private banks $_ Units
- Merchant banks $_ Units
- Global financial services firms $_ Units
- Community development $_ Units
- Community banks $_ Units
- Savings and Loans $_ Units
- Credit unions $_ Units
- Insurance companies $_ Units
- Insurance brokerages $_ Units
- Reinsurance companies $_ Units
- Stock brokerages $_ Units
- Capital market banks $_ Units
- Custody services $_ Units
- Angel investment $_ Units
- Venture capital $_ Units

Water
- Public utilities $_ Units
- Desalination plants $_ Units
- Treatment plants $_ Units
- Equipment manufacturers $_ Units
- Pipe and water control device manufacturers $_ Units

Chemical
- Inorganic chemical production $_ Units
- Organic/Industrial production $_ Units
- Ceramics $_ Units
- Petrochemicals $_ Units
- Agrochemicals $_ Units
- Polymers $_ Units
- Elastomer production $_ Units
- Oleochemicals $_ Units
- Explosives $_ Units
- Fragrance production $_ Units
- Chemical wholesale $_ Units
- Exotic chemicals $_ Units

Commercial facilities
- Hotels $_ Units
- Shopping centers $_ Units
- Stadiums and sport arenas $_ Units
- Schools $_ Units
- Commercial office buildings $_ Units
- Museums $_ Units
- Zoos and Aquariums $_ Units
- Public Libraries $_ Units
- Amusement parks $_ Units

Emergency Services
- Fire Departments $_ Units
- Law enforcement agencies $_ Units
- Search and rescue teams $_ Units
- Ambulance companies $_ Units
- Mountain/Cave/Mine rescue teams $_ Units
- Other technical rescue teams $_ Units
- Bomb disposal units $_ Units
- Blood/Organ transport/supply $_ Units
- Amateur radio emergency comms $_ Units
- Public utility protection providers $_ Units
- Emergency Road services $_ Units
- Emergency Social services $_ Units
- Community emergency response teams $_ Units
- Disaster relief teams $_ Units
- Famine relief teams $_ Units
- Poison Control units $_ Units
- Animal control teams $_ Units
- Welfare services $_ Units

Materials Reactors and...
- Electric utilities $_ Units
- Reactor and associated materials $_ Units
- University and educational institutions $_ Units
- Control systems $_ Units
- Nuclear safety $_ Units
- Waste disposal services $_ Units
- Uranium processors $_ Units
- Protective garment manufacturers $_ Units

Telecommunications
- Telephone/Cell/air services $_ Units
- Satellite data transmission $_ Units
- Broadcasting entities $_ Units
- Broadcast equipment manufacturing $_ Units
- Radio equipment manufacturing $_ Units
- Internet equipment manufacturing $_ Units
- High speed data transmission $_ Units
- Internet service providers $_ Units
- Print media $_ Units
- Internet technology providers $_ Units

Critical Manufacturing
- Iron and Steel mills $_ Units
- Aluminum production and processing $_ Units
- Nonferrous metal production and processing $_ Units
- Engine, Turbine and Power transmission $_ Units
- Electrical Equipment manufacturing $_ Units
- Motor Vehicle manufacturing $_ Units
- Aerospace product & parts manufacturing $_ Units
- Railroad rolling stock $_ Units
- Other Transportation equipment $_ Units

Postal and Shipping Services
- United States Postal Service $_ Units
- High volume document and parcel shipping $_ Units
- Container shipping services $_ Units
- Marine shipping $_ Units
- Trucking industry $_ Units
- Airborne shipping $_ Units
- Distribution services $_ Units

Transportation
- AMTRAK $_ Units
- Commuter rail $_ Units
- Intracity rail services $_ Units
- Commercial airlines $_ Units
- Private air services $_ Units
- Cruise lines $_ Units
- Subway systems $_ Units
- Long-haul maritime shipping $_ Units
- Trucking $_ Units
- Bus services $_ Units
- Freight rail service $_ Units
- Automobile travel $_ Units
- Roads, Highways, bridges and tunnels $_ Units

Information Technology
- Hardware providers $_ Units
- IT Conglomerates $_ Units
- Semiconductor production $_ Units
- Electronics manufacture $_ Units
- IT services $_ Units
- Server and network hardware $_ Units
- Display/digital TV $_ Units
- Software production $_ Units
- Gaming $_ Units
- Information security $_ Units
- Semiconductor equipment $_ Units

Figure 11.1c.   The PAM for the CIKR owners and operators.

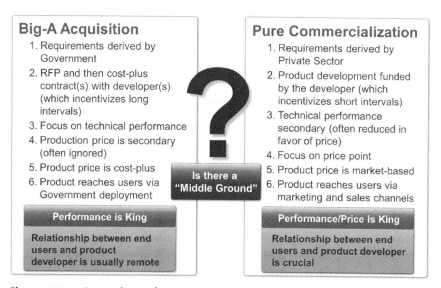

Big-A Acquisition

1. Requirements derived by Government
2. RFP and then cost-plus contract(s) with developer(s) (which incentivizes long intervals)
3. Focus on technical performance
4. Production price is secondary (often ignored)
5. Product price is cost-plus
6. Product reaches users via Government deployment

Performance is King

Relationship between end users and product developer is usually remote

Is there a "Middle Ground"

Pure Commercialization

1. Requirements derived by Private Sector
2. Product development funded by the developer (which incentivizes short intervals)
3. Technical performance secondary (often reduced in favor of price)
4. Focus on price point
5. Product price is market-based
6. Product reaches users via marketing and sales channels

Performance/Price is King

Relationship between end users and product developer is crucial

Figure 11.2. Comparison of "pure acquisition" versus "pure commercialization" models for product/system development and the resultant hybrid model implemented by DHS.

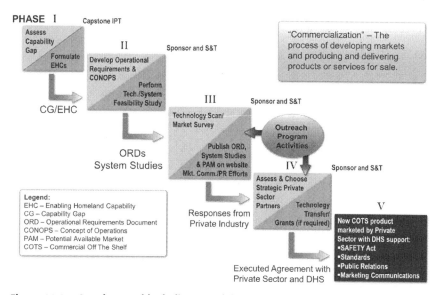

PHASE I

Capstone IPT

Assess Capability Gap

Formulate EHCs

CG/EHC

II

Sponsor and S&T

Develop Operational Requirements & CONOPS

Perform Tech./System Feasibility Study

ORDs
System Studies

III

Sponsor and S&T

Technology Scan/ Market Survey

Publish ORD, System Studies & PAM on website Mkt. Comm./PR Efforts

Outreach Program Activities

IV

Sponsor and S&T

Assess & Choose Strategic Private Sector Partners

Technology Transfer/ Grants (if required)

V

New COTS product marketed by Private Sector with DHS support:
•SAFETY Act
•Standards
•Public Relations
•Marketing Communications

"Commercialization" – The process of developing markets and producing and delivering products or services for sale.

Responses from Private Industry

Executed Agreement with Private Sector and DHS

Legend:
EHC – Enabling Homeland Capability
CG – Capability Gap
ORD – Operational Requirements Document
CONOPS – Concept of Operations
PAM – Potential Available Market
COTS – Commercial Off The Shelf

Figure 11.3. Step-by-step block diagram of the commercialization process developed and adopted by DHS.

Table 11.1.   Benefit Analysis—"Win-Win-Win" The SECURE Program is viewed positively by DHS stakeholders. The success of the program lies in the fact that all participants receive significant benefits.

Taxpayers	Public Sector	Private Sector
1. Citizens are better protected by DHS personnel using mission-critical products	1. Improved understanding and communication of needs	1. Save significant time and money on market and business development activities
2. Tax savings realized through private sector investment in DHS	2. Cost-effective and rapid product development process saves resources	2. Firms can genuinely contribute to the security of the nation
3. Positive economic growth for American economy	3. Monies can be allocated to perform greater number of essential tasks	3. Successful products share in the "imprimatur of DHS"; providing assurance that products really work
4. Possible product "spin-offs" can aid other commercial markets	4. End users receive products aligned to specific needs	4. Significant business opportunities with sizable DHS and DHS ancillary markets
5. Customers ultimately benefit from COTS produced within the Free Market System—more cost-effective and efficient product development	5. End users can make informed purchasing decisions with tight budgets	5. Commercialization opportunities for small, medium and large business

On the following pages several examples of Commercialization-Based Operational Requirements Document are presented as developed for DHS operating components, first responders, and critical infrastructure and key resources owners and operators.

DHS OPERATING COMPONENTS: C-ORD FOR PORTABLE STAND-ALONE WATER PURIFICATION SYSTEM

Contents

1. General Description of Operational Capability
    - *1.1. Capability Gap*
    - *1.2. Overall Mission Area Description*
    - *1.3. Description of the Proposed Product or System*
    - *1.4. Supporting Analysis*
    - *1.5. Mission the Proposed System Will Accomplish*

1.6. Operational and Support Concept
    1.6.1. Concept of Operations
    1.6.2. Support Concept
2. Threat
3. Existing System Shortfalls
4. Capabilities Required
    4.1. Operational Performance Parameters (T: Threshold/ O: Objective)
    4.2. Key Performance Parameters (KPPs)
    4.3. System Performance
        4.3.1. Mission Scenarios
        4.3.2. System Performance Parameters
        4.3.3. Interoperability
        4.3.4. Human Interface Requirements
        4.3.5. Logistics and Readiness
        4.3.6. Other System Characteristics
5. System Support
    5.1. Maintenance
    5.2. Supply
    5.3. Support Equipment
    5.4. Training
    5.5. Transportation and Facilities
6. Force Structure
7. Schedule
8. System Affordability

1. General Description of Operational Capability

Water is a basic necessity for human life. In the event of a natural disaster or terrorist attack, the ability to quickly deliver potable water to communities is of critical importance.

With a cost-effective and ergonomic purification system on-site, government agencies, emergency management professionals, and first responder teams can curb the all-too-often costly and polluting practice of trucking water into affected areas, not to mention eliminating or greatly reducing the burden of having to dispose of many thousands of discarded water bottles and other trash.

The operational capability described in this commercialization-based operational requirements document (C-ORD) will provide users with a self-contained, self-fueling water pumping and purification system that can be deployed and operated in less than thirty minutes after transport to a site by truck, helicopter, or boat. Units shall be operated without specialized training wherever the need for potable water or water displacement arises. A proposed system shall provide an affordable, high-quality, easy-to-use option utilizing reliable technology at significant cost savings over the current methods providing potable water to users in need.

1.1. Capability Gap

The conventional method of providing potable water in the wake of a disaster is often costly and logistically complex. Normally, potable water is distributed to communities by trucking in bottled water or using diesel generator purification systems.

Any proposed system must eliminate many points of failure by presenting a stand-alone design allowing for flexible transport of the unit by air, land, or water, bringing a cost-effective, high-yield water purification capability to potential users incorporating a self-generating power source.

1.2. Overall Mission Area Description

The provision of potable water to communities affected either by natural disasters or terrorist events is understandably a top priority for first responders, emergency management authorities at all levels of government concerned with short- and medium-term disaster response and relief efforts.

Any proposed system shall provide a stand-alone potable water resource to federal, state, local, and tribal preparedness and/or response teams and emergency management professionals. A proposed system shall be transportable using a variety of options (by air, land, and/or water) even in the most adverse conditions. A proposed system shall be easy-to-deploy, easy-to-use, and shall produce potable water from even polluted sources.

Any proposed system shall be low cost, low maintenance, providing high-quality and high-yield output. A system shall primarily be used to pump and purify water for public consumption with ancillary benefits such as self-generating power to operate its pumps as well as provide DC and AC load centers into which other critical equipment could be plugged in and engaged. This is especially required in areas that have been devastated by a natural disaster or terrorist event where infrastructure, electrical, transportation, and water resources have been compromised.

1.3. Description of the Proposed Product or System

A proposed system shall be a self-contained, self-powered water purification system contained in as small as possible a foot-print. The system shall be deployed to any site where there is level ground using forklift, helicopter, truck, or boat and shall easily fit into any shipping container.

No special training shall be required to operate a proposed system, and a system shall be operable, pumping and purifying water and supplying electricity in less than thirty minutes after arrival on site. A proposed system shall eliminate particles and render biological pathogens inert. A multi-thousand-gallon collapsible storage tank shall come standard with each unit, storing water so it is available when needed by first responders and community members. A proposed system shall contain an internal battery bank (or equivalent) so that the system can operate 24/7 and can also provide electricity to run generators, lights, tools, or other command station equipment.

1.4. Supporting Analysis

Countless requests from members of the first responder community know that such kinds of systems have been used effectively in other applications in other venues.

1.5. Mission the Proposed System Will Accomplish

Any proposed system shall provide readily deployable, high-quality, high-yield water purification to disaster-affected communities at a low cost. Any proposed system shall eliminate any and all problems associated with bottled water or more cumbersome fuel alternatives often used to provide potable water. The proposed system shall be easily deployable and operational in a self-contained, self-generating powered platform eliminating the need to supply additional fuel. With the capability of 24/7 operation, potable water needs to be readily available at a site, when and where it is most needed, at a low cost with no pollution. Ancillary power available to operate lights, computers, satellite communications modules, and other equipment is also required.

1.6. Operational and Support Concept

1.6.1. Concept of Operations A proposed system may be deployed after a disaster event to affected areas to purify contaminated water sources or may be transported to a site where it is likely to be needed before the occurrence of a natural event. For instance, if it is likely a hurricane will make landfall in a particular area, a proposed system shall possess the ability to be pre-positioned. A proposed system shall be able to withstand commonly occurring weather conditions without additional hardening or protection. A system safety plan shall be provided for necessary precautions to protect a proposed system from weather disasters such as tornados, hurricanes, etc.

Emergency response teams making use of the system shall identify areas requiring water purification based on local procedures, emergency response plans, and readiness of a water source, including identification of specific deployment locations. Water test kits shall be provided with each unit, and additional kits shall be made available at a low price from the vendor to test pre- and post-filtration water quality.

Operation roles in the field will be determined by local procedures and emergency response plans. A comprehensive, easy-to-understand training manual shall be included with each unit describing the procedures to deploy and operate a system. In the event a more in-depth training session is required, a provider shall host tailored training sessions. A system provider shall provide telephone, e-mail, and on-site assistance plans, as necessary.

Any proposed system shall be capable of utilizing other power sources such as grid or generator, when available, as a "backup" to its self-generating power. Power generated by the unit is used to pump and purify water and can also be used to power ancillary tools, lights, and communication systems.

A system shall be self-contained and self-powered.

1.6.2. Support Concept Any system shall support easy installation and maintenance without the general need for specialized training. Maintenance requirements shall be minimal.

Maintenance and operation roles in the field will be conducted by personnel using local procedures and emergency response plans. A comprehensive operations manual shall be provided with each unit describing when routine maintenance is required and the procedures required to maintain a given system. In the event a more in-depth training session is requested, the vendor hosts regular training sessions. Any supplier shall provide on-site assistance plans as well as telephone and e-mail troubleshooting assistance.

Any system consumables shall be available for up to seven years after original system purchase.

2. Threat

Contaminated water poses a significant health risk to exposed individuals. Exposure to contaminated water can result in sickness and death.

Water infrastructure represents a potential terrorist target. Having in place a system ready to deploy to an affected area a high yield ($\geq$ 30,000 gallons from freshwater sources) of purified water is critical to necessary preparation for providing potable water to communities.

Additionally, water sources are often contaminated during a natural disaster. Hurricane events along the U.S. Gulf Coast, including Hurricane

Katrina (2005) and Hurricane Gustav (2008) regularly impact water resources adversely, leaving communities without access to sanitary water.
Other natural disasters have caused similar devastation to communities
by contaminating water supplies including the 2004 Indian Ocean Tsunami and the earthquake in Sichuan, China (2008).

3. Existing System Shortfalls

The current methods of providing potable water in the wake of a disaster can be both costly and logistically complex. Current methods of
distributing potable water to communities are trucking in bottled water
or using diesel generator purification systems. The shortfalls in these approaches can include the high cost and logistical considerations of buying
and transporting fuel and buying and transporting bottled water, as well
as disposal costs of used bottles. These traditional approaches require
roads and bridges to be passable in order to transport the goods, and also
require ongoing monetary outlay to purchase fuel, transport the goods,
and pay personnel to oversee and fuel generators. A proposed system
shall utilize technology to significantly reduce logistical considerations
inherent in the provision of potable water where clean water is unavailable and also offer significant cost savings.

For example, hurricane, tornado, earthquake, and other disaster response plans have typically provided bottled water to affected communities with potential ongoing difficulties, including:

- Sourcing water vendors
- Costly contracts to purchase bottled water and transportation services
- Fluctuating cost of fuel, making budget planning difficult
- Diluted distribution system that can be difficult to oversee and ensure quality of service delivery
- Unreliable roads and other infrastructure needed to deliver the
bottled water
- Unreliable delivery dates presenting the possibility of no potable
water to distribute
- Costly disposal of discarded water bottles and the resulting increase
of waste diverted to Landfills and/or costs associated with the recy-
cling of discarded bottles

Diesel-only generator purification systems can present similar difficulties in terms of high cost, the necessity of having a readily available and
cheap source of fuel, and an easy, cost-effective means of regularly transporting the fuel to an affected site.

In summary, conventional methods of delivering potable water after a disaster rely on three uncontrollable factors:

1. The identification and ability of a source to supply bottled water or generator fuel
2. The availability of fuel to transport goods
3. An intact transportation infrastructure network to get the goods to an affected site

These three points of potential failure in more typical approaches are present throughout the duration of a disaster response. Any proposed system shall eliminate these potential points of failure by presenting a stand-alone design allowing for flexible transport of the unit by air, land, and/or water, bringing high-yield water purification to an affected site, and using self-generating power capabilities, thus eliminating the need for only external fuel sources for operation.

Current methods present a threat of interrupted service when any one of these factors fails at anytime during the short and medium term of disaster response, leaving communities without life-saving water for undefined periods of time. Current methods rely on functional transportation networks to move bottled water or diesel generator fuel to the site. The transport of these goods can be costly, as is often the purchase of goods (i.e., the bottled waters). Costs associated with the disposal of bottled water containers is another potential shortcoming of this type of approach.

Capabilities needed to address this gap include utilization of a stand-alone water purification system on-site that does not require external fuel sources alone. It is also important that the technology be initially transportable to the site using a variety of transportation methods in order to mitigate impassable roads and bridges. This ensures that potable water is being delivered to affected communities without interruption of service.

4. Capabilities Required

4.1. Operational Performance Parameters (T: Threshold/ O: Objective)

Each system unit will weigh no more than 8,000 pounds (T) and $\leq$ 5,000 pounds (O).

Stowed, the units are no more than 10 foot cube (T), 5 foot cube (O).

Each unit will have a total capacity of $\geq$ 3,000 watts (T), $\geq$ 4,000 watts (O) when fully operational.

Grid power connection to allow for trickle charging during long-term indoor storage (T)/(O).

Ability to run additional equipment from 120 VAC and 12 VDC plugs (T), 120 VAC or 220 VAC and 12 VDC plugs (O).

A system shall pump and purify an average of ≥ 20 gallons per minute (GPM) (T), ≥ 30 gallons per minute (O) from freshwater surface or shallow well sources when fully operational. Capabilities to purify saltwater and brackish water sources shall also be available.

4.2. Key Performance Parameters (KPPs)

Easily transportable to the site using truck (and trailer,) international shipping container, boat, helicopter, and/or forklift (T)/(O).

Easy to use with limited training (T), after review of operation manual (O).

Each unit is self-powered (T)/(O).

A system shall pump and purify an average of ≥ 20 gallons per minute (GPM) (T), ≥ 30 gallons per minute (O) from freshwater surface or shallow well sources when fully operational. Capabilities to purify saltwater and brackish water sources shall also be available.

- Filtration process without using chemicals to purify water (T), providing redundancy for safety and uninterrupted water purification output, without using chemicals to purify water (O).
- Water filtered by a system must meet the standards for Drinking Water Quality set forth by the Environmental Protection Agency (EPA), and provisions of the Safe Drinking Water Act of 1974 and all subsequent amendments (T)/(O).

4.3 System Performance

4.3.1 Mission Scenarios Any proposed system shall work in defined harsh environments and represent a tool for emergency management professionals and disaster relief teams. Any proposed system shall be a self-contained, easily transportable, and easy-to-use system that purifies contaminated water at the source at a low cost while providing the added benefits of being self-powered and providing ancillary power to operate additional AC and DC machinery.

4.3.2 System Performance Parameters

Each unit is self-powered (T)/(O).

The system can pump and purify an average of ≥ 20 gallons per minute (GPM) (T), ≥ 30 gallons per minute (O) from freshwater surface or shallow well sources when fully operational.

There are also capabilities to purify seawater and brackish water sources.

Filtration process shall occur without using chemicals to purify water (T), providing redundancy for safety and uninterrupted water purification output, without using chemicals to purify water (O).

4.3.3 Interoperability Any proposed system shall work independently, without relying solely on any external input. It generates its own electricity to power water pumps, water purification, and other equipment. In order to provide the utmost flexibility to the end user, the system can also be tied in seamlessly to the grid (and use other forms of energy in "backup" modes).

4.3.4 Human Interface Requirements Operator safety is paramount. Safety features shall be incorporated into the unit. A system shall be deployed by no more than two people in ≤ 30 minutes using the easy-to-follow operation manual.

Any proposed system shall require minimal maintenance and oversight, while including safety mechanisms to ensure high quality of potable water output. It only requires periodic visual confirmation from an operator to ensure the system is running optimally, checking system indicators and flow of potable water coming out of the purification system.

4.3.5 Logistics and Readiness Safety features shall be built into a system to ensure the highest-quality water output. Operators shall be easily alerted if any filters or other consumables must be changed or serviced.

4.3.6 Other System Characteristics Any proposed system shall operate in harsh environments and operate in temperatures ranging from at least 32 degrees to above 120 degrees (F), in high-humidity, rainfall, high-wind, and dust-filled environments. Any system or unit shall have at least a five-year guarantee of performance under stated, normal conditions.

5. System Support

5.1 Maintenance

Any proposed system shall be designed to require minimal maintenance and oversight, while including safety mechanisms to ensure high quality of potable water output. Periodic visual checks of a system's self-diagnostic indicators will be conducted by operators or maintenance personnel to ensure the system is running optimally, checking potential gauges, LED light indicators, and flow of potable water coming out of the purification system. Minimal training of personnel is required to ensure proper understanding of system self-diagnostic indicators.

An operation manual shall show the procedures required to maintain/change consumables and accomplish routine maintenance.

5.2 Supply

Operation and maintenance manual(s) shall be provided to an end user with each system. Manuals will include deployment procedures, information on diagnostics, a troubleshooting guide, and consumable replacement procedures. Any supplier shall provide low-cost replacement packages for standard water purification consumables.

5.3 Support Equipment

No additional equipment shall be required for the operation of a system.

5.4 Training

A training manual shall be provided with each system describing when routine maintenance should be performed and procedures required to maintain a system. In the event a more in-depth training session is required, a supplier shall host customizable training session(s). On-site assistance plans, as well as telephone and e-mail troubleshooting assistance shall be provided.

5.5 Transportation and Facilities

Any system shall be transported by truck, trailer, air, in international shipping containers, by boat, by helicopter suspended from installed lift points, or by forklift using the skids built into the base of each system. A system shall be installed at a minimum on level ground or on a trailer bed near a water source.

6. Force Structure

Emergency response teams at the state, local, and/or tribal level are the typical customers. Any proposed system shall not require specialized knowledge or training to operate or maintain.

It is conservatively estimated that the potential available market for such a system is greater than 18,000 units for use by local municipalities, public water systems, water treatment facilities, and emergency management agencies, for example.

7. Schedule

Units or systems shall be available for purchase in twelve months or less after signing SECURE Program agreement. Deployment of the units typically shall require less than thirty minutes after arriving on site. Units can be deployed without any specialized training.

8. System Affordability

Individual system price is not expected to exceed $100,000 at high volume production levels (T), $\leq$ $80,000 for a freshwater system (O).

Systems for the purification of brackish and/or seawater sources shall also be available in less than eighteen months. Replacement consumable parts can be readily purchased from a supplier for at least five years after purchase.

Systems shall also be available to potential users on a lease or lease-to-buy payment scheme.

DHS OPERATING COMPONENTS: C-ORD FOR CRISIS DECISION-SUPPORT SOFTWARE

Contents

1. General Description of Operational Capability
    1.1. Capability Gap
    1.2. Overall Mission Area Description
    1.3. Description of the Proposed System
    1.4. Supporting Analysis
    1.5. Mission the Proposed System Will Accomplish
    1.6. Operational and Support Concept
        1.6.1. Concept of Operations
        1.6.2. Support Concept
2. Threat
3. Existing System Shortfalls
4. Capabilities Required
    4.1. Operational Performance Parameters
    4.2. Key Performance Parameters
    4.3. System Performance
        4.3.1. Examples of Mission Scenarios
        4.3.2. System Performance Parameters
        4.3.3. Interoperability
        4.3.4. Human Interface Requirements
        4.3.5. Logistics and Readiness
5. System Support
    5.1. Maintenance
    5.2. Supply
    5.3. Support Equipment
    5.4. Training
    5.5. Transportation and Facilities

6. Force Structure
7. Schedule
8. System Affordability

1. General Description of Operational Capability

Among the most difficult of decisions are those made in crisis or an unstable situation of extreme danger or difficulty. Examples of crisis decision environments range from emergency response to disaster management, antiterrorism response, emergency room triage, and even military (battlefield) operations. Decision failures can literally cost lives of first responders and members of the public, not to mention billions of dollars in failed missions, ruined infrastructure, and lost economic capability.

Much attention is focused on providing more and better data and information to decision makers. While admirable, there is a compelling and unrecognized need to improve the decision process itself, how decision makers use available information to reach effective decisions in a crisis.

The capability described in this commercialization-based operational requirements document (C-ORD) shall support decision makers in learning and applying effective decision-making techniques in real-world situations. Success is achieved by thinking the way that successful crisis decision makers think and to compress experience by bringing the knowledge of experienced decision makers quickly to bear, even for "crisis management rookies."

The needed system will support decision making for a broad range of crisis-like situations through a plug-and-play software application, deployed as a field-portable hardware/software capability. The system will help decision makers rapidly reach correct "good enough and/or optimal" decisions in high-stress, multiple-distraction environments.

The software may apply the recognition-primed decision model (RpDM) or other similar prediction models, in which observed event characteristics are used to force recognition of a similar scenario from a knowledge base. A major benefit of this method is the search for the first available "good enough" solution rather than more traditional normative decision processes that search all options for the "optimal" answer.

The core of the capability will be an extensive database of decision scenarios—combinations of events, key observable indicators, and resulting decisions. This database will form the knowledge base for the recognition-primed process. The software rapidly "walks" a decision maker through a limited set of questions to a choice of a scenario. An automated interview will terminate as soon as a base scenario is found that adequately matches the limited information available to the decision maker. The decision-support system then adapts the base scenario to actual event conditions as known at decision time, "tuning" the decision for the specific event. Finally, the system will identify key additional information that can significantly refine the decision, focusing the decision maker on extracting critical information from chaos.

1.1. Capability Gap

A gap currently exists in the training and real-time support for effective decision-making processes in crisis situations. Research and observation of operational crisis decision making have shown that excellent decision makers do not normally use traditional "rational choice" decision techniques. Instead, they rely on past or shared experiences to guide them through difficult decisions. They do not pursue perfection, rather they find the first "good enough" solution to a problem, implement it, and move on to the next urgent decision in the crisis. The psychological label given to this natural style of decision making is often referred to as RpDM.

Today's crisis decision makers face specific gaps in decision-making capability:

- Novice decision makers usually do not know how to apply RpDM based on personal experiences in crisis situations and are not always equipped to make the judgments necessary to quickly reach a conclusion and act.
- Experienced decision makers often do not have a personal knowledge base of past or shared experiences broad enough to cover unfamiliar events such as terrorist attacks or natural disasters.

A system is required that can rapidly supply the decision maker with "like experiences" from the past and from others across the field (e.g., fire fighting, earthquake response, hazardous materials response, etc.) and can guide a decision maker to a rapid "good enough" decision. Many systems have been designed to aid decision makers in data collection and organization. However, a user-centric approach matched with an expansive database of past decisions and a proven method to quickly reach critical decisions in high pressure environments for wide operational use is needed in the first-responder community as well as other communities.

1.2. Overall Mission Area Description

Crisis decisions often share a common set of characteristics:

- Time urgency
- Complex event or decision characteristics

- Rapidly changing event or decision conditions
- A chaotic surrounding environment
- High physical and/or emotional stress
- Severe consequences for decision failure
- Poor data availability and quality
- Competing demands for the decision maker's attention
- Frequent interruptions during the decision-making process

Below are a number of diverse activities that require crisis decision making, including:

- Natural disaster response: Bringing together a wide variety of people to solve group-centric problems in time-sensitive and chaotic environments both domestically and abroad
- Antiterrorism response: Crisis and consequence management for domestic and foreign terrorist attacks
- Hazardous materials emergency response: Managing, resolving, and mitigating consequences of hazardous materials releases due to accident, terrorist, or other actions
- Police response: Managing, resolving, and mitigating consequences of criminal, violent, or high-hazard events
- Fire response: Managing, resolving, and mitigating consequences of fires, explosions, and other high-energy events
- Emergency medicine: Managing, resolving, and mitigating consequences of urgent medical crises for individuals and mass casualties
- Search and rescue: Managing, resolving, and mitigating consequences of disasters trapping persons in high-hazard environments

1.3. Description of the Proposed System

The decision-support system shall, through a database-oriented software capability, integrate decision processes, decision-support tools, and a knowledge base needed to make effective decisions in a recognition-primed (or other performance-equivalent or superior types) decision environment. The system will interact with a decision maker to:

- Pose and answer key questions about the event in an interview environment
- Choose an analogous event and decision from a knowledge base
- Modify the analogous event and decision based on the actual conditions
- Provide a recommended decision that a user can quickly and unambiguously implement

The field-portable software system will combine knowledge databases, artificial intelligence database search functions, scenario modification tools, and an interface that operates on hardware platforms and operating systems typically available and used by crisis decision makers (e.g., MS Windows desktop computers, laptop computers, portable digital assistants [PDAs], etc.).

1.4. Supporting Analysis

DHS's experience has shown a genuine interest by various personnel involved in natural or man-made crisis decision making in possessing cost-effective, field-deployable decision tools/systems to aid crisis decision makers save valuable time in order to save lives and property.

1.5. Mission the Proposed System Will Accomplish

The proposed system will accomplish three key decision-support activities for crisis decision makers:

1. Real-time support for crisis decisions that have decision time-frames of greater than five minutes
2. Training support for enhancing decision-making skills and personal knowledge for both novice and experienced decision makers
3. Development and distributed sharing of community-wide (e.g., hazardous materials response community, etc.) decision knowledge bases

1.6. Operational and Support Concept

1.6.1. Concept of Operations A system will support a variety of key decisions across a wide range of crisis decision making. A system will integrate two processes: how decision makers recognize and size up a situation and how they evaluate the course of action by imagining it and rehearsing process and outcomes. The basic decision-making steps directly supported by the software system will be:

1. Size up the situation using available information.
2. Search a knowledge base (of decision maker experience) and recognize the first case that adequately matches the situation at hand.
3. Diagnose the historical case against the situation at hand.
4. Adapt and modify the solution of the historical case to work in the situation at hand.
5. Rehearse the solution to verify that it is likely to realistically work.
6. Put the solution/decision into play.

In practice, the decision maker will work from a decision-making location (e.g., event scene, emergency operations center, etc.). The decision-support system will be resident on a hardware device (e.g., a laptop computer or a PDA device) already in use by the decision maker for other response or functional purposes, etc.

The decision maker likely will follow seven basic operational steps:

1. Size up the event situation, gathering information about the event during a limited period of time.
2. Activate a decision-support software system.
3. Answer questions from the system as it walks the user through a rapid selection of base-event scenarios.
4. Answer further questions from the system as it walks the user through modification of the base-event scenario.
5. Simulate and evaluate the final scenario to confirm applicability.
6. Simulate and evaluate the recommended decisions to confirm appropriateness and practicality.
7. Implement decisions.

1.6.2. Support Concept Maintenance requirements for the system will be minimal. Each unit will be sold as licensed software with implementation and end user support. Follow-on contracts should be available for continued support after an initial included support period. Software design will allow for easy implementation in multiple hardware/operating system configurations and as a purely Web-based application. Upgrades distributed via the Internet will address software bug fixes and product advances.

2. Threat

Response to and management of any terrorist event will involve multiple crisis-type decisions, in both the crisis management and consequence management phases of events. Though not classic "threats" in the terrorism sense of the word, natural disasters, accident-based emergencies, fire response, police response, medical response, and search-and-rescue all involve threats to public health and welfare. Crisis-type decisions will always be involved in these or similar events.

3. Existing System Shortfalls

The classical approach to decision making, termed "rational choice decision making," is a conceptually straight-line (and straightforward) process to:

1. Define the problem and objectives for solution
2. Identify decision options or alternatives

3. Identify methods for evaluating the options against each other
4. Gather necessary data to define and evaluate each option
5. Score the decision options
6. Choose the best decision from among the available options
7. Implement the best decision

This analytical approach, or variations, has been espoused and applied in a variety of fields. This is also the decision-making approach almost universally applied in developing formal methods, processes, and tools for crisis decision making. In particular, emergency management decision makers and battlefield decision makers are taught to use the rational choice approach and provided tools and technology in support.

Much of the effort in decision system development for crisis management has been focused on improving the rational choice method, computer-based comparisons, more data capture, training methods, and so on. Key requirements for this approach include well-defined options, clear objectives, availability of extensive data for event and decision options, uninterrupted time for analysis and comparison of multiple options, and an environment that allows complex mental processes. Very often, none of these requirements is met in real-world decision making.

Some research has shown that the most effective crisis decision makers do not in fact use the rational choice approach, even when taught and required to use it. For instance, a study found that only 30 percent of crisis decisions by fire ground commanders and wildfire incident commanders were made in this way. Additional research with experienced emergency incident commanders has routinely rejected rational choice decision systems, aids, and training, declaring them to be unworkable in the real world.

4. Capabilities Required

4.1. Operational Performance Parameters

This section lists the minimum operational performance parameters (note: T= Threshold and O= Objective).

4.1.1 Operate in Plug-and-Play Mode   Plug-and-play mode allows for different crisis-decision environments with capability to treat both analytical and heuristic decisions. System will:

- Allow interchangeable crisis environment/decision modules, with plug-and-play by end user
- Allow user-authoring of crisis environment/decision modules

- Allow upgrade/revision of knowledge bases from central source
- Support modular, interchangeable processing of analytical decisions and decision components
- Support processing of heuristic decisions and decision components
- Support experienced decision makers
- Support inexperienced decision makers

4.1.2 The First "Good Enough Solution" Is Found and Implemented   The system implements the first "good enough" solution without characterizing or comparing all options to find the optimal solution. System will:

- Develop, incorporate, and maintain a knowledge base of event/decision pairs sufficient in spectrum and depth to support decision-making
- Allow interchangeable event/decision knowledge base modules, with plug-and-play by end user
- Allow user-authoring of event/decision knowledge bases
- Produce decision recommendations within the time allowed for effective decision making
- Allow upgrade/revision of event/decision knowledge bases from central source
- Produce decisions that adequately meet the decision need

4.1.3 Expectations Are Developed for "What Next"   The system will predict outcomes of decisions and, if not matched, the change is quickly captured and the decision modified. System will:

- Predict the envelope of expected inputs for the next stage in the decision process and the envelope of possible decisions (outcomes) based on previous inputs
- Dynamically change predicted envelope of expected inputs for the next stage in the decision process and the envelope of possible decisions (outcomes) as interactive user input process proceeds
- Dynamically inform user of predicted envelope of expected inputs for the next stage in the decision process (O) and the envelope of possible decisions (outcomes) (T)
- Dynamically inform user of trend in convergence/divergence in envelope of possible decisions (outcomes)
- Dynamically identify key inputs that can lead to rapid convergence toward single decision (outcome)
- Dynamically inform user of key inputs that can lead to rapid convergence toward single decision (outcome)

4.1.4 Implement Operational and Training Modes   Both operational and training modes are implemented within the system and user can toggle between them. System will:

- Implement a full training mode for the system
- Capture and present training scores and statistics to the user
- Capture training sessions and grow event/decision knowledge base
- Capture training sessions and grow knowledge base of observation/ decision pathways
- Implement a capability to improve the ability to predict decision (outcomes) from each training session

4.1.5 Produce a System That Is Consistently Reliable   The system must be one that works all the time, always reaches an answer, and produces the same results for the same input information.

- Mean rate of failure to operate ≤ 0.5%
- Mean rate of failure to reach an answer when system operates ≤ 0.5%
- Mean rate of failure to reach expected answer when an answer is reached ≤ 0.5%
- Mean rate of failure to produce identical answers for identical inputs 0%

4.1.6 Produce a System That Is Cost Efficient   Price for system implementation is <$3,000 (T) / < $1,000 (O) in high-volume quantities.

4.2. Key Performance Parameters

This section lists the minimum key performance parameters.

4.2.1 Employ a Naturalistic Decision Model   The decision model is one that matches the psychology of rapid crisis decision making. System will:

- Allow decision maker to characterize event size-up information as a starting point for analysis
- Support user in recognizing an analogous case from a decision knowledge base that is "good enough" for use as a start to decision making
- Support user in analyzing a recognized case to determine if it adequately represents the crisis situation
- Support the user in customizing the selected analogous case to better fit the actual crisis conditions

- Support the user in mentally rehearsing the decision and action steps to evaluate if success is likely
- Support the user in implementing the final decision as an effective course of action

4.2.2 Employ Case-Based Reasoning   Case-based reasoning is used to expedite decision making and take advantage of expertise and past experiences. System will:

- Implement an artificial intelligence or equivalent capability
- Implement a knowledge base of observation/decision pathways
- Populate the knowledge base of observation/decision pathways with sufficient cases to produce target performance by an artificial intelligence or equivalent capability
- Implement a capability to improve its ability to predict decision (outcomes) from each operational session
- Allow interchangeable observation/decision pathways knowledge-base modules, with plug-and-play by end user
- Allow user-authoring of observation/decision pathways knowledge bases
- Allow upgrade/revision of observation/decision pathways knowledge bases from central source

4.2.3 Trigger Recognition with Partial Characterization   By triggering recognition with partial characterization of an event, traditional "paralysis by data collection" is avoided. System will:

- Allow "unknown" or fuzzy inputs
- Recognize an event or event component with specified level of limited information at specified frequency
- Allow a mixture of known and unknown information about an event
- Capture all known information quickly then focus on resolving unknowns

4.2.4 Use Common System Parameters   Use system parameters that the user is likely to already have available. System will:

- Operate on a standard Windows-based laptop computer
- Operate on a standard Windows-based PDA device
- Operate via the Internet from any computer device with an Internet connection and a standard Internet browser

4.2.5 *Establish an Internet-Based capability for Training* A central,
Internet-based capability will be available for training and knowledge
base building. System will:

- Establish an Internet-based, game-oriented version for multiple tar-
geted applications
- Implement a training mode for the Internet-based system
- Capture and present Internet-based training scores and statistics to
the user
- Capture Internet-based training sessions and grow central event/
decision knowledge bases
- Capture Internet-based training sessions and grow knowledge base
of observation/decision pathways
- Implement a capability to improve the system's ability to predict
decisions (outcomes) from each Internet-based training session
- Implement a gaming/competition mode for the Internet-based system
- Capture and present Internet-based gaming/competition scores and
statistics to the user
- Capture Internet-based gaming/competition sessions and grow central event/decision knowledge bases
- Capture Internet-based gaming/competition sessions and grow
knowledge base of observation/decision pathways
- Implement a capability to improve the system's ability to predict
decisions (outcomes) from each Internet-based gaming/competition
session

4.3 System Performance

4.3.1 *Examples of Mission Scenarios* *August 2005: Crisis managers
during the Katrina hurricane response fail to mobilize and employ available
transportation resources (buses and trains) to evacuate the population of New
Orleans.*
The hurricane version of the system would be preloaded with key
indicators of evacuation scenarios. Equipped with the decision-support
system, decision makers will be able to weigh the risk involved in decisions and pull from an extensive knowledge base of past events in order
to characterize the current situation. Once characterized properly, evacuation decisions can be made in the interest of key risk factors. Due to the
rapidly available historical cases, precious time is saved, allowing for
early evacuations of citizens.
*May 2000: Fire managers at the Bandolier National Monument in New Mex-
ico decide to initiate a prescribed burn in spite of forecasted high winds and dry
conditions. Control is quickly lost and the Cerro Grande Wildfire burns hundreds
of families out of their homes, resulting in more than $1 billion in damages.*

The decision-support system would probe decision makers on key indicators in order to provide them with past experiences in very similar situations. The system would then characterize the risk and provide the user with a range of optimal decisions. Managers, noting that risk of fire spread is extremely high, decide to hold off until conditions are more favorable.

2009: A local response team responds to an apparent terrorist attack. A release has occurred from a suspicious package. A number of victims are down and exhibiting a variety of observable symptoms. The perpetrators are arrayed behind buildings wearing gas masks and shooting any responders that come near.

The decision-support system would walk the decision makers through a size-up process to gather key information about symptoms, weather, container type, etc., then help the incident commander identify likely scenarios from an event knowledge base. The incident commander would recognize a likely release of Sarin and further make effective shelter/evacuation/rescue decisions that include the competing risks from terrorist gunfire.

4.3.2 System Performance Parameters
4.3.3 Interoperability   The system shall:

- Operate on a standard Windows-based laptop computer running Windows XP, Windows Vista, or higher
- Operate on a standard Windows-based PDA device
- Operate via Internet from any computer device with an Internet connection and a standard Internet browser, including Windows Internet Explorer (Version 6 or higher), FireFox (Version 2 or higher), or Safari (Version 3 or higher)

4.3.4 Human Interface Requirements   The decision-support system will employ a user-friendly graphical user interface (GUI). The purpose of the GUI will be to walk a user through the RpDM (or performance-equivalent or superior) process using concise and clear interactions. The system will operate using common browser-based interface methods, requiring very little experience to use.

Once the browser-based application is downloaded, direct human interface with the system will be limited to interaction during performance. Installation will require little to no expertise as conventional software download techniques shall be applied. Output data will be provided in concise reports both for training and information management purposes. The reports will be designed by the user and access to them will be at the user's discretion.

4.3.5 Logistics and Readiness   The system shall operate on a wide range of user field equipment (within the hardware/software listed above). This is key in assuring that most users can access and use the

decision-making support without any additional equipment or modifications to existing systems. The system shall operate at a high level of reliability (> 99%) both in the field or at command or operation centers. It must be accessible twenty-four hours a day, seven days a week with no noticeable delay beyond the time necessary to boot up the on-board Internet browser. The system must have a stand-alone backup method of accessing the knowledge base (database) to ensure that reliable operation is ensured if Internet access is lost during a crisis event.

5. System Support

5.1 Maintenance

Maintenance will be provided through automatically downloadable patches. Additions and updates to the extensive knowledge base will be accessible to the user through a download system as well. Since the system is software-based, electronic help systems, electronic (pdf) user guides, and frequently asked questions will be provided to ensure proper installation and to troubleshoot software/hardware interface issues. User support will also be offered through online support forums as well as through direct contact with a system support organization.

5.2 Supply

Backup copies of the decision-support software and knowledge bases for each user will be stored on a central server for download at user convenience. Users will also be able to download copies onto CD for local backup as desired. Manuals will be provided to the operator by the vendor and will include installation procedures, common problems, test cases, download instructions, and data retrieval procedures. When necessary, real-time diagnostics can be performed by system experts to ensure the system is operating properly.

5.3 Support Equipment

No support equipment will be needed for the system. Patches and system updates will be downloadable to ensure that system performance is optimal.

5.4 Training

Because the system will be browser-based, little, if any, training will be required to enable the user to start and operate the application. Offline tutorials (included with system downloads) and evaluated online training scenarios shall be provided to end users. Custom-designed training shall be available, on a mutually agreed fee basis.

5.5 Transportation and Facilities

Transportation will be at the sole discretion of the user, due to the software-based nature of the system. Cross-platform capabilities will be provided to ensure easy and highly reliable integration into the field.

6. Force Structure

The potential end-users of the decision-support system within the Department of Homeland Security (DHS) and DHS-supported crisis management community are extensive. Multiple levels of users exist within each of these groups. For instance, the U.S. Coast Guard might deploy a decision-support system within each rescue helicopter, but they might also have a single or multiple systems within each regional command center to help deal with large amounts of incoming data. Therefore, in many of these organizations, there are needs at both the field-task level and the management or command center level.

For estimation purposes, two units of the system will be needed for each subgroup level in order to ensure maximum efficiency and to provide backup support. Based on estimates of the market, the need is approximately 50,000 units.

7. Schedule

A TRL-9 (fully deployable) product that satisfies user requirements, is required within 12 (T) / 6 (O) months.

8. System Affordability

Price for individual units shall be <$3,000 (T)/ ≤ $1,000 (O).

FIRST RESPONDERS: C-ORD FOR NATIONAL EMERGENCY RESPONSE INTEROPERABILITY FRAMEWORK AND RESILIENT COMMUNICATION SYSTEM OF SYSTEMS

Contents

1. General Description of Operational Capability for a National Emergency Response Interoperability Framework and Resilient Communication System of Systems

1.1. Capability Gap
1.2. Overall Mission Area Description
1.3. The Description of Resilient Portable Communications Responder Kits
1.4. Supporting Analysis
1.5. Mission the Proposed System Shall Accomplish
1.6. Operational and Support Concept
    1.6.1. Concept of Operations
    1.6.2. Support Concept
2. Threat
3. Existing System Shortfalls
4. Capabilities Required
4.1. Operational Performance Parameters
4.2. Key Performance Parameters (KPPs)
4.3. System Performance
    4.3.1. Mission Scenarios
    4.3.2. System Performance Parameters
    4.3.3. Interoperability
    4.3.4. Human Interface Requirements
    4.3.5. Logistics and Readiness
    4.3.6. Other System Characteristics
5. System Support
5.1. Maintenance
5.2. Supply
5.3. Support Equipment
5.4. Training
5.5. Transportation and Facilities
6. Force Structure

1. General Description of Operational Capability for a National Emergency Response Interoperability Framework and Resilient Communication System of Systems

1.1. Capability Gap

Interoperability and compatibility of first-responder communication systems is a mandate of the National Incident Management System (NIMS). However, as of 2009, the only interoperability systems widely in use are expensive and complicated proprietary voice-over-radio systems. These aptly described "patchwork" interoperability systems are unable to scale without additional costly equipment coupled with costly on-site support provided by highly trained technicians. This current mode of operations is not feasible in the critical first minutes and hours of an incident response.

The vast majority of emergency responders are limited in their ability to communicate and collaborate with each other. They are unable to communicate with command, support teams, and other responding organizations present at an incident scene. In 2008, almost seven years after the tragic lessons learned by 9/11, the majority of emergency response organizations (ERO) do not have the basic capability for any of their team members to establish communications at an incident site. They may have to wait hours for large trucks and/or trailers with very expensive and complicated communications equipment delivered to the site. In the case of a catastrophic incident causing a scorched-earth environment, it may take days to get the necessary equipment and communication support personnel to the incident site.

It is not only the complexity and cost of existing systems that inhibit NIMS compliance; most systems often render previous technology investments obsolete or require a need for costly upgrades to legacy systems, proving impractical or unaffordable. A system is required that creates a communications framework enabling not only interoperability of disparate systems, but also the ability to interconnect legacy systems and new systems.

Another major capability gap exists in providing an affordable solution for the interoperability and interconnection of communication systems that support IPv4 routing with those systems that answer the Department of Defense mandate for IPv6 compliance. The cost of phasing out an IPv4 system (which is prevalent in the vast majority of state and local EROs, nongovernment organizations, and private sector security) is not realistic from a budgetary feasibility perspective and would take years to accomplish.

Yet, closing this gap is mandatory. The NIMS mandate for interoperability is unattainable without a cost-effective, easy-to-implement system that provides a framework for the interoperability of data and video between responders and EROs. Data is as critical as voice communications within an incident site. If noise levels inhibit voice communications or silent communications are necessary, instant messaging is an effective tool. Video from an inexpensive webcam on a first responder's laptop may make a critical difference by providing a visual assessment to the ERO. Maps and other files needed at the incident site must get to the response team without the need to deliver files physically via courier, currently the most widely used solution.

Existing interoperable voice, data, and video communications require fixed private networks or access to the Internet via a virtual private network (VPN) requiring authentication servers and server-based network management systems. This requirement for access to remote servers creates an insurmountable capability gap for interoperable communications among responders in the hours or days they must wait for communications trucks and/or trailers to arrive at the incident scene. This commercialization-based operational requirement document (C-ORD) requires a system that provides peer-to-peer interoperability between responders and EROs without the requirement for remote servers or dedicated networks. The requirement is for secure peer-to-peer communication between any responder using any type of voice, video, or data communication device and any other responder or ERO, without requiring the receiving communication to be of similar device type or dedicated network. Responders at an incident site must be able to establish incident area peer-to-peer communications within minutes of responding and interoperate with EROs both at the incident site and/or remotely across readily available disparate communications networks without the need for third-party services or servers.

Even more problematic is the fact that most EROs still depend on vulnerable radio or cellular infrastructure to support expensive communication and command vehicles. Network failures caused by destruction of critical infrastructure, such as radio towers, landlines, and network control centers, represent a major challenge for both the public and private sectors. If they do have systems, the majority are not portable enough for easy transport to the incident scene by a first responder or are so complicated that extensive training is required to operate the system. Very few EROs currently have portable systems whose capabilities allow a responder to establish interoperable voice, data, and video communications at the incident site without technical support in ten to twenty minutes. All EROs require this capability.

The aftermath of the 2004–2005 hurricane season, which resulted in catastrophic damage across the Gulf States, is the ultimate example of not possessing the capability in discussion. Vast areas realized devastating damage to their communications infrastructure. There was no communications resiliency. The available response recovery solutions were inadequate or failed altogether, leaving many areas where lives were at risk without communications for days.

Many critical infrastructure facilities of importance to the security of the region did not have effective communications for weeks. Belle Chase Naval Air Station, critical for the staging of over 30,000 rescue operations south of New Orleans, did not have reliable voice communications for nearly ninety-six hours after the landfall of Hurricane Katrina. With a system that meets the requirements of this C-ORD, the Coast Guard Rescue Operations in New Orleans would have had telephone capability and data communications within ten to twenty minutes of beginning the emergency response. This communication could have been established by anyone at the staging area regardless of whether that person had training in deploying communication networks or not.

Almost all communication systems in 2009 still require some type of fixed infrastructure in order to function and the presence of qualified technicians or engineers is required. Yet many disaster situations result in no usable infrastructure to support either local area or wide area communications.

According to an Associated Press report in 2005, "Downed telephone lines and damaged cellular towers left emergency crews confused and isolated in the aftermath of Hurricane Katrina." The report, quoting experts, said communications systems eroded as the waters rose and only became worse. "We had no way to communicate except by line of sight. Our radios were not operable, most landlines and cell phones were useless and our communications centers were under water. When help arrived, we could not communicate with them either," Juliette Saussy, director of Emergency Medical Service of New Orleans, told regulators. "Some 3 million telephone lines were knocked out as the violent storm hit the Gulf Coast on August 29, 2005. At least thirty-eight 911-call centers went down, and more than 1,000 cellular towers were out of service. As many as 20,000 calls failed to go through the day after the storm, and about 100 TV and radio stations were knocked off the air," FCC chairman Kevin Martin commented.

There must be a framework for enabling communications, interoperability, and collaboration that is affordable. The biggest gap in 2009 is that existing solutions are too expensive for most EROs, and funding for staffing communication technicians to operate these solutions reduces the ability of most EROs to equip and staff for other vital capabilities necessary for mission effectiveness. This C-ORD requires not only that the technology-based solution works, but that it is affordable.

The local incidents, as well as the wide-area natural disasters within the past seven years clearly identify the capability gap to enable first responders to communicate, interoperate, and collaborate with each other, their command and their support teams, or with other organizations present at an incident scene within minutes of arriving at an incident site. This C-ORD provides the system requirements to close this vital gap saving lives and increasing security.

1.2. Overall Mission Area Description

A first emergency response provider (FERP), by definition, is any professional who first arrives at an incident site to provide emergency medical services, security, law enforcement, and assessment of the scope of the incident, and who recommends and coordinates an extended response if required. The mission area covered by this C-ORD is to outline the capabilities needed to enable FERPs to communicate and collaborate with each other and their command and interoperate with mutual aid, support teams, and other responding organizations within minutes of arriving at an incident site. This C-ORD will also address the capabilities needed to provide interoperable voice and data systems to command in control of the incident; to dynamically manage the incident as the response grows and scale communications as required; and to increase collaboration and extend the chain of command across jurisdictions. Finally, this C-ORD will identify the requirements of the proposed system capabilities and provide a communications framework for the creation of a dynamic, interoperable system of systems.

1.3. The Description of Resilient Portable Communications Responder Kits That Create a System of Systems

The primary system solution that closes the capability gap described above and accomplishes the mission of this ORD is a system of systems (SoS). The SoS must meet three primary requirements. First, the SoS must be dynamic, enabling interoperability between any combinations of different communication device types and converge any type or number of disparate networks on demand at any incident site. The SoS also fosters dynamic communications with EROs; elected officials whose districts are affected by the incident; supporting emergency operations centers (EOCs), medical facilities, military bases, etc.; and private sector security involved in the area of the event. There cannot be any operational restrictions on the number of, or combination of, systems available to support the incident response. The requirement is that the EROs and FERPs use the same software-based framework that is freely distributable at the incident site and can be loaded on or accessed by any device in minutes.

In order to create a dynamically interoperable SoS, the SoS must be based on software that converges network protocol types and provides network presence awareness. The SoS is required to enable data interoperability among any combinations of ad hoc, terrestrial data, telephony, or satellite networks that are immediately available to FERPs or will be introduced to the SoS by other FERPs or EROs as the response develops.

The second primary requirement that must be in place to meet the mission of this C-ORD is human portable resilient communication systems that can provide connectivity to the interoperability framework. These systems will be in a kit form that has everything a FERP needs, to be hand-carried to the incident site or transported by car, helicopter, or small watercraft. The kit must be able to provide voice, video, and data communication peer-to-peer among FERPs at the incident site as well as capability across any available network. If normal network infrastructure is unavailable, the kit will contain a broadband satellite system to ensure connectivity beyond the incident site. The resilient portable communications kit (RPCK) will be easy to set up and become operable within ten to twenty minutes by any FERP. The kit will require no technical support to set up. The RPCK shall seamlessly participate in an expanding system of systems. The kit will be available in multiple form factors, providing EROs the flexibility to have kits carried by hand in cases, mounted in vehicles, or installed in mobile EOCs or any other type of response apparatus. If an ERO needs to support large-scale recovery operations, the RPCK will be modifiable to meet the requirement of the ERO.

The communication capabilities of the RPCK require:

- The ability to operate via both AC and DC power without requiring filtering. It will directly connect with any 12-volt battery, vehicle cigarette lighter adaptor, generator, tactical solar array, or tactical fuel cell.
- A full-featured VoIP PBX with at least five handsets (wired or wireless) with the ability to scale the support of VoIP handsets for every FERP at the incident site.
- Wired Ethernet connectivity for a minimum of four external devices.
- Wireless access to the network for any 802.11-enabled COTS computer at the incident site. The system's wireless coverage will be scalable simply by deploying software-definable wireless routers operating on AC or DC power deployable by the FERP.
- Network management software converging data, telephony, and video protocols while interconnecting seamlessly and without configuration with IPv4 and/or IPv6 networks and devices.
- IPv6 and IPv4 network routing with a software firewall as well as allowing external firewalls and VPNs to be used if required.
- Simple operating instructions with color-coded connections allowing any FERP to deploy the network without prior exposure or training to the RPCK.
- The capability to add IP-based devices and peripherals as needed to support an extended response or recovery operation.
- The ability to interconnect with any land mobile radio network (LMR) or cellular "push to talk" (CPT) phone patchwork interoperability system, enabling LMR or CPT devices to interoperate with any other type of device on the SoS, such as a laptop computer. This ability allows EROs utilizing IP-based devices (laptop, PDA, desktop computer, etc.) to have voice communications with LMR or CPT devices.
- Interoperability support with cellular systems.

The third primary requirement is the kit must be affordable and scalable. The SoS will fail if the FERP does not carry resilient communications to the incident. EROs will need multiple RPCKs. If the kits are too expensive, they will not be available where they are needed most as an integral part of any FERP's support equipment. The RPCK should be affordable to rapidly fund the distribution of enough kits across the United States, enabling the deployment of a resilient SoS, which in turn creates a national communication resiliency network (NCRN). Even if parts, or all of the national power and communications infrastructure are compromised or destroyed, the NCRN would survive. Figure 11.4 details the architecture needed to create the SoS framework.

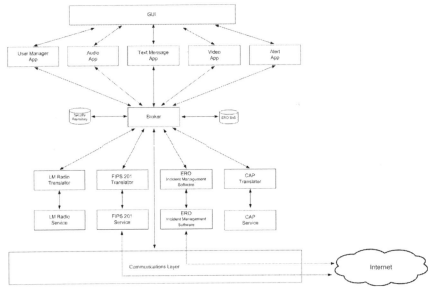

Figure 11.4.

The kits are required to interconnect with any available IPv4 or IPv6 data network that the FERP has authorization to use; providing Wide Area Network (WAN) connectivity without requiring any configuration or modifications by a FERP. By enabling the IPv6 capability, the system provides the ERO the ability to create secure collaboration with supporting agencies anywhere in the world, on-demand. The following diagram details the capability of creating secure peer-to-peer collaboration on demand without the need of a server.

Figure 11.5 is the position of components on the open systems interconnection (OSI) stack necessary to support interoperability. The contingent network in the diagram above is any available WAN connection. If a WAN connection is not available at the incident site, the RPCK will include a small broadband satellite system with active service.

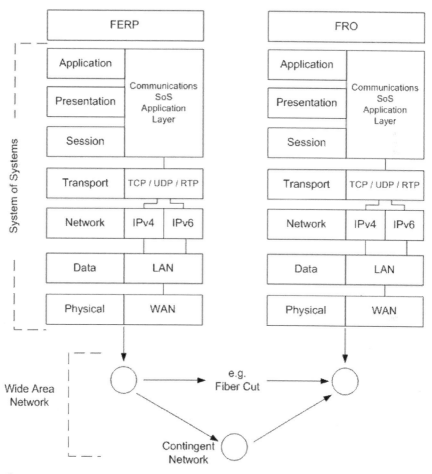

Figure 11.5.

1.4. Supporting Analysis

These requirements have been verified through interviews with DHS and first-responder personnel throughout the United States.

1.5. Mission the Proposed System Shall Accomplish

Homeland Security Presidential Directive 5 (HSPD-5) mandated the National Incident Management System (NIMS) calls for the creation of a system that enables:

> Federal, state and local governments to work effectively and efficiently together to prepare for, respond to and recover from domestic incidents, regardless of cause, size or complexity. To provide for interoperability and compatibility among Federal, state and local capabilities, the NIMS will include a core set of concepts, principles, terminology, and technologies covering the incident command system, multiagency coordination systems; unified command; training; identification and management of resources (including systems for classifying types of resources); qualifications; and certification; and the collection, tracking and reporting of information and incident resources. HSPD-5 (February 2003)

The proposed SoS and RPCK would enable the accomplishment of this directive. If FERPs and EROs cannot communicate, they fail. The proposed system creates the communication resiliency necessary for an "interoperable and compatible response" to an incident.

Specifically the proposed system shall accomplish this mission by:

- Providing a communication framework that creates dynamically interoperable communications on-demand
- Providing any FERP with the capability to communicate at an incident site with other responders and with anyone else who has data or telephony capability anywhere in the country with what the FERP brings to the incident site with no need for additional equipment
- Enabling any responder, even if it is the first time the FERP has used the kit, to set up the system within ten to twenty minutes
- Interoperating with other systems, creating a system of systems for voice, data, and video interoperability
- Providing the ability to log communications among FERPs for reporting purposes interconnecting command systems in a multi-agency response across disparate networks on demand
- Creating visibility among responders to know what resources are available and coordinate the use of those resources
- Enabling the creation of "ad hoc" incident site, area, regional, and national communication networks as needed within minutes providing peer-to-peer communications that enable instant alerts, warnings, and advisories that can be viewed and responded to from anywhere in the country

1.6. Operational and Support Concept

1.6.1. Concept of Operations   The RPCK and a SoS framework shall establish communications anywhere and anytime without any other support. These systems will be a part of the FERP team's basic response tools. The system creates a system of systems with other systems and will interoperate with any other IP-based network. If FERP vehicles in every locality in the country carried the RPCK/SoS system or used the software that provides the system capabilities for legacy systems, in effect, the NCRN is created that provides communication capability even in the aftermath of a large-scale infrastructure disaster. Figure 11.6 illustrates the NCRN.

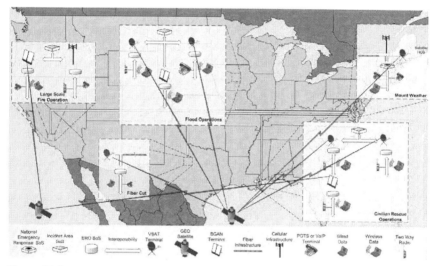

Figure 11.6.

The NCRN shall be available to as many FERPs and EROs as possible on a 24/7 basis. The system creates the communication resiliency and provides the capabilities to accomplish the mission only if the SoS is available to the FERP teams and their commanders. Every EOC, fire station, police station, hospital emergency room, and private security force at critical infrastructure sites could have an RPCK in order to create a system of systems on demand. In addition, key response vehicles, apparatus, and command vehicles could also have systems in order to be apart of the system of systems. Finally, civilian and political leaders who are integral to the NIMS could also travel with the RPCK to guarantee their availability to collaborate by having personal communication resiliency.

Sites and agencies not affected by the loss of communication capabilities but who still need to be a part of the SoS can simply do so by running the proposed system software on their existing systems. This ability to run SoS software on any network from any location will provide the capability of a virtual on-demand NCRN, resilient by design. The SoS communication framework is agnostic of device type or network type. The SoS system framework simply requires a MAC or IP address within an IPv4 or IPv6 network.

Despite the fact that billions of dollars have been spent on interoperability since the NIMS mandate, there is no real capability for interoperability of voice, video, and data that can be used on a local, state, regional, and national basis immediately following an incident. The proposed RPCK/SoS shall provide that capability for far less than the cost of alternative systems that do not have the capability of meeting the mandate. Meeting this requirement has the potential to save hundreds of millions of taxpayer dollars while also being rolled out nationally in less than three years.

1.6.2. Support Concept   The core concept of the SoS deals in providing connectivity when and where it is needed. A staff of network convergence engineers could support the system around the clock. A support engineer shall have the ability to troubleshoot problems in real time. Because one of the major requirements of this ORD is that hardware components be minimized when possible by providing network functionality with software, a support engineer shall run remote diagnostics on any supported system.

Software updates shall be available to all systems in a planned and coordinated manner. Because the SoS is a peer-to-peer framework, updates shall automatically be logged to the support database with an acknowledgment of a successful update. If updates are required at the incident site, a support engineer would have the ability to remotely update the RPCK at the incident.

If there are hardware failures with the RPCK, replacement systems and parts can be staged at regional logistic depots, which would guarantee a maximum delivery time of eight hours to the ERO. Spare parts should be included with each RPCK for repairs that can be made by the FERP.

Live interactive webinars can be held daily on a regional basis allowing any FERP to not only receive training, but also ask for advice and share ideas with other FERPs. These webinars will be coordinated and monitored by a national support staff. Because every RPCK would provide peer-to-peer video capability, enhanced support would be provided to any FERP when needed.

2. Threat

If FERPs and EROs cannot communicate, they cannot respond effectively. Lives have been lost because communications systems were not resilient or could not interoperate with other systems at the incident. Rescue operations cannot be coordinated or assets requested or deployed because valuable time is lost without critical communications capability.

On a local-level incident response, too many missions are compromised because some EROs cannot afford easy-to-use resilient communication systems. The systems sold to them are too expensive and require costly support. Complex systems requiring this type of support take resources away from other critical areas.

In most cases, as communications systems funding becomes available, EROs do not possess the knowledge or experience to adequately obtain a system that addresses all the communication risks they will face in a disaster. There are no current standards published that give them guidance on possible solutions that will meet the demands necessary to implement this C-ORD. Instead, to a large extent they rely on existing relationships with vendors, who quite often are not skilled or adept in disaster recovery communications. Also, companies whose business model relies on proprietary technology that does not allow other manufacturers' products to integrate create obvious issues for the mission of this C-ORD. Additionally, EROs find that what they get is not what they thought they were buying. There are dozens of anecdotal stories of EROs spending millions to deploy systems that do not accomplish the intended mission, and when they voice their dissatisfaction, they are often informed they will need to spend millions more to actually get the system to do what they need, if in fact the system can do what they need. On a state and regional level where interoperability exists, only certain types of radio systems have this ability. These systems depend on an infrastructure with little or no resiliency. Major budget dollars spent on incident management software and services by EROs to manage incidents on a regional or state basis will not work well if they do not have connectivity to the Internet. Alert and warning systems have become a major business since the Virginia Tech tragedy, but they all depend on networks that provide little or no resiliency. If power fails, campus communications fail. You cannot send an SMS alert and have any guarantee the message was received if you are depending on a highly vulnerable cellular network, for example. If one sends an emergency e-mail, there is no way to guarantee that the multiple e-mail servers required for the delivery of the e-mail will be available and able to deliver the increased amounts of e-mail generated due to an event. Not only are many EROs creating plans that will fail without resilient and an interoperable communication framework, they are spending hundreds of millions of dollars building a false sense of readiness.

There is currently no interoperable resilient national communication solution across federal, state, and local EROs. Solutions that will take decades, costing billions of dollars, and do not provide resilient interoperability can become a major threat to homeland security. A response to a pandemic, a major terrorist strike at key infrastructure, a cyber attack on telecommunication centers, super-regional earthquakes, or catastrophic oil shortages planned to cripple the U.S. economy, or any other scenario with national impact, could fail because current communications infrastructure will be compromised or, worse yet, destroyed. Without proper communications, EROs are "blind, deaf, and mute" to any coordinated national response. There is currently no capability to create a national "ad hoc" communications network for a coordinated national response. This inability makes NIMS vulnerable to failing on a catastrophic level.

Finally one of, the greatest threats is ignoring the plurality of our system of government. Incident response always starts at the local level; therefore, expenditures must happen at the local level. It is impractical to implement a federally mandated one-size-fits-all system. William Waugh points out this in his paper "Terrorism, Homeland Security and the National Emergency Management Network":

> On September 11, 2001, officials and agencies that are part of the national emergency management system orchestrated the responses to the collapse of the World Trade Center towers and the fires at the Pentagon. The efforts of local, state, and federal emergency agencies were augmented by nonprofit organizations, private firms, and organized and unorganized volunteers. The system reacted much as it would have for a major earthquake or similar disaster. In the rush to create federal and state offices to deal with the threat of terrorism and, ultimately, to create a Department of Homeland Security, the very foundation of the nation's capacity to deal with large-scale disasters has been largely ignored. Although the human and material resources that the emergency management network provides may again be critical in a terrorist-spawned catastrophe, the new Homeland Security system may not be capable of utilizing those resources effectively. The values of transparency, cooperation, and collaboration that have come to characterize emergency management over the past decade seem to be supplanted in the new command-and-control-oriented Homeland Security system. If that occurs, when the resources of the national emergency management system are needed most, the capacity to utilize the system may be severely damaged and cultural interoperability will be a serious problem.

Avoiding this problem lies in a communication system that is based on the concepts of the type of SoS called for by this C-ORD. All of the efforts of the National Emergency Management Network (NEMN) are wasted without an NCRN. Ham radios alone will not coordinate the management of a national response effort. EROs and FERPs require resilient voice and data communication capability that will interoperate with other EROs and FERPs.

3. Existing System Shortfalls

Why do current systems fall short of providing the capability to meet the NIMS requirements?

To provide for interoperability and compatibility among Federal, state and local capabilities, the NIMS will include a core set of concepts, principles, terminology, and technologies covering the incident command system, multi-agency coordination systems; unified command; training; identification and management of resources (including systems for classifying types of resources); qualifications; and certification; and the collection, tracking and reporting of information and incident resources.

Specifically, current systems fall short in these major areas:

- Most systems are not resilient. Systems that depend on a fixed infrastructure, dedicated networks, and proprietary technology are not reliable in a response to a major disaster or infrastructure failure. Most systems take days if not weeks to restore when they fail. Without communications, NIMS's plans will fail.
- The requirements published for NIMS compliance by EROs lack a communications framework that simplifies the process of implementing a system that meets the requirement for interoperability and compatibility. Most EROs lack the technical resources to filter through the plethora of available systems. In many cases, communications specialists who are making these decisions are only experienced in analog radio systems or telephony and are being forced to make IP networking decisions in which their lack of knowledge leads them to spend their budget on systems that only provide part of the capability they need. EROs need options that work within a communications framework that will guarantee interoperability and compatibility with any agency or ERO.
- Systems are too expensive. The ERO buys a system that is limited by budget or grant potentials. Many have what they can afford, not what they need. Every ERO and FERP need full resilient communications capability.
- Systems are too complicated. For example, one major provider of systems that any ERO would deem reliable is selling a solution that requires several certified technicians to operate. The ERO may have a powerful system that may in fact cost more in five years to operate than it cost to purchase. A FERP will not have the needed communication capability if the technician cannot get to the incident scene. This could take hours in most cases and in the case of a major disaster, days. Many systems rely on proprietary technology that can

only integrate with like devices. The major providers of communication systems provide systems based on proprietary technology that drives up the price for the ERO to not only acquire and support, but also makes it difficult and expensive to interoperate with other EROs. In some scenarios, voice, video, and data interoperability between different proprietary systems is not feasible. Many systems will fail to provide resilient communication because they are so cumbersome they require dedicated power and transportation, rendering them useless to the FERP in the first critical minutes of a response. Semi-trailers cannot easily travel over roads blocked by fallen trees and downed power lines. Due to the flooding, responding to Hurricane Katrina meant having to fly systems and technicians in by helicopter or small planes, taking days to provide communication capabilities for rescue operations. If the systems are simple to use and FERP-portable, they could and should go to the incident site with the FERP.

- Since there is no practical framework to create a system of systems today, even the grant process for funding systems is slowed down. Without a framework, it is a daunting challenge for a multi-agency grant process to verify that what is being bought by the ERO is necessary and will meet the mission requirements. With an SoS, it becomes feasible to require systems be compliant with the framework, making purchasing decisions and grant processes easier.

- Most EROs have system networks that are IPv4 and not IPv6 compliant. The majority of FERPs would not even notice the difference, but a system that is not IPv6 compliant is more difficult to secure in trying to support interoperability. These security concerns by themselves can cause any mutual response to fall short of the requirement for interoperability and compatibility.

- Current systems also fall short because, due to a lack of an interoperability framework supporting systems being apart of a system of systems, it is problematic, if not impossible to allow EROs not only to interoperate with other EROs and FEMA, but National Guard, military, and private sector security as well. Without a communications framework supporting communications across organizations, a mutual-aid response will likely fall short on what is needed for an effective response and rapid recovery.

4. Capabilities Required

4.1. Operational Performance Parameters

The SoS and RPCK shall meet the NIMS mandate. To do so, the RPCK, at a minimum must be able to:

- Converge multiple protocols and networks to provide interconnectivity to any IPv4 or IPv6 network or optimally a system that will interconnect to IPv4 and IPv6 networks wired or wireless, and terrestrial or satellite (O/T)
- Support IPv6 connectivity and be capable of routing to an IPv4 LAN (O/T)
- Run two or more RPCKs at the same incident site (T) to run two or more RPCKs at multiple sites across a large area and support collaboration of every RPCK or IP network being used in the response (O)
- Operate on either AC or DC power (T), directly connect to any 12-volt battery, vehicle cigarette lighter, generator, tactical solar array, or tactical fuel cell (O)
- Support interoperable voice, video, and data applications at the incident site (T), the ability to support secure interoperable voice, video, and data from the incident site with any other location in the country (O)
- Provide two form factors, one portable and one that can be mounted in a mobile transport in less than one hour (T), multiple form factors enabling the ability to put a RPCK anywhere (O)
- Be carried by a FERP to an incident on foot, by small watercraft, car/SUV, helicopter/small plane (T), or the RPCK is small enough to fit in a bag or case that the FERP is using to carry other gear into the incident (O)
- Mount in fire apparatus or emergency response vehicle (T), or small enough to fit in any ERO network rack or any mode of transportation available in the response (O)
- Set up in twenty minutes by the FERP (T), or in less than ten minutes (O)
- Require no more than six steps to set up (T), or no more than three steps to set up (O)
- Provide VoIP calling anywhere in the United States (T), or anywhere in the world (O)
- Provide a software VoIP PBX that supports at least three phone calls at one time using a single toll-free DID (T), or able to support thirty phone calls at one time using a single toll-free DID (O)
- Support extension-to-extension dialing over the incident area (T), or support extension dialing across a WAN (O)
- Create a LAN for the incident site (T), or create a "no set up required" LAN for the incident site with software providing secure IPv4 and IPv6 routing and the ability to support organizational security requirements (O)
- Interconnect with any available network providing Internet connectivity (T), or the ability to connect to multiple networks and rollover

to a backup network when the primary fails or load balance between the two (O)

- Provide 10 mb network connectivity between users on the LAN (T), or 54 mb network connectivity between users on the LAN (O)
- Support interoperable peer-to-peer networking (T), support peer-to-peer video, audio, and data connectivity (O)
- Provide a minimum 400 mw 802.11 a/b/g wireless access point that can support non-line-of-sight wireless access to the incident LAN from up to 100 yards (T), or a minimum 400 mw 802.11 a/b/g wireless access point that can support the same access from up to one mile (O)
- Support up to at least twenty-five users on the network at one time (T), or support up at least to one hundred users on the network at one time per RPCK (O)
- Provide one VoIP handset (T), or five VoIP handsets with the option of adding up to at least twenty-five handsets per RPCK (O)
- Support any IP-over-satellite network access (T), or have the ability to provide satellite service for the RPCK without having to increase the size of the RPCK (O)
- Provide complete instructions for setup and trouble shooting (T), or complete color-coded instructions with pictures that a FERP with an elementary education can setup (O)
- Be affordable enough to purchase and maintain (T), or affordable enough for the ERO to have RPCKs at all supporting sites with enough RPCKs to support every FERP responding to the incident (O)

The SoS at a minimum must:

- Create a system of systems at an incident site simple enough for a FERP to set up in ten to twenty minutes or optimally extend the system of systems to any system in the country if the system has access to the Internet or mutually accessible dedicated network; nothing more should be required other than entering the location code of the SoS
- Create a communications framework for interconnecting disparate local-area data networks, video networks, and radio networks and enable automatic interoperability between all interconnected networks at the incident site or optimally securely interconnect disparate networks anywhere in the country creating a WAN on demand
- Support the interoperability of peer-to-peer communications of voice, video, and data or optimally support peer-to-peer and one-to-many and many-to-many connectivity of all users within the SoS

- Provide a framework for collaboration or optimally a framework for collaboration that can provide application functionality by writing an XML document
- Support presence management and optimally include a self-aware application that several times a minute updates the SoS user list, enabling dynamic collaboration and peer-to-peer communication
- Support multiple applications or optimally multiple applications and services, including multiple security services
- Operate at level 4 of the IP communication layer and optimally as much functionality as possible should operate at layer 5, 6, and 7
- Support the federal efforts to provide extended alerting:
  - Commercial Mobile Alert System (CMAS)
  - Common Alerting Protocol (CAP)
  - Existing broadcast alert services
- Provide a mechanism for Trusted Identity Management:
  - National Incident Management System (NIMS) requirements (SP 800-73, SP 800-78, SP 800-79, IR 6887)
  - Homeland Security Presidential Directive 12 (HSPD-12) and Federal Information Processing Standard (FIPS) 201 compliance and support
  - First Responder Identification Credential (FRAC) support
  - Public Law 110-53 compliance

4.2. Key Performance Parameters (KPPs)

The key performance parameters for the SoS and the RPCK are as follows:

Resiliency—Interoperable communications must be able to establish voice and data communications within fifteen minutes from the time of arrival at the incident site. The system must provide required communications capability even if all communications infrastructure is compromised or destroyed. Redundant communication must be provided with the RPCK. If the VoIP services are not working, the FERP should be able to have peer-to-peer voice capability with anyone on the SoS. If conditions are not favorable for audio communications, the FERP should be able to send private and public instant messages or alerts and advisories using the SoS software.

Accessibility—Communications must be established by a FERP without the need for technical support. No configuration of the software should be required to set up the RPCK. The system will be connected to the best available network and connected to an AC or DC power with phone and Internet services available to all FERPs.

Portability—The FERP shall have a portable solution they can literally carry with them to the incident to assure they will have communications capability immediately upon arrival. RPCKs must be man portable and operate independent of large vehicles and/or trailers.

Interoperability—The SoS provides full interoperable voice, video, and data communications among FERPS and supporting agencies and EROs regardless of communication device types. The interoperability shall be dynamic. Dynamic interoperability is defined as the ability to connect any user across any network and have the ability to connect any IP communication device with any other IP communication device. The interoperability shall be at level 4 or 5 of the communication layer enabling the SoS to connect any network and run on any IP device. The SoS should also enable interoperability between interoperable radio and telephone switching systems and any data user of the SoS.

Expandability—The SoS shall not have any limitation on the number of users it can support. The number of interconnected networks cannot be limited. The RPCK must be scalable either by linking multiple RPCKs together or by running the SoS on a larger Resilient Communication Command System (RCCS). An RCCS should support hundreds of users exactly as an RPCK supports dozens of users. The RCCS must also be tactical and transportable, but the need for greater scalability may limit the method of transportation with an SUV or pickup truck. The RCCS should not only offer the same features and functionality as an RPCK, but also be as easy to set up and be available in a kit form. Because of the greater processing power of an RCCS, the area of coverage shall increase, providing greater flexibility.

Visibility—The SoS must be able to allow span of control and mutual assessment and collaboration at and beyond the incident area site. The software interface must support a span of control over the users, allowing for grouping users into manageable groups and subgroups without compromising security. The ability to group should be as simple as entering a code that will direct the user to their group, while allowing incident command the ability to see all resources. Peer-to-peer voice, video, and data communication must allow users on demand the ability to have private one-on-one communication or private group conversations, while at the same time having incident-wide communications.

Transparency—The SoS must not only enable the interoperability of voice, video, and data communications, but it must also interconnect and support other systems and networks, providing alerts, warnings, and advisories. The SoS software shall enable alerts and advisories between any FERP or ERO without needing anything but the SoS software. The alerts and advisory capability will expand to provide public advisories.

Flexibility—The RPCK must provide a full-featured software PBX that is configurable from an easy-to-use GUI interface providing QoS and options to meet the ERO and FERP requirements. The PBX should provide a toll-free DID and support hundreds of extensions if needed. The PBX will have defined calling features available for configuration by the ERO. The RPCK must support as many simultaneous calls as the backhaul will allow. The SoS should also support both IPv4 and IPv6 networking and the RPCK should provide IPv6 capability to EROs who only have IPv4 capability.

Usability—The RPCK and SoS must work with both AC or DC power, be network agnostic and able to work in any type of weather or climate that the FERP is operating in. The RPCK should require no special environmental conditions. The RPCK must converge the network protocols involved in providing voice, video, and data so that network configurations are automatically provided to the user. The FERP should be able to connect color-coded cable, power the system up, and have full communication capability.

Adaptability—The SoS communication framework must be built using XML to allow for the rapid implementation of services and development or integration of applications used for collaboration. The FERP must be able to create a system of systems, enabling scalability, interconnectivity, and rapid data convergence among all responders in just minutes, for all responding mutual aid agencies, remote support, and chain of command. This capability will not require dedicated technical resources to maintain. The SoS and RPCK must function in any environment without need of other systems if they are not available, but seamlessly interconnect to those systems without requiring the FERP to do anything. The RPCK will turn any vehicle into a forward command post for areas that have been cut-off or are a HAZMET site. The system will go anywhere in the United States and work without modifications or additional configurations.

Affordability—The SoS shall be affordable to the ERO. The software enabling peer-to-peer interoperability will be freely distributed with the ERO only paying for the delivery medium. The cost of the communications framework software should decrease with the number of groups within the ERO's span of control and should be available as a software service if the ERO has limited technical resources for organizational installation and system administration. The RPCK must be COTS compliant and provide volume-pricing incentives.

4.3 System Performance

There are many types of disasters in the United States, but the most common emergencies are:

- Dam failure
- Earthquake

- Fire or wildfire
- Flood
- Hazardous material
- Heat
- Hurricane
- Landslide
- Nuclear power plant emergency
- Pandemics
- Terrorism
- Thunderstorm
- Tornado
- Tsunami
- Volcano
- Winter storm

4.3.1 *Mission Scenarios* Preparation and/or planning for these scenarios are paramount to enable recovery. The first and foremost consideration must be the lives of any potential victims or personnel within the immediate area of the incident site. Secondly, no situation, no matter how small, should ever be viewed in any other terms than worst-case scenario. If emergency responders are prepared for the worst possible situation, they inevitably will increase their odds for success. Those who fail to plan and fail to prepare are our greatest liabilities.

The most frightening and destructive forces of nature (e.g., hurricane, tornado, earthquake, tsunami, wild fires, or flooding) strike suddenly, violently, and many times, in the event of an earthquake or tornado, they occur without warning. If an earthquake or tornado occurs in a populated area, it may cause many deaths, injuries, and extensive property damage. There are no guarantees for safety following a disaster; identifying potential hazards ahead of time and advance planning can save lives and significantly reduce injuries and property damage. In the event of a disaster, EROs are required to do an assessment of the damage prior to allowing safety personnel and restoration groups into the incident area. Most likely, this would require communications in a scorched-earth environment. FERPs would be required to set up and deploy the SoS in the disaster region and communicate to other reporting agencies to coordinate relief and aid.

In the event of a man-made disaster (e.g., terrorist or enemy-nation attack) the ERO would require a number of FERP teams to respond and report. There is now a requirement to have interoperability with these team members to include establishing two-way radio communications and data transmissions to and from multiple agencies, as well as establishing an Incident Area Command Center (IACC) with full voice telephony

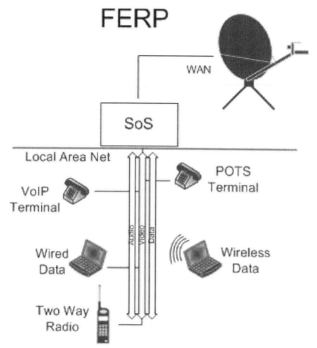

Figure 11.7. The critical functions and interfaces of an interoperability switching system to provide first responders interoperability with each other and the rest of the world.

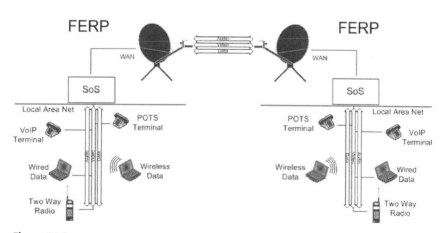

Figure 11.8.

communications mandated. If the immediate responsibility of the ERO is to assess the damages by physically entering the disaster area providing an assessment to the IACC in order to organize and manage the critical next steps of the rescue, video transmission may be required to ascertain the damages and environmental impact.

In all cases of the aforementioned disasters, all EROs need to assess the damage within the incident area, establishing communication to and from the incident site, enabling them to relay information of assessments to decision-making authorities to enable them to conclude on the critical decisions for recovery. This would require that the ERO have minimal setup steps in deploying communications since the focus must be the disaster site itself. The SoS must be able to quickly deploy in different scenarios and adapt to different topologies of networks and environments seamlessly.

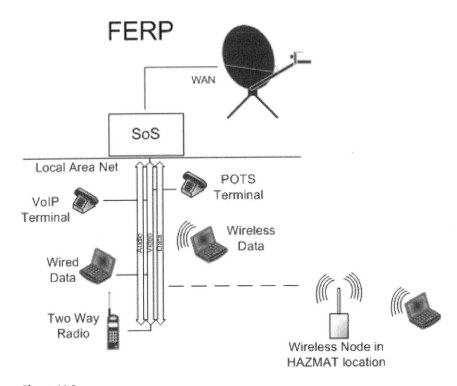

Figure 11.9.

Within ten to twenty minutes of the FERPs' arrival at the incident area, IACC should be able to move into rescue operations. The system must now move to providing LAN and WAN capability, allowing responding personnel and agencies the ability to interoperate immediately.

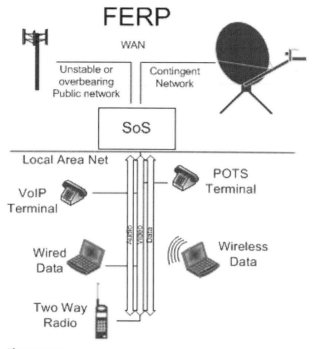

Figure 11.10.

Not all responses are for emergency operations; some exceptions are large-scale events (e.g., national conventions, Super Bowl, national sports events, concerts, demonstrations, or political rallies). These types of events can often cripple existing communication layers with an influx of traffic generated at the event site. The ERO must have the ability to overcome these obstacles easily and seamlessly. The FERP must have the ability to support two-way communications as well as telephony communications. In addition, the FERP must have the ability to send video data to and from the event site. Typically, in these types of situations, FERP members often work with civilian security and/or corporate personnel where interoperability is just a word in the dictionary. Many agencies are responsible for security at large-scale events where tens of thousands of people attend. In many cases, multiple agencies, public and private are "working" the event in some manner. All require a system that establishes a LAN and WAN for all to utilize quickly and easily. In addition, this system must be able to utilize any current network infrastructure or establish its own infrastructure immediately. Other concepts of operations are also acceptable that are not explicitly discussed here.

4.3.2 System Performance Parameters   Key Performance Parameters (KPPs) for the RPCKs:

- Resilient communication is established within ten to twenty minutes.
- No technical support is required for any FERP to set up system.
- Portability: the common form factor should weigh less than 40 lbs and be small enough to be carried on commercial airplane and stored in an overhead compartment.
- Equivalent functionality is available in different form factors.
- Very low power consumption, target 30 watts typical.
- Complies with Part 15 of FCC Rules.
- Extended-temperature operation up to +54°C (130°F) or down to –34°C (–30°F).
- The enclosure must meet or exceed:
  - FED-STD-101C, Method 5007.1, Paragraph 6.3, Procedure A, Level A Tests are superseded and concurrent with ASTM B 4169, DC-18, Assurance Level I, Schedule A.
  - MIL-STD-810F, method 506.4, Procedure II of 4.1.2. FED-STD-101C Method 5009.1, Sec 6.7.1Tests are superseded and concurrent with ASTM B 4169, DC-18, Assurance Level I, Schedule H.
  - ATA 300, Category I, "General Requirements for Category I and II Reusable Containers."
  - Resilient to salt water spray: MIL-STD 810E Method 509.3.
  - Immersion MIL-STD-810F, method 512.4.
  - Qualified to MIL-STD-810 environmental standards.
  - Qualified to MIL-STD 810E Method 516.4. High shock/vibration exist.
  - Qualified to meet Ingress protection (IP67) while in use.
- Consist of at least 2-port WAN connections with fail over and load balancing.
- Provide an easy-to-use administration control GUI or HMI. Consist of at least a four-port fast Ethernet switch.
- Support auto-MDI-MDIX network installations, along with support for auto-crossover, auto-polarity, auto-negotiation, and bridge loop prevention.
- Allow for computing devices to be networked together using 10BaseT or 100BaseTX LAN connections.
- Field programmable, port-based VLAN functionality.
- Allow any combination of LAN ports to be connected together in subnets for use in a small secure or nonsecure network. IEEE 802.3 and IEEE 802.3u compliant.
- Fully independent media access controllers (MACs).
- Embedded frame buffer memory.

- High-speed address look-up engine.
- Qualified to MIL-STD-810 environmental standards.
- Equipped with system status, warning and error indicators.
- Network cable complies with Category 6 standards, providing performance of up to 250 MHz.
- IEEE 802.11a/b/g/n standards (2412-2462MHz) (FCC), (5475-5725MHz) (CE), (5745-5825MHz) (FCC).
- Encryption standard must compile with 802.11i with AES-CCM & TKIP Encryption, 802.1x, 64/128/152bit WEP.
- Wireless data transfer speed up to target of 300 Mbps.
- Wireless nodes peer-to-peer exceed a target of 1 km in range in line of sight environments.
- Port forwarding/tunneling allowing an external user to reach a port on a private IP address (inside the LAN) from the outside WAN connection.
- Administration of the system must support hypertext transfer protocol over secure socket layer (HTTPS) and an additional encryption/authentication layer between the HTTP and TCP.
- VoIP wired terminals support multiline usage with up to 11 line indicators (expandable to 100 lines).
- VoIP wired terminals must support dual 10/100 Mbps Ethernet ports.
- VoIP wired terminals must support basic enterprise call features (e.g., caller ID display or block, call waiting, hold, mute, speaker, transfer [blind or attended], forward, and three-way conferencing).
- Interconnection of radio-over-IP (RoIP) interfaces allowing LMR radio to broadcast over SIP network.
- Connection of analog telephones or POTS terminals.

Call Types Required in the RPCK or RCCS PBX:

- Activity Detection—Activity detect call feature, which provides an integrated voice terminal user a visual indication of voice activity of a particular terminal.
- Alternates/Fail-Over Trunk—Automatic trunking fail-over; if a primary voice trunk, is determined busy, the system will switch to the next available trunk, this operation must be seamless to the terminal.
- Announcement on Hold (AoH)—Allow callers to listen to a recorded announcement(s) to callers on hold or to a predefined extension. The system shall allow for one or more audio channels to be programmed to distribute audio information that is pertinent to the operation.
- Assigned Access—It shall be possible for selected dial terminals to have an assigned access (by class of service) to any combination of

the following: individual nets, public address systems, radio trunks, and PSTN connections. Terminals assigned such access shall be able to obtain the desired connection by keying the appropriate number from the Address Numbering Plan, and terminals that attempt to complete a call to a destination to which access has not been assigned will receive an unavailable tone.

- Automated Attendant (AA)—The PBX shall allow callers to be automatically transferred to a user's extension without the intervention of a live receptionist (e.g., select 1 for EOC, 2 for Field Director).
- Blacklists—The PBX must have the capability of using a list of persons or organizations that have incurred disapproval or suspicion and therefore the call is rejected by the system.
- Call Details—The PBX shall make record and a log of all calls made including:
  ○ Source number, destination number, call duration, date, and time.
- Call Forward—The PBX shall support a telephone call forward capability allowing for the following:
  ○ The user of a particular extension can choose to automatically forward calls to another desired extension or phone if their extension is busy.
  ○ The user of a particular extension can choose to automatically forward calls to another extension if not answered after a defined number of rings.
- Call Groups—The PBX shall support a telephone call groups capability, for:
  ○ Rotary hunting (where an incoming call is automatically rerouted to another terminal in a call group if the first terminal is busy, unavailable, or is not answered during the ring time out period.
  ○ Call pickup within a call group (where any terminal in a call group can pick up a ringing call to a group member, by dialing a designated call pickup number).
- Call Monitoring—A call monitor capability shall be supported to allow supervisors or trusted users to listen or tap into an active call without alerting the other parties of the monitoring.
- Call Queuing—Allows multiple calls to be placed in a queue and answered by the next available call group or extension.
- Call Recording—The PBX shall support recording audio of a phone conversation for later playback or retrieval.
- Call Transfer, Hold—Once a call is connected, it shall be possible to place the call on "Hold" "Transfer" by pressing the feature code.
  ○ The PBX must have the ability to blind transfer a call to another extension without the need to wait for the other extension to pick up.

- ○ The PBX must have the ability to transfer a call to another extension without the need for the other extension to pick up before the call is transferred.
- ○ The PBX must allow a call to be placed on hold. A call hold capability shall be available to all PBX subscribers who are involved in a two party call.
- Caller ID—
  - ○ The specific terminals will display the caller's phone number on the phone's screen.
  - ○ Remote phone must send caller's ID.
  - ○ The specific terminal will display the phone number of a second caller while talking to the first caller.
  - ○ The PBX must have the ability for an administrator to change or correct the outgoing caller ID information.
- Conference Bridging—It shall be possible to host a conference bridge or room that multiple parties at multiple locations using different phone types can access. All conference bridges will have the ability to be password protected by the administrator choice (e.g., conference calls on a local extension, remote fixed line, mobile, and VoIP connection all in one conference).
- Extensions Numbering—The PBX shall have a true flexible numbering plan feature, whereby any number from 0 to 9999 may be assigned to stations or feature codes.
- Hot-line Trunk—The PBX shall have the ability to assign designated trunks to ring designated extensions.
- Interactive Directory Listing (IDL)—IDL allows the inbound callers to look up a person's extension by their name.
- Paging—All terminals will have the ability to "dial direct" to an overhead speaker and/or capable terminal that can be grouped or zoned for announcement or an alert to be made.
- Protocol Conversion—This allows the interconnection of disparate phone networks: (e.g., connect a Telstra call to a VoIP call).
- Standard protocols supported include: TDM, SIP, H.323, LAX, SCCP. Radio Device Connection:
  - ○ The PBX must allow the interconnection of analog terminals (e.g., two-way radio, land mobile radio, and other like devices).
- Remote Call Pickup—This allows a call to be picked up at a remote terminal location.
- Remote Office Support—Ability to connect phones located in a remote office to the office system as local extensions.
- Speed Dialing—Speed dial numbers shall be programmable at both the local level (speed dialing numbers that are applied to a unique

terminal) and at the global level (speed dialing numbers that are applied to all terminals). Each local level speed calling list is unique to a specific terminal, while the global level is available to all configured terminals.

- Three-Way Calling—Connect three people into a mini-conference call.
- Voice-Mail—The PBX must have the ability to record a message from a caller when you are away from your desk. This includes ability to deliver the voice-mail message via e-mail as well as the standard flashing light on your terminal (this feature is terminal specific).
- Satellite services when they are needed.

Key Performance Parameters (KPPs) for Satellite Services for the RPCK:

- VSAT data terminal shall have the capability for Star and SCPC configurations.
- VSAT data terminal shall support at least four public IP addresses.
- VSAT data terminal shall support an eight-port 10/100 Ethernet switch.
- VSAT data terminal shall support Ku-band.
- VSAT data terminal shall support auto antenna acquisition with one-button-push operation.
- VSAT data terminal shall support TCP/IP throughput of transmit of 18 Mbps and receive 4.2 Mbps.
- BGAN data terminal shall support TCP/IP throughput of transmit of 464 kbps and receive 448 kbps.
- BGAN data terminal shall support audible tone signal strength for manual acquisition.
- BGAN data terminal must meet IP-54 rating (dust and spray proof in all directions).

Key Performance Parameters (KPPs) for SoS Framework and Software:

- Provide for modular system development and composition.
- Provide a method for brokering transactions among the composed subsystems.
- Provide translators that act as proxies for services, translating requests/responses into and out of a common, shared format (our XML-based language).
- Provide a method for definition of composition of services.
- Provide for communications among/between asymmetric clients.
- Respond to other well-known communications protocols for discrete info (including, for example, Jabber et al.).

- Be able to render audio and video supplied in various formats.
- Be able to capture audio and video in some number of oft-supported formats.
- Provide a method for publishing availability/capabilities to other possible clients.
- Provide for authentication of credentials and access to identity information.
- Provide for transport of content in cases where peer-to-peer is not possible due to underlying network configuration.
- Provide for ad hoc network creation where indicated.
- Provide for store and forward of data where required (in, for example, cases where a client is not available at the time of original sending).
- Provide a method of finding clients with known characteristics.
- Provide a method for decoupling content itself from the method for transporting said content to other clients.
- Provide for data transport.
- Provide for control/throttling of data transfer (particularly streamed data transfer) to ensure the viability of the local network as a whole.
- Support the federal efforts to provide extended alerting:
  - Commercial Mobile Alert System (CMAS).
  - Common Alerting Protocol (CAP).
  - Existing broadcast alert services.
- Provide a mechanism for Trusted Identity Management.
  - National Incident Management System (NIMS) requirements (SP 800-73, SP 800-78, SP 800-79, IR 6887).
  - Homeland Security Presidential Directive 12 (HSPD-12) and Federal Information Processing Standard (FIPS) 201 compliance and support.
  - First Responder Identification Credential (FRAC) support.
  - Public Law 110-53 compliance.

4.3.3 *Interoperability* Interoperability provided by software that creates a communication framework enables any IP device or system to create a system of systems allowing interconnectivity between any IPv4 or IPv6 user device and multiple IPv4 or IPv6 networks. Any FERP can communicate using voice or video or share data with any other FERP, limited only by the capability of their device (i.e., an LMR would be limited to voice communications only, for example). The FERP can communicate with their ERO and can collaborate with other agencies and FROs, National Guard, military response teams, or private sector security that may be responding to the incident. If responding organizations do not have the software prior to the incident, the SoS software that is included with every RPCK can be freely distributed from any FERP to anyone who needs it. This allows interoperability to be dynamic, changing to meet the communication needs as the response grows and evolves.

The only requirement for interoperability is that the FERP's terminal or device has an IP or MAC address. If the use of analog devices is part of the EROs response plan, the analog network can be given an IP or MAC address by connecting one of the analog terminals using the analog network to a patchwork interoperability switch that in turn is a part of the SoS.

4.3.4 *Human Interface Requirements* Based on the type of communications framework required by this C-ORD, the strength of a system of systems is based on software that will run on any operating system which will run on an IPv4 or IPv6 network. There are no special human interface requirements other than knowing how to use a common phone, an LMR, or computer. If the FERPs can access and use day-to-day computer applications used by the ERO, then they should be able to run the SoS software. It is, in fact easier than sending an e-mail. The FERPs can use devices and terminals they already use.

Since the RPCK standard form factor will weigh less than forty pounds, any FERP can hand-carry the kit, if necessary. The SoS and RPCK should require no specialized personnel at the incident site. Any FERP should be able to set up a RPCK within ten to twenty minutes even if they have no experience or training. No matter how well-designed the system is, systems can require support due to user, hardware, or software malfunction. If for any reason support should be required due to equipment failure, the user must be able to use the troubleshooting guide included with the system. Around-the-clock telephone and online support shall be available from the RPCK provider. The human interface requirement for this system assumes that the FERP is able to read simple instructions.

4.3.5 *Logistics and Readiness* The SoS will be available and utilized constantly by EROs. It can provide interagency interoperability on a daily basis and be in operation when an incident occurs. As the FERP arrives at the incident site, interoperability and collaboration are immediately available just by the FERP turning on the devices they are using as the FERP connects automatically to the SoS.

In order to facilitate interoperability with EROs and FERPs that do not have the SoS software, the software shall be available to every FERP on a USB thumb-drive that can be used to freely install on any computer required to join the SoS. The installation software should also be available to load on ERO servers so that the software can be freely downloaded if necessary. The SoS software should also be downloadable from approved websites with proper security clearance. Installation of the software shall be quick, simple, and intuitive. No training should be necessary for any FERP to install the software and connect to the SoS.

If the device is only able to run on an IPv4 network, free VPN software must be available for installation. Installing and using the VPN should require no configuration. If a VPN is needed, it should be as simple as clicking on "install VPN," and the VPN must automatically install, configure, and connect the FERP to the SoS via the VPN.

If software updates are released for the SoS or RPCK, a release method of free upgrading will be implemented by a vendor.

At least one RPCK should be available to every ERO in the country. Because a requirement for the RPCK is that it be a self-contained kit, distribution of new kits, additional kits, accessories such as additional VoIP handsets, cameras, headsets, cables, and satellite systems may be managed under a contract with a national technology logistics company. Logistics must be handled by an organization that specializes in delivering network technology efficiently to the public/private sector. Efficient distribution and parts should be stored in strategically located sites in order to guarantee delivery to the ERO in less than eight hours. An efficient inventory method should be used to avoid using potential public funds to stockpile systems. A purchasing system should be instituted to guarantee EROs the ability, once a state of emergency is declared, to order additional systems, parts, and accessories immediately.

4.3.6 Other System Characteristics   The SoS and RPCK shall be simple to use and affordable. VoIP services will be provided with a flat-rate annual contract for unlimited calls. Every RPCK will have an available satellite option for resiliency; the cost of constant satellite services will be affordable. Flat-rate contracts with providers for on-demand satellite service when the RPCK is deployed are required. Every system should always be on and able to support a phone call to the national support center requesting that additional bandwidth be provided for the duration of the incident.

5. System Support

5.1 Maintenance

A maintenance agreement should be available on every SoS system and RPCK. The SoS will operate 24/7; if issues arise, users can contact a 24/7 support desk. If updates to the SoS software are needed, the update will be sent directly to the user by the support desk and will also be downloadable from a support website.

The RPCK must be used regularly in everyday operations or be required to be tested at least twice a month to be confident that there are no problems with a kit's performance. The day-and-night support center must have the ability to run remote diagnostics on any kit and if possible repair the system remotely. If a kit has a component failure that cannot be immediately fixed at the users' location with the assistance of the support desk, a loaner will be shipped to the ERO immediately. The ERO will ship the "down" system to the repair depot. Under a support maintenance agreement, a loaner system is provided at no charge until their repair kit is returned and tested by the ERO. A ratio of loaners available to kits in service will be at least 1 to 25.

5.2 Supply

The installation software will also be available on ERO servers so that the software can be downloaded from the ERO server, if necessary. The SoS software should also be downloadable from approved, secure websites with proper authorization. Installation of the software must be quick, simple, and intuitive. No training should be necessary for any FERP to install the software and connect to the SoS.

Because a requirement of the RPCK is "self-containment," distribution of new kits, additional kits, or loaner kits should be available if a RPCK fails. Accessories such as additional VoIP handsets, cameras, headsets, cables, and satellite systems should be managed under a contract with a national technology logistics company that specializes in delivering network technology efficiently to the private/public sector. Efficient distribution requires parts be stored in strategically located depots in order to guarantee delivery to the ERO in less than eight hours. An efficient inventory method is required to avoid using public funds to stockpile systems. An easy-to-use purchasing system is required to guarantee EROs the ability, once a state of emergency is declared, to order additional systems, parts, and accessories immediately.

5.3 Support Equipment

The RPCK will include any equipment necessary for testing, and the system must be available to be tested remotely by support, if needed. The remote diagnostics will require nothing more than a given customer's approval.

5.4 Training

The SoS and RPCK will be simple enough that user training is not required. However, in order to maximize the power of the SoS and to fully understand what the RPCK is capable of, webinars will be held every day on a regional basis covering topics that will improve the effective use of the SoS and RPCK. An online group forum will be available for FERPs to share ideas and ask questions of other FERPs. This service will be a feature of the SoS software.

5.5 Transportation and Facilities

The SoS is software and does not require transportation or storage. The RPCK by design must be small enough to store in the trunk of a car or in a closet in the FERP's office or duty station. It will be able to be stored anywhere with a temperature between –10°C and +50°C. The RPCK will require no special transportation; however, it must be available in a form factor that can be mounted in any vehicle, making that vehicle a mobile resilient communication center. It also will be able to be used anywhere at anytime without any special installation being required and easily be transportable as carry-on luggage on any commercial airline.

6. Force Structure

Many homeland security applications rely on resilient communications; there can be no SoS without communications systems to connect to. In order to implement a national SoS providing national interoperability, enough RPCKs must be distributed across the country to provide resilient communication in enough locations to generate a national emergency communication network. It would take 200,000 RPCKs to provide enough for the following:

Law enforcement agencies in the United States—17,000
Fire departments in the United States—30,000
Incorporated cities in the United States—80,000
Counties and or parish governments in the United States—3,000
School districts and colleges in the United States—20,000
Emergency operation centers in the United States—15,000
Ports of entry in the United States—240
Critical infrastructure and key assets in the United States—33,000
Hospitals in the United States—5,500

FIRST RESPONDERS: C-ORD FOR INTEROPERABLE COMMUNICATIONS SWITCH

Contents

1. General Description of Operational Capability
   1.1. Capability Gap
   1.2. Overall Mission Area Description

1.3. Description of the Proposed System

1.4. Supporting Analysis

1.5. Mission the Proposed System Will Accomplish

1.6. Operational and Support Concept

    1.6.1. Concept of Operations

    1.6.2. Support Concept

2. Threat

3. Existing System Shortfalls

4. Capabilities Required

    4.1. Operational Performance Parameters

    4.2. Key Performance Parameters (KPPs)

        4.2.1. Connectivity

    4.3. System Performance

        4.3.1. Mission Scenarios

        4.3.2. System Performance Parameters

        4.3.3. Interoperability

        4.3.4. Human Interface Requirements

        4.3.5. Logistics and Readiness

        4.3.6. Other System Characteristics

5. System Support

    5.1. Maintenance

    5.2. Supply

    5.3. Support Equipment

    5.4. Training

    5.5. Transportation and Facilities

6. Force Structure

7. Schedule

8. System Affordability

9. Appendixes

List of Figures

Figure 11.7 The Critical Functions and Interfaces of the Interoperability Switching System provide First Responders Interoperability with each other and the rest of the world

Figure 11.8 An Interoperability Switch-Based Facility Communications System Provides Networked Communications Between any Number of Agencies and Personnel

List of Tables

Table 11.2 Matrix for Required Types of Terminal Calls Operations and Services

1. General Description of Operational Capability

As a goal, first responders would like to be able to speak to anyone at any time in any place. With the ubiquitous cell phone, that vision seems to be nearly a reality. There is a natural desire to extend this near reality to the far more complex environments of mobile platforms, remote locations (middle of the ocean, out in the desert, atop mountains), and scenes of destruction (earthquakes, explosions, fires).

While the inability to complete a cell phone call successfully may be an annoyance in a personal situation, the inability to communicate can have deadly consequences in a public safety situation. It is therefore critical that those responsible for communications in these organizations plan ahead for contingencies, set realistic expectations, acquire necessary equipment, and conduct training on a periodic basis.

Regarding expectations, it is realistic to pre-engineer multiple solutions to specific interoperability challenges that can be relied upon in an emergency. It is not realistic to think that on-the-fly personnel can expect to successfully interoperate between communications media that have not been previously analyzed and engineered for interoperability. There are numerous challenges to successful interoperability. The right combination of equipment, knowledge, and training will lead to mission-critical interoperability when it's needed most. Wishful thinking and ignoring the complexities will, in contrast, provide a false sense of security and lead to failure.

The problems and issues associated with different radio systems not being able to communicate with each other have been known to first responders for many years. The communications problems surrounding the terrorist attacks on September 11, 2001, significantly raised the visibility of this issue and have led to numerous and varied attempts to improve communications interoperability among first responders.

1.1 Capability Gap

One primary method of resolving communications interoperability is having all involved parties using the same, or at least interoperable, radios, whether they are cellular, portable, fixed, or mounted. Since many first responders have already invested significantly in their current radio systems, acquiring new radios is often not a practical solution. This leads to the second means of resolving interoperability issues, the use of a gateway or switching type of device or system that can quickly and easily connect two or more otherwise noninteroperable radio systems. This system would allow multiple first responders to talk to each other either directly or via radio nets, all while using their existing radios, cell phones, or telephones.

1.2 Overall Mission Area Description

The mission area covered by this C-ORD is all public safety–related events where first responders must communicate with other first responders using communications media such as radios and telephones that are not normally interoperable. This includes different agencies and types of first responders (police, fire, EMTs, etc.) and first responders from different jurisdictions and/or locations (city, county, state, federal, etc.).

1.3 Description of the Proposed System

Responders in the field need access to a switching system with the capability to integrate voice communications of all types in a special evolution- or command-and-control-type environment such as an emergency operations center (EOC). The proposed interoperability switching system will provide the user the ability to provide advanced private branch exchange–like capabilities between handsets connected through PSTN, IP, local radio systems (e.g., Land Mobile Radio [UHF or VHF]), commercial wireless (cellular/PCS and satellite), and other standard interface systems. The switching system shall include a full range of switching functions for telephony, radio circuits, simultaneous plain and P-25 encrypted circuits, progressive radio and telephone conferencing and netting, extensive administrative support for configuration planning and event and call logging, and a wide variety of system interfaces. It will support a wide range of commercial voice terminals (analog and digital), radios, wireless systems (such as IP-DECT), integrated voice communication terminals, assignable loudspeakers, and virtually any other analog or digital voice source. The switching system will be able to provide interoperability on a much broader scale than simply tying together radio nets. The switching infrastructure must able to bring all the types of voice communications needed by each user together in a single voice terminal. For some, a telephone is sufficient; for others, a multipurpose integrated terminal that can handle both radio and telephone calls is appropriate.

The switching system shall be capable of connecting to all types, brands, and styles of first-responder land-mobile radios in a fixed or mobile communications center. The system will be the hub that connects or networks different types of radios (even radios on different frequency bands) and at the same time allows the local users at the communications center to join multiple radio networks and communicate over telephones, intercom, and landlines, all at the same time. Figure 11.7 shows the critical functions and interfaces of such a system that will allow first responders, and anyone else associated with a particular emergency operations or communications center, to communicate with one another while using different systems.

1.4 Supporting Analysis

This C-ORD is supported by analysis done by DHS S&T.

1.5 Mission the Proposed System Will Accomplish

The proposed system will be able to connect and network different and various types of radios, wireless systems, integrated voice terminals, telephones, and other communications media such as PBXs, VoIP Switches, and the Public Switched Telephone Network (PSTN). Integrated voice terminals are defined as devices that can handle several functions, such as radio calls, telephony, and intercom simultaneously. The proposed system will provide a means for users (first responders and those that need to talk to them) with different communications devices and media to seamlessly communicate and interoperate with one another.

1.6 Operational and Support Concept

1.6.1 Concept of Operations The communications interoperability switch will enable first responders to communicate with each other and with communications center personnel using different types of radios, cell phones, telephones, and other communications means. This system will integrate voice communications so that police, fire, and EMT personnel of all types and from all jurisdictions will be able to easily talk to each other using whatever means of communications they have. Figure 11.8 shows the concept of first responders using various devices all connected to the Interoperability Switch by either wire or wireless, being able to communicate with one another. These communications can be either conferenced, networked (netted), or point to point. The proposed system will typically be located in a fixed communications or command center such as an emergency operations center (EOC) but will also be sized to be able to be located in a mobile station if needed.

The proposed system will provide the following operational capabilities:

1. Enable all agencies and entities to keep their existing radios and other voice terminals, yet integrate them together in a system-of-systems (SoS).
2. Provide the ability for communications operators to quickly and seamlessly connect or disconnect any number of first responders with a few button pushes (no laptop needed).
3. Deliver calls without blocking.

4. Enable managers, and other authorized users, to monitor as many communication channels or circuits as they require (or can personally handle) to achieve maximum situational awareness.
5. Interface with security and encryption, if required, to provide transmission security, and easily control who can hear which conversations.

1.6.2 Support Concept The proposed system shall be maintainable either by the equipment provider or by personnel trained to maintain the system.

The design of the proposed system shall support easy installation by the equipment provider or other trained personnel. Some knowledge of the (fixed or mobile) emergency operation center's interfaces (such as radios, telephones, and power) will be required in order to plan and do the installation.

Maintenance requirements for the system shall be minimal. Each unit shall include basic self-test mechanisms to indicate proper operation. System design shall allow for easy replacement of a defective line replaceable unit (LRU) by a new unit with no need for user-level repair maintenance. Defective LRUs will be returned to the manufacturer for disposition.

Spare parts will be made available by the equipment provider if not available as a commercial-off-the-shelf (COTS) item.

Training shall be provided by the equipment provider to either a system trainer (via a train-the-trainers session) or to the users and operators at the installed site at a time convenient to the users and operators.

2. Threat

The proposed system counters any threat potentially caused or exacerbated by first responders not being able to communicate with one another. In critical situations, the inability of responders to be able to communicate with one another or with command-and-control authorities could cause loss of life. The interoperability provided by this system will eliminate communications breakdown or failure as a source of issues when dealing with the threat or situation.

3. Existing System Shortfalls

Existing systems that provide interoperability have the following weaknesses:

- The number of devices and nets supported is inadequate to serve as a radio switch for all but the very smallest of applications.

- No support is provided for integrated voice terminals. Integrated voice terminals greatly improve the mission effectiveness of users through:
  - Allowing multiple circuits (radio or telephony) to be monitored simultaneously while supporting one channel in active mode.
  - Provision of dynamic key text and color to make communications intuitive and responsive to the specific needs of the user.
  - Supporting advanced interaction with remotely controllable radio terminals. Such interaction requires an intelligent switch.
  - Allowing a member of a conference (using an integrated voice terminal—IVT) to monitor the terminal traffic and dynamically manage the conference by adding members or dropping others out of the conference as circumstances warrant.
- No support is provided for secure voice circuits. Even if secure conferences are not attempted (with multiple radios and encryption devices), these applications do require the switching system to support secure radio circuits at the same time that plain radio circuits are operating. This imposes requirements on the switching equipment that the current systems do not support.
- While the Human-Machine Interface (HMI) for current systems may be adequate for the duration of a specific interoperability net, it is not acceptable for a general radio switch.
  - The HMI for a current system is accomplished using a laptop. Thus, the management of any conference requires someone to use a central gateway laptop for conference setup and management. This requires personnel resources that will not be necessary when each conference can be managed at the voice terminal of the leader of the conference.
  - The ideal managers of specific conferences are likely to be different individuals depending upon the mission served by the conference. Thus, a central laptop is much less effective for HMI than allowing integrated voice terminals to serve the conference managers as needed operationally.

4. Capabilities Required

4.1 Operational Performance Parameters

The proposed system shall provide required voice and control signal connections to support terminal-to-terminal calls, terminal-to-net calls, external system calls to terminals and nets, and combinations of these.

The proposed system shall provide a "nonblocking" architecture such that calls cannot be blocked because of switch limitations.

The proposed system shall support ISDN and POTS lines and trunks, and provide for nonblocking traffic flow among all switch port connections, for up to 2,000 subscribers (configuration dependent).

The proposed system shall be able to provide connections for three classes of terminal devices:

- Direct BRI S/T line connections for user terminals such as integrated voice terminals and ISDN phones
- Direct POTS connections for POTS and analog phones and connections
- Network Termination (NT) adapters for converting between the BRI S/T lines and special analog interface connections such as radios and PA systems.

The proposed system shall provide a primary rate interface (PRI) trunk connection for interfacing to private branch exchange (PBX) systems and radio communication systems (RCS).

The proposed system shall be capable of providing redundancies to ensure protection against single-point failures.

The proposed system shall support full-duplex connections, conferencing, self-test operations, and both plain (unencrypted) and secure modes of operation between designated terminals and systems.

The proposed system shall be created such that users from outside the EOC's area of responsibility are able to communicate with local first responders.

Digital terminals: The proposed system shall support digital/ISDN terminal direct-dial service to other dial terminals and direct-dial access (when properly class marked) to nets and external systems that interface with the Interoperability Switch. Specific communications interoperability switch features available for use by digital terminals will be limited only by the physical configuration of the terminal and the accesses or class marks available to it. Digital/ISDN terminals shall provide an interface to an associated Interoperability Switch in accordance with industry standard digital BRI S/T characteristics and requirements, and to standard accessory connections associated with the terminal (e.g., handsets, headsets, speaker extensions). Integrated voice terminals (IVT) are multifunctional ISDN terminals that will have push-to-talk capability and can therefore make radio calls in addition to making standard telephone and intercom calls. The communications interoperability switch shall provide the power for the ISDN terminals.

Analog Terminals: The communications interoperability switch shall support analog POTS (plain old telephone services) that operate with a standard loop start signaling interface, for connections to POTS terminals, associated FAX machines, and external connections that appear to the

POTS interface as a terminal. Analog POTS terminals shall provide an interface to an associated Interoperability Switch in accordance with the requirements of industry standard EIA/TIA-464B, and to standard accessory connections for the terminal (e.g., handsets). The communications interoperability switch shall provide the power for the analog terminals.

System Features: The proposed switching system shall provide the connection paths for the voice and control signals transmitted and received by dial terminals and net terminals. The types of call connections that shall be provided are as follows:

- Calls from dial terminal to dial terminal: The calling party activates the dial terminal, receives a dial tone or indication, and presses or selects (keys) the appropriate buttons on the terminal for the desired service
- Calls from dial terminal to net terminal: The calling party initiates the call and keys the terminal for the desired service. If the dialed number or single-button access represents a net, the calling party will be connected to the net.
- Designated terminal to external system interface connections (such as PBXs, VoIP Switches or the PSTN)

The proposed system shall provide and support the services and features shown in table 11.2. The lists that follow the table define the service requirements in additional detail.

System Call Processing Requirements: The following lists provide a brief description of call processing types and services for the communications interoperability switch (shown in table 11.2).

Call Hold

- Places an engaged call on hold to allow a subscriber to consult a third party.
- Capability shall be available to all communications interoperability switch subscribers who are involved in a two-party call.

Call Transfer

- Provides a capability to transfer a received call to another terminal, and also permit three-party calls.
- Capability shall be available to all Interoperability Switch subscribers who are involved in a two-party call.
- Shall refer to both a "blind transfer" (transferring party hangs up before the transfer is answered) and an "active transfer" (transferring party waits for the transfer to be answered before completing the

Table 11.2.

	CALL OPERATION OR SERVICE	TERMINAL APPLICABILITY		
		Integrated Voice Terminal	ISDN COTS Terminal	POTS or Analog Terminal
1	Call Hold	X	X	X
2	Call Transfer	X	X	X
3	Abbreviated Addressing	X	X	X
4	Progressive Conference	X	X	X
5	Preset Conferencing	X	X	X
6	Meet-me Net	X	X	X
7	Privacy/Auto Override	X	X	X
8	Call Forwarding	X	X	X
9	Call Waiting	X	X	X
10	Assigned Access	X	X	X
11	Access Restriction	X	X	X
12	Alternates	X	X	X
13	Plain or Secure Calls	Either	Plain	Plain
14	Call Monitor (Simultaneous)	X	-	-
15	Push To Talk	X	X	X
16	Intercom Announcing	X	-	-
17	Intercom Hotline	X	-	-
18	Emergency Reporting	X	X	X
19	Speed Calling Lists	X	X	X
20	Call Groups	X	X	X
21	Discriminating Ringing	X	X	X
22	Caller ID	-	X	
23	Activity Detection	X	-	-
24	Analog connection	X	X	X
25	PA Announcing System connection	X	X	X
26	Alarm System Connection	X	-	-
27	Radio Net access	X	X	X
28	Radio Progressive Conferencing	X	X*	X*
29	Assignable Speaker	X	-	-
30	Voice Recorder – Record	X	-	-
31	Voice Recorder – Playback	X	-	-

X Required
- Not Required
* Does not need to initiate a Radio Progressive Conference, but can be added by an Integrated Voice Terminal

transfer). Active transfer is also known as a transfer with introduction.

- Transfers to PSTN Lines, nets, conferences, and multiparty calls shall not be allowed.
- Transfers from nets and conferences shall not be allowed.
- Subscribers currently connected to nets or in conferences shall not have the capability of call transfer.

Abbreviated Addressing (Speed Dialing)

- Gives designated dial terminals the capability to use abbreviated addresses for dialing. Entering a designated abbreviated addressing code into a terminal keyboard (typically two digits preceded by an asterisk) shall initiate a call from the dial terminal.

- Speed dial numbers shall be programmable at both the local level (speed dialing numbers that are applied to a unique terminal) and at the global level (speed dialing numbers that are applied to all terminals). Each Local-Level Speed Calling List is unique to a specific terminal, while the global level is available to all configured terminals.
- The system administration terminal software (SAT) shall allow for the configuration of up to 10 local-level speed dial numbers per terminal, and the SAT shall allow for the configuration of up to 80 (T) global-level speed dial numbers.
- Each integrated voice terminal shall provide the ability to program up to 20 (T)/25 (O) preprogrammable dial keys or buttons, local to the integrated voice terminal, that are to be used for speed dial. Additionally, most ISDN telephone terminals provide the ability to program speed dial keys available on the terminals.

Privacy/Automatic Override

- It shall be possible to assign a privacy override capability so that the "busy" condition of a called dial terminal, and call waiting, if applicable, can be overridden by someone with the proper authority.
- Privacy override will allow selected users to exercise preemption capabilities to cut into or override terminals being used for calls with lower precedence levels. Two methods shall be available for initiating privacy override in designated terminals:
  1. After receiving dial tone, the subscriber depresses the # key and then keys in the called terminal directory number; or
  2. After keying the called terminal directory number and receiving busy, the subscriber depresses the # key within three seconds after receiving busy tone.
- A one-second override tone shall be placed on the existing connection, such that all members of the connection hear the tone, before connecting the override call.
- An overridden terminal with the call-waiting capability that is active on one call appearance shall have the previously active call placed on hold.

Call Forwarding

- Dial terminals designated or class marked for call forwarding shall be able to have all incoming calls routed to another dial terminal, through subscriber implementation.
- Three types of call forwarding shall be available:

1. Unconditional, where calls will be automatically rerouted;
2. Call forwarding busy, which reroutes an incoming call only if the called terminal is busy;
3. Call forwarding no reply, which reroutes an incoming call if there is no answer within a specified amount of time.

- To implement call forwarding, the subscriber shall dial a configurable special service code appropriate to the type of call forwarding, followed by the four-digit number of the terminal to which the calls are to be forwarded.
- Upon the completion of a terminal call forwarding to a valid terminal, the subscriber shall be notified with a confirmation tone.
- To cancel call forwarding on a terminal, the subscriber shall dial the configurable special service code assigned for canceling call forwarding.

Call Waiting

- A call waiting capability shall be available for designated terminals that provide a visual and/or audible indication at a terminal engaged in an established call, to alert it that an incoming call is awaiting connection. A single user action at the designated terminal shall place the engaged call on hold and connect to the waiting call.

Assigned Access

- It shall be possible for selected dial terminals to have an assigned access (by class of service) to any combination of the following: individual nets, public address systems, radio trunks, and PSTN connections.
- Terminals assigned such access shall be able to obtain the desired connection by keying the appropriate number from the address numbering plan, and terminals that attempt to complete a call to a destination to which access has not been assigned will receive an unavailable tone.

Access/Class Mark Restrictions

- It shall be possible to assign access restriction (class mark) categories to all Interoperability Switch line connections, circuits, and terminals for the purpose of controlling intercommunications to or between them. Class marks (CM) provide a means for software to control user accesses and privileges (such as call waiting, call forward, and override).
- An assigned or default class mark shall apply for each terminal, circuit, or call feature so that if the CM appears within the class of service (COS) restricted category for a calling party (CLG) terminal,

the CLG terminal will be prevented from connecting to the called terminal, circuit, or call feature.
- COS and CM assignments for individual terminals will be provided from the SAT (via the communications interoperability switch).

Alternates

- It shall be possible to designate three alternate terminals to be tested in the event that the primary terminal is busy, unavailable or idle, for a minimum of 16 (T) / 32 (O) dial terminals.
- If the primary terminal is busy or unavailable when called, the alternate terminals shall be checked in order and the first idle alternate rung.
- If an idle alternate is rung and not answered before the ring period timeout, the next alternate terminal shall be rung.
- If the last alternate is idle and not answered, a calling ISDN terminal will be placed on-hook while a POTS terminal shall receive unavailable tone.
- If the dialed terminal and all alternates are busy, the calling party shall receive busy tone.
- If the dialed terminal and all alternates are busy and the caller chooses to override within three seconds of receiving busy tone, the dialed terminal shall be overridden.

Call Groups

- The Interoperability Switch shall support a telephone call groups' capability, for:
  1. Rotary hunting (where an incoming call is automatically rerouted to another terminal in a call group if the first terminal is busy, unavailable, or is not answered during the ring timeout period.
  2. Call pickup within a call group (where any terminal in a call group can pick up a ringing call to a group member, by dialing a designated call pickup number), for at least 16 (T) / 32 (O) groups with a minimum of 16 (T) / 20 (O) subscriber members per group.

Plain or Secure Calls

- Controls for integrated voice terminals only shall be provided to permit calls in both plain and secure modes of operation.
- When a circuit transitions to secure mode, all plain-only ports connected to the secure circuit shall have their audio reception blocked until the circuit transitions back to plain mode.
- Transmission of plain-only ports shall still occur to the secure circuit. The communications interoperability switch will be responsible for

security by configuring, connecting, tracking, and disconnecting circuits. When an incompatible security connection is attempted, the integrated voice terminal shall display a security mismatch with a security mode indication on the display.

- An integrated voice terminal shall not have the capability to change the security mode of a call while its PTT is depressed or while the PTT of a terminal connected to the circuit is depressed.
- When a radio net is switched to secure mode, all plain-only terminals in the net shall:
  1. Be disconnected from the net.
  2. Receive a security mismatch (Unavailable) tone.
- If a plain-only terminal attempts to override a terminal with at least one call appearance in a secure radio net, the following shall occur:
  1. The override is unsuccessful and there is no disturbance to the net.
  2. The plain-only terminal gets Unavailable tone.

Call Monitor

- A call monitor capability shall be supported with integrated voice terminals that permit an integrated voice terminal with an existing call connection to accept or originate a new call connection without disconnecting the existing call.
- The first key or button pressed in accepting or originating a call will move an existing call into the monitor mode, where it is held and monitored while the user participates in the new call.
- The first key pressed in accepting or originating a call shall move the existing call into the monitor mode on the ISDN Bearer 2 channel.
- The integrated voice terminal shall be able to monitor calls on the Bearer 2 channel while the user participates in an active call on the Bearer 1 channel.

Discriminating Ringing

- The communications interoperability switch shall support a discriminating ringing capability.
- Capability will be user-selected and applicable for calls originating within the system, originating outside the system (PSTN), or from interface connections (e.g., wireless system).

Caller ID

- The communications interoperability switch shall provide a calling line identification capability (Caller ID) on all ISDN terminals equipped with a user display (reference ANSI T1.625 as a guide).

Activity Detection

- The communications interoperability switch shall provide an activity-detect call feature that provides an integrated voice terminal user a visual indication of voice activity on a monitor channel.
- The operator shall be provided the ability to toggle this feature on and off from the integrated voice terminal.
- When enabled, only the integrated voice terminal keys or buttons that are occupied with calls in monitor mode (illuminated amber) shall blink when audio is being received on the channel associated with the key. This makes it possible for the user to be active in one call while knowing exactly where the monitor audio in the speaker is originating.
- When this feature is disabled, monitor calls shall remain solid amber even when audio is being received.

A capability for *conferences and nets* shall be provided as detailed in the lists below.

Progressive Conference

- For a subscriber terminal that is properly class marked, it shall be possible to set up a full-duplex Progressive Conference capability, whereby terminals are called to join a conference.
- A minimum of 15 (T) / 20 (O) progressive conferences in progress or in setup at one time shall be allowed, for 12 (T) / 14 (O) conferees per conference.
- Setup of a conference will be initiated by a conference originator, and add-on permitted by any conference member with the proper permissions (the members Class of Service is not restricted from performing a progressive conference).

Preset Conference (and Command Net Call)

- A preset conference is a call between a set number of previously designated terminals. At least 15 (T) / 20 (O) preset conferences of 12 (T) / 15 (O) terminals each shall be supported.
- Dialing the preset conference directory number from one of the designated terminals shall ring the other designated terminals.
- Each designated terminal (of a predefined conference member) shall be added to the preset conference if it goes off-hook before the end of the ring period, which shall be programmable up to a maximum of 45 seconds.
- Command net call is similar to a preset conference except that it does not allow automatic privacy override.

- At least 15 (T) / 20 (O) Command Nets of 12 (T) / 15 (O) terminals each shall be supported.

Meet-Me (Voice) Net

- A meet-me net capability shall be provided, whereby participating terminals are not pre-assigned to the net but will enter it with a single action depression (on an integrated voice terminal) or defined programmable directory number with no additional user action.
- Dialing a defined meet-me number shall immediately connect a terminal to the meet-me net.
- Every terminal that dials the meet-me net directory number shall be connected into the net with the ability to disconnect and reconnect without disturbing other net participants.
- Each net shall support a capacity of at least 12 (T) / 15 (O) participants. The minimum simultaneous net capacity shall be at least 15 (T) / 20 (O) nets.

Emergency Nets/Calls

- An emergency reporting net capability of up to 3 (T) / 4 (O) nets shall be provided to receive emergency calls from any dial terminal, with one terminal assigned to each emergency net for handling incoming emergency calls on that net, and identified as the responsible dial terminal (RDT).
- When a called RDT goes off-hook, it will be connected to its emergency net, and any subsequent calls to the emergency number or associated net number will be connected to the emergency net and be able to converse with other net members.
- Emergency reporting shall be possible for each of five "readiness" conditions, and under each condition of readiness a particular RDT may be designated as responsible for handling emergency calls on one or more emergency reporting nets.
- An emergency reporting net shall be identified by up to two emergency telephone numbers (i.e., 2211 and 911) in addition to a net number.
- The following call/connection procedures shall be implemented:
  - Any terminal calling the emergency number and RDT is not-busy, shall receive a ring-back tone until the RDT operator goes off-hook (or integrated voice terminal equivalent), at which time both parties shall be connected to the corresponding emergency net.
  - Subsequent callers calling the emergency number or the emergency net number shall be connected to the corresponding emergency net and be able to converse with other net members.

○ If the call to the RDT cannot be completed due to equipment problems or settings, the operator of the calling terminal shall receive an unavailable tone.

○ If an emergency call is made to the RDT while it is busy on a call to other than its assigned emergency net, all parties on the existing call shall hear a one-second emergency tone added to their conversation in progress, and then will be placed on hold while the RDT is automatically connected to the Emergency Net.

○ The RDT shall be overridden by an emergency net call even if the RDT is currently on a nonoverridable call on its nonemergency number. The RDT operator may then retrieve any of the parties on hold.

○ The RDT shall continue to be connected to the corresponding emergency reporting net even if the calling terminal should go on-hook.

○ The RDT's connection to the net shall be broken only when the RDT goes on hook or deactivates.

○ At least 3 (T) / 4 (O) Emergency Nets of 12 (T) / 15 (O) terminal participants each shall be supported.

Address Numbering Plan

- Capability will be provided that permits each terminal, net, interface channel, or service code to be identified by a discrete four-digit number.
- The address numbers are to be used in switch service operations for identification purposes and by the subscriber for service requests.
- The numbering plan will typically be divided into two parts: a fixed or reserved set of numbers, and a directory set of numbers.

A capability for *PTT and intercom* connections shall be provided as detailed by the lists below.

Push-to-Talk (PTT)

- A push-to-talk (PTT) capability shall be supported for integrated voice terminal connections and radio mode calls.
- A voice operated transmission (VOX) PTT shall be implemented for POTS and BRI/ST Interface Boards.

Intercom Announce

- Intercom capability shall be supported for integrated voice terminals, as a dedicated nonblocking service feature that establishes a talk-back connection between designated terminal users.

- The calling integrated voice terminal alerts the called subscriber with an audible tone. An integrated voice terminal permits a called party to hear the calling party even if the called integrated voice terminal is busy, and a single action at the called integrated voice terminal establishes a connection in the reverse direction to permit the called party to talk to the calling party.
- The initiator of the IC call shall have an immediate half-duplex connection to the monitor channel of the other integrated voice terminals in the IC group. The other integrated voice terminals will hear the originator without any action on their part.
- An integrated voice terminal key in the IC ringing state shall beep and continue flashing until answered or the caller disconnects.
- IC ringing shall not time out. If not answered, the call shall remain in the ringing state until the calling party disconnects.
- Pressing the IC key or button on a called integrated voice terminal shall establish full-duplex audio between the terminal, the initiating terminal, and any other integrated voice terminals that have answered.
- If other members disconnect, leaving one remaining member, the call shall remain active.
- An integrated voice terminal shall have the ability to leave the IC call and reenter the call by depressing the IC key.
- An integrated voice terminal operator who presses the IC key to return to an active IC call shall be immediately connected.
- At least 15 (T) / 20 (O) total intercom circuits of 12 (T) / 15 (O) participants each shall be supported.

Auto Answer

- Applicable to ISDN terminals with auto answer capability, an incoming ring signal shall automatically activate the terminal if its mode switch is set to "auto-answer," allowing the terminal to ring once and the calling party to start speaking.
- The integrated voice terminal shall include a locally enabled auto-answer feature, whereby the terminal automatically answers incoming telephone and Intercom Announce calls without any user action required.

A capability for *external connection calls* shall be provided to permit dial terminals that are appropriately class marked to dial a connection to an interfacing external system, as described in the lists that follow (such as to a public address (PA) system, radio net, or access to a PSTN trunk using a dialed access code).

Public Address (PA) and Alarm System Connection

- Connection shall be to a PA or alarm system from designated voice terminals by keying (dialing, with PTT) a designated PA or alarm system termination number.
- At least 8 (T) / 12 (O) total PA or alarm system nets of 12 (T) / 15 (O) participants at least each shall be supported.

Radio Net Connection

- The communications interoperability switch shall provide a radio, analog NT interface capability (application dependent) that permits a secure mode connection via the communications interoperability switch, from an integrated voice terminal to a site-provided voice radio device.
- The NT circuit shall present an interface that consists of BRI S/T-to-analog converter circuits and discrete control lines, for an appropriate radio channel connection that has a standardized interface.
- At least 15 (T) / 20 (O) total Radio Nets of 12 (T) / 15 (O) participants at least each shall be supported.

PSTN Connection

- A capability shall be provided for accessing PSTN trunks from dial terminals and integrated voice terminals that are appropriately class marked, by dialing an access code.
- The PSTN side shall provide the required dial tone.

Traffic handling capabilities for the communications interoperability switch will have minimum (threshold) baseline characteristics as specified in the lists that follow:

Traffic Handling

- Traffic load and distribution—During the busiest hour the communications interoperability switch shall be capable of handling:
  a. 0.004 terminal-to-terminal calls originated per dial terminal per second (equates to one new call per terminal every 4 minutes), with an average holding time of 30 seconds; and
  b. 0.002 line-to-net calls originated per dial terminal per second (approximately one new call every 8 minutes), with an average holding time of 2 minutes. It is assumed that the percentage of these calls completed within the originating node is equal to 100

percent divided by the number of nodes, and that the traffic load imbalance between multiple nodes does not exceed 1.5 to 1.

- Call Busy Factor Adjustment—A call busy factor of 25 percent is assumed, to reflect the number of dial terminals unable to make or receive calls because the line is occupied with a previously established call.
- Call Initiation Delay—The busy hour call initiation delay measured from call initiation to receipt of dial tone shall be less than 3.0 seconds.
- Call Completion Delay—The busy hour call completion delay measured from the last digit dialed to ring forward shall be less than 0.5 second for calls at one node, or less than 2.5 seconds for calls between nodes.
- Blocking—An interoperability switch shall provide a traffic handling capability of less than one call in one thousand lost or blocked (equates to a call not going through) as a result of an error in the controller, or a false trunk, switch, or station signal.
- Misrouting—For security requirements, the probability of call misrouting (call sent to another terminal) due to an interoperability switch error shall be less than one in 106.

The *radio progressive conference (RPC)* feature provides a means to establish a true two-way conference call between multiple radios, integrated voice terminals, and other terminals.

This feature enables an integrated voice terminal user to join two or more radio nets together to form one large net. As an example, a VHF link from one land-based agency to a helicopter could be joined to a UHF link from the same agency back to other agencies in the area. The extended network would be half-duplex, but participants on the VHF and UHF links can all hear transmissions and transmit on either link. This represents a concatenation of two nets.

In addition, the feature can be used to bring another terminal into a radio net. For example, the originator may be participating in a law enforcement UHF net and decide that someone on another IVT needs to join the conversation. That operator can call the other IVT and then conference that IVT into the radio progressive conference.

The term *progressive* in the title implies that additional members (Radio Nets or terminals) may be progressively added (or dropped) one at a time. These conferences can also be referred to as ad hoc conferences. RPC requirements are detailed in the list that follows.

RPC Requirements

- The proposed switching system shall provide radio progressive conferencing with 15 (T) / 20 (O) preset conferences. Each preset conference shall support at least 12 (T) / 15 (O) terminals.

- The SAT shall have the capability to configure the radio progressive conference feature for any integrated voice terminal.
- If a radio net or a terminal is already involved in a radio progressive conference, attempting to conference that radio net or terminal shall result in an unavailable tone at the attempting integrated voice terminal.

Assignable Speaker/Voice Recorder (AS/VR)

- The assignable speaker/voice recorder (AS/VR) feature of the proposed system shall enable a user to assign speakers or a voice recorder to an interoperability switch radio net, public address net, or voice net for monitoring and recording purposes.
- The proposed system shall be able to interface with a public address announcing system using industry standard interfaces.
- The proposed system shall be able to interface with an alarm system using industry standard interfaces.
- The proposed system shall be able to interface to a voice recording device using industry standard interfaces, for the purposes of recording any of the circuits or calls that are routed through the switch.
- The voice recorder's record port shall be able to be connected to a net (via the communications interoperability switch) such that all voice transmission on the net is recorded.
- The voice recorder's playback port shall be able to be connected to a net (via the communications interoperability switch) such that multiple integrated voice terminals and dial terminals can listen to the playback audio.
- The connection of the speaker and/or the voice recorder to a net (via the interoperability switch) shall be configurable from the SAT (offline or online) or from the integrated voice terminal.

4.2 Key Performance Parameters (KPPs)

4.2.1 Connectivity The interoperability switching system shall provide at least:

- Connectivity to radios—16 (T) / 32 (O)
- Connectivity to integrated voice terminals—24 (T) / 48 (O)
- Connectivity to telephones—16 (T) / 32 (O)
- Connectivity to wireless systems—4 (T) / 8 (O)
- Connectivity to public switched telephone networks—1 (T) / 2 (O)
- Connectivity to recording systems—2 (T) / 3 (O)

4.3 System Performance

4.3.1 Mission Scenarios The interoperability switching system will typically be located at fixed area or mobile communications centers that handle emergency events such as an emergency operation center (EOC). Systems will be installed and can be up and in operation at all times in order to minimize the time needed to establish communications in the event of an emergency.

4.3.2 System Performance Parameters The interoperability switching system shall provide at least:

- Connectivity to radios—16 (T) / 32 (O)
- Connectivity to integrated voice terminals—24 (T) / 48 (O)
- Connectivity to telephones—16 (T) / 32 (O)
- Connectivity to wireless systems—4 (T) / 8 (O)
- Connectivity to other switches via a PRI interface—1 (T) / 2 (O)
- Connectivity to public switched telephone networks—1 (T) / 2 (O)
- Connectivity to public address systems—2 (T) / 4 (O)
- Connectivity to other interoperability switches via a trunk—1 (T) / 2 (O)
- Connectivity to recording systems—2 (T) / 3 (O)
- Connectivity to voice over IP (VoIP) systems—1 (T) / 2 (O)

4.3.3 Interoperability The communications interoperability switch will be able to interface to all radios, wireless systems, integrated voice terminals, telephones, PBXs, VoIP switches, PA systems, recording devices, and other communications media that utilize industry standard interfaces.

4.3.4 Human Interface Requirements An integrated voice terminal (IVT) will be the primary and most functional human machine interface (HMI) connected to the communications interoperability switch for connecting and establishing radio/wireless and telephone calls, circuits, conferences, and nets.

Analog and digital telephones (also known as dial terminals) will be additional HMI devices connected to the communications interoperability switch for the purpose of making and receiving calls and connecting to conferences, and nets.

A system administration terminal (SAT) will act as the HMI for system configuration data entry, system configuration reports, system status reports, and failure interrogation.

The SAT can be either continuously connected to the communications interoperability switch for permanent ongoing system status reporting or be capable of being placed in offline mode during user absence or for configuration database updating (for a later database transfer to the communication interoperability switch).

When the SAT is not online, communications interoperability switch status and failure events shall be stored in the communications interoperability switch for batch transfer to the SAT when it is returned to online status.

An SAT connection shall be able to interface to a local or networked printer, if part of the configuration, for hardcopy printouts of system status.

The SAT can be any PC that is operable from 115 VAC, is available with backup battery option, provides printer and Ethernet interface connections, and is capable of running the communications interoperability switch SAT software under Microsoft Windows.

The SAT shall provide for communications interoperability switch setup and management and for initiating switch built-in-test (BIT) operations.

The SAT shall provide a status screen displaying the latest status of the communications interoperability switch. The SAT status screen shall contain the communications interoperability switch call and fault logs.

The SAT shall provide the user a capability to manage the system tests and view the status of the tests.

Accepted industry standards shall be applied as guidance for human engineering design criteria in the design of the proposed system, to achieve safe, reliable, and effective performance by operator, supervisor, and maintenance personnel, and to minimize personnel skill requirements and training time.

4.3.5 Logistics and Readiness The proposed system is required to be operational for several days of continuous operation without interruption. No user level maintenance or spare-part replacement is required. Spare PWAs should be available in case replacement is required.

Mean time between failures (MTBF) shall be 1,500 hours (T) 1,800 hours (O).

System availability (Ai) requirement shall be 0.999995 (T), 0.999997 (O) based on the following formula:

$$Ai = \frac{MTBF}{MTBF + MTTR}$$

4.3.6 Other System Characteristics Design drivers are the interfaces and the ability of the proposed communications interoperability switch to interface to all types of radios, wireless systems, telephones, and other communications media. Cost drivers are the interface cards for the many and varied systems to be connected to the proposed system. Risk drivers are the ability of the communications interoperability switch to interface with many and varied different systems using readily available off-the-shelf interface boards without the need of designing or building new boards.

5 System Support

5.1 Maintenance

The proposed system shall be designed for unattended operation. Routine, scheduled maintenance will be performed online, except for specified infrequent cleaning operations. Scheduled maintenance checks shall not be required more than once every twenty-four hours. Scheduled maintenance may include, but not be limited to: air filter cleaning and replacement, battery cleanliness and battery voltage level checks, daily semiautomatic system tests from the SAT, lamp and meter checks, and general cleanliness requirements.

The total twenty-four-hour normal maintenance burden for an operating system, scheduled and unscheduled, shall not average more than two man-hours (T) / one man-hour (O).

5.2 Supply

User Manuals will be provided to the operators and maintenance technicians by the equipment provider (vendor) and will include operator procedures, diagnostic testing/SAT use, and replacement procedures. No special tools or diagnostic equipment will be required for equipment replacement.

5.3 Support Equipment

Standard support equipment for the interoperability switch is the system administration terminal (SAT) described in section 4.3.4, HMI, which will handle system diagnostic testing. No special test equipment will be required to maintain or operate the unit. The vendor will provide software upgrades as needed/required and will provide software development services to the buyer for new features as requested.

5.4 Training

Training will be provided by the equipment provider to a system trainer (via a train-the-trainers session) and to the users and operators at the installed site at a time convenient to the users and operators. The training curriculum will be designed to ensure users understand and are fully capable of operating and using all features of the system. Knowledgeable staff members of the equipment provider will also be made available by phone (via a help desk–type arrangement) should a user or operator need assistance with any part of the proposed system.

5.5 Transportation and Facilities

It is anticipated that this system will most often be used in a fixed station. If the proposed system is to be mobile or used in the field, it will be transportable via truck or van and will be able to be lifted by two or fewer personnel. Sufficient 115V power and cables will be needed to connect the communications interoperability switch to the radios and other equipment necessary to provide connectivity and interoperability commensurate with the event. Any training needed in the field can be provided as on-the-job training with no special facilities needed.

6. Force Structure

One interoperability switch system will typically be required at each emergency operating center (EOC) or similar-type communications center. The proposed system will be modular and scalable (or sizable) to have enough capacity and interface boards necessary to interface all of the radios, integrated voice terminals, telephones, and other communications devices needed by the center personnel to conduct their mission.

Additional systems can be supplied to mobile platforms (vans or trucks) if an EOC or other shore-based center is not within communications range of the event.

The high reliability of the system (sect. 4.3.5) dictates only a minimum amount of spares needed for interface boards, power supplies, and communications devices.

7. Schedule

Demonstration of an initial operational capability is required within 3 months (T) / 1 month (O) after executed SECURE agreement. For the purpose of this effort, initial operational capability is defined as installation and field demonstration of one fully operational communications interoperability switch system to include one SAT and at least two radios, two integrated voice terminals, two telephones, and one other wireless device (such as a cell phone.)

A fully operational system will be required within 9 months (T) / 6 months (O). A fully operational system includes the communications interoperability switch with interface boards, system administration terminal (SAT), and all necessary integrated voice terminals supplied by the proposed system vendor. Radios and other communications devices (telephones, wireless systems) to interface with the communications interoperability switch are typically separate from the communications interoperability switch system and may have different lead times if they are not already available at the site.

8. System Affordability

An Individual unit price cost for such a communications interoperability switch shall cost less than $200K (T) / $150K (O).

9. Appendixes

List of Acronyms

CM—Class Mark
COS—Class of Service
COTS—Commercial-Off-the-Shelf Equipment
EOC—Emergency Operations Center
ISDN—Integrated Services Digital Network
KPP—Key Performance Parameter
MTBF—Mean Time Between Failures
POTS—Plain Old Telephone System
PSTN—Public Switched Telephone Network
RDT—Responsible Dial Terminal
SAT—System Administration Terminal
IVT—Integrated Voice Terminal

CRITICAL INFRASTRUCTURE AND KEY RESOURCES (CIKR): C-ORD FOR INTEGRATED INTRUSION PROTECTION (IIP)

Contents

1. General Description of Operational Capability
    1.1. Capability Gap
    1.2. Overall Mission Area Description
    1.3. Description of the Proposed Product or System
    1.4. Supporting Analysis
    1.5. Mission the Proposed System Shall Accomplish
    1.6. Operational and Support Concept
        1.6.1. Concept of Operations
        1.6.2. Support Concept
2. Threat
3. Existing System Shortfalls
4. Capabilities Required
    4.1. Operational Performance Parameters
        4.1.1. Effective Intrusion detection
        4.1.2. False Alarm rate
        4.1.3. Intruder characterization

4.1.4. Real-time intruder information

4.1.5. Intrusion Site Change Characterization

4.1.6. Automated Operation

4.1.7. Highly Adaptable Surveillance Coverage

4.1.8. Sensors

4.1.9. Sensor signal receivers

4.2. Key Performance Parameters (KPPs)

4.2.1. Cost-Effectiveness

4.2.2. Deployment Schedule

4.2.3. Maximum Coverage Area

4.3. System Performance

4.3.1. Mission Scenarios

4.3.2. System Performance Parameters

4.3.2.1. Sensors

4.3.2.2. Sensor signal receivers

4.3.2.3. "Sensor fusion" processor

4.3.3. Interoperability

4.3.4. Human Interface Requirements

4.3.5. Logistics and Readiness

4.3.6. Other System Characteristics

5. System Support

5.1. Maintenance

5.2. Supply

5.3. Support Equipment

5.4. Training

5.5. Transportation and Facilities

6. Force Structure

7. Schedule

8. System Affordability

1. General Description of Operational Capability

Currently, the overall surveillance function for the Department of Homeland Security (DHS) is performed using a variety of technologies including video, infrared, sound, pressure, and vibration sensing. Each of these solutions, with its advantages and vulnerabilities, is useful for a narrow range of specific surveillance needs. However, the need exists for an adaptable, scalable surveillance capability that provides automated, real-time protection for a wide range of operational scenarios. DHS must also be able to leverage use of non-real-time intelligence data associated with any suspicious activity or perceived preparations prior to a critical event. In addition, the full cadre of surveillance delivery systems must be considered. An integrated intrusion protection (IIP) system is necessary.

This advanced capability must effectively support different types of protection without the need for 24/7 staffing. It must also be simple and quick to deploy, effective for a variety of surveillance area types and sizes, and require little maintenance. Finally, it must be cost-effective to use, even for temporary protection needs. This capability is useful to missions performed by the DHS National Protection and Programs Directorate (NPPD) (specifically the Office of Infrastructure Protection), the Transportation Security Administration (TSA), the U.S. Customs and Border Protection (CBP), the U.S. Coast Guard, and the Federal Emergency Management Agency (FEMA), as well as critical infrastructure/key resources (CIKR) owners and operators and first responders.

1.1. Capability Gap

Current surveillance technology does not adequately address the variety of surveillance needs. For example, most surveillance systems, including video surveillance, require major investments in time, materials, and staffing to deploy. Additionally, a video surveillance system requires thorough planning for effective installation to overcome its normally limited coverage area; requires constant monitor staffing; and is usually costly due to technology, installation, and maintenance costs. After a major disaster, for example, FEMA must establish surveillance of geographic areas very rapidly and with minimum overhead for multiple reasons. For instance, if a post-disaster neighborhood presents critical, life-threatening hazards that were not present prior to the disaster, FEMA may decide to prohibit unauthorized personnel from entering the area until it is secured. In order to enforce this, surveillance of the area may need to be established to notify authorities if an intruder enters. The same paradigm applies when a user must keep an area from being looted after a disaster. A rapidly deployable, wide-area surveillance system is necessary to meet these needs.

Another example includes supplies that are forward-deployed in preparation for a disaster. These supplies require protection from theft or sabotage. Ideally, a surveillance system to protect these supplies would provide sufficient warning to apprehend or deter the intruder before a theft or sabotage occurs. However, if these supplies are stored in existing commercial storage units next to a street with frequent foot and vehicular traffic, a surveillance perimeter large enough to provide such warning may be impractical. Therefore, security may arrive on site after the intruder has departed. Information to characterize an intrusion, such as whether the intruder was on foot or not and/or whether the intruder removed supplies or left an object behind to commit an act of sabotage is useful to arriving security forces. Such a system would need to cover the site internally and externally and be staffed persistently. In this case, an adaptable and automated surveillance capability that provides intrusion characterization to security forces after the actual intrusion may be more cost-effective.

As previously mentioned, this capability gap is not confined to FEMA alone. For example, a critical requirement for the Office of Infrastructure Protection is protection surveillance for critical infrastructure; such as a dam that provides power or water for a major urban area. Access to a dam often involves rough terrain and a wide geographic area. Traditional surveillance technology such as video, infrared, pressure, and sound sensors do not usually cover large areas of rough terrain effectively. In addition, to maximize protection, surveillance must detect an intruder early enough to enable security to prevent the intruder from reaching the dam. Therefore, the traditional solution is often security patrols. Such random patrols are costly and labor-intensive and require training of patrol personnel. Patrol vehicles require a major investment and regular, costly maintenance. An automated, real-time, readily deployable, wide-area surveillance system is more persistent and cost-effective and would make better use of limited security personnel.

1.2. Overall Mission Area Description

The IIP system shall address infrastructure protection and incident management mission needs. It shall be used to protect national and local infrastructure, storage facilities, and geographic areas when benign intrusion does not frequently occur unexpectedly, i.e., authorized personnel do not regularly enter the surveillance area without notification. Therefore, IIP users shall primarily be first responders and security personnel at the national, state, local, or tribal levels.

An IIP system shall provide rapidly deployable and reliable surveillance over large geographic areas. It may effectively detect intruders sufficiently early for authorized personnel to intercept them prior to an intruder penetrating the target or may be used to detect changes to the protected area when intruders cannot be prevented from reaching the site. In addition, the IIP system shall characterize (time, location, type) the intrusion to enable alarms and an appropriate security response. Finally, an IIP shall provide different types of automated alarms so that security personnel are notified and involved only when needed. For instance, an IIP system may be configured to provide warnings when a suspicious person is walking toward the protected area and an alarm when that person has become an intruder by entering the protected area. The system does not require around-the-clock staffing to monitor the surveillance area.

1.3. Description of the Proposed Product or System

The IIP system shall be composed of the following major subsystems:

1. A sensor array
2. One or more sensor signal receivers
3. A central processor
4. A communication system

Whenever possible, the sensors shall be COTS products. These sensor arrays shall be distributable around the protection perimeter and any specific areas of interest, such as a road, or the geographic area to be monitored. In addition, these sensor arrays may be fastened to walls of storage units to sense reductions or additions to the unit contents.

The sensor signal receiver(s) shall be composed of COTS products. These receivers shall either receive signals sent from the sensors or interrogate sensors for a response. Mobile sensors may be deployed to supplement permanently deployed sensors, if required.

A "sensor fusion" processor shall also be a COTS product. This processor shall be used to define a characteristic surveillance baseline and representative intruder responses from a sensor set. As responses are received from the sensor signal receivers, the processor shall match these responses with characteristic baseline and intruder responses. If a response matches the baseline within defined thresholds, the processor shall simply wait for the next signal set. If the response matches an intruder within defined thresholds, the processor shall notify security via the communication system of that intrusion type. Intrusion types include, for example, one or more intruders on foot or vehicles. An anomalous response type shall also be defined to alert security of uncharacterized intrusions, other surveillance area changes (e.g., a tree falling in the woods is heard), or IIP equipment failures.

1.4. Supporting Analysis

These capability gaps have been verified through interviews with DHS, CIKR, and first-responder personnel throughout the United States.

1.5. Mission the Proposed System Shall Accomplish

The IIP system shall provide an easily deployable, adaptable, and low-maintenance solution for the surveillance of various geographic areas related to actions of harmful or illegal intent. It shall provide reliable, effective detection of intruders and characterize them according to predefined intrusion categories. Dependent on the protection level required and site specifics, this automated intrusion detection system may establish a perimeter to provide sufficient lead time for authorized personnel to intercept the intruder before the target area is breached. The IIP system shall also determine if the intruder removed or left something at the site and where it was placed. The IIP system shall be cost-effective and most, if not all, of its components may be reused for subsequent surveillance deployments. It shall be capable to use as a stand-alone surveillance system or may be easily integrated with additional surveillance technologies.

1.6. Operational and Support Concept

1.6.1. Concept of Operations IIP is intended as a surveillance system in a "security toolbox." It has the advantages of:

1. Providing surveillance of large areas
2. Characterizing intrusions for authorized responders
3. Providing early intrusion warnings
4. Responding automatically, so that continuous staffing is not required
5. Being rapidly deployable with minimal planning for various terrains
6. Being adaptable to different surveillance areas
7. Requiring little training to deploy and operate
8. Requiring minimal maintenance
9. Using COTS technology
10. Providing cueing to other security systems such as video systems, once an intrusion has been detected

The IIP system most effectively protects areas that are typically low density in terms of human and vehicle operations. If supply storage or infrastructure is situated near a busy footpath, street, or highway on a small plot, other surveillance methods may be more appropriate for protection from intruders at the current time. For example, many public storage facilities are near busy streets, and during the daytime, high-profile public sites such as the Washington Monument are constantly surrounded by tourists.

The current low-density constraint is due to the need to control false alarms. For instance, if a supply storage facility is located near a busy street, each pedestrian and passing vehicle may interact with the sensor array, causing an atypical response, and thus notifying security of a possible intruder. However, if the supply storage facility is separated from nearby traffic by some distance, IIP could be an appropriate solution. We are interested in solutions that minimize false alarms with high foot or vehicular traffic.

The IIP deployment attributes listed above make it ideal for situations requiring rapid deployment (e.g., during emergencies and disasters). For example, an agency may decide to deploy IIP for multiple scenario classes. One would be to protect forward-deployed supply storage. In the event of a potential emergency such as an impending hurricane, one may decide to pre-deploy supplies to reduce the loss of life and property in the event of hurricane impact. In addition, after a disaster has occurred, officials may also determine that specific geographic areas must be protected. For instance, one may decide to deny access to areas that have become hazardous or are potential looting sites.

Another application may be to choose to deploy IIP over large geographic areas to protect critical national infrastructure. Such infrastructure includes defense industrial bases; energy; national monuments and icons; dams; commercial nuclear reactors, materials, and waste; telecommunications; transportation systems; and other government facilities.

In each case, sensors may be deployed by distributing them around the perimeter of the area to be protected and areas of special interest such as access roads. If intruders are to be intercepted by security prior to reaching the protected site, planning is required to determine the perimeter distance from the target to assure adequate response time. If interception is not required, the perimeter may be deployed around a smaller area. If a stealth configuration is desired, sensors shall be able to be easily hidden or camouflaged. These sensors may also be fastened to the protected site itself if there is a concern for sabotage or a desire to learn if something has been removed from a storage building.

Sensor signal receiver(s) are installed within range of the sensors. Since the sensor signal receiver(s) may be connected to the processor by either wireless or Internet cable, the processor may be located at the protected site, at the local security site, or anywhere with network connectivity. When the sensors have been distributed, the sensor signal receiver(s) responses are processed by the processor to define a "baseline" response pattern. This process calibrates the IIP to recognize a nominal, non-intrusion state.

Over time, most sites shall undergo changes. To accommodate such changes, the processor shall provide the option to "reset" the baseline either manually or at preset intervals. The processor enables IIP to be self-learning based on updated information and disposition of the area of interest. The system shall go through a calibration sequence each time "reset" is initiated in order to establish a new baseline. After the baseline has been established, the system responses to intrusion types of interest are also defined if desired. System responses to each intruder type are characterized using actual intruder approaches and entrances of the IIP surveillance area.

As IIP operates, each time a non-baseline state (including unlawful intrusions) is identified, the system response information is recorded. Intrusion and non-baseline state information may be retrieved from the processor using a standard network interface.

1.6.2. Support Concept An IIP system shall be designed to require minimal maintenance. All sensors and detection array pieces shall be extremely rugged and produced to withstand extreme temperatures and physical changes. These sensor products need to be optimized for use under a wide range of environmental conditions and may be fastened or placed on almost any surface. If one of these sensors fails operationally, this shall be reflected as an anomalous condition by the processor. As the replacement of a failed sensor power unit is the primary IIP maintenance required, sensor batteries are the only significant spares required.

System function is regularly reported to security if the system response is nominal, thereby automatically testing system function and communications. Diagnostics for the IIP-specific components shall be built-in and may be executed automatically. Baseline response recalibration may also be configured to be executed automatically after a specified interval or may be performed manually as necessary.

2. Threat

Intruders may be civilians returning to the scene of a disaster, looters, saboteurs, or potentially international/domestic terrorists.

The evidence for people returning to hazardous disaster areas is well documented. People return for a variety of reasons, such as searching for a relative or pet or to retrieve a possession. These people put themselves, and potentially rescue workers in harm's way. Hazards include the remains of buildings after collapsing during an earthquake, wild animals after a flood, contagions after a hurricane, or poisonous chemical exposure after a terrorist attack. Intruders create a health hazard that may result in the loss of life.

The evidence for looters invading a disaster area is also well documented. Looters rob from unattended sites, including disaster sites as well as unattended supply storage units. Their methods often result in property damage as well as theft of property. In addition, they create a situation in which the risk of injury or loss of life to themselves and to the other people present is dramatically increased. These risks result from their looting methods or conflicts resulting from such looting. Saboteurs and terrorists may attack infrastructure or intrude disaster sites. They may intrude disaster areas to create the potential for further disaster. These means may include chemical or biological agents that may be more vulnerable to theft, during or after a disaster.

3. Existing System Shortfalls

Existing systems do provide effective intrusion detection within range of their sensors. For infrared (IR), this range is extremely short, as background IR energy overcomes the source energy. Sound also suffers from the same range limitations and is problematic in an outdoor setting. For video, the effective range is limited by the need for an identifiable image. Although video sensor coverage area may be increased by the use of wide-angle lenses, the range of an identifiable image diminishes rapidly as the lens angle increases. Many current solutions also store collected data to be retrieved only after an event occurs. This may help identify the culprit, but not prevent the disaster. None of these systems automatically detects how an intruder may have changed the protected site—e.g., placed something at the site such as a bomb or removed something from the site. It is essential that surveillance data be collected and processed prior to and during potential suspicious events.

Therefore, traditional surveillance sensor types are inadequate to cover diverse geographic areas without the added (and often prohibitive) expense of planning and the installation of large numbers of costly sensors. Deployment of each of these systems requires expert analysis of the coverage area due to their small, interactive coverage areas. In addition, if sufficient warning time for security response is required, these sensor types may have to be installed in multiple layers, at a minimum with a warning layer and an actual intrusion layer. Each technology requires significant time to deploy and test. Operation of sound and infrared systems may provide cost-effective automatic detection for limited range. Video may provide automatic detection, but is prone to spoofing and costs much more than the same capability for sound or infrared systems. Therefore, operations for video systems are costly due to the need for continuous staffing during the threat period as well as the expense of the technology. Substantial training is required to deploy and maintain video systems. Further, video systems require regular maintenance due to scanning platforms and the need to clean the lenses of outdoor systems. Sound and infrared systems are much cheaper to operate and maintain due to their automatic capability and the cost of the technology.

In summary, infrared and sound systems provide limited coverage but tend to be cost-effective. Video systems provide intrusion identification, have larger coverage areas, yet tend to be costly to deploy, operate, and maintain.

4. Capabilities Required

4.1. Operational Performance Parameters

Operational Performance parameters are labeled as either Threshold (T) or Objective (O). Threshold parameters are the minimum parameters to be met for system utility. Objective parameters are the desired values for system operation. If a parameter is marked without a T or O indicator, it is an Objective parameter.

4.1.1. Effective Intrusion Detection The IIP system shall provide the capability to detect 98% (T) / 99.9% (O) of defined intrusions within a defined protected area.

The IIP system shall provide the capability to read data from each sensor in real time. The IIP system shall provide the capability to locate intrusions to ≤ 20 meters (T) / ≤ 3 meters (O) of their true location. Location accuracy is dependent on sensor placement.

4.1.2. False Alarm rate The IIP system shall generate ≤ 0.1% (T) / ≤ 0.01% (O) false alarms.

4.1.3. Intruder Characterization The IIP system shall provide the capability to identify intrusions by human beings, animals, vehicles, and/ or robots.

4.1.4. Real-Time Intruder Information The IIP system shall provide the capability to send real-time intruder warning messages to security. "Warning" messages are sent when intruders approach (i.e., before they enter) the coverage area.

The IIP system shall provide the capability to send real-time intruder alarm messages to security. "Alarm" messages are sent when intruders penetrate the coverage area.

The IIP system shall provide the capability to send real-time updates of intruder information to investigating security personnel.

4.1.5. Intrusion-Site Change Characterization The IIP system shall provide the capability to detect changes to the protected site. These changes include (1) adding something, (2) removing something, or (3) physically changing the site in a preset limit involving minimal size and weight and the type of object. Please specify the size, weight, and type of object specifications.

4.1.6. Automated Operation The IIP system shall provide the capability to continuously monitor a defined area automatically.

The IIP system shall provide the capability to identify intrusions (see 4.1.5) automatically.

The IIP system shall provide the capability to send multiple intrusion alarm levels automatically.

4.1.7. Highly Adaptable Surveillance Coverage   The IIP system shall provide the capability to provide effective surveillance for any area with sensors deployed by less than their maximum range.

4.1.8. Sensors   The IIP system sensors shall operate normally in temperate ranges from ≥ 140°F (60°C) to ≤ - 35°F (-37°C).

4.1.9. Sensor Signal Receivers   The IIP system sensor signal receiver shall normally receive sensor data from a range of ≥ 100 meters (T) / ≥ 1 kilometer (O).

4.2. Key Performance Parameters (KPPs)

4.2.1. Cost-Effectiveness   The IIP system kit shall provide surveillance of at least 10,000 square meters for ≤ $8,000 (in volume production quantities). Additional kits may be combined to monitor larger coverage areas.

4.2.2. Deployment Schedule   The IIP system shall provide the capability to deploy, configure, and test an area of ≥ 10,000 square meters in surveillance coverage, with operational status within 24 hours.

4.2.3. Maximum Coverage Area   The IIP system shall provide surveillance coverage capability of any size area. Larger areas shall require additional sensors and sensor signal receivers, or their equivalent.

4.3 System Performance

4.3.1 Mission Scenarios   Two primary scenarios were posited in the operations concepts section: (1) a pre-disaster deployment to protect forward-deployed supply storage and (2) a post-disaster deployment to deny access to areas that have become hazardous or are potential looting sites. The IIP system may also be deployed to provide surveillance for large geographic areas necessary to protect critical national infrastructure.

4.3.2 System Performance Parameters

4.3.2.1. Sensors

All IIP system sensors shall be COTS products (T).
All IIP system sensors shall operate continuously using self-contained power for a minimum ≥ 6 months (T)/ ≥ 24 months (O).

4.3.2.2. Sensor Signal Receivers

The IIP system sensor signal receiver shall be composed of COTS hardware (T).
The IIP system sensor signal receiver software shall execute on a COTS lower-cost personal computer (T).

4.3.2.3 "Sensor Fusion" Processor

The IIP system processor shall be composed of COTS hardware (T).
All IIP system software shall execute on a COTS personal computer (T).
The IIP system processor shall be capable of storing intrusion data for
≥ 3 months (T)/ ≥ 6 months (O).

4.3.3 *Interoperability* The IIP system processor shall be capable of
communication using a hardwired or wireless network, using standard
TCP/IP protocols.

4.3.4 *Human Interface Requirements* The IIP system human interface
shall comply with Windows GUI standards. The processor shall provide
the human interface to the entire system including the configuration and
diagnostics for the sensor signal receiver.

4.3.5 *Logistics and Readiness* The system shall be operational for long
periods of continuous operation without interruption. Independent of
individual sensor failures, the mean time between failure (MTBF) shall be
≥ 5,000 hours (T) / ≥ 25,000 hours (O).

4.3.6 *Other System Characteristics* The system shall be designed for
(1) unattended and automatic operation, (2) rapid deployment, (3) low
maintenance, (4) use of low-cost components, (5) use of easily replaceable
components, (6) use of readily available components, (7) rapid, simple
deployment, (8) deployment by staff with little or no prior training, (9)
operation by staff with little or no prior training, and (10) maintenance by
staff with little or no prior training.

5. System Support

5.1 Maintenance

Each IIP system shall provide both visual and auditory indications of
system anomalies. Diagnostics may be executed automatically or manually from the processor user interface. Manual execution requires minimal
training. The processor user interface shall provide user access to diagnostic results.

Diagnostics shall identify IIP subsystems that require maintenance,
including sensors that require consumable replacement. Replacement of
specific sensors or sensor batteries/other consumables shall be performed
by personnel with minimal or no training. Other maintenance shall be
performed by replacing the subsystem.

5.2 *Supply*

No special tools or support equipment shall be required for deployment or subsystem replacement. Manuals shall be provided to the operator by the vendor and shall include deployment procedures, information on diagnostic indicators (both automatic and manual diagnostics) and replacement procedures. The manuals shall also provide information on system data retrieval.

5.3 *Support Equipment*

All diagnostics shall be provided by the system. No external support equipment shall be required for the operator to maintain and operate the system.

5.4 *Training*

Users shall be instructed on the deployment, operation, and routine maintenance of system, interpretation of diagnostic indicators (both automatic and manual), and data retrieval procedures. In addition, manuals and written procedures supplied by the system developer shall be of sufficient detail to enable the execution of each of these activities by untrained personnel.

5.5 *Transportation and Facilities*

Transportation of IIP system components is expected and shall be well within individual carriage limitations for standard automobiles. Sensor equipment shall be small and light, and the sensor signal receivers and processor shall be no larger than the size of a desktop computer. The needs for cables, wires, etc., for most installations shall be minimal.

Once deployed, IIP system components shall remain in place until removed or replaced. The number of sensors required shall depend on the surveillance coverage area size, shape, terrain, and existing access among other factors.

Transportation of retrieved digital media shall require no special technical capability but should be conducted consistent with applicable procedures to preserve chain of custody when data retrieval is conducted for use in legal proceedings (e.g., criminal prosecution or civil litigation).

Facilities for housing the sensor signal receiver(s) and the processor shall require standard 110 V 60 Hz AC and protection from the elements. Fixed buildings, mobile units, and tents shall suffice, given the other requirements.

6. Force Structure

Each IIP system deployment can be unique, dependent on the protection mission and the geographical coverage area. For instance, the value of the protected infrastructure shall determine the distance of the protection perimeter from this target, the depth of the perimeter, and the density of sensors deployed within the perimeter. The required security response time shall define the distance of the perimeter from the target.

Sensor placement is dependent on a number of factors. The complexity of existing access to the target shall guide additional sensor placement to monitor this access and the areas around this access. The coverage area shall dictate sensor placement, as its size, shape, and terrain shall determine the number of sensors and how they are to be deployed. Finally, the sensor type shall establish deployment choices. The sensor type, active or passive (simple transponders), shall determine sensor transmission range and maintenance schedule. Sensors may be placed outdoors on a solid surface or may be shallowly buried. Sensors may also be mounted on vertical or overhead surfaces to achieve specific surveillance requirements. Sensors may not be submerged underwater.

Sensor signal receiver(s) shall be deployed based on sensor signal receiver type (how many sensors may be processed by the type), the number of sensors deployed, and the range limits of the sensors and the receiver. Sensor signal receivers shall require protection from the elements and standard 110 V 60 Hz AC power. Sensor signal receivers shall require cable or wireless network access to the processor, but are not required to be co-located with it. A single processor shall be deployed to process data from each of the deployed sensor signal receivers. It shall require protection from the elements and standard 110 V 60 Hz AC power. It shall also require cable or wireless network access to the sensor signal receivers. Assuming a communications infrastructure is accessible and readily available, it shall require duplex access to security forces via cable or wireless network, telephone, or radio.

7. Schedule

An operational capability shall be defined as the demonstration of enough deployed sensors to monitor at least a 10,000-square-meter area, the necessary sensor signal receiver(s) and a processor (or equivalent signal processing equipment) within one year.

8. System Affordability

The price of an IIP system kit shall be ≤ $8,000 based on high-volume production. This price shall include the software; hardware; and documentation to deploy, operate, and maintain the system kit. The system kit components include: (1) sufficient sensors to cover an area of at least 10,000 square meters, (2) sufficient receiving and processing equipment to monitor the sensor array, and (3) software on compact disc for installation on computers as required.

The price is all inclusive. No special consulting fees/services for the system kit are permitted for any scenario the vendor accepts.

CRITICAL INFRASTRUCTURE AND KEY RESOURCES (CIKR): C-ORD FOR BLAST RESISTANT AUTONOMOUS VIDEO EQUIPMENT (BRAVE)

Contents

1. General Description of Operational Capability
   1.1. Capability Gap
   1.2. Overall Mission Area Description
   1.3. Description of the Proposed System
   1.4. Supporting Analysis
   1.5. Mission the Proposed System Will Accomplish
   1.6. Operational and Support Concept
       1.6.1. Concept of Operations
       1.6.2. Support Concept
2. Threat
3. Existing System Shortfalls
4. Capabilities Required
   4.1. Operational Performance Parameters (T: Threshold / O: Objective)
       4.1.1. Form Factor
       4.1.2. Resolution
       4.1.3. Frame Rate
       4.1.4. Field of View/Focal Length
       4.1.5. Data Format
       4.1.6. Tamper Resistance
       4.1.7. Power Source
       4.1.8. Environmental
       4.1.9. Blast Survivability
   4.2. Key Performance Parameters (KPPs)
       4.2.1. Cost
       4.2.2. Storage Capacity
   4.3. System Performance
       4.3.1. Mission Scenarios
       4.3.2. Interoperability
       4.3.3. Human Interface Requirements
       4.3.4. Logistics and Readiness

5. System Support
    5.1. Maintenance
    5.2. Supply
    5.3. Support Equipment
    5.4. Training
    5.5. Transportation and Facilities
6. Force Structure
7. Schedule
8. System Affordability

1. GENERAL DESCRIPTION OF OPERATIONAL CAPABILITY

The rapid development of low-cost forensic camera systems for use by the first-responder community and ancillary markets will give state, local, tribal, and transit authorities the ability to determine incident cause at a low total cost of ownership in numerous applications. While technologies are currently being explored and developed at locales like Chicago, L.A., Seattle, and other metropolitan areas, a low-cost alternative with high rapid potential deployment to more users compared to these more costly systems is attractive for many reasons. In one example, mass transit vehicles and networks represent a potentially attractive target to terrorists and a unique challenge for law enforcement and transit personnel, due to their relative openness and large user base. Recent attacks in London, Madrid, and elsewhere around the world have demonstrated the devastating impacts of attacks carried out on mass transit vehicles. The investigation of the July 2005 attacks in London also demonstrated the forensic power of employing video surveillance data to successfully identify the terrorists directly and indirectly involved in such an attack. While many communities and transit agencies in the United States have implemented the use of video surveillance systems within their transit infrastructure, uniformity of coverage is lacking. Financial, technical, and policy challenges continue to limit the implemented coverage. As a result, the requirement exists to enhance the capability to obtain, store, and protect video surveillance information gathered from mass transit systems for forensic purposes. The operational capability described herein will provide user communities with a self-contained, low-cost video surveillance option that can be implemented as an adjunct to an existing system or as a primary source for forensic video surveillance information. The system will support greater surveillance implementation and meet a range of surveillance requirements for operators in applications where infrastructure-intensive approaches are impractical.

1.1. Capability Gap

A gap currently exists in the surveillance coverage of national critical infrastructure. For example, the majority of major mass transit systems are not able to reliably collect, store, and protect video surveillance of potential future terrorist attacks throughout their transit networks. While specific technical capabilities exist, coverage is limited in many localities due to high costs and infrastructure requirements of existing systems. Except in select localities (e.g., Chicago), most cities have video surveillance capabilities in a small percentage of mass transit buses and often less in rail applications. This coverage gap directly limits the ability to investigate, pursue, and prosecute terrorists following a potential terrorist act involving noncovered conveyances. Infrastructure-intensive technical approaches present a capability gap for mobile platforms (e.g., buses and trains) where sufficient transmission bandwidth may not be available, is cost prohibitive, and may raise security concerns. Existing surveillance approaches typically require an extensive wired (or wireless) network to support high-bandwidth transmission of data to centralized processing and storage facilities. Centralized networked systems also incur intensive manpower requirements for installation, monitoring, and maintenance. Pursuit of the system described herein will facilitate the closing of the coverage gap in video surveillance coverage by providing a low-cost capability to supplement existing capabilities and coverage or a stand-alone system in the case where no legacy capability exists. The intended end users of the system are the impacted local transit authorities (represented within DHS by Transportation Security Administration—Rail and Surface Transportation), transit and local law enforcement officers, and the federal agencies involved in the forensic investigation of a terrorist attack.

1.2. Overall Mission Area Description

Video surveillance systems are currently used by mass transit operators and associated law enforcement departments for a wide range of missions. Mission applications include support of transit operations, criminal investigation, litigation support, enforcement of passenger regulations, training, and improved safety of passengers and employees due to a deterrent effect. The system identified herein will have the additional capability to protect recorded video surveillance data, without external infrastructure, in the event of a terrorist attack, and to support forensic investigation of the same. The system is expected to provide coverage of areas not currently reached by video surveillance and in some cases to provide supplementary blast-resistant video coverage in areas currently serviced by other systems. In addition to post–terrorist attack forensics, the system is expected to extend coverage of other mission applications including criminal investigation and litigation support to newly covered areas. Due to its decentralized approach, however, the system will not directly support mission applications requiring real-time monitoring of data (e.g., support to transit operations).

1.3. Description of the Proposed System

The proposed system will be a stand-alone fixed video surveillance unit that will produce and maintain a continuous video recording of a designated transit vehicle, infrastructure component, access control point, or other location of interest within its designated field of view. It is expected that multiple such units will be necessary to provide full coverage of individual transit vehicles and other areas of interest. Each unit will record continuously and store data for a specified period of time, after which data will automatically be overwritten as necessary. Following installation, the system will not require user intervention to maintain continued operation. In the event of a terrorist attack or catastrophic event, the unit will protect the recorded data from damage or tampering until retrieval by authorities. Only survival of the video data sufficient for retrieval and playback of the collected video surveillance is expected. The system will also allow for data retrieval by authorized individuals as required for other mission applications. Each BRAVE unit will be a self-contained device that includes a camera, removable data storage, and protective hardening for the data storage. System power may be provided by the installed platform (e.g., bus) or by an included power source. In the case of an external power option, a transformer, as necessary, will be included within the system housing.

1.4. Supporting Analysis

This C-ORD is supported by "Application of Video Surveillance Technology in Public Transit Systems" submitted to DHS S&T through the U.S. Army Natick Soldier Research Development and Engineering Center (NSRDEC) and prepared by the Center for Technology Commercialization. The analysis is further supported by visits to transit authorities in Seattle, WA; Washington, DC; New York, NY; and Chicago, IL, conducted by NSRDEC and DHS S&T representatives in February 2008.

1.5. Mission the Proposed System Will Accomplish

The proposed system will provide a low-cost option for provision of a blast-resistant video surveillance capability to mass transit platforms without such a capability. Once installed, BRAVE will support investigation of terrorist and criminal activities conducted within the visual coverage of the deployed system. The system will serve primarily to visually record all activity within its field of view for a designated period of time. Video data will be recorded continuously during designated operational periods. Video data stored beyond the designated storage duration will be overwritten as necessary to provide storage for more recent video data. In the event of an explosion caused by a terrorist attack, the system will protect the data from blast and other damage and allow recovery of the video data for purposes of forensic investigation and/or prosecution.

1.6. Operational and Support Concept

1.6.1. Concept of Operations BRAVE will be used by local transit authorities and law enforcement officials to supplement video surveillance coverage in areas and vehicles not currently covered by legacy systems. Localities making use of the system will identify areas requiring coverage based upon their local procedures, including identification of specific installation locations. Transit maintenance or contracted personnel will install units in identified locations including connection to locally available power source as applicable. Upon installation, each unit will provide continuous video recording whenever powered. User support and maintenance will be minimal. Retrieval of data will use commercially standard interfaces (e.g., Secure Digital card, or USB connection) to retrieve data. Video will similarly be stored in a commercially standard, nonproprietary format to facilitate easy review of data in a range of commercially available software applications.

1.6.2. Support Concept The design will support easy installation by transit service maintenance or contracted personnel. No special skills except knowledge of the interfacing platform's power system will be required. Maintenance requirements for the system will be minimal. Each unit will include basic self-test mechanisms to indicate proper operation visually (e.g., through the use of LEDs). System design allows for easy replacement of defective unit by a new unit with no need for user-level maintenance. Defective systems will be returned to the manufacturer for disposition. No user-installed spare parts are expected. Memory cards, if used to meet storage requirements, will be compatible with existing commercially available formats.

2. Threat

Public transportation systems continue to be targets of terrorist attacks. Recent attacks including London (2005), Madrid (2004), and elsewhere around the world demonstrate a general persistent terrorist threat to mass transit systems. In particular, transit systems provide a potentially attractive target to terrorists by virtue of their access to large populations with currently less restrictive access controls than airline and other transportation methods.

3. Existing System Shortfalls

Existing video surveillance systems provide a variety of technical capabilities including systems that meet or exceed specific technical capabilities required herein. However, system and supporting infrastructure costs and maintenance requirements for these systems are often high enough that implementation and system coverage has been limited, thereby reducing the system-wide surveillance capability. Existing fixed systems include those placed in stations, in tunnels, on bridges, and at access control points. These systems typically rely on a hardwired infrastructure to transmit data away from the point of interest for storage, processing, and commonly viewing. Onsite backup storage is optional but is not often employed. In cases where onsite backup is employed currently, the level of protection in the event of a terrorist attack is largely unknown.

4. Capabilities Required

4.1. Operational Performance Parameters (T: Threshold / O: Objective)

4.1.1. Form Factor   Each BRAVE unit will occupy a volume of less than 3" by 3" by 2" (T) / 2" x 2" x 1.5" (O).

4.1.2. Resolution   The system will record and store color video data at a resolution of at least 1CIF (T) / 4 CIF (O).

4.1.3. Frame Rate   Video data recorded and stored by BRAVE will have a frame rate of at least 7.5 FPS (T) / 30 FPS (O). The frame rate will be adjustable at time of installation (O).

4.1.4. Field of View/Focal Length   The system will be capable of recording video at focal lengths ranging from 3 to 50 ft. Focal length will be set at installation (T) / adjust automatically (O).

4.1.5. Data Format   Video data will be stored in a format in a manner suitable to meet evidentiary requirements (T/O). Recorded data will include a calibrated time stamp that can be used during data retrieval and review (T/O). The system will produce a message digest or "digital fingerprint" of recorded data using cryptographic hash function MD5 or SHA-1 (T/O) to assist in preserving the evidentiary status of the recorded data. Stored videos shall be accessible with standard commercial and open-source video playback software (O).

4.1.6. Tamper Resistance BRAVE units will be constructed to prevent unauthorized access to stored data, device power, and device activation mechanism (T/O).

4.1.7. Power Source BRAVE units will be compatible with 48V DC, 120 AC, and 12V DC power sources and include any necessary transformer with the system (T). Device will provide self-contained power capability (e.g., solar cells) (O).

4.1.8. Environmental BRAVE will demonstrate capability to perform within the full range of environmental conditions without degraded performance. System will meet all environmental requirements specified in IEEE 1478 Standard for Environmental Conditions for Transit Rail Car Electronic Equipment for the E3 (Vehicle Exterior, Body Mounted) and E4 (Vehicle Interior, Non-Conditioned) environments. Temperature: In addition to the requirements of IEEE 1478, the system will experience no degraded performance due to rapid changes in temperature of 20°C. Dust: Blowing sand and dust testing will include testing with steel sand and dust particulates. EMI/EMC: System performance will not be degraded due to electromagnetic interference from external devices.

4.1.9 Blast Survivability The BRAVE memory component will demonstrate a capability for stored data to survive a blast for the purposes of reading video imagery. Parameters for this section will be provided separately.

4.2. Key Performance Parameters (KPPs)

4.2.1. Cost Individual unit cost will not exceed $200 (T) / $100 (O) based on production quantities of 100,000 or more. Costs of support equipment and software to operate and access data on individual surveillance units will not exceed $1,000 (T) / $0 (O) per 100 units in use.

4.2.2. Storage Capacity Data storage will be sufficient for data storage of continuous video recording for a period of 7 days (T) / 14 days (O).

4.3 System Performance

4.3.1 Mission Scenarios BRAVE units will be located on mass transit vehicles or infrastructure (e.g., tunnels and bridges). Units will be installed to continuously monitor a designated area with minimal human intervention required until data retrieval or unit replacement is required. BRAVE will operate in a range of environmental conditions including large temperature swings, humidity, rainfall, vibration/shock, dust, and EMI/EMC considerations. Units will also be capable of recording in low light conditions. In the event of a terrorist attack, when catastrophic data retrieval is required, video storage will be recovered and transferred from the potentially damaged housing of the units of interest. Recorded video data will be reviewed and analyzed as part of the forensic investigation as appropriate. In noncatastrophic data retrieval scenarios, such as data use in a criminal investigation or forensic investigation from a unit not damaged by the attack, the unit housing and electronics will be reused. In these cases, the operator will remove the current memory card, taking care to document the proper chain of evidence, and replace it with a new unused memory card. Periodic visual checks of the system's self-diagnostic indicator will be conducted by operators or maintenance personnel. Minimal training of personnel is required to ensure proper understanding of system self-diagnostic indicators.

4.3.2 Interoperability   Recorded data will be compatible with existing commercial and open-source file formats including MPEG2, MPEG4, or H264 (T/O). Stored videos shall be accessible with standard commercial and open-source video playback software (O).

4.3.3 Human Interface Requirements   Once installed, direct human interface with the system will not be required except for data retrieval. Installation will require basic mechanical skills to attach and position the unit. Knowledge of the interfacing power system will also be required. Data access and retrieval will require basic to intermediate computer skills and familiarity with using memory cards or USB storage mediums (dependent of final design). Human interface is also required to periodically check maintenance self-check indicators. If needed, unit replacement will require similar skills to installation.

4.3.4 Logistics and Readiness   The system is required to be operational for long periods of continuous operation without interruption. No user-level maintenance or spare part replacement is required. Replacement units and memory cards should be available in case replacement is required. Mean Time Between Failure (MTBF): 40,000 hours (T) 80,000 hours (O).

5. System Support

5.1 Maintenance

Each BRAVE unit will have the capability to visually indicate to a minimally trained individual that it is no longer functioning and needs repairs or replacement. User-level maintenance shall be limited to monitoring of self-diagnostic indicator and installation, removal, and replacement of the system. All other maintenance will be vendor provided as necessary.

5.2 Supply

No special tools or support equipment are required for installation or replacement. Manuals will be provided to the operator by the vendor and will include installation procedures, information on diagnostic indicators of unit self-test, and replacement procedures. Manual will also provide information on routine and catastrophic (i.e., after a terrorist attack) data retrieval.

5.3 Support Equipment

All self-test diagnostic tests will be contained within the unit. No external support equipment will be required to maintain and operate the unit. Suitable computer equipment will be required to review data retrieved from the system. Specific hardware and software requirements will depend on the level of analysis to be conducted and the quantity of video data to be analyzed.

5.4 Training

Users will be instructed on the installation and replacement of units; interpretation of self-test diagnostic indicators; and data retrieval procedures by manuals and written procedures supplied by the unit manufacturer.

5.5 Transportation and Facilities

Once installed, individual units will remain in place until removed or replaced. Transportation of individual units for installation or replacement is expected to be well within individual carriage limitations and will be dependent on the local installation point. Transportation of retrieved digital media will require no special technical capability but should be conducted consistent with applicable procedures to preserve chain of custody when data retrieval is conducted for use in legal proceedings (e.g., criminal prosecution or civil litigation). Facilities and suitable computer equipment will be required to review data retrieved from the system. Facility sophistication and size will depend on the level of analysis to be conducted and the quantity of video data to be analyzed.

6. Force Structure

Video surveillance cameras are typically positioned on vehicles to cover each entrance and the length of the vehicle in each direction. Cameras can also be positioned to show vehicle exteriors. Each standard bus is expected to make use of a minimum of 4 units. Longer articulated buses will use 7 or more units, while train cars can make use of 6 or more units. Based on current public transportation fleet size and current video surveillance usage rates, approximately 200,000–300,000 units would be required to provide the discussed video surveillance capability to mass transit vehicles without a current video surveillance capability. Additional systems will be required within each locality based upon the demonstrated reliability rate to ensure that replacement systems are on hand for quick replacement of faulty units. An additional quantity of the appropriate removable memory cards will be necessary as well, to ensure availability of replacement cards when data is removed for forensic and other purposes. Additional systems may be required for station, infrastructure, and other surveillance purposes.

7. Schedule

Demonstration of an initial operational capability is required within 4 (T) / 3 (O) months. For the purpose of this effort, initial operational capability is defined as installation and field demonstration of 100 fully operational units in an identified major city transit system.

8. System Affordability

Individual unit cost will not exceed $200 (T) / $100 (O), based on production quantities of 100,000 or more. Costs of support equipment and software to operate and access data on individual surveillance units will not exceed $1,000 (T) / $0 (O) per 100 units in use.

NOTE

1. See T. Cellucci, "Opportunities for the Private Sector," 2008, 43pp. Available online at www.dhs.gov/xres/programs/gc_1211996620526.shtm; and R. Margetta, "S&T Official Working to Move Product Development Out of DHS, Into Private Sector," *Congressional Quarterly Homeland Security*, June 27, 2008.

Chapter 12

FutureTECH in Action

Due to the popularity of the SECURE Program introduced by the recently formed Commercialization Office, the U.S. Department of Homeland Security (DHS) Science and Technology (S&T) Directorate has now introduced a "sister program" called FutureTECH. The SECURE Program leverages the experience and resources of the private sector to develop fully deployable (i.e., technology readiness level nine, [TRL-9]) products and/or services based on DHS-generated and vetted detailed commercialization-based operational requirements documents (C-ORDs) and a conservative estimate of the potential available market (represented by DHS operating components and ancillary markets comprised of first responders, critical infrastructure/key resources [CIKR] owners/operators and other DHS stakeholders). The FutureTECH Program, on the other hand, is reserved for those critical research/innovation focus areas that could be inserted eventually into DHS acquisition or commercialization programs when development reaches TRL-6 based on metrics and milestones more specific than those of a broad technology need statement alone, yet not as specific as a detailed C-ORD. FutureTECH uses what is referred to as a 5W template—where W stands for "Who," "What," "Where," "Why," and "When."

FutureTECH identifies and focuses on the future needs of the department, as fully deployable technologies and capabilities, in many cases, are not readily available in the private sector or federal government space. While the SECURE Program is valuable to all DHS operating components, organizational elements, and DHS stakeholders, FutureTECH is intended for DHS S&T use only, particularly in the fields related to research and innovation.

DHS S&T BASIC RESEARCH,
INNOVATION, AND TRANSITION

DHS S&T's basic research activities create fundamental knowledge for enhancing homeland security, normally at a time frame exceeding eight years. These efforts emphasize (but are not limited to) university fundamental research and governmental lab discovery and invention. Basic research programs are executed in the Directorate's divisions, facilitated by the Office of National Laboratories and the Office of University Programs and are closely coordinated with other government agencies.

Typically, the basic research efforts at S&T are motivated by one or more of the following:

1. The research addresses an important DHS issue without a viable near-term solution.
2. The research pursues a creative solution that addresses a unique, long-term DHS need that is not addressed elsewhere.
3. The research exploits new scientific breakthroughs (e.g., from universities, laboratories, or industry) that could strengthen homeland security.

The research leads in S&T's divisions developed basic research focus areas that represent the technological areas in which S&T seeks to create and/or exploit new scientific breakthroughs. These focus areas, generated with input from the research community and vetted through S&T's Research Council, will help guide the direction of the S&T basic research thrust, within resource constraints, to provide long-term science and technology advances for the benefit of homeland security.

DHS S&T's innovation activities focus on homeland security research and development (R&D) that could lead to significant technology breakthroughs that could greatly enhance DHS operations and "support basic and applied homeland security research to promote revolutionary changes in technologies that would promote homeland security; advance the development, testing and evaluation, and deployment of critical homeland security technologies; and accelerate the prototyping and deployment of technologies that would address homeland security vulnerabilities."

Personnel work closely with the undersecretary for science and technology, S&T divisions, DHS components, industry, academia, and other government organizations to determine topic areas for projects. Table 12.1 shows a current delineation of innovation project areas.

The DHS S&T transition activities focus on the identification, evaluation, and management of the near-term technology portfolio to develop and deliver advanced capabilities to DHS operating components, stakeholders, and end users for homeland security improvements. The Capstone Integrated Product Team (IPT) process is the framework that determines that developed capabilities meet operational needs, analyzes gaps in strategic needs and capabilities, determines operational requirements, and develops programs and projects to close capability gaps and expand mission competencies. This process is a DHS customer-led forum through which the identification of functional capability gaps and the prioritization of these gaps across the department are formalized. The IPTs oversee the research and development efforts of DHS S&T and enable the proper allocation of resources to the highest priority needs established by the DHS operating components and first responders.

FutureTECH PROGRAM DETAILS

Scope

This program enables DHS S&T to efficiently and cost-effectively leverage the resources, skills, experience, and productivity of the private sector and other non-DHS entities to develop technologies/capabilities in alignment with research/innovation focus areas obtained from DHS S&T (see above for examples). These technologies/capabilities, when successfully developed, may ultimately be used by DHS, the first responder community, critical infrastructure/key resources (CIKR) owners/operators, and other DHS stakeholders. In essence, FutureTECH provides a "window of visibility" or "preview" of research/innovation focus areas that DHS and its stakeholders believe are essential in future products and services where detailed C-ORDs cannot be fully developed at this time. The program also provides insight into areas where Independent Research and Development (IRAD) monies could be spent by firms possessing funding to address DHS research/innovation focus areas.

Analogous to the popular SECURE Program, FutureTECH is another innovative private-public partnership and outreach program that outlines focus areas for which current technology only exists at earlier stages on the technology readiness scale (TRL 1–6). Technologies developed in alignment to stated focus areas could lead to cost-effective and efficient product development (TRL 7–9) when detailed requirements contained in C-ORDs are available. Like the SECURE Program, DHS will provide information to the public in an open and free way. The private sector and

Table 12.1. Description of Innovation Project Areas Categorized as High Impact Technology Solutions (HITS) and High Innovative Prototypical Solutions (HIPS) Projects.

High Impact Technology Solutions (HITS) Projects	
Cell-All Ubiquitous Chem/Bio Detect	Examines proofs-of-concept for integrating miniaturized chemical and biological agent detectors into personal devices, such as cellular telephones, in order to create a widely distributed network for detection, classification, and notification in the event of a chemical release, and with possible extensions to detect chemical components of some biological agents. Individual device owners on the network would control the detection and transmission of the data, sensor timing, and global positioning satellite (GPS) location information. The goals of this project include significant improvement to chemical and biological detectors' integration, size, costs, power, maintenance, durability, and response characteristics.
Wide Areas Surveillance	Focuses on surveillance and tracking in densely populated infrastructure settings and urban landscapes (such as airports, train stations, city streets, and squares) to protect the nation's highest priority infrastructure. In FY 2008, the project constructed an array of multiple high-resolution cameras that are digitally integrated into a single view with an overall resolution of 100 megapixels. The system provides high-resolution imagery and allows multiple operators to simultaneously view and manipulate (e.g., zoom and scan) regions of the scene in high-resolution detail while maintaining a full 360-degree field of view. The system includes automated change detection capabilities, and users can rapidly scan video images for forensic analysis. In FY 2009, the project planed to conduct a demonstration to evaluate the effectiveness of the system in a densely populated environment and also significantly advance the system hardware to more than double the current resolution and ultimately improve system cost-effectiveness.
Resilient Tunnel Project	The project focuses on designing an inflatable tunnel plug to protect mass transit tunnels from fires, smoke and flooding. In FY 2008, the project initiated a partnership with the Washington Metropolitan Area Transit Authority (WMATA) and conducted a demonstration in a WMATA subway tunnel in August 2008. The results illustrated that a full-scale plug can be inflated quickly and efficiently in a real-world transit environment and that the plug effectively seals against the tunnel walls. In FY 2009, the project plans to conduct numerical modeling to optimize plug structure and performance; construct new small-scale plugs with stronger materials and optimized geometries; and subject these plugs to pressurized testing in the laboratory to simulate tunnel flooding.
Tunnel Detect Project	Develops detection technologies to locate clandestine underground tunnels that are used for cross-border illegal activities such as smuggling. In FY 2008, the project conducted a series of demonstrations of an electromagnetic gradiometer (radio frequency)

mounted on an unmanned aircraft system, which was planned for further evaluation by Customs and Border Protection (CBP) and Immigration and Customs Enforcement (ICE) in FY 2009. Research and development activities include incorporating other sensors such as a hyper-spectral camera that detects differences in the environmental characteristics (e.g., moisture) at or near the tunnels that are indicators of the presence of a tunnel. The project initiated a parallel effort to prototype and test advanced ground-penetrating radar for tunnel detection. In FY 2009, S&T planned to test and demonstrate an advanced ground-penetrating radar and investigate additional technologies by leveraging Department of Defense (DoD) tunnel-detection efforts for border protection applications.

Homeland Innovative Prototypical Solutions (HIPS) Projects	
Future Attribute Screening Technologies Mobile Module (FASTM2) (formerly Future Attribute Screening Technologies) Project	Develops real-time, mobile screening technologies to automatically and remotely detect behavior indicative of intent to cause harm (identified as malintent) at screening checkpoints. In FY 2008, the project identified potential behavioral (illustrative gestures, gait, blinking, eye-gaze, etc.), physiological (change in heart beat, respiration, thermal, etc.), and paralinguistic cues that are likely indicative of malintent and identified remote sensors capable of detecting the associated physiological signals. The feedback from initial peer review and independent, nationally recognized subject matter experts was positive.
	In FY 2008, the project demonstrated the FAST laboratory module which is a functional test laboratory for the development, integration, and implementation of real-time, mobile screening and future sensing technologies. In FY 2009, the project continued validating and updating the malintent theory, sensors, and the module environment and incorporate the initial elements of data fusion and machine learning to improve screening accuracy. Independent peer review will be an ongoing element of the project to promote objectivity and ensure all aspects of the project are addressed. In FY 2009, the project conducted an operational demonstration of a real-time intent detection capability.
Hurricane & Storm Surge Mitigation Project	Develops methods to better understand and accurately predict the behavior of a hurricane to help better predict its future track and to reduce the intensity and/or duration of a hurricane or storm. The focus will be on understanding the dynamics of storms as they grow from depressions to full hurricanes, and to try to determine if any of the dynamic variables can be used or manipulated against the storm itself in order to prevent further growth in strength. State and local officials will be able to more accurately and quickly determine which areas to evacuate. This project will focus on discovering variables to affect that could reduce the intensity and/or duration of a hurricane or storm before the storm reaches a point of runaway growth in strength. This project, in partnership with the National Oceanic and

(continued)

Atmospheric Administration (NOAA), will apply knowledge gained in the last 25 years (since the last attempt to modify hurricanes) to understand and model the life cycle of a hurricane and identify/evaluate the effects of salt seeding, carbon black aerosol, upper ocean cooling, ion generators and monolayer films. The goal is not to stop hurricanes, which are an important part of the natural cycle, but to mitigate damage to life and property.

Levee Strengthening & Damage Mitigation Project

Develops techniques to rapidly repair breaches. Innovation has been able to work with S&T's Infrastructure and Geophysical Division to demonstrate technology for rapid repair.

In September of FY 2008, the project successfully demonstrated technologies for rapid repair of levee breaches at the United States Department of Agriculture (USDA) facilities in Stillwater, Oklahoma. This proof-of-concept attracted the attention of potential end users and will lead to the development of full-scale systems. In FY 2009, the project further developed the rapid repair prototypes for a full-scale demonstration and developed a concept of operations.

Resilient Electric Grid (REG) Project

Demonstrates Inherently Fault Current Limiting High-Temperature Superconducting (IFCL-HTS) technologies for reliable distribution and protection of electrical power. This technology would save millions to billions of dollars by providing continuous power in the event of a terrorist attack, brownouts, or blackouts, and provide more efficient power distribution in the course of normal day-to-day operations.

In FY 2008, the project conducted proof-of-concept demonstrations of a 3-meter, IFCL-HTS cable. The first demonstration in December 2007 showed that an HTS cable could transmit power with no electrical losses and simultaneously prevent cascading failures under normal conditions (i.e., no current overloads). Subsequently, the February 2008 demonstration was an important Go/No-go decision point because it confirmed that the HTS cable provides significant fault current limiting and also identified potential challenges due to higher than expected Alternating Current (AC) losses in the HTS cable. The project team conducted additional experiments and demonstrations in May 2008 to isolate the causes of the higher than expected AC losses and a third 3-meter cable was tested in August 2008. The results justified going forward with a 25-meter demonstration in FY 2009 at Oak Ridge National Laboratory. The project team successfully demonstrated the fault current limiting capability of the 25-meter test cable in March 2009. The project is planning an in-grid demonstration of the IFCL-HTS cable in the Manhattan grid for evaluation under operational conditions.

Safe Container (SAFECON) Project

Investigates various technologies, including probe systems that detect and identify dangerous cargo and could be mounted on cranes used for on- and off-loading ship-carried containers. SAFECON also looks for sensors and specialized container materials designed to make screening more effective. The project aims to provide the capability to scan containers entering the country while minimizing the impacts to commerce; high reliability, high-throughput detection of weapons of mass destruction (WMD), explosives, contraband, and human cargo; and immediate detection and isolation of suspected threat containers.

In FY 2008, the project completed threat characterization and container characterization studies at the ports of Charleston, South Carolina, and Boston, Massachusetts, to inform decisions on sensor and prototype development. SAFECON also began the development of a remote vapor inspection system using advanced laser techniques to detect and identify threat chemicals and explosives. In FY 2009, the project demonstrated integrated chemical and explosives sensor performance in a laboratory.

In addition to the approach described above for rapid detection while the container is being moved by crane, DHS S&T is also looking at an alternative approach that takes advantage of the long transit time most shipping containers experience as they transit from their port of origin to the United States. This part of the SAFECON program is called Time Recorded Ubiquitous Sensor Technology (TRUST). It would allow detection of Chemical, Biological, Radiological, Nuclear, Explosive, and Personnel (CBRNE/P) threats within any container while in its port of embarkation or in transit, thus enabling authorities to route a suspect container to a safe location for special handling and an entry determination prior to entering a U.S. port.

Scalable Common Operational Picture Experiment (SCOPE) Project

Leverages an existing effort by DOD. The DOD effort, called the Joint Concept Technology Demonstration for Global Observer, is developing a high-altitude, long-endurance unmanned aircraft system (GO UAS). This aircraft-mounted system will enable homeland security personnel at the federal, state, and local levels to collectively see what is happening during an event and potentially provide a communication platform for regions where infrastructure has been destroyed. This will allow responders to quickly understand the extent of a natural disaster or terrorist attack, enable communications and provide sufficient time to make critical decisions and mount a coordinated response. Today, no such capability exists.

In FY 2008, the project developed and integrated modular sensor and communication payloads and began the formal GO Critical Design Review (CDR). In early FY 2009, the project successfully completed CDR and will conduct a series of operational utility assessments that will serve as a proof-of-concept for DHS operational security needs.

Rapid Liquid Component

Uses ultra-low-field Magnetic Resonance Imaging (MRI) technology to screen baggage for liquid explosives. To mitigate the liquid

(continued)

**Detector
(MagViz) Project**

explosives threat, airline passengers currently must pack liquids or gels (such as certain toiletries and medicines) in containers that are 3 ounces or smaller. Those containers must be placed in a 1-quart-sized, clear plastic, zip-top bag; and only 1-bag-per-traveller is allowed. These are known as "3-1-1 bags," which undergo an X-ray inspection and possibly secondary screening using multiple methods, such as visual inspection. The goal of MagViz is to eliminate the 3-1-1 rule and allow passengers to place liquids in their carry-on baggage. MagViz will scan and identify individual materials that may be packaged together or separately as they go through the scanning process and evaluate them against a database that will differentiate between those items considered safe for carrying onto an aircraft (e.g., benign liquids and gels like mouthwash, toothpaste, etc.) and harmful ones. The intent is for the detection of liquids in baggage to be noncontact and to occur at the same rate as current X-ray machines, thus not hindering passenger throughput.

In FY 2008, the project built and demonstrated a 3-1-1 bag-screening prototype in a lab. The August 2008 laboratory demonstration of this system showed that it can recognize and compare a wider range of liquids to a stored database and discriminate between harmful and benign liquids and gels with greater sensitivity and discrimination capability than previous demonstrations by overcoming operational challenges such as the orientation of containers and containers within containers.

In December 2008, the project conducted a full demonstration of the 3-1-1 bag-screening prototype in an airport to assess its ability to detect liquid explosives within baggage in an operational setting. This public demonstration successfully showed that the prototype could distinguish between liquids in an operational environment overcoming challenges that could affect its sensitivity. Also in FY 2009, the project will build an exhaustive database of liquids through magnetic characterization and further address clutter in the operational environment; evaluate the capability of MagViz to detect dangerous solids; and demonstrate the capability of its research prototype to inspect at a depth of 20 cm. In FY 2010, the project plans to continue building the magnetic characterization database of liquids and demonstrate the capability of MagViz to seamlessly screen segregated liquids (without the 3-1-1 bag constraint) in an operational environment and subsequently evaluate termination or transition options.

other non-DHS entities may use their own resources (including IRAD) to develop technologies/capabilities that will be of potential benefit to the DHS mission. Like the SECURE Program, DHS may enter into a simple CRADA (Cooperative Research and Development Agreement) document with an organization that shows it has the ability to deliver technology aligned with the research/innovation focus area sought after by DHS.

To state it simply, the SECURE Program focuses on product/service development to create products and services to protect our nation in the shorter term, while FutureTECH focuses on science and technology development related to critical research/innovation focus areas. Like all of the Commercialization Office's programs, all parties "win" in the FutureTECH Program—the private sector and other non-DHS entities by receiving valuable insight into future research/innovation focus areas needed by DHS and its stakeholders. DHS "wins" because it will leverage the valuable skills, experience, and resources of the private sector and others to expedite efficient and cost-effective technology development; the non-DHS entities "win" because they receive valuable information useful for their own strategic plans; and most importantly, all American taxpayers "win" because this innovative partnership yields valuable technologies/capabilities aligned with research/innovation focus areas developed in a more cost-effective and efficient way saving taxpayer money.

Overall Process

Figure 12.1 is a graphical representation of the overall outreach process the Commercialization Office continues to implement to stimulate and engage the private sector and other non-DHS entities to use their resources to rapidly develop technology aligned with research/innovation focus areas that can yield significant benefits for DHS S&T with a speed-of-execution not typically observed in the public sector.

OUTREACH TO THE PRIVATE SECTOR

Program Process

DHS S&T provides this FutureTECH vehicle by which the private sector and other non-DHS entities can identify or develop technology aligned with research/innovation focus areas ranging from TRL-1 through TRL-6 (not fully developed TRL-9 products and/or services) based on DHS S&T's insight and knowledge mainly through its research and innovation portfolios/areas. This approach enables DHS S&T to collaborate on the development of technology aligned with several research/ innovation focus areas in an open and free way. The private sector and other non-DHS entities receive information on what new technologies will be required over the horizon to protect our nation, removing much of the "guess work" normally associated with predicting future needs.

Contact with the Private Sector

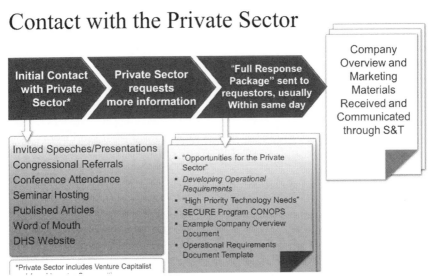

Figure 12.1. Overview of S&T Directorate private sector outreach process.

As with the popular SECURE Program, DHS will review third-party, recognized test and evaluation data to ensure that all milestones/objectives of an executed CRADA agreement are met and DHS will place a given research/innovation focus area solution developed by an entity on the FutureTECH website demonstrating that the research/innovation focus area has met DHS's broadly defined requirements contained in a 5W template, detailed below (in contrast to the SECURE Program where products or services must demonstrate compliance to detailed operational requirements contained in a C-ORD).

Expression of Interest

In the adherence to fairness of opportunity, and in order to capitalize on the free-market system, DHS S&T intends to publish this program and all ancillary requirements documents/information on the DHS website. These materials will be accessible by *all*. Given this information, the private sector and other non-DHS entities may contact DHS S&T if they are interested in developing or enhancing their technology within a research/innovation focus area in cooperation with DHS S&T. Potential research/innovation focus areas for this program (along with a simple CRADA agreement used in the SECURE Program) are provided on our website. The private sector organization or non-DHS entity must provide DHS S&T with basic, nonproprietary business information, contact information, and demonstrate their potential alignment to widely available DHS S&T research/innovation requirements that are more detailed than what are commonly referred to as technology need statements, yet not as detailed as a well-defined ORD.

Acceptance

In order to be fully considered by DHS S&T for cooperative research/ innovation focus area technology development:

- An entity must demonstrate they either possess technology at TRL-1 or higher (i.e., basic research) or possess the ability to develop a technology aligned with the research/innovation focus area to TRL-6 for later technology insertion into a potential acquisition or commercialization program.
- The private sector and other non-DHS entities must propose a research/innovation focus area technology development effort that has clear and substantial alignment with any published DHS S&T requirements delineated above.

A DHS committee will be established to review the private sector and/ or non-DHS entities' potential alignment to DHS research/innovation focus areas, and monitor the mutually agreed-upon roles and responsibilities of partnership participants. The committee will consider these and other DHS proprietary metrics for determining which opportunities to pursue.

CRADA

The private sector and/or non-DHS entity and DHS S&T could execute a simple, straightforward, and binding CRADA whereby the non-DHS entity details milestones with dates and, in most cases, agrees to bear full and total financial responsibility to develop its technology aligned within the research/innovation focus area to a TRL-6 state. Under the Stevenson-Wydler Act (which is the statutory authority enabling DHS to enter into CRADAs), agencies may not contribute funds under a CRADA; however, they may contribute know-how, expertise, materials, and equipment. It is important to mention that the execution of a CRADA agreement is at the sole discretion of the corresponding DHS S&T program manager. Additionally, a CRADA with DHS S&T will not necessarily lead to any follow-on contract actions or solicitations by DHS or other government agencies. Any solicitations for funding agreements related to technology areas collaborated upon in a CRADA would be subject to full and open competition. DHS S&T will publish on the DHS S&T website the factual finding(s) of any final assessment. DHS S&T has the right to cancel an agreement if the non-DHS entity does not fulfill/achieve its milestones or performance objectives by the mutually agreed-upon dates.

Publication of Results

It is apparent that the private sector and other non-DHS entities highly value DHS S&T's potential assessment of a given technology's recognized third-party test and evaluation (T&E) data. DHS S&T will openly publish summary findings and an acknowledgment of an entity's attainment of performance objectives on the DHS public web portal for review by the DHS operating components, first responder communities, CIKR owners and operators, and other potential users.

FUTURETECH: PUTTING IT TO THE TEST . . .

Let's examine a few 5Ws to see how to use FutureTECH effectively.

Critical Research/Innovation Focus Area Document: Deter and Predict U.S. Department of Homeland Security, Science and Technology (S&T) Directorate

Who?

Identify any DHS component stakeholders that contain or represent potential end users. Also name any Capstone IPT (refer to www.dhs.gov/xres/programs/ gc_1234200779149.shtm and the article entitled "Making It Easier to Work with DHS"), if any, which identified a capability gap related to this research/innovation focus area.

The U.S. Department of Homeland Security (DHS) leads for CIEDs (Counter-Improvised Explosive Devices) are the Office for Bombing Prevention and United States Secret Service (USSS). The corresponding DHS Science and Technology (S&T) Capstone IPT that identified capability gaps related to this focus area is entitled "Counter-IED."

What?

Describe a required technology/capability. Describe how a technology will provide the capabilities and functional improvements needed to address the DHS

need. Do not describe a specific technical solution. Instead, describe a conceptual technology for illustrative purposes. Define typical missions that the proposed technology could be utilized to accomplish.

Today's analytical tools are based largely upon static models and lack a dynamic ontology or associated taxonomy. On the international stage, our adversary's agile and adaptive tactics, techniques, and procedures (TTPs) have succeeded repeatedly against this static approach. A dynamic computational framework that employs a science-based social and behavioral analytical approach is essential to better understanding and anticipating the IED threat.

A robust predictive capability must support the following near real-time capabilities: (1) recognition of radicalization-related indications and warnings through social science–based pattern extraction, analysis, and visualization; (2) prediction of cultural- and adversary-based target and staging areas based upon contiguous United States (CONUS) and outside the contiguous United States (OCONUS) patterns of adversary-specific behaviors and TTP; and (3) prioritization of intelligence, surveillance, and reconnaissance (ISR) assets through formulation and testing of customized hypotheses given particular attack variables.

The capabilities should be flexible and scalable to ensure that the resulting tools and information are usable throughout the IED community of interest including federal, state, local, tribal, and territorial responders and policy makers. These capabilities should integrate privacy protections in all phases of design, development, and deployment.

A computational framework that better reflects the adversary's agile and adaptive behavior is needed. Recognition of radicalization-related indications and warnings through social science-based pattern extraction, analysis, and visualization will require the development of: a data structure that integrates individual, group, and community-level indicators of radicalization and incorporates multiple modeling, simulation, and visualization techniques; validated radicalization models that span the group formation life cycle; and radicalization-related data extraction and content analysis technologies.

Prediction of cultural- and adversary-based target and staging areas adapted from CONUS and OCONUS patterns of adversary-specific behaviors and TTP will require: a data structure that integrates behavioral, demographic, and cultural factors with traditional geospatial and network analysis; validated targeting models (group, culture, and tactic specific); validated staging areas models (group, culture, and tactic specific); and near real-time capability to integrate and analyze emerging geospatial and behavioral data.

Prioritization of ISR assets through customized hypothesis formulation and testing will require: an interactive interface to support hypothesis generation, analysis, and visualization of threat patterns, and to prioritize intelligence, surveillance, and reconnaissance assets; an ability to leverage the near real-time geo-behavioral analytical capability referenced above.

Why?

Describe the analysis and rationale for requiring a new technology/capability. Describe why existing technologies cannot meet current or projected requirements. Describe what new technologies/capabilities are needed to address the gap between current capabilities and required capabilities.

Currently, there is not an effective ability to identify active radicalized individuals or groups, or terrorist support networks within the United States or reliably recognize activities that indicate preparations are underway for an IED attack.

An improved understanding and anticipation of IED threats will enable the United States authorities to predict potential actors, behaviors, targets, and timing more accurately for the purposes of interdiction, prevention, and protection.

DHS must draw on this abundance of information to improve the ability to identify the operational signatures of individuals, groups, or networks and predict potential targets and staging areas consistent with applicable law including those laws relating to privacy and confidentiality of personal data.

To deploy our limited resources most efficiently, we must study the enemy as thoroughly as they have studied us and strive to develop an ability to identify behaviors and TTPs that radicalized individuals/groups and networks might take under various conditions. This requires the development of models that reflect our adversary's behavior, capturing elements from radicalization to acts of terrorism, and including detailed patterns of behavior ranging from group formation through dissolution.

When?

If a technology/capability is intended as a countermeasure to a threat, summarize the threat to be countered and how the technology could be used (i.e., concept of operations). If applicable, provide a schedule/time frame to capture when the technology/capability is needed in order to address the DHS gap.

Worldwide intelligence gathering activities and investigations of IED events have generated volumes of data related to the activities involved in planning for terrorist attacks and to the TTPs used to execute bombings. *Please note that as more details are available, DHS will post updated research/innovation focus area overviews on the FutureTECH website. This is a pre-decisional draft document of the NSTC Subcommittee on Domestic IEDs.*

Where?

Describe the projected threat environment in which the technology/capability may be potentially deployed.

The domestic environment is an open, complex, multicultural setting for which no fundamental baseline description of the society based on sound social and behavioral scientific principles has been established. The applicability of approaches used in foreign settings has not yet been demonstrated within the United States.

Critical Research/Innovation Focus Area Document:
Detection of Homemade Explosives (HMEs)
Counter-Improvised Explosive Devices (CIED)
U.S. Department of Homeland Security, Science and Technology
(S&T) Directorate

Who?

Identify any DHS component stakeholders that contain or represent potential end users. Also name any Capstone IPT (refer to www.dhs.gov/xres/programs/ gc_1234200779149.shtm and the article entitled "Making It Easier to Work with DHS"), if any, which identified a capability gap related to this research/innovation focus area.

The U.S. Department of Homeland Security (DHS) leads for counter-improvised explosive devices (CIEDs) are the Office for Bombing Prevention and United States Secret Service (USSS). The corresponding DHS Science and Technology (S&T) Capstone IPT that identified capability gaps related to this focus area is entitled "Counter-IED."

What?

Describe a required technology/capability. Describe how a technology will provide the capabilities and functional improvements needed to address the DHS need. Do not describe a specific technical solution. Instead, describe a conceptual technology for illustrative purposes. Define typical missions that the proposed technology could be utilized to accomplish.

Sampling and detection methods are needed that are able to screen at a fast rate (nominally <5 seconds) while maintaining a low false-alarm rate (false positives) and a high enough rate of detection (true positives) to deter terrorist use of HMEs.

Ideally, the sampling and detection methods should be usable in various venues with an emphasis on transportation (air) checkpoints (most critical due to the small amount of explosive needed to create catastrophic damage), but also for screening at large crowd venues such as sports events. It would be preferable to have both a fixed and portable version of the equipment with real-time response for screening people and baggage.

The introduction of the technological solution should enable the end user to maintain current tactics, techniques, and procedures without major changes to their current practices. The deliverable sought for this requirement should include the following: (1) underlying science for the sampling and detection of HMEs and their precursors that are applicable under a wide range of environmental conditions at stand-off and screening checkpoints; (2) systems architecture capable of addressing the known HME threats and extendable to new materials and/or classes of HMEs in the future; (3) comprehensive characterization data on the relevant characteristics of vapor and surface contamination from known or expected HMEs to enable development of the sampling and detection methods; and (4) listing of materials and chemical classes the technological solution addresses and could be expanded to in the future.

References

a. HSPD-19: Sections 4b and 5e.
b. National Strategic Plan for U.S. Bomb Squads, December 2007, National Bomb Squad Commanders' Advisory Board, page 19, Section 7.
c. National Research Council, *Containing the Threat from Illegal Bombings: An Integrated National Strategy for Marking, Tagging, Rendering Inert, and Licensing Explosives and Their Precursors*, National Academies Press, 1998.

Why?

Describe the analysis and rationale for requiring a new technology/capability. Describe why existing technologies cannot meet current or projected requirements. Describe what new technologies/capabilities are needed to address the gap between current capabilities and required capabilities.

The terrorist threat facing our nation's critical infrastructure can take many forms including HMEs. In fact, for over twenty years terrorists have used HMEs to target U.S. interests with notable success and devastating consequences. Considering likely events based on available intelligence and past experiences, HMEs will continue to be used by terrorist groups against U.S. interests due primarily to the wide availability of improvised bomb-making materials, the ability to conceal large amounts of explosives, the ease of getting the IED to the target, the proliferation of bomb-making instructions, and the history of success, which increases repetition and imitation.

The diversity of materials that can potentially be used to devise HMEs and their normal presence in streams of commerce make detection of these materials particularly challenging. Improvised explosive devices (IEDs) can be constructed from bottles of liquid medical essentials, flammables, industrial gases, explosives, or reactive/energetic chemicals. The main challenge for finding a solution to the detection problem is that the only common thread for these materials may be their energetic/reactive nature.

While DHS, the Bureau of Alcohol, Tobacco, Firearms and Explosives (ATF), and the Federal Bureau of Investigation (FBI) have agreed on nine explosives chemical precursors as having the largest quantities in unregulated distribution as well as the highest destructive potential, the detection of HME and their precursors cannot be limited to this set.

The detection of the wide range of materials that can be used in constructing HMEs is challenging, and a successful solution may require multiple technologies. The integration of multiple technologies into a system that can give comprehensive coverage against known threats and be adaptable to cover new threats as they emerge will require a strong systems architecture approach from the start.

The term HME has been used to cover a wide range of materials from pure explosive compounds, such as triacetonetriperoxide (TATP), that can be synthesized from readily available articles of commerce to homemade variants of explosives, such as ammonium nitrate (ANFO), that are used in very large commercial blasting operations. The former is a very sensitive material and so ordinarily is not made in large quantities. The latter is relatively insensitive and can be made in very large quantities. In non-transportation applications, the detection of the precursors of the explosives in a way that allows discrimination between legitimate use of those precursors and illegal use to make explosives is extremely challenging.

At this time there is no standoff or remote detection of classes of liquid explosives or flammables for use in screening and portal environments. There is also a need in security and operational law enforcement environments to detect explosives, including HMEs, from a safe standoff distance for a given quantity of explosives.

When?

If a technology/capability is intended as a countermeasure to a threat, summarize the threat to be countered and how the technology could be used (i.e., concept of operations). If applicable, provide a schedule/time frame to capture when the technology/capability is needed in order to address the DHS gap.

The need is immediate with the ability for adaptability to meet potential emerging threats of the future.

Where?

Describe the projected threat environment in which the technology/capability may be potentially deployed.

The solution must provide a capability to detect HMEs and their precursors in a variety of venues and situations. The solution will be utilized at a security checkpoint where inspection of persons is conducted and the envisioned users will be security personnel who are nonscientists so the technology must be adaptable for use by people who have not been technically trained.

The need for HME detection goes far beyond screening in a transportation venue. There is also the need to detect HME precursors and their relative quantities in other environments in such a way as to allow a decision to be made regarding what action should be taken to protect the first responders and others in the vicinity. In particular, transportation (air) checkpoints, but also for screening at large crowd venues.

Critical Research/Innovation Focus Area Document:
Standoff Rapid Detection of Person-Borne Improvised Explosive Devices (PBIEDs)
Counter-Improvised Explosive Devices (CIED)
U.S. Department of Homeland Security, Science and Technology (S&T) Directorate

Who?

Identify any DHS component stakeholders that contain or represent potential end users. Also name any Capstone IPT (refer to www.dhs.gov/xres/programs/ gc_1234200779149.shtm and the article entitled "Making It Easier to Work with DHS"), if any, which identified a capability gap related to this research/innovation focus area.

The U.S. Department of Homeland Security (DHS) leads for CIEDs are the Office for Bombing Prevention and United States Secret Service (USSS). The corresponding DHS Science and Technology (S&T) Capstone IPT that identified capability gaps related to this focus area is entitled "Counter-IED."

What?

Describe a required technology/capability. Describe how a technology will provide the capabilities and functional improvements needed to address the DHS

need. Do not describe a specific technical solution. Instead, describe a conceptual technology for illustrative purposes. Define typical missions that the proposed technology could be utilized to accomplish.

A solution is needed that provides the ability for security personnel to detect PBIEDs at a sufficient distance, to a reasonable degree of certainty, and in sufficient time to allow reasoned decisions to be made and effective actions to be taken to safely deal with the threat posed by that device in a public venue.

The solution must be unobtrusive because if the bomber knows that they are being observed, they are likely to detonate causing as much damage as possible. Ideally, the solution will require no cooperation from the subjects under observation.

When the individual carrying an improvised explosive device (IED) is in a crowd, the solution must be able to detect the device without impeding pedestrian traffic flow.

The solution must have a high probability of detection and low false-alarm rate. False positives—an indication that there is a PBIED when there is not one—are acceptable within limits. False negatives—an indication that there is not a PBIED when there is one—are not.

The solution may provide stationary, portable, or mobile adaptations and/or all three if possible.

The solution must be easy to use, require minimum training, and be cost-effective.

References

a. HSPD-19 Requirement 5(d): Improving Capabilities to Combat Terrorist Use of Explosives within the United States.
b. High Priority Technology Needs, June 2008, Science and Technology Directorate, Department of Homeland Security, page 10, Counter-IED.
c. National Strategic Plan for U.S. Bomb Squads, December 2007, National Bomb Squad Commanders' Advisory Board, page 12, Section 5.1.1; page 19, Section 7.

Why?

Describe the analysis and rationale for requiring a new technology/capability. Describe why existing technologies cannot meet current or projected requirements. Describe what new technologies/capabilities are needed to address the gap between current capabilities and required capabilities.

Countering PBIEDs is a particularly difficult problem in a free and open society such as ours where individuals are free to travel without leave or hindrance, and where the Fourth Amendment to our Constitution guarantees protection from unreasonable searches and seizures. Fourth Amendment rights pose particular challenges in the context of protecting the public from PBIEDs in a public venue where they are most likely to be used.

Portal-based solutions to PBIED detection require proximity to the suspected bomber and the cooperation of the individuals going through the portal thereby impeding traffic flow and causing people to collect in a relatively small area making them potential targets for PBIEDs. Increased range for the detection of PBIEDS either remotely or at standoff distances is desirable to minimize the accumulation of people and to give additional time to react to a detected threat.

The main challenges associated with PBIEDs are the need for detection before the bomber is in a position to carry out his mission and with enough time to allow an effective response once the PBIED is detected. PBIEDs can have a large lethal radius, much more than the fifteen meters nominally assigned to handguns, with instantaneous effect. The problem is further complicated by the fact that PBIEDs are usually concealed, so the detection methodology must be able to cope with clothing or other cover as well as the possibility that the aspect presented to the detector may hide the device or other materials being probed.

Since they can have minimal metal content, PBIEDs are hard to detect with technologies that presume the presence of metallic components and rely on that feature for positive detection.

When?

If a technology/capability is intended as a countermeasure to a threat, summarize the threat to be countered and how the technology could be used (i.e., concept of operations). If applicable, provide a schedule/time frame to capture when the technology/capability is needed in order to address the DHS gap.

Response to a PBIED is a more complex undertaking particularly for domestic law enforcement agencies than dealing with other types of deadly force situations such as those involving handguns. The PBIED is ordinarily concealed under clothing/other cover and may not be exposed before the device is detonated. Whatever approach is taken to the identification of a PBIED and subsequent incapacitation of the bomber must have a degree of certainty that is legally sufficient to justify the use of whatever means of incapacitation is employed up to and including deadly force.

Where?

Describe the projected threat environment in which the technology/capability may be potentially deployed.

PBIEDs are terror weapons that are typically employed in venues where large concentrations of individuals congregate such as at major sporting events, airports, and/or shopping malls. The presence of a crowd makes the detection problem more difficult due to clutter and possible interferences.

Many of the venues in which detection of PBIEDs is conducted are outdoors and do not have controls over environmental conditions (temperature, humidity, precipitation, dust, etc.). Any proposed solution must be able to detect PBIEDs that have minimal metal content under a variety of clothing, in all weather, day or night, outdoors, and that may contain a variety of different types of explosives.

Critical Research/Innovation Focus Area Document: Vehicle-Borne Improvised Explosive Devices (VBIED) Detection Counter-Improvised Explosive Devices (CIED) U.S. Department of Homeland Security, Science and Technology (S&T) Directorate

Who?

Identify any DHS component stakeholders that contain or represent potential end users. Also name any Capstone IPT (refer to www.dhs.gov/xres/programs/ gc_1234200779149.shtm and the article entitled "Making It Easier to Work with DHS"), if any, which identified a capability gap related to this research/innovation focus area.

The U.S. Department of Homeland Security (DHS) leads for CIEDs are the Office for Bombing Prevention and United States Secret Service (USSS). The corresponding DHS Science and Technology (S&T) Capstone IPT that identified capability gaps related to this focus area is entitled "Counter-IED."

What?

Describe a required technology/capability. Describe how a technology will provide the capabilities and functional improvements needed to address the DHS need. Do not describe a specific technical solution. Instead, describe a conceptual technology for illustrative purposes. Define typical missions that the proposed technology could be utilized to accomplish.

The problem of VBIED detection can be split into two operational categories: (1) checkpoint screening applications wherein the detection system occupies a fixed location and observes all vehicles passing through the checkpoint for evidence of the presence of a VBIED; and (2) mobile or portable applications that may be needed to determine from a distance whether or not a suspicious vehicle is a VBIED. The applicable technologies for these two categories may be the same or different, but the implementation will differ based on operational considerations.

The desired VBIED detection solution:

- Must provide rapid, noninvasive, standoff explosives detection capabilities across the threat spectrum, in a noisy environment, in sufficient time (minutes if not seconds) for effective action to be taken to neutralize the threat at a sufficient distance to place the operator and target outside of the hazard zone for that category of device. Optimally, it also will identify the location of the explosives within the vehicle.
- For mobile applications, the solution should be compact enough to be transported on a bomb squad response vehicle or trailer, require minimal effort to set up and operate, and have a small footprint. Ideally, it would be handheld or at least small and light enough to be deployed by a robot or carried and set up by an individual wearing a bomb suit.
- Should require minimal training to operate and maintain.
- Should be able to quickly screen suspect vehicles without having to scan each side of the vehicle separately.
- Must be able to quickly adjust screening capabilities to accommodate any size vehicle.
- Must not be affected by: the physical condition of the vehicle; emissions that are given off from the subject vehicle, or any other vehicles in the vicinity; elements such as water, salt, dirt, sand, and other grime that is commonly found on vehicles. It must be able to operate in all environments and weather conditions.
- Must not pose an unacceptable safety risk to the operator, bystanders, or occupants of the vehicle being surveyed. Safety considerations both with regard to operation and disposal of nuclear materials would seem to make nuclear-based solutions unsuitable for use by state and local agencies. Must be cost-effective. Science and technology (S&T) will support the development and testing of VBIED explosives detection solutions to standards that meet the minimum requirements of end users.

Among the key contributions that may be provided by S&T are:

- Development of concepts for rapid and nonintrusive imaging of the contents of a vehicle
- Approaches to standoff detection of improvised explosive devices (IED) components through electromagnetic signatures or other characteristics of the initiation system

- Development of methods of access that are minimally disruptive and have a low probability of initiating an IED accidentally
- Standoff methods of detecting explosives residues deposited on the vehicle
- Characterization of the likely distribution and quantity of explosives residues on vehicles bearing IEDs

References

a. HSPD-19 Requirement 5(d): Improving Capabilities to Combat Terrorist Use of Explosives within the United States.
b. High Priority Technology Needs, June 2008, Science and Technology Directorate, Department of Homeland Security, page 10, Counter-IED.
c. National Strategic Plan for U.S. Bomb Squads, December 2007, National Bomb Squad Commanders' Advisory Board, page 12, Section 5.1.2.; page 19, Section 7.

Why?

Describe the analysis and rationale for requiring a new technology/capability. Describe why existing technologies cannot meet current or projected requirements. Describe what new technologies/capabilities are needed to address the gap between current capabilities and required capabilities.

All existing solutions to remotely confirm the presence of a VBIED require proximity. No known existing solutions provide the ability to detect a VBIED with any reasonable degree of assurance at a sufficient distance and in sufficient time to allow actions to be taken to safely deal with the threat posed by that device. A sufficient distance depends on the size and nature of the explosive device(s) carried in the vehicle, but can safely be assumed to be on the order of 100s of meters.

Bomb squads rely on visual confirmation with either a bomb technician or preferably a robot in close proximity to a vehicle. Confirmation will often require punching a hole in the vehicle and inserting a probe risking premature detonation and placing the bomb technician in great danger.

There are numerous challenges associated with detecting VBIEDs. One challenge is that there is not a standard type of vehicle associated with VBIEDs. Thus any proposed solution must be applicable to any of the types of vehicles likely to be encountered where the detection system is deployed. Vehicle selection usually depends on several factors: ability of the vehicle to blend in with the normal traffic at the target; vehicle availability; and the security surrounding the intended target.

For instance, "hardened" facilities with good physical security measures (including barriers to ensure significant standoff distances) may require the terrorist to use trucks with large, enclosed cargo areas. A vehicle of this size provides increased explosives capacities capable of generating damaging air blast effects over a large distance.

Secondly, there are not standard explosives associated with VBIEDs. If the proposed solution focuses on detection of the explosives rather than device components (e.g., wires, batteries, and other electronic components), then the explosives detection technologies must be able to detect a spectrum of threats including homemade explosives (HMEs). Additionally, these technologies must possess standoff detection capabilities in a fast-paced environment with dynamic backgrounds and must be able to achieve low false-alarm rates. Furthermore, detection systems cannot be static. They must include the capability to easily upgrade system algorithms to respond to new explosives threats and background conditions as well as threats actively attempting to defeat the system and security measures.

Other challenges in detecting VBIEDs with explosive detection technologies:

1. The reduction of false-alarm rates while maintaining detection capability is central to a solution for this need. Insufficient signal-to-noise on the detector and interference with detection capabilities from frequently carried commodities cause high false-alarm rates and have the capability to obscure explosive threats. High false-alarm rates can result in operators clearing or ignoring alarms and have the potential to cause major delays to ground transportation.
2. Explosives with low vapor pressures may be particularly difficult to detect depending on the basis of the detection technology.
3. Vehicle checkpoint throughput rates are low and detection technologies are not able to rapidly screen vehicles of various sizes (ranging from cars to trucks).
4. There are difficulties in penetrating various materials/commodities to screen concealment areas in vehicles.
5. Depending upon the technology, passengers may not be able to stay inside the vehicle while it is being screened because of safety concerns. Furthermore, exclusion areas are required for equipment operators, vehicle occupants, and the general public; this requires a large operational footprint.
6. Detection technologies tend to be expensive to purchase, operate, and maintain. X-ray imaging systems are much less susceptible to false alarms than explosive detection technologies, but share many of their other limitations including safety and high cost. They also tend to be large and cumbersome.

When?

If a technology/capability is intended as a countermeasure to a threat, summarize the threat to be countered and how the technology could be used (i.e., concept of operations). If applicable, provide a schedule/time frame to capture when the technology/capability is needed in order to address the DHS gap.

Over the last two decades, terrorists have used VBIED tactics (sometimes in sophisticated simultaneous attacks) to target global suppliers of critical resources and U.S. interests around the world. This tactic has impacted our government's ability to protect its citizens and workers of host nations and provide vital services, and it has created the potential for using system-disruption tactics as a method of strategic warfare. Gauging by the number of casualties and amount of property damage, VBIEDs have been the most successful means of terrorist attack both domestically and internationally, except for the September 11, 2001, attacks. Available intelligence based on global events and terrorist trends and past experiences, such as the bombing of the Murrah Federal Building, suggests that terrorist networks will most likely use VBIED tactics to attack our homeland. Factors contributing to the popularity of VBIEDs among terrorists are the wide availability of materials used to make IEDs; the ability to conceal large amounts of explosives; the ease of getting the vehicle to the target; the proliferation of bomb-making instructions; and a history of extensive experience and success, which increases repetition and imitation.

Where?

Describe the projected threat environment in which the technology/capability may be potentially deployed.

The solution must be able to operate in all environments and weather conditions.

Critical Research/Innovation Focus Area Document: Improvised Explosive Device (IED) Access and Defeat Counter-Improvised Explosive Devices (CIED) U.S. Department of Homeland Security, Science and Technology (S&T) Directorate

Who?

Identify any DHS component stakeholders that contain or represent potential end users. Also name any Capstone IPT (refer to www.dhs.gov/xres/programs/ gc_1234200779149.shtm and the article entitled "Making It Easier to Work with DHS"), if any, which identified a capability gap related to this research/innovation focus area.

The U.S. Department of Homeland Security (DHS) leads for CIEDs are the Office for Bombing Prevention and United States Secret Service (USSS). The corresponding DHS Science and Technology (S&T) Capstone IPT that identified capability gaps related to this focus area is entitled "Counter-IED."

What

Describe a required technology/capability. Describe how a technology will provide the capabilities and functional improvements needed to address the DHS need. Do not describe a specific technical solution. Instead, describe a conceptual technology for illustrative purposes. Define typical missions that the proposed technology could be utilized to accomplish.

The preservation of human life is paramount in conducting improvised explosive device (IED) defeat operations. To the greatest extent possible, IED access and render-safe procedures are performed remotely in order to reduce risk of harm to personnel. In most instances, this is accomplished through the use of robotic platforms which are controlled by either radio or fiber-optic cables. However, the use of non-radio-frequency (RF) methods of remote control for robots and other explosive ordnance disposal (EOD) tools is required to address the remote-control improvised explosive device (RCIED) threat.

Due to the potential for creation of an infinite number and variety of IEDs, bomb technicians require a wide range of tools in order to be prepared for all possible scenarios. These tools range from simple hand tools to radiographic equipment and in some cases disruption charges that weigh hundreds of pounds when assembled. Therefore, in addition to remotely operated tools, IED defeat operators need the ability to quickly and easily transport tools, equipment, and the technician themselves to the incident site and subsequently down range. This is especially true for larger tools such as those used for vehicle-borne improvised explosive devices (VBIEDs).

Every IED defeat operation carries some risk of a high-order detonation, but proper training of bomb disposal personnel helps mitigate this potential. However, training alone may not ensure that IED defeat operators are able to quickly and easily select the most appropriate tool to render safe a given device depending on the sophistication of the device, the complexity of the tool, and the experience level of the technician. Because of this, access and defeat tools should be sufficiently characterized to allow operators to select the appropriate tool based on the device's construction and its placement.

Science and technology can contribute to the problem of access and defeat of IEDs in a number of areas by developing:

1. Approaches to access the device that are minimally disruptive and hence unlikely to cause unintended initiation of the IED.
2. Approaches to protecting operators who must approach the IED to do manual defeat.
3. Methods of mitigating blast when defeat must be done in a location where collateral damage must be minimized (e.g., in an urban setting).
4. Tools that can function in the presence of and interoperable with electronic countermeasures (ECM) equipment.
5. Defeat techniques that do not require substantial amounts of explosive (which carries with it a hazard of its own) or water (which may not be readily available in large quantities at the site).

References

a. HSPD-19 4 (b, c, d), 9; HSPD-19 I-Plan (Draft) Task Ref: 3.2.1, 3.2.2, 3.2.3, 3.2.4, 3.2.5.
b. National Guidelines for Bomb Technicians (Revised 4/06).
c. National Strategy for U.S. Bomb Squads (December 2007) page 19, Section 7.
d. FBI Special Technicians Bulletin 2007-3: Vehicle-Borne Improvised Explosive Device Response Bomb Squad Readiness.
e. Bomb Squad Response to Suicide Bombers and Vehicle-Borne Improvised Explosive Devices: Categories of Situations and Strategies for Each Category.

Why?

Describe the analysis and rationale for requiring a new technology/capability. Describe why existing technologies cannot meet current or projected requirements. Describe what new technologies/capabilities are needed to address the gap between current capabilities and required capabilities.

IED design is unpredictable, and IED defeat operations do not follow rigid courses of action. Today's devices and those developed by future bomb makers will likely contain not only a high explosive charge and improvised initiator, but a power source and activation mechanism that reflects state-of-the-art technology. However, as newer and more technologically advanced devices emerge, the simple device consisting of readily obtainable low explosive or pyrotechnic materials and a rudimentary firing mechanism will remain a deadly variant in the bomber's arsenal. Therefore response technologies must address the entire spectrum of possible threats, not just the latest devices design and employment strategy.

Bomb technicians and other IED defeat operators must penetrate the barrier materials or structures surrounding or containing the item of primary concern (gain access to), as well as the contents and components of suspect packages in order to decide upon the selection of appropriate tools to disrupt or disable the device without causing the device to function as designed.

Gaining access to critical components and materials is an integral part of the render-safe procedure. This requires that IED defeat operators receive standardized training and equipment in order to access and perform render-safe procedures on all types of IEDs, including VBIEDs and RCIEDs.

When?

If a technology/capability is intended as a countermeasure to a threat, summarize the threat to be countered and how the technology could be used (i.e., concept of operations). If applicable, provide a schedule/time frame to capture when the technology/capability is needed in order to address the DHS gap.

The range of IEDs that may be encountered is very broad from tens of pounds of explosive that might be found in a leave-behind IED to thousands of pounds that might be present in a VBIED. The energetic materials used in the devices also range in sensitivity from fairly insensitive (e.g., ammonium nitrate [ANFO]) to extremely sensitive (e.g., acetone peroxide [TATP]). Approaches to defeating one of these materials might initiate the other. A variety of tools applicable to the range of IEDs is needed.

Where?

Describe the projected threat environment in which the technology/capability may be potentially deployed.

Threats identified in urban areas or areas where a high-order detonation would not be warranted require careful planning for access and defeat.

Critical Research/Innovation Focus Area Document: Radio Controlled Improvised Explosive Device (RCIED) Countermeasures Counter-Improvised Explosive Devices (CIED) U.S. Department of Homeland Security, Science and Technology (S&T) Directorate

Who?

Identify any DHS component stakeholders that contain or represent potential end users. Also name any Capstone IPT (refer to www.dhs.gov/xres/programs/gc_1234200779149.shtm and the article entitled "Making it Easier to Work with

DHS"), if any, which identified a capability gap related to this research/innovation focus area.

The U.S. Department of Homeland Security (DHS) leads for CIEDs are the Office for Bombing Prevention and United States Secret Service (USSS). The corresponding DHS Science and Technology (S&T) Capstone IPT that identified capability gaps related to this focus area is entitled "Counter-IED."

What?

Describe a required technology/capability. Describe how a technology will provide the capabilities and functional improvements needed to address the DHS need. Do not describe a specific technical solution. Instead, describe a conceptual technology for illustrative purposes. Define typical missions that the proposed technology could be utilized to accomplish.

The solution to this need must be deployable by the majority of medium bomb robots deployed with U.S. bomb squads and, if necessary, must be capable of being carried to the scene and emplaced by a bomb technician.

It must be able to preclude the radio-control device from initiating a detonation within a meaningful radius of operation without affecting radio frequencies outside of that radius to a high degree of certainty.

It must allow communication with deployed bomb robots and, if required, bomb technicians operating within that radius of operation.

The solution must have meaningful mission duration and be cost-effective and compliant with any applicable regulations.

It must require minimal training and be easily employed by the average public safety bomb technician.

RCIED Countermeasures include:

1. Optimization and characterization of the current electronic countermeasures (ECM) system on the standardized platform with the current antenna technologies.
2. Development of alternative approaches to interfering with the ability of terrorists to control the initiation of improvised explosive devices (IEDs) with electromagnetic radiation. This may involve more highly targeted intervention with the specific devices of interest rather than jamming.

References

a. HSPD-19 Requirement 5(d): Improving Capabilities to Combat Terrorist Use of Explosives within the United States.

b. 28 U.S.C. § 533; 28 C.F.R., § 0.85(l). DOJ/ FBI Counterintelligence and Counterterrorism Authority.
c. Executive Order 12333—United States Intelligence Activities (December 4, 1981) (E.O. 12333).
d. PPD-39—U.S. Policy on Counterterrorism (June 21, 1995).
e. National Strategic Plan for U.S. Bomb Squads, December 2007, National Bomb Squad Commanders' Advisory Board, page 13, Section 5.1.3

Why?

Describe the analysis and rationale for requiring a new technology/capability. Describe why existing technologies cannot meet current or projected requirements. Describe what new technologies/capabilities are needed to address the gap between current capabilities and required capabilities.

The radio-controlled improvised explosive device (RCIED) threat continuously proliferates for several reasons. One reason is the wide range of commercially available radio-controlled equipment readily available and adaptable to IED triggers, and another reason is the standoff distance the RCIED gives to the terrorist. It is a technical challenge to meet the changing and evolving domestic and global radio frequency (RF) threats. The domestic use of any ECM system must be in compliance with applicable laws and regulations. With each technical modification in terms of responding to or anticipating a change in the RCIED threat, the potential exists to run afoul of regulatory constraints. Regulatory responsibility for the radio spectrum is divided between the Federal Communications Commission (FCC) and the National Telecommunications and Information Administration (NTIA). The FCC, an independent regulatory agency, is assigned responsibility for the regulation of nongovernment interstate and foreign telecommunications. The presidential authority for federal government RF spectrum use has been delegated to the administrator of the NTIA, an operating unit within the Department of Commerce. Several other federal spectrum stakeholders—such as Federal Aviation Administration (FAA), National Aeronautics and Space Administration (NASA), and the Department of Defense (DoD)—also have concerns when it comes to the RF jamming.

When?

If a technology/capability is intended as a countermeasure to a threat, summarize the threat to be countered and how the technology could be used (i.e., concept of operations). If applicable, provide a schedule/time frame to capture when the technology/capability is needed in order to address the DHS gap.

The RCIED is a very real and formidable terrorist threat facing our homeland as was demonstrated in the attack on a women's clinic in Birmingham, Alabama, in 1998. RF has been used in a number of ways to trigger conventional IED(s) and vehicle-borne improvised explosive devices (VBIEDs). ECM systems to jam RCIEDs, which were developed initially for the military, are a necessary tool in accessing and defeating RCIEDs. The efficacy of ECM systems is continually challenged, as terrorists are forever reinventing and redeveloping RCIED technology.

Where?

Describe the projected threat environment in which the technology/capability may be potentially deployed.

A hurdle in the effort to bring this capability to American cities is the confidence in the performance of the system. To properly build this confidence in federal spectrum stakeholders, sufficient data is needed in the characterization of the current ECM platform used by Public Safety Bomb Squads.

Characterization combined with new antenna technologies on the standardized vehicle platform will help expedite the ECM capability to future bomb squads.

Critical Research/Innovation Focus Area Document: Improvised Explosive Device (IED) Assessment and Diagnostics Counter-Improvised Explosive Devices (CIED) U.S. Department of Homeland Security, Science and Technology (S&T) Directorate

Who?

Identify any DHS component stakeholders that contain or represent potential end users. Also name any Capstone IPT (refer to www.dhs.gov/xres/programs/ gc_1234200779149.shtm and the article entitled "Making It Easier to Work with DHS"), if any, which identified a capability gap related to this research/innovation focus area.

The U.S. Department of Homeland Security (DHS) leads for CIEDs are the Office for Bombing Prevention and United States Secret Service (USSS). The corresponding DHS Science and Technology (S&T) Capstone IPT that identified capability gaps related to this focus area is entitled "Counter-IED."

What?

Describe a required technology/capability. Describe how a technology will provide the capabilities and functional improvements needed to address the DHS

need. Do not describe a specific technical solution. Instead, describe a conceptual technology for illustrative purposes. Define typical missions that the proposed technology could be utilized to accomplish.

Technologies and techniques that require the technician to approach the device should allow the operator to safely collect useful information while minimizing the time required in close proximity to the device. Furthermore, for a technology to be usable near an improvised explosive device (IED), consideration must be given to its functionality in an electronic countermeasures (ECM) environment.

Personnel protective equipment necessary for working near an IED limits not only movement, but vision and hearing as well. All equipment should be easy to operate while the technician/operator is in a bomb suit regardless of proximity to the device. The logistical burden associated with the tools and techniques for assessment and diagnosis of the IED should be kept to a minimum.

With respect to the detection of potential explosives contained within a device, special consideration should be given to identification of improvised explosives because of their potential sensitivity to influences such as heat, shock, friction, and static discharge.

The development of advanced assessment and diagnostic tools/techniques in the following areas is desired:

- Novel imaging approaches to identify the precise location of IEDs whether by detection of the explosive filler, energized or unenergized circuitry, or some other yet-to-be-identified signature
- Approaches to standoff diagnostics
- Identification of characteristics of IEDs that provide information that can be used in the selection of an approach for defeating the IED
- Approaches to assessment and diagnosis suitable for use by responders who may not have the scientific or technical background to interpret quantitative data, and will therefore be dependent on qualitative information

References

a. HSPD-19, paragraphs 4 (b, c, d), 9.
b. HSPD-19 I-Plan Tasks: 3.2.1, 3.2.2, 3.2.3, 3.2.4, 3.2.5.
c. National Guidelines for Bomb Technicians (Revised 4/06).
d. National Strategy for U.S. Bomb Squads (December 2007), page 13, Section 7.
e. FBI Special Technicians Bulletin 2007-3: Vehicle-Borne Improvised Explosive Device Response Bomb Squad Readiness.

f. Bomb Squad Response to Suicide Bombers and Vehicle-Borne Improvised Explosive Devices: Categories of Situations and Strategies for Each Category

Why?

Describe the analysis and rationale for requiring a new technology/capability. Describe why existing technologies cannot meet current or projected requirements. Describe what new technologies/capabilities are needed to address the gap between current capabilities and required capabilities.

Bomb makers do not normally choose a "best design" to meet their needs; they adapt what already exists. The ability to analyze IED firing systems and circuitry (diagnostics) and evaluate not only the potential for destruction but likelihood of detonation (assessment) is critical to developing appropriate IED response plans and render safe procedures. Technologies for assessment and diagnostics performed on IEDs must undergo a sustained development, testing, evaluation, and improvement process in order to mitigate the impact of new and emerging IED threats, and offset the technological adaptations and defeat countermeasures developed by the enemy.

When?

If a technology/capability is intended as a countermeasure to a threat, summarize the threat to be countered and how the technology could be used (i.e., concept of operations). If applicable, provide a schedule/time frame to capture when the technology/capability is needed in order to address the DHS gap.

The makeup of an IED is no longer limited to conventional explosives such as trinitrotoluene (TNT). Devices designed and built by bomb makers today can incorporate improvised explosives and detonators, modified ordnance and hazardous materials such as industrial toxic chemical, radiological materials, or substances that enhance the effect of the explosive materials. In addition, IED designs may span the range of simple pressure-plate devices to systems that use microprocessor-controlled sensor circuitry. Assessment and diagnostic tools that provide qualitative and quantitative information on the threat is critical for planning access and defeat procedures.

Where?

Describe the projected threat environment in which the technology/capability may be potentially deployed.

Assessment and diagnostic procedures should be performed outside the blast and fragmentation range of the IED in order to keep bomb technicians out of harm's way.

Critical Research/Innovation Focus Area Document: Detect and Defeat Waterborne Improvised Explosive Devices (WBIEDs) Counter-Improvised Explosive Devices (CIED) U.S. Department of Homeland Security, Science and Technology (S&T) Directorate

Who?

Identify any DHS component stakeholders that contain or represent potential end users. Also name any Capstone IPT (refer to www.dhs.gov/xres/programs/ gc_1234200779149.shtm and the article entitled "Making It Easier to Work with DHS"), if any, which identified a capability gap related to this research/innovation focus area.

The U.S. Department of Homeland Security (DHS) leads for CIEDs are the Office for Bombing Prevention and United States Secret Service (USSS). In addition, the United States Coast Guard (USCG) is the federal organization most responsible for domestic maritime security. The corresponding DHS Science and Technology (S&T) Capstone IPT that identified capability gaps related to this focus area is entitled "Counter-IED."

What?

Describe a required technology/capability. Describe how a technology will provide the capabilities and functional improvements needed to address the DHS need. Do not describe a specific technical solution. Instead, describe a conceptual technology for illustrative purposes. Define typical missions that the proposed technology could be utilized to accomplish.

Domestic response is not the U.S. Navy Explosive Ordnance Disposal's (EOD) primary mission, and nearly 70 percent of its forces are currently deployed in support of other missions, reducing domestically stationed detachments to the minimum manning levels permissible to maintain operational status.

The USCG is the federal organization most responsible for domestic, maritime security. In addition to its normal shore stations, USCG maintains thirteen terrorism-focused Maritime Safety and Security Teams, established through the Maritime Transportation Security Act, that possess explosives detection canine teams. It has consolidated its diving resources into two Deployable Operations Groups (DOG) located in Norfolk, Virginia, and San Diego, California. The USCG has some UHD search capability, but limited maritime or underwater explosive device preparedness and response capability.

In a number of areas of the country, public safety dive teams (PSDT) and their bomb squad counterparts have moved to develop local solutions to the need represented by issues previously described. Today, none of those programs has produced the capability that can replace a U.S. Navy EOD team in the WBIED render-safe role. Further, the responsibility for render-safe of waterborne military ordnance will likely continue to reside primarily with the U.S. Navy.

The response community in the maritime domain today expands to include those who have the daily responsibility for port security diving; their bomb technician diver counterparts, who have ultimate local responsibility for handling render-safe issues within their areas of operation; and the U.S. Navy EOD technicians, who will likely always remain the ultimate reach-back capability for WBIED response.

DHS must develop technology and associated training for public-safety divers, bomb technician divers, and other dive resources who may respond to domestic UHDs, since DHS cannot expect U.S. Navy EOD technicians to continue as the sole providers of assistance to conventional dive teams possessing minimal render-safe capabilities. The ability to locate and validate possible threats is the minimum acceptable level of response.

Desired technology will provide capabilities to detect, diagnose, and disrupt or disable IEDs by remote, semi-remote, or manual means in a maritime environment. Technology must address IEDs attached to ship hulls at depth and devices attached to small craft afloat that may be used themselves as explosive devices.

Where such IED placements affect maritime traffic, including shipping and passenger cruise ships, critical infrastructure/key resources (CIKR), national security activities, etc., technology must address devices emplaced where the presence of water changes the buried or ground-emplaced characteristics of a classic device, e.g., in drainage conduits, wetlands, shallow areas of fresh- or saltwater, on bridge supports, etc.

Technology development should provide material for developing threat characterizations, tool performance testing and standards.

Why?

Describe the analysis and rationale for requiring a new technology/capability. Describe why existing technologies cannot meet current or projected requirements. Describe what new technologies/capabilities are needed to address the gap between current capabilities and required capabilities.

Over 2 billion tons of domestic cargo move through U.S. ports annually, and a significant portion of domestically produced commodities and products are shipped by water. Nearly two-thirds of all U.S. wheat and wheat flour, one-third of soybean and rice, and almost two-fifths of domestic cotton production is exported via U.S. ports. Records indicate that approximately 4.2 million passenger cars, vans, SUVs, and light trucks pass through U.S. seaports annually.

More than 4 million Americans work in port-related jobs that generate $44 billion in annual personal income and $16.1 billion in federal, state, and local taxes. Port activity also contributes more than $723 billion annually to the gross domestic product. Additionally, public ports serve national security functions. The DoD routinely uses public ports for the mobilization, deployment and resupply of U.S. armed forces. Many naval installations are based in U.S. ports, creating a unique set of cross-sector challenges.

Within the Public Safety Dive Teams (PSDT) community there is a lack of national standards in both the equipment and training necessary to provide an effective response throughout U.S. ports, which puts both the diver and port at risk. A response must be successful in adverse operational conditions that may include unstable vessels or platforms, cold water, offshore locations, poor visibility, and the possibility that a device or hazard is entirely submerged.

Each of the various conditions under which bomb technician divers operate requires them to possess specific skills, tools, and standard operating procedures that currently do not exist nationally. To complicate this mission further, many PSDTs are created as a collateral duty responsibility, and therefore divers are often multitasked within their respective departments.

Recognized standards for tools and operating procedures do exist nationally for bomb technicians involved in nonwaterborne render-safe procedures. The development of those tools and procedures falls under the purview of the staff at the Federal Bureau of Investigation's (FBI) Hazardous Devices School (HDS). While HDS staff work in coordination with the Department of Defense and the NBSCAB to set standards, develop tools, and train render-safe personnel, this is the only such school or organization with responsibility for this function within the entire United States.

In recognition of the value of this existing set of national tools and standards, which are rare in any other public service, the FBI has initiated a process to begin to assess the training or actual deployment techniques currently being used by bomb squad divers across the United States. The FBI, in collaboration with DHS, has simultaneously developed and implemented a nationally consistent training process to equip PSDTs with the skills and procedures they need to operate more safely in the WBIED environment and to seamlessly integrate with bomb squad assets during a WBIED event.

To develop a national standard for WBIED operations, there is a need to develop a set of tools and operating standards that may become the subject of enhanced training for bomb squad divers at the FBI's HDS. This new set of tools and procedures will be integrated with existing and/ or enhanced training for public safety dive teams in order to provide a single, vertically integrated approach to WBIED incidents in U.S. ports or other maritime infrastructure.

Related Requirements

- Maritime Operational Threat Response (MOTR) for the National Strategy for Maritime Security: "DHS will plan for the prevention and detection of sea mining and swimmer operations in waters subject to the jurisdiction of the United States."

References

a. HSPD-19 4 (b, c, d), 9.
b. HSPD-19 I-Plan (Draft) Task Ref: 3.2.2.
c. National Strategy for Maritime Security. September 2005.

When?

If a technology/capability is intended as a countermeasure to a threat, summarize the threat to be countered and how the technology could be used (i.e., concept of operations). If applicable, provide a schedule/time frame to capture when the technology/capability is needed in order to address the DHS gap.

The terrorist threat facing our nation's critical infrastructure can take many forms, including bombs used in a maritime environment. Over the last two decades, terrorists have used WBIEDs to target U.S. interests with notable success and devastating consequences, including the deadly suicide bombings of the USS *Cole* and a French oil tanker off the coast of Yemen. Considering likely events based on available intelligence and experience, terrorist groups will continue to use WBIEDs on land and in a maritime environment against U.S. interests.

Where?

Describe the projected threat environment in which the technology/capability may be potentially deployed.

Accessibility by water as well as land, proximity to vast metropolitan centers and inherent integration into transportation hubs present additional multifaceted security challenges for ports. DHS understands that drug smugglers use divers as a means of attaching and retrieving contraband, and it is not unreasonable for DHS to recognize that terrorist combat swimmers and boat operators may act alone or in teams to attach explosive devices or limpet mines to ship hulls, bridge supports, dams, levees, locks, or oil rigs. Recently, the Sri Lankan government was targeted successfully by a suicide scuba diver who wore, placed, and detonated against the hull of a fast patrol boat in Trincomalee Harbor a device, resulting in its sinking.

In the maritime environment, the ability to detect the presence of explosives or explosive devices, locate the explosive or device precisely, diagnose the device to determine its components and how they function, and defeat the device using the best tool to eliminate the threat is made more difficult by the water environment. Not only may there be more variables to consider than in a nonmaritime environment, but also the presence of the water changes the implications of variables that are part of DHS's understanding developed on land.

Critical Research/Innovation Focus Area Document: Improvised Explosive Device (IED) Warnings Counter-Improvised Explosive Devices (CIED) U.S. Department of Homeland Security, Science and Technology (S&T) Directorate

Who?

Identify any DHS component stakeholders that contain or represent potential end users. Also name any Capstone IPT (refer to www.dhs.gov/xres/programs/ gc_1234200779149.shtm and the article entitled "Making It Easier to Work with DHS"), if any, which identified a capability gap related to this research/innovation focus area.

The U.S. Department of Homeland Security (DHS) leads for CIEDs are the Office for Bombing Prevention and United States Secret Service (USSS). The corresponding DHS Science and Technology (S&T) Capstone IPT that identified capability gaps related to this focus area is entitled "Counter-IED."

The threat of an improvised explosive device (IED) attack is shared almost universally by U.S. communities, private sector enterprises and public sector agencies, and across the eighteen sectors of the nation's critical infrastructure and key resources (CIKR) owners and operators. Consequently, the community of interest for this research effort includes public officials and agency leads across the range of U.S. jurisdictions and communities at the federal, state, regional, and local levels.

What?

Describe a required technology/capability. Describe how a technology will provide the capabilities and functional improvements needed to address the DHS need. Do not describe a specific technical solution. Instead, describe a conceptual technology for illustrative purposes. Define typical missions that the proposed technology could be utilized to accomplish.

Government officials, civic leaders, media representatives, law enforcement officials and emergency managers need to properly delineate and issue hazard/risk warnings to the public prior to an imminent or suspected IED attack and provide appropriate protective actions and post-attack instructions.

Specific stakeholders in this effort include:

Office of the President and White House Staff
Department of Homeland Security
DHS/FEMA
Department of Justice
Equivalent agency heads at the state, regional, and local levels
Governors' offices nationwide
Local elected officials, e.g., mayors and county executives
Local law enforcement, public safety, and emergency management officials

The development of a data structure and analysis program (and accompanying training materials) that will support federal, state, local, tribal, and private sector partners having specific roles and responsibilities within their communities for public safety and security against IED attacks is required. Development of hazard and risk warnings to the public in imminent threat of or immediately after a terrorist IED attack will incorporate the following requirements:

- Detailed responses and methodologies to appropriately inform and protect the public during terrorist explosive attacks—should involve members of professional press and media with local officials and emergency managers
- Consistent and repeatable methods to inform and employ the public in identifying suspicious circumstances or abnormal conditions in local communities that could serve as warnings to local authorities of terrorist attack planning or potential IED events
- Development and testing of guidelines for government and civic leaders in issuing effective emergency communications in the event of an IED attack
- Technology that will rapidly provide accurate status information from forensic and law enforcement agencies to government officials and leadership, and public safety and security personnel with near real-time updates

- Preplanned responses and messages that have been crafted, analyzed, tested, and rehearsed by civic officials and members of the media and press corps to provide accurate instructions and reassurances to the public
- Development of local models and simulation-based games to exercise first responders and local government leaders in potential scenarios and test courses of action to support and protect local populations
- Development of simulations to analyze effects on transportation and public infrastructures, local economies, and tempo of civic life in the event of an IED attack or terrorist campaign employing IEDs, and to analyze and test alternate approaches to managing the consequences

References

a. HSPD-19 Section 4(a, d).
b. HSPD-19 Implementation Plan (draft) Task Ref: 2.3.4, 3.

Why?

Describe the analysis and rationale for requiring a new technology/capability. Describe why existing technologies cannot meet current or projected requirements. Describe what new technologies/capabilities are needed to address the gap between current capabilities and required capabilities.

The United States has little experience in dealing with an immediate threat of attack that could affect individual American citizens in their own communities. Likewise, civic officials have very little awareness or training in how to instruct the public properly regarding the safety measures they should take during terrorist attacks or similar extraordinary events. Officials' experience is generally centered on managing public information and security during serial murders or kidnappings; civil unrest, gang violence, and inner-city crime waves; and rare events exemplified by the 1979 Three Mile Island event, the Unabomber attacks from 1978 to 1995, and the anthrax and sniper attacks in the Washington, D.C., metropolitan area in 2001 and 2002 respectively. Criminologists or terrorism experts serving local law enforcement or the FBI have formulated most instructions to the public and senior law enforcement officials have issued them.

The ability to provide information quickly and accurately is critical to preserving public confidence at the local level and generating awareness, cooperation, and support of the public in identifying abnormal or suspicious events that might indicate imminent danger or precursor activities to an IED attack.

There are two challenges involved in this effort: (1) protecting the public from initial and successive IED events especially in the face of a general lack of official knowledge of the unfolding scenario; and (2) maintaining public confidence in the face of potential threats. Public confidence is important in preserving public conviction at the local level and generating awareness, cooperation, and support of the public at the local level in identifying abnormal or suspicious events that might indicate imminent danger or precursor activities to an IED attack.

When?

If a technology/capability is intended as a countermeasure to a threat, summarize the threat to be countered and how the technology could be used (i.e., concept of operations). If applicable, provide a schedule/time frame to capture when the technology/capability is needed in order to address the DHS gap.

The terrorist threat facing our nation's critical and civic infrastructure can take many forms including vehicle bombs, suicide attacks, or combinations thereof. This includes attacks such as those seen in the Beslan School or the Moscow Theater, which combine armed attackers, hostages, and IEDs. In the event that IED attacks were to occur—or worse, that a campaign of terrorist use of explosives employing such methods were to be launched on U.S. soil—authorities must quickly provide the American people with accurate information about the nature of the threat. Authorities also must provide guidance on protective actions and precautions that Americans might take to improve security in their communities and reduce the risks to them and their families.

Where?

Describe the projected threat environment in which the technology/capability may be potentially deployed.

If terrorists stage a coordinated attack or multiple attacks against the American people using IEDs, vehicle-borne improvised explosive devices (VBIEDs), or suicide bombers against targets within communities and public gathering places, the problems presented will be significantly more complex and will likely have national implications. In a free and open society, it is impossible to ensure the constant safety of people and the certain protection of targets against terrorist attacks. Nevertheless, there are in fact steps that authorities can and should take at the local, regional, and national levels to inform the public and manage the security problem posed by terrorism.

Critical Research/Innovation Focus Area Document: Improvised Explosive Device (IED) Threat Characterization and Signatures Counter-Improvised Explosive Devices (CIED) U.S. Department of Homeland Security, Science and Technology (S&T) Directorate

Who?

Identify any DHS component stakeholders that contain or represent potential end users. Also name any Capstone IPT (refer to www.dhs.gov/xres/programs/ gc_1234200779149.shtm and the article entitled "Making It Easier to Work with DHS"), if any, which identified a capability gap related to this research/innovation focus area.

The U.S. Department of Homeland Security (DHS) leads for CIEDs are the Office for Bombing Prevention and United States Secret Service (USSS). The corresponding DHS Science and Technology (S&T) Capstone IPT that identified capability gaps related to this focus area is entitled "Counter-IED."

What?

Describe a required technology/capability. Describe how a technology will provide the capabilities and functional improvements needed to address the DHS need. Do not describe a specific technical solution. Instead, describe a conceptual technology for illustrative purposes. Define typical missions that the proposed technology could be utilized to accomplish.

Our ability to analyze improvised explosive device (IED) threats requires common definitions and lexicon, a detailed process for testing and characterizing the performance of IEDs and IED countermeasures, the ability to simulate IED threats, and the development of IED threat models.

A repository of data obtained under controlled conditions is necessary to conduct the analysis required for this characterization and modeling. Collecting data on vehicles used as devices and on devices in vehicles (person-borne, placed, etc.) will require a standard set of procedures for surface sampling to characterize the extent of surface contamination occurring during the IED construction process and an instrumented range to test small vehicles with progression toward larger vehicles.

Analysis of test data will provide an understanding of why and how various components can be used in device construction as well as measurements of the effects of blasts conducted under different physical configurations.

Threat characterization requires analytic tools that incorporate prediction and pattern assessment.

The development of a comprehensive body of common standards can be achieved by searching out the standards that may exist, evaluating their effectiveness, ensuring their consistency, and using them to develop additional necessary standards that are missing.

Comprehensive instrumentation and instrumentation protocols and standards for existing testing facilities are needed to provide reliable and well-understood characterizations.

Scientific analysis of accumulated test data can provide an understanding of why and how various components can be used in device construction. Measurements of the effects of blasts conducted under different physical configurations can be used to model the consequences of IED blasts.

Correlation of standardized characterizations to post-event forensics and real-time event data will assist in identification of ongoing planning activities by the terrorist.

References

a. HSPD-19 I-Plan (Draft) Tasks: 3.1.2.
b. HSPD-19, Paragraphs 8, 9.

Why?

Describe the analysis and rationale for requiring a new technology/capability. Describe why existing technologies cannot meet current or projected requirements. Describe what new technologies/capabilities are needed to address the gap between current capabilities and required capabilities.

The IED community requires an ability to obtain, access, and analyze detailed and authoritative performance data on IED threat devices based on the design, assembly, and detonation of IED threat devices in a laboratory and/or testing environment.

The following challenges limit our ability to characterize and understand the nature of IED threats: (1) lack of unrestricted access to fully instrumented explosives test ranges has limited the capability to conduct multiple tests of IED devices under controlled conditions and to collect well-understood data; and (2) lack of a common lexicon and data standards for defining measurements and storing and analyzing data prevents us from comparing and using test results and analyzing previous, current, and future test data to determine overall effectiveness of CIED solutions.

When?

If a technology/capability is intended as a countermeasure to a threat, summarize the threat to be countered and how the technology could be used (i.e., concept of operations). If applicable, provide a schedule/time frame to capture when the technology/capability is needed in order to address the DHS gap.

To develop the capability to counter IED attacks, we must integrate our understanding of two aspects of the threat—the actor and the tool. Despite the worldwide proliferation of IED attacks, little standardized data exists that can be used to characterize the construction of the IEDs or the resulting blast effects under various conditions and methods of delivery. There is no commonly accepted set of test criteria on IED detonations or a database of recent performance data.

Where?

Describe the projected threat environment in which the technology/capability may be potentially deployed.

A repository of data obtained under controlled conditions is necessary to conduct the analysis required for this characterization and modeling.

Chapter 13

"Change Ain't Easy"—But It's Possible

If there's one consistent theme to this book it's that change for the better is possible—even in government. SECURE and FutureTECH represent real-world examples of programs developed from a well-thought-out commercialization model that has at its core the premise that participants can "win." This axiom of any and all participants in a program, or joint venture benefitting from it is the key ingredient to the success of commercialization in governments throughout the world. Below is a set of discussion points used to articulate how we achieved the impressive results we did in a relatively short amount of time. Please take the time to review them thoroughly and pass them on for the next set of "change agents."

CHANGE AIN'T EASY

The art of progress is to preserve order amid change and to preserve change amid order.

—Alfred North Whitehead

Those who expect moments of change to be comfortable and free of conflict have not learned their history.

—Joan Wallach Scott

If you want to make enemies, try to change something.

—Woodrow Wilson

Why a Commercialization Office?
S&T Commercialization Office—Four Major Activities
Creating and Demonstrating Value

Why a Commercialization Office?

S&T Commercialization Office -- Four Major Activities
Creating and Demonstrating Value

Parameter	Requirements Development Initiative	Commercialization Process	SECURE Program	S&T Private Sector Outreach
1) Increases speed-of-execution of DHS programs/projects	✓	✓	✓	✓
2) DHS and its stakeholders receive products more closely aligned to specific requirements/needs	✓	✓	✓	✓
3) Increases effective and efficient communication	✓	✓	✓	✓
4) End users can make informed purchasing decisions	✓	✓	✓	✓
5) Large savings of cost and time for DHS and its stakeholders	✓	✓	✓	✓
6) Increases goodwill between taxpayers, private sector and DHS	✓	✓	✓	✓
7) Fosters more opportunities for small, medium and large businesses	✓	✓	✓	✓
8) Large taxpayer savings	✓	✓	✓	✓
9) Possible product "spin-offs" can aid other commercial markets	✓	✓	✓	✓
10) Promotes open and fair competition	✓	✓	✓	✓

Return-on-DHS Investment is LARGE!

Why SECURE Program

Multiuse:

- Provides private sector, in an open and transparent way, with what they need most—business opportunities
- Provides assurance to DHS, first responders, and private sector users (like CIKR) that products/services perform as prescribed (and provides vehicle for first responders, CIKR owners and operators to voice their requirements)
- Augments the value of the SAFETY Act

Saves money:

- Private sector uses its own resources to develop products and services to the benefit of the taxpayer and the federal government.

Creates jobs:

- Detailed articulation of requirements coupled with funded large potential available markets yield *opportunity* that yields job creation (it's better to teach a person to fish than to give them a fish).
- Enables small firms with innovative technologies to partner with larger firms, venture capitalists, and angel investors because of the

credibility of having government show detailed requirements with associated market potential (instead of just their own business plans).

Efficient use of government funds:

- Articulating detailed requirements saves time and money. It is better for government to spend funds to procure products or services that are available for sale and rigorously tested than to spend money and time to develop new solutions for ill-defined problems.

SECURE Program Benefit Analysis
"Win-Win-Win"

Taxpayers	Private Sector	Public Sector
1. Citizens are better protected by DHS personnel using mission critical products	1. Save significant time and money on market and business development activities	1. Improved understanding and communication of needs
2. Tax savings realized through Private Sector investment in DHS	2. Firms can genuinely contribute to the security of the Nation	2. Cost-effective and rapid product development process saves resources
3. Positive economic growth for American economy	3. Successful products share in the "imprimatur of DHS"; providing assurance that products really work	3. Monies can be allocated to perform greater number of essential tasks
4. Possible product "spin-offs" can aid other commercial markets	4. Significant business opportunities with sizeable DHS and DHS ancillary markets	4. End users receive products aligned to specific needs
5. Customers ultimately benefit from COTS produced within the Free Market System – more cost effective and efficient product development	5. Commercialization opportunities for small, medium and large business	5. End users can make informed purchasing decisions with tight budgets

Let's Make it Happen

Commercialization Office Major Activities	Potential Benefits
Requirements Development Initiative enables easy-to-use guidelines for articulating detailed operational requirements used throughout the Department to enhance internal and external communications for program/project development and execution, procurement and private sector outreach programs.	Net Impact: Savings of >$2.5 Billion annually in DHS resources
S&T Commercialization Process ensures the cost-effective and efficient development of products/services for DHS, First Responders, and Critical Infrastructure/Key Resources owners with the aid of the private sector's resources.	Net Impact: When implemented across DHS, conservative savings in current and opportunity costs > $10 Billion annually.
SECURE Program is an innovative public-private partnership in which DHS relays detailed operational requirements and a conservative estimate of potential available markets for a given need in exchange for the private sector to develop widely distributed product/service at their own expense.	Net Impact: To date, over $261 Million has been conservatively invested in DHS projects for the SECURE Program pilot.
S&T Private Sector Outreach is a concerted effort to engage the private sector in understanding DHS detailed needs and establish a large repository of technologies/products/services aligned with DHS needs.	Net Impact: Savings of >$350 Million in S&T Budget and opportunity costs.

Commercialization Office: Major Activities

Commercialization Office

Requirements Development Initiative	Commercialization Process	SECURE Program	Private Sector Outreach
•Requirements Development Book(s) •Operational Requirements Document Template •Training for end users and engineers	•"Hybrid" Commercialization Model •Product Realization Chart •Commercialization Framework and "Mindset"	•Concept of Operations •Website Development •Internal processes developed and socialized •Requirements and Conservative Potential Market Available Estimates Communicated	•Invited Speeches •Meetings with business executives •Numerous articles written and published regarding observations and programs in practice. •Repository of currently available products, services and/or technologies in the private sector aligned to Capstone IPT Capability Gaps

Homeland Security

http://www.dhs.gov/xabout/structure/gc_1234194479267.shtm

It All Starts with a Plan:
Objectives, Strategies and Tactics

Objectives
1. Create a "Commercialization Mindset" throughout DHS by enacting Management Directive(s) consistent with our Commercialization Process by December 2009.
2. Enter into agreements/contracts related to a minimum of six products aligned to DHS ORDs by December 31, 2008.
3. Post a minimum of ten DHS sponsored ORDs (and accompanying market estimates) on SECURE website by March 2009.

Strategies
1. Develop "top-down" and "bottom-up" awareness and use of commercialization processes through briefings to Senior Executives, S&T Corporate Board and Transition and Program Managers.
2. Continue to meet with S2/G-7 Senior leadership to receive projects/ ideas for possible commercialization throughout the Department.
3. Work with Private Sector Office to expand outreach to Private Sector entities and develop policies for commercialization initiatives
4. Expand exposure of SECURE Program on DHS.gov through media, speaking appearances, press releases, and other PR and marketing communications initiatives.
5. Develop internal processes to expedite the use of SECURE Program.

Tactical Elements
1. Distribute *Requirements Development Guide* and *Developing Operational Requirements* to personnel in and associated with DHS – e.g. Operating Components, First Responders and S&T with assistance from Office of Public Affairs/Corporate Communications (on-going)
2. Conduct small group training for S&T Division Heads, Transition Managers and Program Managers on requirements development and the context in which requirements fit into product development and commercialization lifecycles (due by October 31, 2008)
3. Assist in creation of a directive for S&T staff to receive training on requirements development (by March 2009)
4. Assist in creation of a directive for all projects resulting in end-user products to require ORDs before appropriation of monies by Jan 31, 2009
5. Assist in creation of a directive outlining the "hybrid" Commercialization Process for use in DHS product development cycles by April, 2009
6. Inform Members of Congress and Senate with updates on commercialization initiative progress on a quarterly basis (on-going)
7. Provide regular updates to Deputy Secretary (S2) and G-7 on commercialization initiative progress on a monthly basis (on-going)
8. Develop and implement a mechanism to inform and make available to S&T personnel company overview documents received as part of Private Sector outreach efforts (due by July 31, 2008)
9. Develop process by which conservative estimates of potential available markets are generated (due by September 30, 2008)
10. Develop process by which Operational Requirements Document are reviewed and placed on SECURE website (due by September 30, 2008)
11. Develop process by which third party independent T&E is evaluated and results reported on SECURE website (due by October 31, 2008)
12. Work with Office of Public Affairs (OPA) to place articles in more media outlets, post "Opportunities for the Private Sector" brief online, and expand content of SECURE website (due by August 31, 2008)
13. Collaborate with Operating Components and First Responders to write ORDs for problems not addressed by current S&T projects. (on-going)
14. Monitor progress against goals and update OST (on-going)

Top-Down, Bottom-Up Socialization

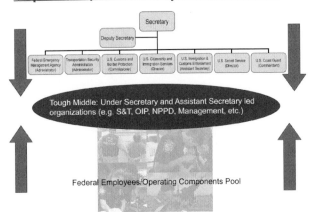

Public Vs. Private Sector
Typical Drivers and Motivators

Public Sector	Private Sector
• Advancing Public Good	• Sales Opportunities
• Fulfilling Needs of Stakeholders/ Constituents	• Market Development
• Following clear processes and methods	• Profit Margins
• Power of the Purse Strings	• Raising capital
• Strive for Perfection	• Increasing shareholder value
• Job Security	• Efficiency and Cost-Effectiveness
• Commitments/Obligations/ Expenditures	• Speed of Execution
	• Results/Output

Challenge: Enabling and fostering common goals to facilitate mutually beneficial programs

Critical Role of Metrics

- Number of Products/Services Developed and Deployed
- Number of Technologies Transitioned
- Return on Investment
- Taxpayer Money Saved
- Speed of Execution – ORD draft, review process and development of product/service

"If you can't measure it, you can't manage it"

Let Others Take the Credit

- Success has a thousand fathers
- SECURE Pilot "Primed the Pump"
- Headquarters takes ownership of ORDs
- People want to be productive and efficient
- Imitation is the sincerest form of flattery

Innovate and Automate

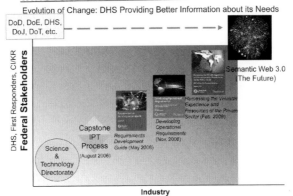

Evolution of Change: DHS Providing Better Information about its Needs

Lessons Learned:

- Communicate and iterate, iterate, and iterate.
- Strive for excellence, not perfection!
- Have a backup to the backup of the backup.
- Expect the unexpected.
- Plan, measure and report.
- Education is key.
- Demonstrate benefits for all parties.
- Put it in writing.

Things to Come

- Semantic Web 3.0
- Communities of practitioners
- Continued outreach/interaction with stakeholders and private sector
- Leveraging new R&D opportunities with universities, national labs, regional technology consortiums, etc.

Summary:

- Make it easy/keep it simple.
- Never (ever) give up.
- Innovate.
- Reiterate.
- Contemplative-in-action.

Appendix A

Infrastructure Geophysical Division (IGD)
Overview

Infrastructure and Geophysical Division
Science and Technology Directorate
Department of Homeland Security

DHS Science & Technology Directorate Technical Divisions

Basic Research

Discovery and Invention to Enable Future Capabilities

- Brings the capabilities, talent and resources of the Homeland Security Centers of Excellence, DOE National Laboratories and DHS Labs to bear to address the long-term R&D needs for DHS in sciences of enduring relevance

- This type of focused, protracted research investment has potential to lead to paradigm shifts in the nation's homeland security capabilities

Innovation

High Risk, High Gain, Game Changers for Leap-Ahead Results

- Promotes revolutionary changes in technology

- Focus on prototyping and deploying critical technologies

Includes:

- HSARPA – Homeland Security Advanced Research Projects Agency

  Visit https://baa.st.dhs.gov

- Small Business Innovation Research program

  Visit http://www.sbir.dhs.gov

DHS S&T Solicitations also posted at:

http://www.FedBizOpps.gov

Product Transition

Enabling Capabilities, Supporting Mission Critical Needs of DHS

Integrated Product Teams (IPTs)

13 Capstone IPTs form the centerpiece of the S&T's customer- or patron-driven approach to product transition

Engage DHS customers, acquisition partners, S&T technical division heads, and end users in product research, development, transition and acquisition activities

Identify our customers' needs and enable and transition near-term capabilities for addressing them

Capstone Integrated Product Teams (IPTs)

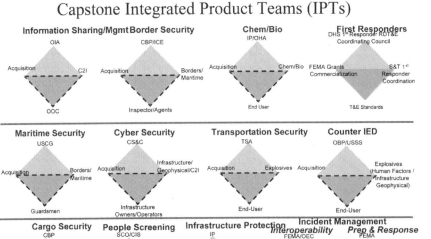

Infrastructure Geophysical Division (IGD) Mission

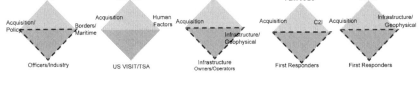

Infrastructure and Geophysical Division will increase the Nation's **preparedness for and response** to natural and man-made threats through superior situational awareness, enhanced emergency responder capabilities, and **critical infrastructure protection**

The IGD Transition Business Model

4 Customer driven
-Office of Infrastructure Protection (IP)
-Federal Emergency Management
Agency (FEMA)

Prep & Response

4 User oriented
-Infrastructure owners and operators
-First responders and emergency
managers

Infrastructure Protection

Infrastructure Protection
Collaboration & Coordination

The DHS Office of Infrastructure Protection (IP) serves as the
bridge between the 18 CIKR Sectors and the DHS Science and
Technology Directorate

R&D needs

- 18 CIKR Sectors
  - Sector Specific Agencies
  - Sector Coordinating Councils
  - Government Coordinating Councils
  - Office of Infrastructure Protection Divisions
    - Office for Bombing Prevention

- DHS Science and Technology
  - IP led or co-led Capstone IPTs
    - Infrastructure Protection Capstone IPT
    - Chemical and Biological Defense Capstone IPT
    - Counter-IED Capstone IPT

*critical infrastructure
protection technologies*

Critical Infrastructure Sectors & Lead Agencies

Sector-Specific Agency	Sector
Department of Agriculture Department of Health and Human Services	Agriculture and Food
Department of Defense	Defense Industrial Base
Department of Energy	Energy
Department of Health and Human Services	Public Health and Healthcare
Department of Interior	National Monuments and Icons
Department of Treasury	Banking and Finance
Environmental Protection Agency	Water
Department of Homeland Security Office of Infrastructure Protection	Chemical Commercial Facilities Dams Emergency Services Nuclear Reactors, Materials, and Waste Critical Manufacturing
Office of Cyber Security and Telecommunications	Information Technology Communications
Transportation Security Administration	Postal and Shipping
Transportation Security Administration, United States Coast Guard	Transportation Systems
Immigration and Customs Enforcement, Federal Protective Service	Government Facilities

The National Infrastructure Protection Plan (NIPP) R&D Process

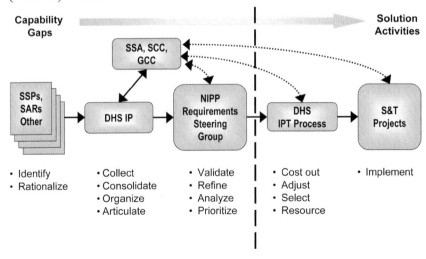

IGD Thrust Areas

4 Infrastructure Protection (IP)

4 Preparedness and Response

4 Geophysical Sciences

IGD Preparedness and Response (P&R) Program Areas

4 Integrated modeling, mapping, and simulation

4 Personnel Monitoring

4 Incident management enterprise system

4 Logistics management tool

IGD Infrastructure Protection (IP) Program Areas

4 Interdependencies and cascading
   consequences

4 Blast analysis and protection

4 Advance surveillance

4 Rapid mitigation and recovery

4 Critical utility components

4 Community based critical infrastructure
   protection institute

IGD Geophysical Program Areas

4 Southeast Region
   Research Initiative
   (SERRI)

4 Rapid Levee Repair
4 Overhead Imagery

Emerging Areas of Interest

4 Cyber-Physical System Security

4 Advanced Materials Research

Questions?

Appendix B

Typical New Product Development Process Used in the Private Sector

	FEASIBILITY PHASE	OPTIMIZATION PHASE	DEVELOPMENT PHASE	PILOT PHASE	SALES RELEASE PHASE
OVERVIEW	**Objective:** To investigate new product ideas (or technologies) when marketing and/or engineering risks are significant. **Inputs:** A value proposition statement and concise description of the investigation. **Output:** A written report of findings and recommendations.	**Objective:** To develop a detailed product plan. **Input:** A preliminary product plan. **Output:** A detailed product plan.	**Objective:** To complete the design and development of the product through the release of an engineering documentation package and manufacturing plan. **Input:** A detailed product plan. **Outputs:** Engineering documentation package release and manufacturing plan.	**Objective:** Demonstrate that the product can be manufactured within cost and on schedule. **Inputs:** Completed engineering documentation and manufacturing plan. **Outputs:** Customer-desired, defect-free product package.	**Objective:** Prove that a defect-free product can be promoted, sold, manufactured and tracked according to its product plan. **Input:** Completed manufacturing plan release package **Outputs:** Commercially available-defect-free product and finalized product plan
RESEARCH & DEVELOPMENT	• Establish technical objectives and milestones (including go / no-go decision points) • Conduct preliminary IP review • Select team and estimate required resources	Develop Engineering Plan to include: • Detailed performance specifications • Agreement by Marketing and Sales • Product Cost Estimate • User Interface(s) • Packaging considerations • Accessories • Detailed schedule and budget	Complete the following: • Design product to specifications with several design reviews • Prepare and complete engineering documentation • Build engineering prototypes • Design and build support tooling and test fixtures • Demonstrate ease-of-manufacturability	Complete the following: • Support required testing and assembly training • Support manufacturability / design change(s) • Offer assistance to other functional areas when required (e.g., help in finalizing sales literature or tools)	Complete the following: • Any ECOs implemented • Ensure application engineering / technical support trained and tested • Assist other functional areas if required
PRODUCTION	• Provide list of any potentially required tools, materials or new processes. • An advisor on subjects such as "design for test", manufacturability and ways to cost-effectively produce a product / technology platform	Develop Manufacturing Plan to include: • Product Cost Estimate • Manufacturability issues • Detailed schedule and budget • Capital / facilities requirement • Product structure / architecture	Complete the following: • Set up product routings • Design and fabricate process tooling • Order long-lead items • Develop and test assembly procedures • Finalize manufacturing plan	Complete the following: • Finalize tooling and set up manufacturing routings • Measure and track pilot engineering changes • Ensure material and production systems • Provide producibility feedback to R&D • Train applications engineering personnel	Complete the following: • All QA / testing finalized • All tooling and processes frozen • Final manufacturing and assembly routines / procedures are frozen
MARKETING & SALES	• Establish marketing objectives and milestones (including go / no-go decision points) • Estimate required resources and select team from Marketing and Sales • Develop rough draft of features, benefits and "reasons to buy" • List potential derivative products / technologies • Provide draft of prospective customers	Develop Marketing Plan to include: • Detailed market size(s) and forecasts • Product introduction • Detailed competitive analysis • Alpha and Beta site plan • Product launch plan • Features, benefits and "reasons to buy" • Advertising / promotion plan • Detailed market research (primary and secondary)	Complete the following: • Develop sales / distribution plan • Manage and report on Alpha and Beta sites • Develop first draft of User's Manual • Develop sales literature and tools • Develop integrated marketing communications strategy • Finalize product strategy • Develop sales training plan	Complete the following: • Initiate worldwide sales training • Approve user manual • Prepare sales release package • Update / include product in corporate literature / web site / etc. (demo only) • Review / edit promotion strategy	Complete the following: • All integrated marketing activities are finalized • Worldwide sales materials, tools and training are complete (internal and external) • All corporate materials are updated • Finalize marketing plan
QUALITY CONTROL	Ensure the qualification of tools / materials / processes and suppliers as required	Develop Quality Plan to include: • Standards / Conformance • Calibration requirements • Packaging / shipping requirements • Lifetime / reliability testing	Complete the following: • Develop and implement test plan • Define regulatory requirements • Design and build inspection tooling • Conduct shipping tests	Complete the following: • Develop preliminary QA test procedures • Audit key suppliers • Edit and approve manuals	Complete the following: • Finalize all QA / test procedures • Finalize all QA / test tooling • Finalize quality plan
FINANCE	Provide team with any financial data or information required	Complete a Financial Analysis to include: • NPV / ROI • Cash Flow • Sensitivity / Scenario Analysis	Complete the following: • Conduct preliminary cost roll-up	Complete the following: • Complete cost roll-up	
REVIEW OF CORPORATE "DELIVERABLES"	Review of Corporate "Deliverables": 1. The written report of findings and recommendations to corporate reviewers is to be distributed to corporate reviewers at least one week prior to the scheduled review meeting. 2. The Feasibility Review meeting will be attended by each corporate officer, the "product / technology champion" and a designated representative of each functional area. 3. Results / follow-up actions of the review meeting will be communicated to the organization by the champion. Approved preliminary product plans continue to the Optimization Phase and approved new technology roadmaps are given to the CTO and / or VP R&D for further development and implementation.	Review of Corporate "Deliverables": 1. The written product plan is to be distributed to corporate reviewers at least one week prior to the scheduled review meeting. 2. The Optimization Review meeting will be attended by each corporate officer, "the product champion" and a designated representative of each functional area. 3. Results / follow-up actions of the review meeting will be communicated / coordinated by the champion.	Review of Corporate "Deliverables": 1. The engineering documentation package release and manufacturing plan is to be distributed to corporate reviewers at least one week prior to the scheduled review meeting. 2. The Development Phase review will be attended by each corporate officer, the "product champion" and a designated representative of each functional area. Note: Ample time must be allocated for sharing of details of not only the engineering and manufacturability plan, but also of progress / updates from the functional areas. 3. Results / follow-up actions of the review meeting will be communicated / coordinated to the organization by the champion.	Review of Corporate "Deliverables": 1. The manufacturing plan release package is to be distributed to corporate reviewers at least one week prior to the scheduled review meeting. 2. The Pilot Phase review will be attended by each corporate officer, the "product champion" and a designated representative of each functional area. 3. Results / follow-up actions of the review meeting will be communicated / coordinated to the organization by the champion.	Review of Corporate "Deliverables": 1. The finalized product plans sales release package is to be distributed to corporate reviewers at least one week prior to the scheduled review meeting. 2. The Sales Release Phase review will be attended by each corporate officer, the "product champion" and a designated representative of each functional area. Ample time must be allocated to the processes to ensure flawless execution of the acceptance, shipment, and after-sales support of the new product. 3. Results / follow-up actions of the review meeting will be coordinated / communicated to the organization by the champion.

Figure B.1. © Cellucci Association, Inc.

Appendix C

Product Realization Guide

Figure C.1.
Product Realization Guide detailing the steps required to deploy a product or service for use in the Homeland Security Enterprise (HSE).

DHS S&T Portfolio	N/A	Basic Research			Technology Development			Innovation and Transition		Product Development		
Technology Phase	Needs Assessment	Science											
Technology Readiness Level (TRL)	N/A	TRL 1 – TRL 3			TRL 4 – TRL 6			TRL 7 – TRL 9		TRL 7 – TRL 9			
Manufacturing Readiness Level (MRL)	N/A	MRL 1 – MRL 3			MRL 4 – MRL 6					TRL 7 – MRL 10			
		TRL 1	TRL 2	TRL 3	TRL 4	TRL 5	TRL 6	TRL 7		TRL 8	TRL 9	
Key Objectives		MRL 1	MRL 2	MRL 3	MRL 4	MRL 5	MRL 6	MRL 7		MRL 8	MRL 9/10	
Key Deliverables												
Management Review												

FutureTECH™ Program (TRL 1-6)   SECURE™ Program (TRL 6-9)   SAFETY Act   Designation: TRL 6-9 & Certification: TRL 9-Deployment

Product Realization Guide

- This guide is designed as a resource to assist in project execution relative to technology development. This systematic approach facilitates efficient and effective product development by reducing the risk of unidentified errors and product development shortfalls. It is intended that this guide be incorporated as an easy-to-use resource to ensure due diligence throughout the product development life cycle. Please note that this guide presents a general framework for product realization and that individual projects may require a tailored product realization path.

- Additional information on TRLs, MRLs and other product development related resources can be found at the following links:

  – Technology Readiness Assessment (TRA) Deskbook, July 2009 - https://acc.dau.mil/CommunityBrowser.aspx?id=18545

  – Definition of Technology Readiness Levels - http://esto.nasa.gov/files/TRL_definitions.pdf

  – Technology Readiness Levels NASA white paper, April 1995 - http://www.hq.nasa.gov/office/codeq/trl/trl.pdf

  – Using the Technology Readiness Levels Scale to Support Technology Management in the DoD's ATD/STO Environments. September 2002 - http://www.sei.cmu.edu/reports/02sr027.pdf

  – DHS S&T Technology Readiness Level Calculator (ver 1.1.) - http://www.homelandsecurity.org/hsireports/DHS_ST_RL_Calculator_report200910?0.pdf

  – DAU TRL Calculator - https://acc.dau.mil/CommunityBrowser.aspx?id=25811

  – Manufacturing Readiness Assessment (MRA) Deskbook, May 2009 - https://acc.dau.mil/CommunityBrowser.aspx?id=18231

  – Assessing Manufacturing Risk - https://acc.dau.mil/CommunityBrowser.aspx?id=18231

  – GAO Report – Defense Acquisitions: Assessment of Selected Major Weapons Programs - http://www.gao.gov/new.items/d08361.pdf

  – About Manufacturing Readiness Assessments - http://www.wpafb.af.mil/library/factsheets/factsheet.asp?id=9757

Figure C.2.   Notes and additional information for the Product Realization Guide.

Appendix D

DHS's Private Sector Resources Guide

LETTER FROM ASSISTANT SECRETARY DOUGLAS A. SMITH

May 10, 2010

Dear Private Sector Partner,

To better facilitate your organization's access to the resources you need to help keep our country secure, DHS has developed this catalog. The first to be targeted specifically towards private sector partners and encompass all of DHS, this document collects the training, publications, guidance, alerts, newsletters, programs, and services available to the private sector across the department. It is organized by component and resource type and a comprehensive index is available to facilitate locating resources. Additionally, contact information across the department is available in Appendix A. Recognizing the diversity of the available resources as well as the continually evolving work of the department, this catalog will be updated regularly to publicize new resources and to increase private sector awareness.

In order to face the new threats and evolving hazards of today's security environment, we must develop and maintain critical homeland security capabilities at all layers of our society. We all share the responsibility to build all-hazards preparedness and resiliency into our way of life. As outlined in the Quadrennial Homeland Security Review Report released earlier this year, this *enterprise* approach is composed of multiple partners whose roles and responsibilities are distributed and shared among a broad-based community with a common interest in the public safety and well-being of America and American society.

The private sector is a critical partner in our homeland security efforts and my office is committed to strengthening the Department's relationship with organizations such as yours. As primary advisor to the Secretary on issues related to the private sector, including academia, non-profits, NGOs, and businesses, the Private Sector Office (PSO) coordinates active engagement between DHS and the private sector.

Regardless of where your organization fits into the homeland security enterprise, the Private Sector Office is committed to providing you with the assistance and support you require. You can contact our office at any time with requests, comments, questions, issues or concerns at private .sector@dhs.gov, (202) 282-8484.

Sincerely,
[Signed]
Douglas A. Smith
Assistant Secretary for the Private Sector

DEPARTMENT-WIDE RESOURCES

The Blog @ Homeland Security provides an inside-out view of what we do every day at the U.S. Department of Homeland Security. The Blog lets us talk about how we secure our nation, strengthen our programs, and unite the Department behind our common mission and principles. It also lets us hear from you. Visit www.dhs.gov/journal/theblog/.

Commercialization Office is responsible for the development and implementation of a commercialization process and for the execution of two innovative public-private partnerships that leverage research and development efforts in the private sector that are aligned to detailed operational requirements from Department stakeholders. The Commercialization Office also spearheads DHS Science and Technology's (S&T) outreach efforts that inform the private sector on "How to do business with DHS." See www.dhs.gov/xabout/structure/gc_1234194479267.shtm. Contact: SandT_Commercialization@hq.dhs.gov, 1-(202) 254-6749.

Cooperative Research and Development Agreements (CRADAs) are part of the national Technology Transfer Program, designed to assist federal laboratories in leveraging taxpayer dollars. As a designated federal laboratory and a member of the Federal Laboratory Consortium, the Federal Law Enforcement Training Center (FLETC) can provide personnel services, facilities, equipment and other resources to support research and development that is beneficial to both FLETC and the CRADA partner.

FLETC uses the CRADA program to establish partnerships for research and development in areas with potential to advance the nation's ability to train law enforcement personnel. The CRADA program can be used to identify and evaluate emerging technologies and training methodologies that can be incorporated into law enforcement and security training. See http://www.federallabs.org or contact FLETC-CRADAProgramOffice@ dhs.gov, (912) 267-2100.

DHS Center for Faith-Based and Community Initiatives (CFBCI) builds, sustains, and improves effective partnerships between government sectors and faith-based and community organizations. Located within FEMA, CFBCI is a vital communication link and engagement partner for faith-based and community organizations across the entire Department of Homeland Security. Visit www.dhs.gov/fbci. *For more information or to sign up to receive Information Updates,* e-mail Infofbci@dhs.gov.

DHS Office of Infrastructure Protection (IP) leads the national effort to mitigate risk to America's critical infrastructure from the full spectrum of 21st-century threats and hazards. IP coordinates with government and critical infrastructure owners and operators across 18 diverse sectors to enhance critical infrastructure resilience, strengthen protective programs, and share vital information. For more information on IP programs and resources visit www.dhs.gov/criticalinfrastructure.

DHS Private Sector Office As primary advisor to the Secretary on issues related to the private sector, including academia, nonprofits, NGOs, and businesses, the Private Sector Office coordinates active engagement between DHS and the private sector to build strong partnerships, shape policy, and enhance internal and external dialogue. For more information, contact the private sector office at private.sector@dhs.gov, (202) 282-8484.

DHS Private Sector Community Preparedness Updates The DHS Private Sector Office sends a weekly update e-mail collecting homeland security news and resources. To subscribe, see https://service.govdelivery.com/ service/subscribe.html?code=USDHS_99. For more information, contact private.sector@dhs.gov, (202) 282-8484.

DisabilityPreparedness.gov is the Disability Resource Center of the Interagency Coordinating Council on Emergency Preparedness and Individuals with Disabilities (ICC). Maintained by the DHS Office for Civil Rights and Civil Liberties (CRCL), this site is the main repository for information related to the activities of the ICC, including bimonthly updates regarding federal programs and services relevant to individuals with disabilities and emergency preparedness. The site also contains information to assist individuals with disabilities in personal preparedness planning; provides emergency managers, first responders, and other disaster service providers with resources relevant to working with individuals who have disabilities; and offers tips regarding how individuals with disabilities can get involved in preparedness activities within their communities. This resource can be accessed at www.disabilitypreparedness.gov. For more information, contact Disability.preparedness@dhs.gov, (202) 357-8483.

Electronic Crimes Task Force (ECTF) Program brings together not only federal, state, and local law enforcement, but also prosecutors, private industry, and academia. The common purpose is the prevention, detection, mitigation and aggressive investigation of attacks on the nation's financial and critical infrastructures. The U.S. Secret Service's ECTF and Electronic Crimes Working Group initiatives prioritize investigative cases that involve electronic crimes. These initiatives provide necessary support and resources to field investigations that meet any one of the following criteria: significant economic or community impact, participation of organized criminal groups involving multiple districts or transnational organizations, or the use of schemes involving new technology. For more information, see www.secretservice.gov/ectf.shtml.

E-Verify and Unfair Labor Practices The DHS Office for Civil Rights and Civil Liberties (CRCL) staff provides training on the responsibilities imposed upon the private sector when using E-Verify. Training includes best practices, examples of unlawful practices against workers, and preparing an HR Department to use E-Verify. The training assists employer understanding of how to use E-Verify in a responsible manner without violating prohibitions against discrimination. For more information, contact CRCL at crcltraining@dhs.gov, (202) 357-8258.

Homeland Security Information Network (HSIN) is a user-driven, Web-based, sensitive but unclassified (SBU) information sharing platform that connects a broad range of homeland security mission partners. One portal of the HSIN enterprise is HSIN-CS, managed by the Office of Infrastructure Protection. DHS has designated HSIN-CS to be its primary information-sharing platform between critical infrastructure and key resource sector stakeholders. HSIN-CS enables DHS and critical infrastructure owners and operators to communicate, coordinate, and share sensitive and sector-relevant information to protect their critical assets, systems, functions, and networks at no charge to sector stakeholders. Vetted critical infrastructure private sector owners and operators are eligible to access HSIN-CS. To request access to

HSIN-CS, please e-mail CIKRISEAccess@hq.dhs.gov. When requesting access, please indicate the critical infrastructure sector to which your company belongs and include your name, company, official e-mail address, and supervisor's name and phone number. For more information, see www.dhs.gov/hsin or contact hsin.helpdesk@dhs.gov, (866) 430-0162.

Intelligence and Analysis Private Sector Partnership Program The Office of Intelligence and Analysis (I&A) strives to synchronize information sharing of timely, accurate, and actionable intelligence information with the private sector across the spectrum of business and security operations with respect to protecting privacy and civil rights and civil liberties. I&A provides private sector businesses, groups, and trade associations with tailored threat briefings to meet their security information needs. Additionally, the office creates intelligence products that are posted on the Homeland Security Information Network-Critical Sectors (HSIN-CS) portal for use by vetted critical infrastructure owners and operators. For more information, see www.dhs.gov/hsin. To request access to HSIN-CS, e-mail CIKRISEAccess@hq.dhs.gov. When requesting access, please indicate the critical infrastructure sector to which your company belongs and include your name, company, official e-mail address, and supervisor's name and phone number. For more information, contact I&APrivateSectorCoordinator@hq.dhs.gov or call (202) 447-3517 or (202) 870-6087.

Lessons Learned and Information Sharing (LLIS.gov), a U.S. Department of Homeland Security (DHS)/Federal Emergency Management Agency program, is the national online network of lessons learned, best practices, and innovative ideas for the emergency response and homeland security communities. This information and collaboration resource helps emergency response providers and homeland security officials prevent, protect against, respond to, and recover from terrorist attacks, natural disasters, and other emergencies. To register for LLIS, please visit www.llis.gov, contact the program via e-mail feedback@llis.dhs.gov, or call (866) 276-7001.

Office of Small and Disadvantaged Business Utilization (OSDBU) serves as the focal point for small business acquisition matters and works closely with all DHS components to implement the program. OSDBU makes available forecasts of contract opportunities, vendor outreach sessions, a list of component small business specialists, DHS prime contractors, and information about the DHS mentor-protégé program. See www.dhs.gov/openforbusiness or contact OSDBU, (202) 447-5555.

DHS Open Source Enterprise Daily Intelligence Reports provide open source information on several topics of interest. The following are currently available open source reports: *The DHS Daily Digest Report, The DHS Daily Cyber Report, The DHS Daily Infectious Diseases Report, The DHS Daily Human Trafficking and Smuggling Report, The DHS Daily Drug Trafficking and Smuggling Report,* and *The Daily Illicit Commercial Trafficking and Smuggling Report.* These reports may be accessed on the Homeland Security Information Network (HSIN) or private sector partners may request that they be added to distribution by e-mailing OSINTBranchMailbox@hq.dhs.gov with subject line reading "Request DHS Daily [name] Report."

The National Information Exchange Model (NIEM) Program is a federal, state, local, and tribal interagency initiative providing a national approach and common vocabulary for information exchange. NIEM has a robust training curriculum that is accessible both in classroom and online. The primary audience for the NIEM Training Program is executives, project and program managers, architects, and technical implementers within federal, state, local, tribal, and private entities. Additional information on the training courses and NIEM can be obtained by visiting www.NIEM.gov or e-mailing NIEMPMO@NIEM.gov.

Ready Business The U.S. Department of Homeland Security and the Advertising Council launched the *Ready Business* Campaign in September 2004. This extension of the successful *Ready* Campaign, *Ready Business* helps owners and managers of small- and medium-sized businesses prepare their employees, operations, and assets in the event of an emergency. For free tools and resources, including how to create a business emergency plan, please visit www.ready.gov.

Traveler Redress Inquiry Program (DHS TRIP) provides a single point of contact for individuals who have inquiries or seek resolution regarding difficulties they experienced during their travel screening at airports, train stations, or crossing U.S. borders. To initiate an inquiry, please log on to DHS TRIP's interactive website www.dhs.gov/trip. For more information, contact the TSA Contact Center, (866) 289-9673.

U.S. CITIZENSHIP AND IMMIGRATION SERVICES (USCIS)

U.S. Citizenship and Immigration Services (USCIS) is the government agency that oversees lawful immigration to the United States. USCIS will secure America's promise as a nation of immigrants by providing accurate and useful information to our customers, granting immigration and citizenship benefits, promoting an awareness and understanding of citizenship, and ensuring the integrity of our immigration system. www .uscis.gov.

USCIS Asylum Program resources include an information guide for prospective asylum applicants available in a number of languages. For more information, visit www.uscis.gov/asylum.

E-Verify is an Internet-based system that allows an employer, using information reported on an employee's Form I-9, to determine the eligibility of that employee to work in the United States. For most employers, the use of E-Verify is voluntary and limited to determining the employment eligibility of new hires only. There is no charge to employers to use E-Verify. Available resources include a demonstration video, fact sheets, weekly webinars, an overview presentation, brochures and posters for employers and employees, and a rights and responsibilities guide. See www.dhs.gov/everify. Contact E-Verify@dhs.gov, (888) 464-4218 with any questions or comments.

U.S. Civics and Citizenship Online Resource Center for Instructors provides information about USCIS's Resource Center to help instructors prepare students for naturalization and incorporate civics into ESL instruction. See www.uscis.gov/files/nativedocuments/M-662.pdf.

Civics and Citizenship Toolkit—A Collection of Educational Resources for Immigrants contains a variety of educational materials designed to help permanent residents learn more about the U.S. and prepare for the naturalization process. For more information, visit www.citizenshiptoolkit .gov.

Expanding ESL, Civics, and Citizenship Education in Your Community: A Start-Up Guide provides an overview and recommendations to help organizations design and offer ESL and civics/citizenship classes for immigrants. See www.uscis.gov/files/nativedocuments/M-677.pdf.

USCIS Genealogy Program is a fee-for-service program providing family historians and other researchers with timely access to historical immigration and naturalization records. The USCIS Genealogy Program offers two services: Index Search, using biographical information provided by the researcher, and a Record Copy Request, where researchers with valid record citations (USCIS file numbers), gained through a USCIS Genealogy Program index search or through independent research, may request copies of historical immigration and naturalization records. Questions

about the USCIS Genealogy Program may be sent to Genealogy.USCIS@
dhs.gov. For more information, see www.uscis.gov/portal/site/uscis/
menuitem.eb1d4c2a3e5b9ac89243c6a7543f6d1a/?vgnextoid=d21f3711ca5
ca110VgnVCM1000004718190aRCRD&vgnextchannel=d21f3711ca5ca110
VgnVCM1000004718190aRCRD.

Guide to Naturalization contains information about the naturalization
process, laws, and regulations. See www.uscis.gov/files/article/M-476
.pdf.

If You Have the Right to Work, Don't Let Anyone Take it Away Poster
is a poster with Department of Justice information regarding discrimination in the workplace. See www.uscis.gov/files/nativedocuments/
e-verify-swa-right-to-work.pdf.

USCIS Information for Employers and Employees on the employment
authorization verification process and the immigration petition process.
See   www.uscis.gov/portal/site/uscis/menuitem.eb1d4c2a3e5b9ac8
9243c6a7543f6d1a/?vgnextoid=ff1d83453d4a3210VgnVCM100000b92ca
60aRCRD&vgnextchannel=ff1d83453d4a3210VgnVCM100000b92ca60aR
CRD. For more information contact Public.Engagement@dhs.gov.

USCIS Office of Public Engagement (OPE) seeks to focus on open, can-
did, and constructive collaboration with community stakeholders at all
levels. OPE coordinates and directs USCIS-wide dialogue with external
stakeholders to advance the Agency's vision of customer inclusiveness
by actively engaging stakeholders to ensure information flow and to in-
stitutionalize a mechanism whereby their input will be considered in the
process of policy formulation, priority calibration, and assessment of organizational performance. The goal of the office is to provide information
and invite feedback to inform our work. See the Outreach tab at www
.uscis.gov. For more information contact Public.Engagement@dhs.gov.

USCIS Resources USCIS offers a variety of resources for our customers,
the organizations that serve them and the public. USCIS is committed
to supporting the resource needs of stakeholders, including Congress,
community-based organizations and legal practitioners, and educators
and researchers. Resources include customer guides, videos, citizenship
toolkits, an immigration law glossary, reports and studies, civics and
citizenship education resources, and a historical library. See the "Resources" section at www.uscis.gov. For more information contact Public
.Engagement@dhs.gov.

Welcome to the United States: A Guide for New Immigrants With this landmark publication, the federal government reaches out to new immigrants with essential orientation materials needed to adjust to life in America. It also contains basic history and civics information that introduces new immigrants to U.S. history and the system of government. See www.uscis.gov/files/nativedocuments/M-618.pdf.

CITIZENSHIP AND IMMIGRATION SERVICES OMBUDSMAN (CIS OMBUDSMAN)

The CIS Ombudsman is a separate office within the Department of Homeland Security dedicated to improved national security, efficiency, and customer service in the immigration benefits process. The CIS Ombudsman provides recommendations for resolving individual and employer problems with the United States Citizenship and Immigration Services (USCIS). The CIS Ombudsman assists individuals and employers in resolving problems with USCIS; identifies areas in which individuals and employers have problems in dealing with USCIS; and proposes changes to mitigate identified problems. Please note that the CIS Ombudsman is not part of USCIS. The CIS Ombudsman is dedicated to open and accessible communication with both individuals and employers and not only welcomes, but encourages your comments. Comments, examples, and suggestions may be sent to the Ombudsman at cisombudsman@dhs.gov .www.dhs.gov/cisombudsman.

CIS Ombudsman Annual Reports to Congress By June 30 of each calendar year, the Annual Report is delivered to the House and Senate Committees on the Judiciary without any prior comment or amendment from any administrative agency official including: the secretary, deputy secretary, or director of USCIS. The Ombudsman's annual reports focus on identifying systemic issues that cause delay in granting immigration benefits as well as pervasive and serious problems faced by individuals and employers in their interactions with USCIS. The Annual Report contains cumulative analysis and recommendations and provides details on activities undertaken by the Ombudsman during the reporting period of June 1 through May 31 of the calendar year. See www.dhs.gov/xabout/structure/gc_1183996985695.shtm.

CIS Ombudsman's Community Call-In Teleconference Series provides an opportunity to discuss your interactions with U.S. Citizenship and Immigration Services (USCIS) and share your comments, thoughts, and suggestions as well as any issues of concern. For more information, including questions and answers from previous teleconferences and a schedule of upcoming calls, visit www.dhs.gov/xabout/structure/ gc_1171038701035.shtm. To participate in these calls, please RSVP to cisombudsman.publicaffairs@dhs.gov specifying which call you would like to join. Participants will receive a return e-mail with the call-in information.

CIS Ombudsman Updates share information on current trends and issues to assist individuals and employers in resolving problems with US-CIS. See www.dhs.gov/xabout/structure/gc_1221837986181.shtm.

Previous Recommendations by the CIS Ombudsman are intended to ensure national security and the integrity of the legal immigration system, increase efficiencies in administering citizenship and immigration services, and improve customer service in the rendering of citizenship and immigration services. Problems reported to the Ombudsman by individuals and employers (during the Ombudsman's travels), discussions with immigration stakeholders, and suggestions of USCIS employees themselves provide the basis for many of the recommendations. To view the recommendations as well as USCIS responses, see www.dhs.gov/ files/programs/editorial_0769.shtm.

Send Your Recommendations to the CIS Ombudsman. Your recommendations are accepted and encouraged. The Ombudsman is dedicated to identifying systemic problems in the immigration benefits process and preparing recommendations for submission to U.S. Citizenship and Immigration Services (USCIS) for process changes. The Ombudsman believes that process change recommendations from individuals like you represent one of the best sources for identifying systemic problems in the immigration benefits process. Ideally, your recommendations for process changes should not only identify the problem you are experiencing, but should also contain a proposed solution that will not only benefit your individual case, but others who may be experiencing the same problem as well. Send your comments, examples, and suggestions to cisombudsman@dhs.gov or to the following mailing address:

Citizenship and Immigration Services Ombudsman
ATTN: Recommendations
United States Department of Homeland Security
Mail Stop 1225
Washington, D.C. 20528-1225

Submit a Case Problem to the CIS Ombudsman. If you are experiencing problems during the adjudication of an immigration benefit with U.S. Citizenship and Immigration Services (USCIS), you can submit a case problem to the CIS Ombudsman using DHS Form 7001 (CIS Ombudsman Case Problem Submission Form). To submit a case problem on behalf of somebody other than yourself, you should ensure that the person the case problem is about (the applicant for a USCIS immigration benefit, or the petitioner who seeks to obtain an immigration benefit for a third party) consents to your inquiry (see Submitting a Case Problem using DHS Form 7001: Section 15 Consent). See www.dhs.gov/files/programs/editorial_0497.shtm.

U.S. COAST GUARD (USCG)

For over two centuries the U.S. Coast Guard has safeguarded our Nation's maritime interests in the heartland, in the ports, at sea, and around the globe. We protect the maritime economy and the environment, we defend our maritime borders, and we save those in peril. This history has forged our character and purpose as America's Maritime Guardian—*Always Ready* for all hazards and all threats. www.uscg.mil.

America's Waterways Watch is a combined effort of the U.S. Coast Guard and its Reserve and Auxiliary components to enlist the active participation of those who live, work, or play around America's waterfront areas. For more information, contact aww@uscg.mil; visit www.americaswaterwaywatch.us. To report suspicious activity call 877-24WATCH (877-249-2824).

U.S. Coast Guard Auxiliary is the uniformed volunteer component of the United States Coast Guard. Created by an Act of Congress in 1939, the Auxiliary directly supports the Coast Guard in all missions, except military and law enforcement actions. The Auxiliary conducts safety patrols on local waterways, assists the Coast Guard with homeland security duties, teaches boating safety classes, conducts free vessel safety checks for the public, as well as many other activities. The Auxiliary has members in all 50 states, Puerto Rico, the Virgin Islands, American Samoa, and Guam. For more information, visit www.cgaux.org/.

U.S. Coast Guard Maritime Information eXchange ("CGMIX") makes U.S. Coast Guard (USCG) maritime information available on the public Internet in the form of searchable databases. Much of the information on the CGMIX website comes from the USCG's Marine Information for Safety and Law Enforcement (MISLE) information system. See http://cgmix.uscg.mil/.

U.S. Coast Guard Navigation Center provides services for safe, secure, and efficient maritime transportation by delivering: enhanced situational awareness through continuous monitoring and managing of vessel movement system, quality positioning, navigation and timing signals, accurate and timely maritime information services, and system requirements and performing operational oversight of premier navigation services. See www.navcen.uscg.gov/. For more information use the e-mail Inquiry located at www.navcen.uscg.gov/misc/NIS_contact_us.htm or call (703) 313-5900.

HOMEPORT is an Internet repository of detailed information of interest to the Port Community. Specific Homeport topics include: Containers, Domestic Vessels (U.S. Flag Vessels), Environmental, Facilities, Incident Management and Preparedness, Investigations (Maritime Casualties and Incidents), Marine Safety, Maritime Domain Awareness (MDA) & Information Sharing (IS), Maritime Security, Merchant Mariners, Port State Control, Ports and Waterways, Regulations/Administrative Adjudications, Strategic Initiatives, USCG Sector (Field Unit) Directory, Vessel Standards, Counter Piracy, International Port Security (IPS) Program, Maritime Transportation Security Act (MTSA), Marine Safety Center, Mariner Credential Verification, and Mariner Credential Application Status. See http://homeport.uscg.mil.

USCG National Maritime Center (NMC) issues Merchant Mariner Credentials (MMC) to fully qualified U.S. mariners, approves and audits training programs and courses offered by mariner training organizations throughout the United States, and provides information about merchant mariner records. For more information, see www.uscg.mil/nmc or contact NMC Customer Service Center: (888) IASKNMC (1-888-427-5662).

National Vessel Movement Center (NVMC) provides the maritime industry with a method to submit electronically a Notice of Arrival and a Notice of Departure, which fulfills USCG and the Customs and Border Protection's (CBP) requirements. See www.nvmc.uscg.gov or contact the NVMC sans@nvmc.uscg.gov, (800) 708-9823 or (304) 264-2502.

Vessel Documentation (for U.S. Flag Vessels) The National Vessel Documentation Center facilitates maritime commerce and the availability of financing while protecting economic privileges of United States citizens through the enforcement of regulations, and provides a register of vessels available in time of war or emergency to defend and protect the United States of America. See www.uscg.mil/hq/cg5/nvdc/. For more information call (800) 799-8362 or (304) 271-2400 (7:30 a.m. to 5:00 p.m. Eastern Time).

U.S. CUSTOMS AND BORDER PROTECTION (CBP)

CBP is one of the Department of Homeland Security's largest and most complex components, with a priority mission of keeping terrorists and their weapons out of the U.S. It also has a responsibility for securing and facilitating trade and travel while enforcing hundreds of U.S. regulations, including immigration and drug laws. www.cbp.gov.

CBP Publications and Guidance

AIRBUST program provides awareness of suspicious small aircraft and behaviors. The AIRBUST Card is a pocket-sized laminated card displaying the phone number that people can call to report suspicious or low-flying aircraft, 1-866-AIRBUST (1-866-247-2878). This number rings directly to the CBP Air and Marine Operations Center (AMOC) floor, and anyone can use the phone number for reporting. On one side of the card are drawings of single- and twin-engine aircraft often used to transport contraband. The opposite side of the card lists helpful information to note when reporting. The AIRBUST poster, CBP Publication 0000-0716, is an 8.5 x 11 poster with the 1-866-AIRBUST (1-866-247-2878) phone number. It also lists four general items of interest that can tip off a general aviation airport employee or law enforcement official that a particular aircraft or pilot may be involved in illicit activity. For more information, or to order these publications, call 951-656-8000.

CBP Directives Pertaining to Intellectual Property Rights are policy guidance documents that explain CBP's legal authority and policies implementing certain laws and regulations. They are distributed to CBP personnel to clarify implementation procedures and are made available to the public to explain CBP's policies. To access these directives, please visit www.cbp.gov/xp/cgov/trade/legal/directives/. For additional information, or e-mail CBP IPR Policy and Programs at iprpolicyprograms@dhs.gov.

Entry-Level Test Study Guides for CBP Job Applicants CBP provides study guides and test preparation materials for applicants to several core occupations. Applicants for Border Patrol Agent, Customs and Border Protection Officer & Agriculture Specialist, and Intelligence Research Specialist positions will find these resources beneficial during their application process. These resources provide test-taking hints, helpful information on how to prepare for a test, and practice tests. For more information, please visit: http://cbp.gov/xp/cgov/careers/study_guides/.

Intellectual Property Rights (IPR) Seizure Statistics CBP maintains statistics on IPR seizures made by the Department of Homeland Security (CBP and ICE) at: www.cbp.gov/xp/cgov/trade/priority_trade/ipr/pubs/seizure/. For any specific questions or concerns, please contact CBP by e-mail at: iprpolicyprograms@dhs.gov or ipr.helpdesk@dhs.gov.

U.S. Border Patrol Checkpoints Brochure provides information for the public about Border Patrol checkpoints available at: www.cbp.gov/linkhandler/cgov/newsroom/fact_sheets/border/border_patrol/bp_checkpoints.ctt/bp_checkpoints.pdf.

CBP Alerts and Newsletters

Informed Compliance Publications are available on a specific trade issue, which summarizes practical information for the trade community to better understand their obligations under Customs and related laws. These publications are available at: www.cbp.gov/xp/cgov/trade/legal/.

U.S. Border Patrol Blotter, Newsletter, and Alerts compiles the latest information on noteworthy occurrences documenting apprehensions of criminals, seizures of illegal drugs, rescue missions, and many other Border Patrol success stories from around the country. These highlights can be found at: http://cbp.gov/xp/cgov/border_security/border_patrol/weekly_blotter/. The border patrol also publishes a newsletter: www.cbp.gov/xp/cgov/newsroom/publications/frontline_magazine/ and alerts: www.cbp.gov/xp/cgov/newsroom/advisories/.

CBP Technical Assistance

1-800 BE ALERT The public is welcome to actively participate in helping to secure our nation's borders by reporting suspicious activity to the U.S. Border Patrol via a toll free telephone reporting system: "BE ALERT". To report suspicious activity: Call (800) BE ALERT or (800) 232-5378. For more information on U.S. Border Patrol Checkpoints: Call (877) 227-5511. International Callers Call +1 (703) 526-4200.

Automated Commercial Environment (ACE) National Help Desk provides customer technical support services 24 hours a day, seven days a week, including information about ACE Secure Data Portal account access, account management, and report generation. The ACE Help Desk is the first point of contact for all ACE users experiencing system difficulties. To reach the ACE Help Desk, please call: (800) 927-8729.

Cargo Systems Messaging Service (CSMS) is an active, live, searchable database of messages that are of interest to Automatic Broker Interface (ABI) filers, Automated Commercial Environment (ACE) event participants, ACE Portal Accounts users, ACE reports users, air carriers, ocean carriers, Periodic Monthly Statement participants, and rail and truck carriers. CSMS is augmented by an e-mail subscription service, which is available at: https://service.govdelivery.com/service/multi_subscribe .html?code=USDHSCBP&custom_id=938&origin=https://apps.cbp .gov/csms.

CBP Client Representatives are the first points of contact for importers, exporters, transportation providers, and brokers wishing to automate any of their Customs processes. Client representatives are the contact point for all system-related problems and questions from trade partners. For more information about client reps and the services offered to members of the trade, please visit: www.cbp.gov/xp/cgov/trade/automated/ automated_systems/client_reps.xml or contact the CBP Client Representative Office at: (571) 468-5000.

CBP INFO Center Self Service Q&A Database is a searchable database with over 600 answers to commonly (and not so commonly) asked questions about CBP programs, requirements, and procedures. If visitors to the site are unable to find an answer to their question, they may also submit an inquiry or complaint for personal assistance. To use the searchable database, please visit https://help.cbp.gov/cgi-bin/customs.cfg/php/ enduser/home.php?p_sid=YeyXThOj. Or call the CBP INFO Center at (877) CBP-5511 or (703) 526-4200.

Entry Process into United States CBP welcomes more than 1.1 million international travelers into the United States at land, air, and seaports on an average day. U.S. citizens and international visitors should consult the following publications and factsheets for information to simplify their entry into the United States. For information about international travel, visit www.cbp.gov/xp/cgov/travel/. For more information, please contact the CBP Information Center at (877) 227-5511.

Importing into the United States CBP will facilitate about $2 trillion in legitimate trade this year while enforcing U.S. trade laws that protect the economy and the health and safety of the American people. We accomplish this through close partnerships with the trade community, other government agencies, and foreign governments. See www.cbp.gov/linkhandler/cgov/newsroom/publications/trade/iius.ctt/iius.pdf. For information about CBP Trade programs, visit www.cbp.gov/xp/cgov/trade/.

CBP Programs and Services

Automated Commercial Environment (ACE) is the United States' commercial trade processing system designed to automate border processing, to enhance border security, and to foster our nation's economic security through lawful international trade and travel. ACE will eventually replace the current import processing system for CBP, the Automated Commercial System (ACS). ACE is part of a multi-year CBP modernization effort and is being deployed in phases. For more information about ACE, please visit www.cbp.gov/xp/cgov/trade/automated/modernization/.

Automated Commercial System (ACS) is a data information system used by CBP to track, control, and process commercial goods imported into the United States. Through the use of Electronic Data Interchange (EDI), ACS facilitates merchandise processing for CBP and the private sector. ACS is accessed through the CBP Automated Broker Interface (ABI) and permits qualified participants to electronically file required import data with CBP. ABI is a voluntary program available to brokers, importers, carriers, port authorities, and independent service centers. For more information about ACS, please visit www.cbp.gov/xp/cgov/trade/automated/automated_systems/acs/. For additional information specific to ABI, please contact the CBP Client Representative Office at (571) 468-5000.

Automated Export System (AES) is the electronic way to file export declarations and ocean manifest information with CBP. For more information about AES, including technical documentation, software vendors, and other items of interest, please visit www.cbp.gov/xp/cgov/trade/automated/aes/.

Automated Manifest System (AMS) is a multi-modular cargo inventory control and release notification system. AMS facilitates the movement and delivery of cargo by multiple modes of transportation. Carriers, port authorities, service bureaus, freight forwarders, and container freight stations can participate in AMS. Sea AMS allows participants to transmit manifest data electronically prior to vessel arrival. CBP can then determine in advance whether the merchandise merits examination or immediate release. Air AMS allows carriers to obtain notifications of releases, in-bond authorizations, general order, permit to proceed, and local transfer authorization upon flight departure or arrival from the last foreign port. Rail AMS allows rail carriers to electronically transmit information to CBP. When all bills on a train are assigned, the rail carrier transmits a list of the bills and containers in standing car order. For more information about AMS, please visit www.cbp.gov/xp/cgov/trade/automated/automated_systems/acs/acs_ams.xmlACS.

Carrier Liaison Program (CLP) This program provides standardized training and assistance to international air carriers related to admissibility and fraudulent document detection in order to encourage carrier compliance with U.S. Immigration Laws. For more information about CLP, please visit www.cbp.gov/xp/cgov/travel/inspections_carriers_facilities/clp/, e-mail CLP@dhs.gov, or call (202) 344-3440.

Customs-Trade Partnership Against Terrorism (C-TPAT) is a voluntary government-business initiative to strengthen and improve the overall international supply chain and U.S. border security. C-TPAT recognizes that CBP can provide the highest level of cargo security only through close cooperation with the ultimate owners of the international supply chain such as importers, carriers, consolidators, licensed customs brokers, and manufacturers. Through this initiative, CBP is asking businesses to ensure the integrity of their security practices, communicate, and verify the security guidelines of their business partners within the supply chain. For more information, or to apply online, please visit www.cbp.gov/xp/cgov/trade/cargo_security/ctpat/. For questions or concerns, please contact the CBP Industry Partnership Program at (202) 344-1180, or by fax (202) 344-2626 or e-mail, industry.partnership@dhs.gov.

eAllegations provides concerned members of the public a means to confidentially report suspected trade violations to CBP. For more information, or to initiate an investigation, please visit https://apps.cbp.gov/eallegations/, or contact the Commercial Targeting and Enforcement, Office of International Trade at: (800) BE-ALERT.

Electronic System for Travel Authorization (ESTA) is a free, automated system that determines the eligibility of visitors to travel to the U.S. under the Visa Waiver Program. The ESTA application collects the same information collected on Form I-94W. ESTA applications may be submitted at any time prior to travel, though it is recommended travelers apply when they begin preparing travel plans. To apply online, please visit: https://esta.cbp.dhs.gov/. For additional information, please call: (202) 344-3710.

Global Entry is a pilot program managed by CBP which allows preapproved, low-risk travelers, expedited clearance upon arrival into the United States. Although this program is intended for "frequent travelers" who make several international trips per year, there is no minimum number of trips an applicant must make in order to qualify. For more information about Global Entry, please visit: www.cbp.gov/xp/cgov/travel/trusted_traveler/global_entry/ or apply online at: https://goes-app.cbp.dhs.gov/. For additional questions or concerns, please contact CBP by e-mail, cbp.goes.support@dhs.gov, or by phone, (866) 530-4172.

Importer Self-Assessment Program (ISA) is a voluntary approach to trade compliance. The program provides the opportunity for importers to assume responsibility for monitoring their own compliance in exchange for benefits. Public information regarding this program, including frequently asked questions, policy information, best practices, and requirements can be found at www.cbp.gov/xp/cgov/trade/trade_programs/importer_self_assessment/.

Importer Self-Assessment Product Safety Pilot (ISA-PS) CBP and the Consumer Product Safety Commission (CPSC) have a strong history of partnership in combating unsafe imports and have worked together on significant product recalls. CBP announces a new partnership with CPSC and importers to prevent unsafe imports from entering the United States. For more information, please visit www.cbp.gov/xp/cgov/trade/trade_programs/importer_self_assessment/isa_safety_pilot.xml.

Intellectual Property Rights (IPR) Enforcement: A Priority Trade Issue The trade in counterfeit and pirated goods threatens America's innovation economy, the competitiveness of our businesses, the livelihoods of U.S. workers, national security, and the health and safety of consumers. The trade in these illegitimate goods is associated with smuggling and other criminal activities, and often funds criminal enterprises. For more information, please visit www.cbp.gov/xp/cgov/trade/priority_trade/ipr/.

Intellectual Property Rights (IPR) e-Recordation and IPR Search The first step in obtaining IPR protection by CBP is to record validly registered trademarks and copyrights with CBP through the Intellectual Property Rights e-Recordation (IPRR) online system. CBP's online recordation allows intellectual property owners to electronically record their trademarks and copyrights with CBP, and makes IPR recordation information readily available to CBP personnel, facilitating IPR seizures by CBP. CBP uses recordation information to actively monitor shipments and prevent the importation or exportation of infringing goods. For more information please visit: http://iprs.cbp.gov/. For additional information, please e-mail at hqiprbranch@dhs.gov or call (202) 325-0020.

Intellectual Property Rights (IPR) Continuous Sample Bond CBP established a new continuous bond option for Intellectual Property Rights (IPR) sample bonds. Under CBP regulations, CBP may provide samples of certain merchandise suspected of bearing infringing trademarks, trade names, or copyrights of imports seized for such violations, to trademark, trade name, and copyright owners. A sample bond template can be downloaded at: www.cbp.gov/xp/cgov/trade/trade_programs/bonds/ipr_bonds_samples/. For additional information, please contact CBP's Revenue Division, Office of Finance by e-mail at: cbp.bondquestions@dhs.gov, or by phone at (317) 614-4880 or by fax at (317) 614-4517.

Intellectual Property Rights (IPR) Help Desk can provide information and assistance for a range of IPR-related issues including: IPR border enforcement procedures, reporting allegations of IPR infringement, assistance for owners of recorded IPRs to develop product identification training materials, and to assist officers at ports of entry in identifying IPR-infringing goods. To reach the CBP IPR Help Desk, please call at (562) 980-3119 ext. 252, or e-mail at ipr.helpdesk@dhs.gov.

Intellectual Property Rights (IPR) and Restricted Merchandise Branch oversees the IPR recordation program and provides IPR infringement determinations and rulings. For legal questions about CBP's IPR recordation program, please e-mail at: hqiprbranch@dhs.gov, or call (202) 325-0020.

Intellectual Property Rights (IPR) U.S.–EU Joint Brochure and Web Toolkit for Trademark, Copyright Owners To promote strong and effective border enforcement of Intellectual Property Rights, CBP and Customs Officials in the European Union have jointly developed a brochure and Web toolkit to assist intellectual property owners in working with Customs to enforce their rights and to prepare information to help U.S. and E.U. Customs Agencies determine whether goods are counterfeit or pirated. To access the Protecting Intellectual Property Rights at Our Borders brochure, please visit: www.cbp.gov/linkhandler/cgov/trade/priority_trade/ipr/pubs/cpg_final_090306.ctt/cpg_final_090306.pdf. To access the Toolkit, please visit: www.cbp.gov/linkhandler/cgov/trade/priority_trade/ipr/cpg_final_090306.ctt/cpg_final_090306.pdf. For additional questions or concerns, please contact the IPR Help Desk by e-mail, ipr.helpdesk@dhs.gov or phone, (562) 980-3119 ext. 252.

CBP Laboratories and Scientific Services coordinates technical and scientific support to all CBP trade and border protection activities. For more information, please visit www.cbp.gov/xp/cgov/trade/automated/labs_scientific_svcs/.

National Gang Intelligence Center is a multi-agency effort that integrates the gang intelligence assets of federal, state, and local law enforcement entities to serve as a centralized intelligence resource for gang information and analytical support. The mission of the NGIC is to support law enforcement agencies through timely and accurate information sharing and strategic/tactical analysis of federal, state, and local law enforcement intelligence focusing on the growth, migration, criminal activity, and association of gangs that pose a significant threat to communities throughout the United States. The NGIC concentrates on gangs operating on a national level that demonstrate criminal connectivity between sets and common identifiers and goals. Because many violent gangs do not operate on a national level, the NGIC will also focus on regional-level gangs. The NGIC produces intelligence assessments, intelligence bulletins, joint agency intelligence products, and other non-standard intelligence products for our customers. For more information, please contact the NGIC, (703) 414-8600.

Private Aircraft Travel Entry Programs The *Advance Information on Private Aircraft Arriving and Departing the United States* final rule requires that pilots of private aircraft submit advance notice and manifest data on all persons traveling on board. Required information must be submitted to CBP via an approved electronic data interchange system no later than 60 minutes prior to departure. The CBP.gov website offers information about current CBP policies, regulations, documentary requirements, and ports of entry. For more information, please visit www.cbp.gov/xp/cgov/travel/inspections_carriers_facilities/apis/. For additional questions or concerns, please contact CBP via e-mail at Private.Aircraft.Support@dhs.gov.

Secure Freight Initiative (SFI) and Importer Security Filing and additional carrier requirements (10+2) The Secure Freight Initiative (SFI), through partnerships with foreign governments, terminal operators, and carriers enhances DHS's capability to better assess the security of U.S.-bound maritime containers by scanning them for nuclear and other radioactive materials before they are laden on vessels bound for the

United States. For the domestic CBP officers, SFI provides additional data points that are used in conjunction with advanced data, such as 24-hour rule information, 10+2, Customs-Trade Partnership Against Terrorism information, and the Automated Targeting System to assess the risk of each container coming to the United States. For more information, please visit www.cbp.gov/xp/cgov/trade/cargo_security/secure_freight_ initiative/, or e-mail questions to securefreightinitiative@dhs.gov.

CBP Trade Outreach The Office of Trade Relations supports communications between CBP and the private sector, and provides information for new importers, exporters, and small businesses. For more information, please visit www.cbp.gov/xp/cgov/trade/trade_outreach/.

Trusted Traveler Programs (TTP) include FAST-Driver, NEXUS, SENTRI, and Global Entry. TTP provide expedited travel for preapproved, low-risk travelers through dedicated lanes and kiosks (NEXUS at Canadian Pre-Clearance ports). Program members received RFID-embedded cards that facilitate border processing by confirming membership and identity and running law enforcement checks. For more information about a CBP's trusted traveler programs, please visit www.cbp.gov/xp/ cgov/travel/trusted_traveler/.

Visa Waiver Program (VWP) enables citizens and nationals from 34 countries to travel to and enter the United States for business or visitor purposes for up to 90 days without obtaining a visa. For more information about the Visa Waiver Program, please visit www.cbp.gov/xp/ cgov/travel/id_visa/business_pleasure/vwp/.

Western Hemisphere Travel Initiative (WHTI) requires all travelers, U.S. citizens, and foreign nationals to present a passport or other acceptable documents that denote identity and citizenship when entering the United States. For more information about WHTI, please visit: www .getyouhome.gov/, or contact CBP Customer Service at (877)227-5511 or (703) 526-4200, TDD: (866) 880-6582.

CYBERSECURITY AND COMMUNICATIONS (CS&C)

The **Office of Cybersecurity and Communications (CS&C)** is responsible for enhancing the security, resiliency, and reliability of the nation's cyber and communications infrastructure. CS&C actively engages the public and private sectors as well as international partners to prepare for, prevent, and respond to catastrophic incidents that could degrade or overwhelm these strategic assets. www.dhs.gov/xabout/structure/ gc_1185202475883.shtm.

CS&C Training and Education

Control Systems Security Program (CSSP) Instructor-Led Cybersecurity Training is provided through an introductory course for IT professionals or a five-day advanced course that includes hands-on instruction in an actual control system environment. For more information, see www .us-cert.gov/control_systems/cstraining.html, or contact CSSP@dhs.gov.

Cyber Education and Workforce Development Program (CEWD) As cyber threats and their sophistication increase, the demand for qualified IT security professionals increases as well. In response, the National Cyber Security Division's Cyber Education and Workforce Development program (CEWD) developed the IT Security Essential Body of Knowledge (EBK). The IT Security EBK is an umbrella framework that links competencies and functional perspectives to IT security roles to accurately reflect a national perspective. See www.us-cert.gov/ITSecurityEBK/.

CS&C Publications and Guidance

Cybersecurity Information Products and Recommended Practices provide current cybersecurity information resources and recommend security practices to help industry understand emerging control systems cybersecurity issues and mitigate vulnerabilities. This information will help users reduce their exposure and susceptibility to cyber attacks and exploits. For a complete list and access to cybersecurity information products, visit www.us-cert.gov/control_systems/csdocuments.html. An interactive site with recommended practices for control system networks can be found at http://csrp.inl.gov/. For more information, contact CSSP@dhs.gov.

Cybersecurity Public Trends and Analysis Report provides awareness of the cybersecurity trends as observed by the U.S. Computer Emergency Readiness Team (US-CERT). The analysis in this report is based on incident information that has been reported to US-CERT, incidents identified by US-CERT, and public/private sector information identified when correlating and analyzing the data. For more information, see www.us-cert .gov/reading_room/index.html#news. Contact US-CERT at info@us-cert .gov, (888) 282-0870

Cyber Security Evaluation Tool (CSET) is a desktop software tool that guides users through a step-by-step process for assessing the cybersecurity posture of their industrial control system and enterprise information technology networks. CSET is available in DVD format. To learn more, visit www.us-cert.gov/control_systems/satool.html. To obtain a DVD copy of CSET, send an e-mail with your mailing address to CSET@dhs.gov.

Emergency Communications Guidance Documents and Methodologies
The DHS Office of Emergency Communications develops stakeholder-driven guidance documents and methodologies to support emergency responders across the nation as they plan for and implement emergency communications initiatives. These resources identify and promote best practices on improving statewide governance, developing standard operating procedures, managing technology, supporting training and exercises, and encouraging usage of interoperable communications, among other topics. Each is available publicly and is updated as needed. Examples include: *Establishing Governance to Achieve Statewide Communications Interoperability* and the *Formal Agreement and Standard Operating Procedure Template Suite.* For more information, contact the Office of Emergency Communications at oec@hq.dhs.gov or visit www.safecomprogram.gov.

Industrial Control System Cybersecurity Standards and References
provide an extensive collection of cybersecurity standards and reference materials as a ready resource for the industrial control system stakeholder community. The collection provides a one-stop location for accessing papers, reports, references, and standards associated with industrial control system cybersecurity. To view the collection, visit www.us-cert.gov/control_systems/csstandards.html. For more information, contact CSSP@dhs.gov.

Information Technology Sector Risk Assessment (ITSRA) The National Cyber Security Division (NCSD), in partnership with public and private sector partners from the IT Sector Coordinating Council (IT SCC) and the IT Government Coordinating Council (IT GCC), released the baseline ITSRA in 2009. The ITSRA provides an all-hazards risk profile that public and private IT sector partners can use to inform resource allocation for research and development and other protective measures that enhance the security and resiliency of the critical IT sector functions. By increasing the awareness of risks across the public and private sectors, the Baseline Risk Assessment is the foundation for ongoing national-level collaboration to enhance the security and resiliency of the critical IT sector functions. See www.dhs.gov/xlibrary/assets/nipp_it_baseline_risk_assessment.pdf. For more information, contact ncsd_cipcs@hq.dhs.gov.

Information Technology Sector Specific Plan (IT SSP) the National Cyber Security Division (NCSD), in partnership with private sector members of the IT sector, has developed the IT SSP to outline the IT sector security partners' joint implementation of the NIPP risk management framework. It describes an approach for identifying, assessing, prioritizing, and protecting critical IT sector functions, establishing shared IT sector goals and objectives, and aligning initiatives to meet them. To view the IT SSP, visit www.dhs.gov/xlibrary/assets/IT_SSP_5_21_07.pdf. For more information, contact ncsd_cipcs@hq.dhs.gov.

National Emergency Communications Plan (NECP) is a strategic plan that sets goals and identifies key national priorities to enhance governance, planning, technology, training and exercises, and disaster communications capabilities. The NECP establishes specific national priorities to help state and local jurisdictions improve communications interoperability by adopting a series of goals and milestones that measure interoperability achievements over a period of years, beginning in 2008 and ending in 2013. In order to successfully implement the NECP, increased collaboration between the public and private sector will be needed. As a result, the plan establishes specific initiatives and milestones to increase such collaboration. For more information, see www.dhs.gov/xlibrary/assets/national_emergency_communications_plan.pdf or contact the Office of Emergency Communications, oec@hq.dhs.gov.

National Interoperability Field Operations Guide (NIFOG) is a technical reference for radio technicians responsible for radios that will be used in disaster response applications, and for emergency communications planners. The NIFOG includes rules and regulations for use of nationwide and other interoperability channels, frequencies and channel names, and other reference material, formatted as a pocket-sized guide for radio technicians to carry with them. The NIFOG can be accessed online at www.npstc.org/psdocs.jsp#nifog. For more information, contact the Office of Emergency Communications, oec@hq.dhs.gov.

SAFECOM Guidance for Federal Grant Programs The Department of Homeland Security Office of Emergency Communications, in coordination with the Office for Interoperability and Compatibility, develops the annual *SAFECOM Guidance for Federal Grant Programs*. Although SAFECOM is not a grant-making body, the guidance outlines recommended allowable costs and applications requirements for federal grant programs providing funding for interoperable emergency communications. The guidance is intended to ensure that federal grant funding for interoperable communications aligns with national goals and objectives and ensures alignment of state, local, and tribal investment of federal grant funding to statewide and national goals and objectives. See www.safecomprogram

.gov/NR/rdonlyres/31A870C0-0C9D-4C29-86F8-147D61AF25CF/0/
FY_2010_SAFECOM_Recommended_Guidance__111809__Final.pdf. For
more information, contact the Office of Emergency Communications at
oec@hq.dhs.gov.

U.S. Computer Emergency Readiness Team (US-CERT) Monthly Activity Summary summarizes general activity as well as updates made to the
National Cyber Alert System each month. This includes current activity
updates, technical and nontechnical alerts, bulletins, and tips, in addition
to other newsworthy events or highlights. See www.us-cert.gov/reading_
room/index.html#news, contact US-CERT at info@us-cert.gov, (888) 282-
0870.

U.S. Computer Emergency Readiness Team (US-CERT) Security Publications provide subscribers with free, timely information on cybersecurity vulnerabilities, the potential impact of those vulnerabilities, and
action required to mitigate the vulnerability and secure their computer
systems. See www.us-cert.gov/reading_room, contact US-CERT at info@
us-cert.gov, (888) 282-0870.

U.S. Computer Emergency Readiness Team (US-CERT) Vulnerability Notes Database includes technical descriptions of the vulnerability, as
well as the impact, solutions and workarounds, and lists of affected vendors. See www.kb.cert.org/vuls, contact US-CERT at info@us-cert.gov,
(888) 282-0870.

CS&C Alerts and Newsletters

Current Cybersecurity Activity is a regularly updated summary of the
most frequent, high-impact types of security incidents currently being
reported to the US-CERT. See www.us-cert.gov/current/, contact US-
CERT at info@us-cert.gov, (888) 282-0870.

Critical Infrastructure Information Notices are intended to provide
warning to critical infrastructure owners and operators when a particular
cyber event or activity has the potential to impact critical infrastructure
computing networks. This document is distributed only to those parties
who have a valid "need to know," *a direct role in securing networks or systems that enable or support U.S. critical infrastructures.* Access is limited to a
secure portal (https://portal.us-cert.gov) and controlled distribution list.
For more information, contact the US-CERT Secure Operations Center at
soc@us-cert.gov; (888) 282-0870.

National Cyber Alert System offers a variety of information for users with varied technical expertise including Technical Cybersecurity Alerts and Bulletins or more general-interest pieces such as Cybersecurity Alerts and Tips on a variety of cyber-related topics. See www.uscert.gov/cas/alldocs.html. Contact US-CERT at info@us-cert.gov, (888) 282-0870.

CS&C Technical Assistance

U. S. Computer Emergency Readiness Team (US-CERT) Operations Center Report cybersecurity incidents (including unexplained network failures), the discovery of malicious code, and vulnerability information at https://forms.us-cert.gov/report/. Contact the US-CERT Operations Center at soc@us-cert.gov; (888) 282-0870.

Cyber Resiliency Review (CRR) is an assessment offered by the Cyber Security Evaluation Program to measure and enhance the implementation of key cybersecurity capacities and capabilities of critical infrastructure and key resources (CIKR). The purpose of the CRR is to gather information regarding cybersecurity performance from specific CIKR in order to gain an understanding of the relationships and impacts of CIKR performance in protecting critical infrastructure operations. The CRR serves as a repeatable cyber review, while allowing for an evaluation of enterprise-specific cybersecurity capabilities. The results can be used to evaluate a provider independent of other assessments, used with regional studies to build a common perspective on resiliency, and used to examine systems-of-systems (i.e., large and diverse operating and organizing models). The key goal of the CRR is to ensure that core process-based capabilities exist, are measureable, and are meaningful as predictors for an organization's ability to manage cyber risk to national critical infrastructure. For more information about the CRR, contact the CSEP program at CSE@dhs.gov.

Cyber Security Advisors act as principal field liaisons in cybersecurity and provide a federal resource to regions, communities, and businesses. Their primary goal is to assist in the protection of cyber components essential within the nation's critical infrastructure and key resources (CIKR). Equally important is their role in supporting cybersecurity risk management efforts at the state and local homeland security initiatives. CSAs will work with established programs in state and local areas, such as Protective Security Advisors, FEMA emergency management personnel, and fusion center personnel. For more information, contact the program at CSE@dhs.gov.

Cyber Security Evaluation Program (CSEP) conducts voluntary cybersecurity assessments across all 18 CIKR sectors, within state governments, and for large urban areas. CSEP affords CIKR sector participants a portfolio of assessment tools, techniques, and analytics, ranging from those that can be self-applied to those that require expert facilitation or mentoring outreach. The CSEP, in alignment with the DHS National Infrastructure Protection Plan (NIPP), works closely with and coordinates efforts with internal and external stakeholders to measure key performances in cybersecurity management. The Cyber Resiliency Review is being deployed across all 18 critical infrastructure sectors (as denoted by DHS), state, local, tribal, and territorial governments. For more information, visit www .dhs.gov/xabout/structure/editorial_0839.shtm or contact the program at CSE@dhs.gov.

Cybersecurity Vulnerability Assessments through the Control Systems Security Program (CSSP) provide on-site support to critical infrastructure asset owners by assisting them to perform a security self-assessment of their enterprise and control system networks against industry-accepted standards, policies, and procedures. To request on-site assistance, asset owners may e-mail CSSP@dhs.gov.

Industrial Control Systems Technology Assessments provide a testing environment to conduct baseline security assessments on industrial control systems, network architectures, software, and control system components. These assessments include testing for common vulnerabilities and conducting vulnerability mitigation analysis to verify the effectiveness of applied security measures. To learn more about ICS testing capabilities and opportunities, e-mail CSSP@dhs.gov.

CS&C Programs and Services

Control Systems Security Program (CSSP) reduces industrial control system risks within and across all critical infrastructure and key resource sectors. CSSP coordinates cybersecurity efforts among federal, state, local, and tribal governments, as well as industrial control system owners, operators, and vendors. CSSP provides many products and services that assist the industrial control system stakeholder community to improve their cybersecurity posture and implement risk mitigation strategies. To learn more about the CSSP, visit www.us-cert.gov/control_systems/ or e-mail CSSP@dhs.gov.

Critical Infrastructure Protection–Cyber Security (CIP-CS) leads efforts with public and private sector partners to promote an assured and resilient U.S. cyber infrastructure. Major elements of the CIP-CS program include: managing and strengthening cyber critical infrastructure partnerships with public and private entities in order to effectively implement risk management and cybersecurity strategies, teaming with cyber critical infrastructure partners in the successful implementation of cybersecurity strategies, and promoting effective cyber communications processes with partners that result in a collaborative, coordinated approach to cyber awareness. For more information, contact CIP-CS at cip_cs@dhs.gov.

Global Supply Chain Risk Management (GSCRM) Program provides recommendations to standardize and implement risk management processes for acquiring information and communications technologies (ICT) for the federal government and processes to reduce the threat of attacks to federal ICT through the supply chain. Your organization can help with this initiative by applying sound security procedures and executing due diligence to provide integrity and assurance through the vendor supply chain. For more information, visit www.dhs.gov/files/programs/gc_1234200709381.shtm or contact the Global Supply Chain Program at Kurt.Seidling@hq.dhs.gov.

National Vulnerability Database (NVD) is the U.S. government repository of standards-based vulnerability management data represented using the Security Content Automation Protocol (SCAP). This data enables automation of vulnerability management, security measurement, and compliance. NVD includes databases of security checklists, security-related software flaws, misconfigurations, product names, and impact metrics. For more information, visit http://nvd.nist.gov/ or contact nvd@nist.gov.

SAFECOM Program is a communications program that provides research, development, testing and evaluation, guidance, tools, and templates on interoperable communications-related issues to local, tribal, state, and federal emergency response agencies. The SAFECOM website provides members of the emergency response community and other constituents with information and resources to help them meet their communications and interoperability needs. The site offers comprehensive information on topics relevant to emergency response communications and features best practices that have evolved from real-world situations. See www.safecomprogram.gov, contact SAFECOM@dhs.gov.

Software Assurance Program Software Assurance (SwA) is the level of confidence that software is free from vulnerabilities, either intentionally designed into the software or accidentally inserted at any time during its life cycle, and that the software functions in the intended manner. Grounded in the National Strategy to Secure Cyberspace, the Department of Homeland Security's Software Assurance Program spearheads the development of practical guidance and tools and promotes research and development of secure software engineering, examining a range of development issues from new methods that avoid basic programming errors to enterprise systems that remain secure when portions of the system software are compromised. Resources including articles, webinars, podcasts, and tools can be found at the SwA Community Resources and Information Clearinghouse located at https://buildsecurityin.us-cert .gov/swa/. For more information, contact software.assurance@dhs.gov.

FEDERAL EMERGENCY MANAGEMENT AGENCY (FEMA)

FEMA's mission is to support our citizens and first responders to ensure that as a Nation we work together to build, sustain, and improve our capability to prepare for, protect against, respond to, recover from, and mitigate all hazards. www.fema.gov.

FEMA Training and Education

Are You Ready? An In-depth Guide to Citizen Preparedness provides a step-by-step approach to disaster preparedness by walking the reader through how to get informed about local emergency plans, how to identify hazards that affect their local area, and how to develop and maintain an emergency communications plan and disaster supplies kits. Other topics include what to do before, during, and after each hazard type, including Natural Hazards, Hazardous Materials Incidents, Household Chemical Emergencies, Nuclear Power Plant, and Terrorism (including Explosion, Biological, Chemical, Nuclear, and Radiological hazards). For more information visit www.fema.gov/areyouready or call **(800) 480-2520** to order materials. Questions regarding the Citizen Corps program can be directed to citizencorps@dhs.gov.

Center for Domestic Preparedness (CDP) offers several programs that are designed for people that have emergency response and health care responsibilities, or meet the criteria specified in the website cited below. CDP offers courses in chemical, biological, radiological, nuclear, and explosive (CBRNE) incident response, toxic agent training, health care response for mass casualty incidents, Radiological Emergency Preparedness (REP) Program courses, Field Force Operations, and the National Incident Management System (NIMS). CDP offers integrated training that includes the opportunity to train in the only live agent training facility dedicated to the civilian response community. CDP's health care courses include exercises in a training hospital dedicated solely to preparedness and response. CDP offers residential training at its Anniston, Alabama, facility and off-campus training throughout the United States. CDP has an integrated training approach that is free of charge to state, local, and tribal agencies. Individuals from federal and international agencies and the private sector are encouraged to attend; however, they must pay a tuition fee for the courses in addition to their own transportation and lodging fees. For more information, see http://cdp.dhs.gov/index.html or call (866) 213-9553.

Community Emergency Response Team (CERT) This program helps train people to be better prepared to respond to emergency situations in their communities. It is a resource for the private sector to use to ensure its employees are prepared for all hazards. When emergencies happen, CERT members can give critical support to first responders, provide immediate assistance to survivors, and organize spontaneous volunteers at a disaster site. CERT members can also help with nonemergency projects that help improve the safety of the community. For more information visit www.citizencorps.gov/cert or contact cert@dhs.gov.

FEMA Emergency Management Institute Independent Study Program The Emergency Management Institute (EMI) offers self-paced courses designed for people who have emergency management responsibilities and for the general public. FEMA's Independent Study Program offers courses that support the nine mission areas identified by the National Preparedness Goal: Incident Management, Operational Planning, Disaster Logistics, Emergency Communications, Service to Disaster Victims, Continuity Programs, Public Disaster Communications, Integrated Preparedness, and Hazard Mitigation. For more information on EMI's training courses, please visit http://training.fema.gov/IS/ or contact us (301) 447-1200.

FEMA Emergency Management Institute Programs The Emergency Management Institute (EMI) offers several programs that are designed for people who have emergency management responsibilities or meet the criteria specified at the website cited below. The training is free of charge; however, individuals from private sector or contractors to state, local or tribal governments must pay their own transportation and lodging fees. EMI has an integrated training approach and we encourage individuals from the private sector to participate in our courses. EMI's programs include, but are not limited to, the Master Trainer Program, Master Exercise Practitioner Program, Professional Development Series, Applied Practices Series and FEMA's Higher Education Program. For more information, see www.training.fema.gov/Programs/ or call (301) 447-1286.

FEMA Learning Resource Center (LRC) provides current information and resources on fire, emergency management and other all-hazards subjects. With its collection of more than 180,000 books, reports, periodicals, and audiovisual materials, the LRC houses the most extensive collection of fire service literature in the United States. Internet users may access the LRC's Online Public Access Catalog to perform literature searches and download over 17,000 documents. The LRC's collection of books and research reports may also be accessed by requesting interlibrary loan through a local library. For more information visit www.lrc.fema.gov or contact the program via phone (800) 638-1821 or by e-mail netclrc@dhs.gov.

U.S. Fire Administration's National Fire Academy Training Programs enhance the ability of fire and emergency services and allied professionals to deal more effectively with fire and related emergencies. NFA offers courses in the following subject areas: Arson Mitigation, Emergency Medical Services, Executive Development, Fire Prevention: Management, Fire Prevention: Public Education, Fire Prevention: Technical, Hazardous Materials, Incident Management, Management Science, Planning and Information Management, and Training Programs. NFA offers residential training at its Emmitsburg, Maryland, facility and off-campus training throughout the United States, as well as online self-study courses free of charge. For more information, see www.usfa.dhs.gov/nfa/index.shtm or call (301) 447-1000.

First Responder Training & Exercise Integration are delivered in the following formats: Resident—instructor-led classroom training is provided at a training facility; Mobile—also referred to as nonresident, mobile training can be performed by FEMA-funded instructors at any location; Web-Based—Web-based or "online" training is done via the Internet and is often self-paced (no instructor); or Indirect—indirect training includes training courses taught by instructors (non-FEMA or training partner staff) that have completed "Train the Trainer" courses. For more information, visit www.firstrespondertraining.gov or contact the program via phone (800) 368-6498 or e-mail askCSID@dhs.gov.

FEMA Alerts and Newsletters

FEMA Private Sector E-alert The FEMA Private Sector Division, Office of External Affairs, publishes periodic e-alerts providing timely information on topics of interest to private sector entities. The FEMA Private Sector Web Portal aggregates FEMA's online resources for the private sector. Content includes best practices in public-private partnerships, weekly preparedness tips, links to training opportunities, planning and preparedness resources, information on how to do business with FEMA, and more. For more information visit www.fema.gov/privatesector or sign up for the alert at FEMA-Private-Sector-Web@dhs.gov.

Citizen Corps E-mail Alerts provide weekly Community Preparedness news and events from various departments of the federal government and our national Citizen Corps partners and affiliates. For more information, visit www.citizencorps.gov or sign up for the alert at citizencorps@dhs.gov.

FEMA Publications

FEMA Library is a searchable Web-based collection of all publicly accessible FEMA information resources, including thousands of CDs, DVDs, audio tapes, disability resources, posters, displays, brochures, guidance, policy papers, program regulations, guidelines, and forms. Users can search the collection by Subject, Audience Category including categories specific to private sector audiences, Hazard Type, and other categories. For more information, visit www.fema.gov/library/ or call (800) 480-2520.

FEMA Programs and Services

Community Preparedness–Citizen Corps is FEMA's grassroots strategy to bring together government and community leaders to involve citizens in all-hazards emergency preparedness and resilience. Citizen Corps asks each individual to embrace the personal responsibility to be prepared; to get training in first aid and emergency skills; and to volunteer to support local emergency responders, disaster relief, and community safety. There are currently 2,433 Councils that serve over 227 million people or 80 percent of the total U.S. population. For more information on how you can participate, e-mail citizencorps@dhs.gov or visit www.citizencorps.gov.

Donations and Volunteers Information FEMA offers information on the best way to volunteer and donate during disaster response and recovery. For more information, see www.fema.gov/donations.

DisasterAssistance.gov is a secure, user-friendly U.S. government Web portal that consolidates disaster assistance information in one place. If you need assistance following a presidentially declared disaster that has been designated for individual assistance, you can now go to www.DisasterAssistance.gov to register online. Local resource information to help keep citizens safe during an emergency is also available. Currently, 17 U.S. government agencies, which sponsor almost 60 forms of assistance, contribute to the portal. For website technical assistance, contact (800) 745-0243.

The Emergency Lodging Assistance Program provides prompt lodging payments for short-term stays in the event of a declared disaster. The program is administered by Corporate Lodging Consultants, a federal government contractor and the largest outsourced lodging services provider in North America. For more information, see http://ela.corplodging .com/programinfo.php, contact femahousing@corplodging.com, or call (866) 545-9865.

The Emergency Food and Shelter National Board Program was created in 1983 to supplement the work of local social service organizations within the United States, both private and governmental, to help people in need of emergency assistance. This collaborative effort between the private and public sectors has provided over $3.4 billion in federal funds during its 27-year history. For more information, visit www.efsp.unitedway.org/.

The FEMA Industry Liaison Program is a point-of-entry for vendors seeking information on how to do business with FEMA during disasters and non-disaster periods of activity. The program coordinates vendor presentation meetings between vendors and FEMA program offices, establishes strategic relationships with vendor-supporting industry partners and stakeholders, coordinates Industry Days, conducts market research, responds to informal congressional requests, and performs vendor analysis reporting. Vendors interested in doing business with FEMA should take the following steps: Register in the Central Contractor Registration (CCR) at www.ccr.gov, contact the FEMA Industry Liaison Program at www.fema.gov/privatesector/industry/index.shtm, or call the Industry Liaison Support Center at (202) 646-1895.

FEMA Flood Map Assistance Center (FMAC) provides information to the public about National Flood Insurance Program rules, regulations, and procedures. The FMAC is often the first point of contact between FEMA and various flood map users. The FMAC's goal is to provide the appropriate information to callers to help them understand the technical issues involved in a particular situation. In addition to taking incoming telephone calls, map specialists respond to mapping-related e-mail inquiries, and also review and process Letter of Map Amendment (LOMA), Letter of Map Revision Based on Fill (LOMR-F), and Letter of Determination Review (LODR) requests. There are available resources for engineers/surveyors, insurance professionals and lenders, and floodplain managers. For more information, call (877) FEMA-MAP (877-336-2627) or e-mail FEMAMapSpecialist@riskmapcds.com.

FEMA Regulatory Materials FEMA publishes its regulations, containing FEMA's procedures and requirements from the public, in Title 44 of the Code of Federal Regulations (CFR). These regulations are typically open for public comment before they go into effect. The public can access the regulations that are currently in effect electronically, by selecting Title 44 from the drop down menu at http://ecfr.gpoaccess.gov/cgi/t/text/text-idx?c=ecfr&tpl=%2Findex.tpl. The public can submit and view comments submitted by other individuals at www.regulations.gov. For more information on federal agency rulemaking, visit www.reginfo.gov or to contact FEMA regulatory officials e-mail FEMA-RULES@dhs.gov.

FEMA Small Business Program Small business vendors are routed to the FEMA Small Business Analyst for notification, support, and processing. Small Business inquiries can be sent to FEMA-SB@dhs.gov.

U.S. Fire Administration (USFA) Fire Prevention and Safety Campaigns delivers fire prevention and safety education programs to reduce the loss of life from fire-related hazards, particularly among the very young and older adults. The campaigns encourage Americans to practice fire safety and to protect themselves and their families from the dangers of fire. In addition, they provide dedicated support to public fire educators and the media to facilitate community outreach to targeted audiences. For more information, visit www.usfa.dhs.gov/campaigns/ or call (301) 447-1000.

U.S. Fire Administration Publications encourage Americans including private sector constituents to practice fire safety and protect themselves and their families from the dangers of fire. Order online at www.usfa.dhs.gov/applications/publications/ or contact the U.S Fire Administration via e-mail, usfa-publications@dhs.gov or phone, (800) 561-3356.

Freight Rail Security Grant Program funds freight railroad carriers and owners and officers of railroad cars to protect critical surface transportation infrastructure from acts of terrorism, major disasters, and other emergencies. For more information, visit www.fema.gov/government/grant/ or contact the program by e-mail, askcsid@dhs.gov or phone, (800) 368-6498.

Intercity Bus Security Grant Program provides funding to create a sustainable program for the protection of intercity bus systems and the traveling public from terrorism. The program seeks to assist operators of fixed-route intercity and charter bus services in obtaining the resources required to support security measures such as enhanced planning, facility security upgrades and vehicle and driver protection. For more information, visit www.fema.gov/government/grant/ or contact the program at askcsid@dhs.gov or (800) 368-6498.

Intercity Passenger Rail Grant Program creates a sustainable, risk-based effort to protect critical surface transportation infrastructure and the traveling public from acts of terrorism, major disasters, and other emergencies within the Amtrak rail system. For more information visit www .fema.gov/government/grant/ or contact the program at askcsid@dhs .gov or (800) 368-6498.

National Dam Safety Program Led by FEMA, the National Dam Safety Program (NDSP) is a partnership of the states, federal agencies, and other stakeholders to encourage individual and community responsibility for dam safety. Since the inception of the NDSP in 1979, FEMA has supported a strong, collaborative training program for dam safety professionals and dam owners. With NDSP training funds, FEMA has been able to expand existing training programs, begin new initiatives to keep pace with evolving technology, and enhance the sharing of expertise between the federal and state sectors. For more information, visit www.fema.gov/plan/prevent/ damfailure/ndsp.shtm or www.damsafety.org/.

National Incident Management System (NIMS) provides a systematic, proactive approach to guide departments and agencies at all levels of government, nongovernmental organizations, and the private sector to work seamlessly to prevent, protect against, respond to, recover from, and mitigate the effects of incidents, regardless of cause, size, location, or complexity, in order to reduce the loss of life and property and harm to the environment. Website: www.fema.gov/nims. Questions regarding NIMS should be directed to FEMA-NIMS@dhs.gov or (202) 646-3850.

National Response Framework (NRF) is a guide to how the nation conducts all-hazards response. It is built upon scalable, flexible, and adaptable coordinating structures to align key roles and responsibilities across the nation, linking all levels of government, nongovernmental organizations, and the private sector. It is intended to capture specific authorities and best practices for managing incidents that range from the serious but purely local to large-scale terrorist attacks or catastrophic natural disasters. For more information, visit www.fema.gov/nrf.

National Flood Insurance Program focuses on flood insurance, flood-plain management and flood hazard mapping. Nearly 20,000 communities across the United States and its territories participate in the NFIP by adopting and enforcing floodplain management ordinances to reduce future flood damage. In exchange, the NFIP makes federally backed flood insurance available to homeowners, renters, and business owners in these communities. See www.floodsmart.gov. Flood insurance agents interested in the program please visit www.agents.floodsmart.gov or e-mail asktheexpert@riskmapcds.com.

Nonprofit Security Grant Program provides funding support for target-hardening activities to nonprofit organizations that are at high risk of a terrorist attack and are located within one of the specific UASI-eligible urban areas. It is also designed to promote coordination and collaboration in emergency preparedness activities among public and private community representatives, state and local government agencies, and Citizen Corps Councils. For more information, visit www.fema.gov/government/grant/nsgp or contact the program by e-mail, askcsid@dhs.gov or phone, (800) 368-6498.

Port Security Grant Program is a sustainable, risk-based effort to protect critical port infrastructure from terrorism, particularly attacks using explosives and nonconventional threats that could cause major disruption to commerce. The PSGP provides grant funding to port areas for the protection of critical port infrastructure from terrorism. This program is primarily intended to assist ports in enhancing maritime domain awareness; enhancing risk management capabilities to prevent, detect, respond to, and recover from attacks involving improvised explosive devices, chemical, biological, radiological, nuclear, explosive, and other nonconventional weapons; providing training and exercises; and Transportation Worker Identification Credential implementation. For more information, visit www.fema.gov/government/grant/ or contact the program by e-mail, askcsid@dhs.gov, or phone, (800) 368-6498.

QuakeSmart is designed to encourage business leaders and owners in areas of the United States that are at risk from earthquakes to take actions that will mitigate damage to their businesses, provide greater safety for customers and employees, and speed recovery in the event of an earthquake. The goal of QuakeSmart is to build awareness within the business community of the risk and to educate businesses, particularly small and emerging businesses, on the relatively simple things they can do to reduce or mitigate the impact of earthquakes and support community preparedness. Business leaders and owners interested in finding out how to reduce or mitigate the impact of earthquakes on their business should visit www.quakesmart.org.

Ready Business The U.S. Department of Homeland Security and the Advertising Council launched the *Ready Business* Campaign in September 2004. An extension of the successful *Ready* Campaign, *Ready Business* helps owners and managers of small- and medium-sized businesses prepare their employees, operations, and assets in the event of an emergency. For free tools and resources, including how to create a business emergency plan, please visit www.ready.gov.

Radiological Emergency Preparedness Program (REP) Program helps to secure the health and safety of citizens living around commercial nuclear power plants. REP is responsible for reviewing and approving all community radiological emergency plans. The REP program is a leader in areas of policy guidance, planning, training, public education, and preparedness for nuclear power plants. For over three decades, local and state responders have relied on REP's leadership to correct preparedness plans, monitor rigorous training regimens, and support effective performance in the unlikely event of a radiological emergency. For more information, visit www.fema.gov/hazard/nuclear/index.shtm.

Technical Assistance (TA) Program seeks to build and sustain capabilities through specific services and analytical capacities through the development, delivery, and management of TA services that support the four homeland security mission areas (i.e., prevention, protection, response, and recovery), in addition to homeland security program management. TA is offered to a wide variety of organizations and grantees through an extensive menu of services responsive to national priorities. To best accommodate the wide variety of TA needs and deliverables, three levels of TA are provided. Level I/II services can be made available to private sector organizations and include general information, models, templates, and samples. Level III services, available to private sector organizations that may be DHS grantees, provide onsite support via workshops and interaction between TA providers and recipients. For more information, visit www.fema.gov/about/divisions/pppa_ta.shtm or contact (800) 368-6498 or e-mail FEMA-TARequest@fema.gov.

Transit Security Grant Program is a sustainable, risk-based effort to protect critical surface transportation infrastructure and the traveling public from acts of terrorism, major disasters, and other emergencies. For more information, visit www.fema.gov/government/grant/ or contact the program by e-mail, askcsid@dhs.gov or phone (800) 368-6498.

Tornado Safety Initiative assesses building damages and identifies lessons learned after tornadoes occur; funds research on shelter design and construction standards; develops best practices and technical manuals on safe rooms and community shelters; and produces public education materials on tornado preparedness and response. FEMA produces technical manuals for engineers, architects, building officials, and prospective shelter owners on the design and construction of safe rooms and community shelters. For more information, visit www.fema.gov/plan/prevent/saferoom/index.

Unified Hazard Mitigation Assistance (HMA) Grant Programs present a critical opportunity to reduce the risk to individuals and property from natural hazards while simultaneously reducing reliance on federal disaster funds. While the statutory origins of the programs differ, all share the common goal of reducing the risk of loss of life and property due to natural hazards. HMA programs are subject to the availability of appropriation funding or funding based on disaster recovery expenditures, as well as any directive or restriction made with respect to such funds. HMA programs include Hazard Mitigation Grant Program, Pre-Disaster Mitigation program, Flood Mitigation Assistance program, Repetitive Flood Claims (RFC) program and Severe Repetitive Loss program. See www.fema.gov/government/grant/hma/index.shtm.

U.S. IMMIGRATION AND CUSTOMS ENFORCEMENT (ICE)

U.S. Immigration and Customs Enforcement (ICE) is the largest investigative agency in the U.S. Department of Homeland Security (DHS). Formed in 2003 as part of the federal government's response to the 9/11 attacks, ICE's mission is to protect the security of the American people and the homeland by vigilantly enforcing the nation's immigration and customs laws. ICE combines innovative investigative techniques, new technological resources, and a high level of professionalism to provide a wide range of resources to the public and to our federal, state and local law enforcement partners. www.ice.gov.

Forced Labor Resources The ICE Office of International Affairs investigates allegations of forced labor in violation of the Tariff Act of 1930 (Title 19 USC §1307). To request more information or a copy of *A Forced Child Labor Advisory* booklet and brochure, please contact: ice.forcedlabor@dhs.gov. When contacting ICE to report instances of forced labor, please provide as much detailed information and supporting documentation as possible, including the following: a full statement of the reasons for the belief that the product was produced by forced labor and that it may be or has been imported to the United States; a detailed description of the product; and all pertinent facts known regarding the production of the merchandise abroad. For the location of ICE foreign offices, go to the ICE website at www.ice.gov, click *About Us*, click *Office of International Affairs* and select your country. ICE maintains a 24/7 hotline at (866) DHS-2-ICE.

Human Rights Violators and War Crimes Center has a mission to protect the public by targeting war criminals and those who violate human rights, including violators living both domestically and abroad. The assigned staff of ICE investigators and intelligence analysts dedicated to the Center work with governmental and nongovernmental agencies. They accept tips and information from those who report suspected war criminals and human rights violators. Individuals seeking to report these abuses of human rights may contact the Center at HRV.ICE@DHS.GOV.

Human Trafficking: "Hidden in Plain Sight" is the ICE human trafficking public outreach campaign that heightens awareness of human trafficking through announcements via billboards and posters on public transportation, bus stops, and in businesses. The Hidden in Plain Sight campaign provides critical human trafficking information to the public and gives people a method for reporting suspected human trafficking activity. ICE's Office of Investigations (OI) designed a one-minute video Public Service Announcement (PSA), which is a broadcast message used for public outreach. ICE uses the PSA during presentations to provide information to the general public and human trafficking–related organizations. The PSA is accessible to the public via the ICE website at www.ice.gov and it is also distributed to the public on DVD during training and presentations worldwide. See the flash video at www.ice.gov/flash-movie/human-trafficking/plain-sight.htm.

Human Trafficking: Indicators Pamphlet is currently produced in English, Spanish, and Portuguese and is distributed during presentations and trainings worldwide. See www.ice.gov/pi/news/factsheets/humantrafficking.htm.

Human Trafficking: Awareness Resources ICE is the primary agency within the Department of Homeland Security that fights human trafficking. Trafficking in Persons (TIP) is a modern-day form of slavery. Human trafficking is defined by Section 103 of the Trafficking Victims Protection Act of 2000 as "(A) sex trafficking in which a commercial sex act is induced by force, fraud, or coercion, or in which the person induced to perform such acts has not attained 18 years of age; or (B) the recruitment, harboring, transportation, provision, or obtaining of a person for labor or services, through the use of force, fraud, or coercion for the purpose of subjection to involuntary servitude, peonage, debt bondage, or slavery." ICE is committed to a victim-focused approach to trafficking investigations that places equal importance on protecting the victims and prosecuting the traffickers. Part of this strategy includes an aggressive public outreach campaign to raise awareness of the issue and provide a mechanism for the public to report suspected trafficking activity. ICE also conducts continuous outreach and training to U.S. and foreign law enforcement, nongovernmental, and international organizations, in order to provide awareness and the latest investigative techniques and victim assistance practices. The public is encouraged to report all suspicious activity to ICE at (866) DHS-2ICE (1-866-347-2423). Informational material on human trafficking is produced in a variety of languages, and is available to law enforcement and NGOs and includes the following: a public service announcement; human trafficking brochure; human trafficking indicator wallet cards; and human trafficking indicators for law enforcement brochure. See www.ice.gov/pi/investigations/publicsafety/humantrafficking.htm.

Human Trafficking: Trafficking in Persons (TIP) Card ICE currently distributes human trafficking material, known as the human trafficking in persons (TIP) card. This plastic business card helps distinguish between the crime of human trafficking versus the crime of human smuggling, listing indicators of each as the two crimes are often confused. The TIP card includes the ICE telephone number for individuals to call for guidance or to report suspicious activity. The TIP card is currently produced in 17 different languages. To request the TIP card, contact your local ICE office. The TIP cards are also distributed during presentations and training offered worldwide. For more information visit the ICE website at www.ice.gov. For ICE principal field offices across the country, see www.ice.gov/about/investigations/contact.htm.

ICE LINK Portal The ICE National Incident Response Unit (NIRU) for incident awareness, continuity of operations, exercises, incident response, special event coordination, and many other homeland security requirements administers a Web-based communications and collaboration platform called the ICE LINK Portal. The ICE LINK Portal is a robust, sensitive, but unclassified information-sharing network used as a force multiplier to enhance coordination with federal, state, local, and tribal priorities. ICE LINK Portal users include federal agencies, fusion centers, military components, Interpol, and the intelligence community. Additionally, the ICE LINK Portal can be used for critical infrastructure and key resources (CIKR) first-responder personnel in the private sector in the event of a national crisis or incident. For more information and/or assistance, contact NIRU at niru@dhs.gov.

ICE Mutual Agreement between Government and Employers (IMAGE) Program is a joint government and private sector voluntary initiative that enhances employer compliance and corporate due diligence through training and sharing best practices regarding hiring practices. The goal of IMAGE is for the government to work with employers to develop a more secure and stable workforce and restore the integrity of the U.S. immigration system. More information can be found at ICE's website at www.ice .gov/image. Contact: IMAGE@dhs.gov or Section Chief Adam Wilson at (202) 732-3064.

ICE Office of Public Affairs (ICE OPA) is dedicated to building understanding and support for the agency's mission through outreach to DHS employees, the media, and the general public. ICE OPA is headquartered at Potomac Center North (PCN), 500 12th St. SW, in Washington, D.C. ICE field public affairs officers are located throughout the country and are responsible for regional media relations in specific geographic areas. For more information, see www.ice.gov or contact PublicAffairs.IceOfficeOf@ dhs.gov, (202) 732-4242.

ICE Privacy Office sustains privacy protections and the transparency of government operations while supporting the ICE mission. The ICE Privacy Office ensures that the Privacy Impact Assessments and System of Records Notices complies with key federal privacy laws and policies. Members of the public can contact the Privacy Office with concerns or complaints regarding their privacy in regard to the mission of ICE. See www.ice.gov/about/privacyoffice/contact.htm. For more information, contact ICEPrivacy@dhs.gov, (202) 732-3300.

ICE Tip-Line is a 24/7 toll free number enabling the public to report violations of customs and immigration laws, sexual and economic exploitation of children and adults, threats to national security, and other activities considered illegal or suspicious in nature. Please assist DHS in maintaining the security and integrity of the nation by reporting illegal activity. More information regarding ICE programs can be found at the ICE website www.ice.gov or www.ice.gov/pi/topics/index.htm or by calling (866) DHS-2ICE (1-866-347-2423) or outside the United States: +1 (877) 347-2423.

ICE Victim Assistance Program (VAP) provides information and assistance to human trafficking victims. The VAP provides information about post-correctional release or removal of criminal aliens from ICE custody. The VAP provides brochures for victims of trafficking and its victim notification program. To request copies of the brochures, please contact the VAP at (866) 872-4973.

The National Intellectual Property Rights (IPR) Coordination Center is the federal government's central point of contact in the fight against IPR violators and the flow of counterfeit goods into the United States since 2000. The new center in northern Virginia is the high-tech home of a partnership between government, private industry, and law enforcement communities. More information can be found at www.ice.gov/pi/iprctr/index.htm. Report an IPR violation at www.ice.gov/partners/cornerstone/ipr/IPRForm.htm or contact the IPR Center at (866) IPR-2060 or (866) 477-2060.

Money Laundering and Operation Cornerstone U.S. Immigration and Customs Enforcement (ICE) recognizes that the private sector represents America's first line of defense against money laundering. In Operation Cornerstone, the ICE Office of Investigations reaches out to the U.S. business community, along with state and federal agencies to combat financial and trade crimes. Operation Cornerstone identifies and eliminates vulnerabilities within the U.S. financial, trade, and transportation sectors—vulnerabilities that criminal and terrorist organizations could exploit to finance their illicit operations and avoid being detected by law enforcement. The ICE Financial Programs/Cornerstone Unit publishes the Cornerstone Report, a quarterly newsletter. This report provides current trends and financial crimes identified by law enforcement and the private sector. To subscribe to the Cornerstone Report or for more information visit: www.ice.gov/cornerstone. Report suspicious activity by calling (866) DHS-2-ICE.

Project Shield America (PSA) is the first line of defense against those who compromise U.S. national security by violating export laws, sanctions, and embargoes. Specifically, ICE's Counter-Proliferation Investigations Unit reaches out to applicable high-tech industries to monitor weapons of mass destruction and their components that are potential targets for illegal trafficking. Through PSA, ICE works in partnership with U.S. Customs and Border Protection (CBP) and U.S. companies that manufacture, sell, or export strategic technology and munitions. See www.ice.gov/doclib/investigations/pdf/cpi_brochure.pdf (pdf 192 KB). For additional information, please contact ICE Headquarters, PSA Program Manager at ICE Headquarters at (202) 732-3765 or (202) 732-3764. Report suspicious activity at the ICE tip line (866) DHS-2-ICE (1-866-347-2423).

Student and Exchange Visitor Program (SEVP) was established in 2003 as the Department of Homeland Security's frontline effort to ensure that the student visa system is not exploited by those wishing to do harm to the United States. SEVP's key tool in this effort is the Student and Exchange Visitor Information System (SEVIS), a Web-based information management system that allows ICE to monitor the status of nonimmigrant student and exchange visitors in the United States. SEVP collects, maintains, and provides the information so that only legitimate foreign students or exchange visitors gain entry to the United States. The result is an easily accessible information system that provides timely information to the Department of State, U.S. Customs and Border Protection, U.S. Citizenship and Immigration Services, and ICE. For more information, visit www.ice.gov/sevis/. For inquiries by phone, call the SEVP Response Center at (703) 603-3400 or via e-mail at: SEVIS.Source@DHS.gov.

OFFICE OF INFRASTRUCTURE PROTECTION (IP)

From energy systems that power our neighborhoods, to transportation networks that move us around our communities and the country, to facilities that provide our families with safe drinking water, critical infrastructure and key resources (CIKR) impact nearly every aspect of our daily lives. In short, CIKR is an umbrella term referring to the assets of the United States essential to the nation's security, public health and safety, economic vitality, and way of life. CIKR is divided into 18 separate sectors, as diverse as agriculture and food, emergency services, and cyber networks. Because this critical infrastructure provides our country with the enormous benefits and services and opportunities on which we rely, we are very mindful of the risks posed to CIKR by terrorists, pandemic diseases, and natural disasters. At the Department of Homeland Security, we know that these threats can have serious effects, such as cutting populations off from clean water, power, transportation, or emergency supplies. Secretary Napolitano is working to raise awareness about the importance of our nation's critical infrastructure and to strengthen our ability to protect it. The department oversees programs and resources that foster public-private partnerships, enhance protective programs, and build national resiliency to withstand natural disasters and terrorist threats. www.dhs.gov/criticalinfrastructure.

IP Training and Education

Active Threat Recognition for Retail Security Officers This 85-minute presentation produced by the Office for Bombing Prevention is split into easy-to-understand modules and uses specific foreign and domestic case studies to explain lessons learned and to discuss specific considerations for retail and shopping centers. The training discusses signs of criminal and terrorist activity, types of surveillance, and suspicious behavioral indicators. The presentation is available with guest log-in capabilities on the DHS Homeland Security Information Network (HSIN). To access the presentation, please register at: https://connect.hsin.gov/attrrso/event/registration.html. After submitting the short registration information to include setting a password of your choice, you will receive an e-mail confirmation with instructions for logging in to view the material. For more information, contact the Commercial Facilities Sector-Specific Agency at CFSteam@hq.dhs.gov.

Bomb Event Management Web Training is a 60-minute online session produced by the Office for Bombing Prevention that provides an overview of risks and risk mitigation considerations related to improvised explosive devices (IED) threats and planning. This Web training is available to vetted private sector critical infrastructure owners and operators with a demonstrated need to know through the Homeland Security Information Network-Critical Sectors (HSIN-CS) (https://cs.hsin.gov/) online secure portal. For more information, contact the Commercial Facilities Sector-Specific Agency at CFSteam@hq.dhs.gov.

Bombing Prevention is a one-day workshop, intended for regional-level public and private stakeholders and planners from emergency management, security, and law enforcement, designed to enhance the effectiveness in managing a bombing incident. This workshop reviews the current development of strategies and brings together best practices from regions across multiple localities, disciplines, and levels of government. The guided scenario discussion establishes the foundation for the stakeholders within the region to implement a Bombing Prevention Plan. This workshop can accommodate up to 50 participants. To request training, contact the DHS Office for Bombing Prevention at OBP@dhs.gov, (703) 235-5723.

Chemical Sector Explosive Threat Awareness Training Program The Chemical Sector-Specific Agency (SSA) is offering a series of one-day vehicle-borne improvised explosive device (VBIED) training sessions to chemical facility security officers. This course is offered in six locations in

FY10 (Dallas, Orlando, New Orleans, St. Louis, Seattle, and Buffalo). Contact the Chemical SSA for more information at ChemicalSector@dhs.gov.

Counterterrorism Protective Measures Course is a two-day course designed to enhance commercial sector awareness on how to devalue, detect, deter, and defend facilities from terrorism, by providing the knowledge and skills necessary in understanding common vulnerabilities and employing effective protective measures. The Protective Measures Course includes lessons learned and industry best practices in mitigating terrorist attacks. It serves as a follow-up to the Soft Target Awareness Course, focusing more on implementation than awareness. This course can accommodate 35 participants. To request training, contact the DHS Office for Bombing Prevention, OBP@dhs.gov, (703) 235-5723.

Critical Infrastructure and Key Resources (CIKR) Learning Series features one-hour infrastructure protection (IP) Web-based seminars on current topics and issues of interest to CIKR owners and operators and key government partners. Over 5,000 partners/stakeholders have registered for the Learning Series since its inception in August, 2008. The list serve for this series includes more than 27,000 interested individuals. See www.dhs.gov/files/programs/gc_1231165582452.shtm. For more information, contact IP_Education@hq.dhs.gov.

Critical Infrastructure and Key Resources (CIKR) Training Module provides an overview of the National Infrastructure Protection Plan (NIPP) and CIKR Annex to the National Response Framework. The module was developed for inclusion in the FEMA Integrated Emergency Management and other incident management related courses. This document is available upon request in PowerPoint format with instructor and participant guides and can be easily integrated into existing training programs. A Spanish version is also available. To request the training module, contact IP_Education@hq.dhs.gov.

DHS/Commercial Facilities Training Resources Guide pamphlet was developed to promote classroom and independent study programs for DHS partners and private sector stakeholders that build functional skills for disaster response effectiveness. Subject matter includes cybersecurity, weapons of mass destruction, and natural disaster planning. Available on request, contact the Commercial Facilities Sector-Specific Agency at CFSteam@hq.dhs.gov.

DHS Retail Video: "What's in Store—Ordinary People/Extraordinary Events" is a multimedia training video for retail employees of commercial shopping venues alerting them to the signs of suspicious behavior in the workplace that might lead to a catastrophic act. See www.dhs.gov/multimedia/dhs_retail_video.wmv. For more information, contact the Commercial Facilities Sector-Specific Agency at CFSteam@hq.dhs.gov.

DHS Training Video "Check It! Protecting Public Spaces" is a training video for frontline event staff at large public venues. The video demonstrates the proper procedures for conducting bag searches and recognizing suspicious behavior at public gathering spaces like sports venues. The video is available for viewing and download at www.dhs.gov/files/programs/gc_1259859901230.shtm#4 or by contacting the Commercial Facilities Sector-Specific Agency at CFSTeam@hq.dhs.gov.

Emergency Services Sector Training Catalog describes public and private resources and programs that are applicable to first responders. Printed catalogs are available by contacting the Emergency Services Sector-Specific Agency ESSTeam@hq.dhs.gov.

Improvised Explosive Device (IED) Awareness / Bomb Threat Management Workshop IED attacks remain the primary tactic for bombers, terrorists, and criminals seeking relatively uncomplicated, inexpensive means for inflicting mass casualties and maximum damage. This four-hour presentation is designed to enhance and strengthen the participant's knowledge, skills, and abilities in relation to the threat of IEDs. The information presented outlines specific practices associated with bomb threat management including IED awareness, explosive incidents, and bombing prevention. This workshop is designed to provide two four-hour sessions, morning and afternoon, with 50 participants for each session. To request training, contact the DHS Office for Bombing Prevention at OBP@dhs.gov, (703) 235-5723.

Improvised Explosive Device (IED) Awareness Web Training This 60-minute IED Awareness Web Training, produced by the Office for Bombing Prevention and similar to the IED Awareness Course, is designed to enhance and strengthen the participant's knowledge, skills, and abilities in relation to the threat of IEDs. Topics addressed during the Web training include the use of IEDs as a popular terrorist attack method; types of explosives and explosive effects; construction, components, and categories of IEDs; and IED-related safety measures. This Web training is available to vetted private sector critical infrastructure owners and operators with a demonstrated need to know through the Homeland Security Information Network-Critical Sectors (HSIN-CS) (https://cs.hsin.gov/)

online secure portal. For more information, contact the Commercial Facilities Sector-Specific Agency at CFSteam@hq.dhs.gov.

Improvised Explosive Device (IED) Search Procedures Workshop This eight-hour Workshop, consisting of lecture and practical exercises, is designed for security personnel and facility managers of sites hosting any event that requires increased IED security preparedness. The information provided during the workshop focuses on general safeties used for specialized explosives searches and sweeps, and can be tailored to meet the requirements for supporting any event. The workshop can accommodate 25 participants. To request training, contact the DHS Office for Bombing Prevention: OBP@dhs.gov, (703) 235-5723.

Independent Study Course IS-821 "Critical Infrastructure and Key Resources (CIKR) Support Annex" provides an introduction to the CIKR Support Annex to the National Response Framework. See http://training.fema.gov/emiweb/is/is821.asp; for more information, contact IP_Education@hq.dhs.gov.

Independent Study Course IS-860.a National Infrastructure Protection Plan (NIPP) presents an overview of the NIPP. The NIPP provides the unifying structure for the integration of existing and future CIKR protection and resiliency efforts into a single national program. This course has been updated to align with the NIPP that was released in 2009. Classroom materials are also available for this course. For more information, visit http://training.fema.gov/emiweb/is/is860a.asp or contact IP_Education@hq.dhs.gov.

Independent Study Course IS-870: Dams Sector: Crisis Management Overview is Web-based training focused on information provided within the Dams Sector Crisis Management handbook. See http://training.fema.gov/EMIWeb/IS/IS870.asp. For more information, contact the Dams Sector-Specific Agency, dams@dhs.gov.

Integrated Common Analytical Viewer (iCAV) Web-based Training provides instruction on the use of the iCAV Next Generation geospatial visualization tool, including access and use of DHS geospatial resources and data. Users are guided through system "buttonology" to gain a feel for the types of imagery, infrastructure, and situational awareness data available through iCAV Next Generation, as well as some of the analytical tools that users can leverage to understand infrastructure in a domestic response context. More information on iCAV Next Generation is available at www.dhs.gov/icav, and the training itself is available at www.jsrts .org/dhs/icav.

Private Sector Counterterrorism Awareness Workshop is a one-day workshop designed to improve the knowledge of private sector security professionals by providing exposure to key elements of soft target awareness, surveillance detection, and improvised explosive device (IED) recognition. The workshop's training materials enhance and reinforce participants' knowledge, skills, and abilities related to preventing, protecting against, responding to, and recovering from terrorist threats and incidents. The workshop outlines specific counterterrorism awareness and prevention actions that reduce vulnerability and mitigate the risk of domestic terrorist attacks. This workshop can accommodate 100 to 250 participants. To request training contact the DHS Office for Bombing Prevention, OBP@dhs.gov at (703) 235-5723.

Soft Target Awareness Course is designed to enhance individual and organizational awareness of terrorism and help facilitate information sharing at commercial facilities considered soft targets, such as shopping malls and hotels. Commercial infrastructure facility managers, supervisors, operators, and security staff gain a better understanding of their roles in deterring, detecting, and defending their facilities from terrorism. Participants choose from five focus areas according to their specific affiliation: Stadiums and Arenas; Places of Worship; Education; Malls and Shopping Centers; and Large Buildings, Hotels, and Medical Facilities. Each of these focus areas is comprised of a four-hour session of combined informal lecture and capstone-guided discussions. Each session can accommodate 35 participants or can be modified for one general session for up to 175 participants. To request training, contact the DHS Office for Bombing Prevention at OBP@dhs.gov, (703) 235-5723.

Surveillance Detection Training for Commercial Infrastructure Operators and Security Staff Course is a three-day course that explains how protective measures can be applied to detect and deter potential threats to critical infrastructure and key resources (CIKR), as well as the fundamentals for detecting surveillance activity. The course is designed for commercial infrastructure operators and security staff of nationally significant CIKR facilities. This course can accommodate 25 participants. To request training contact the DHS Office for Bombing Prevention at OBP@ dhs.gov, (703) 235-5723.

Surveillance Detection Training for Municipal Officials, State and Local Law Enforcement Course is a three-day course that provides the knowledge and skills necessary to establish surveillance detection operations to protect critical infrastructure and key resources (CIKR) during periods of elevated threat. Comprised of five modules of informal lecture and two exercises, it provides participants with an awareness of terrorist tactics and attack history and illustrates the means and methods to detect surveillance through practical surveillance detection exercises. This Surveillance Detection Course is designed for municipal security officials and state and local law enforcement with jurisdictional authority over nationally significant CIKR facilities. This course can accommodate 25 participants. To request training contact the DHS Office for Bombing Prevention, OBP@dhs.gov, (703) 235-5723.

Surveillance Detection Web Training is a 60-minute online session produced by the Office for Bombing Prevention that addresses the threat of hostile surveillance on critical infrastructure. Topics addressed during the Web training include basic private sector threat awareness, surveillance and surveillance detection defined, recognition of the types and patterns of behavior associated with terrorist activity, signs of terrorist activity, and suspicious activity reporting. This Web training is available to vetted private sector critical infrastructure owners and operators with a demonstrated need to know through the Homeland Security Information Network-Critical Sectors (HSIN-CS) (https://cs.hsin.gov/) online secure portal. For more information, contact the Commercial Facilities Sector-Specific Agency at CFSteam@hq.dhs.gov.

Threat Detection and Reaction by Retail Staff (Point of Sale) This 20-minute presentation is intended for point-of-sale staff, but is applicable to all employees of a shopping center, mall, or retail facility. It uses case studies and best practices to explain suspicious behavior and items; how to reduce the vulnerability to an active shooter threat; and the appropriate actions to take if employees notice suspicious activity. To access the 20-minute presentation, visit: https://connect.hsin.gov/p21849699/.

Web-Based Chemical Security Awareness Training Program is an interactive tool available free to chemical facilities nationwide to increase security awareness. The training is designed for all facility employees, not just those traditionally involved in security. Upon completion, a certificate is awarded to the student. See https://www.chemicalsecuritytraining.com/. Contact the Chemical Sector-Specific Agency at 1-877-CHEMSEC, ChemicalSector@dhs.gov.

IP Guidance Documents/Publications

Active Shooter—How To Respond is a desk reference guide, a reference poster, and a pocket-size reference card to address how employees, managers, training staff, and human resources personnel can mitigate the risk of and appropriately react in the event of an active shooter situation. See www.dhs.gov/files/programs/gc_1259859901230.shtm. For more information, contact the Commercial Facilities Sector-Specific Agency at CFSteam@hq.dhs.gov.

Bomb-Making Materials Awareness Program (BMAP)/Suspicious Behavior Cards These joint FBI-DHS private sector advisory cards offer simple concise tips and images helping retailers identify and report suspicious activity and sale of household items that can be used in making homemade explosives (HMEs) and improvised explosive devices (IEDs). The register cards give front-end store employees guidance on precursor materials and what to look for regarding suspicious purchases. See www .dhs.gov/files/programs/gc_1259938444548.shtm. To request materials or additional information, contact the DHS Office for Bombing Prevention at OBP@dhs.gov, (703) 235-5723.

Chemical Facility Anti-Terrorism Standards (CFATS) Frequently Asked Questions were developed and continue to be regularly updated as a means of assisting facilities in complying with the CFATS regulation. The FAQs are searchable and categorized to further benefit the user and can be found at http://csat-help.dhs.gov/pls/apex/f?p=100:1:7096251139780888. For more information, contact the CFATS Help Desk at cfats@dhs.gov, (866) 323-2957.

Chemical Facility Anti-Terrorism Standards (CFATS) Presentations The Infrastructure Security Compliance Division (ISCD) reaches out to people and companies in the chemical industry and those interested in chemical security. Those interested in a live presentation about CFATS by ISCD personnel can find more information about such presentations at DHS's chemical security website: www.dhs.gov/files/programs/gc_1224766914427.shtm. For more information, contact the CFATS Help Desk at cfats@dhs.gov, (866) 323-2957.

Chemical Facility Anti-Terrorism Standards (CFATS) Risk-Based Performance Standards (RBPS) The Infrastructure Security Compliance Division (ISCD) provides outreach to key stakeholders with interest or involvement in chemical facility security. Those interested in a live presentation about CFATS by ISCD personnel can find more information and request a presentation by visiting www.dhs.gov/files/programs/

gc_1224766914427.shtm. For more information, contact the CFATS Help Desk at cfats@dhs.gov, (866) 323-2957.

Chemical-Terrorism Vulnerability Information (CVI) is the information protection regime authorized by Section 550 of Public Law 109-295 to protect from inappropriate public disclosure of any information developed or submitted pursuant to Section 550. This includes information that is developed and/or submitted to DHS pursuant to the Chemical Facility Anti-Terrorism Standards (CFATS) regulation which implements Section 550. See www.dhs.gov/chemicalsecurity. For more information, contact the CFATS Help Desk at csat@dhs.gov, (866) 323-2957.

Commercial Facilities Sector Pandemic Planning Documents for use by public assembly sector stakeholders detailing key steps and activities to take when operating during a pandemic influenza situation, a process tracking and status template, and a checklist of recommendations for pandemic response plan development. The products were created in partnership with International Association of Assembly Manager's Academy for Venue Safety and Security. Materials are available on request by contacting the Commercial Facilities Sector-Specific Agency at CFSteam@ hq.dhs.gov.

Dams Sector Resources provide owners/operators with information regarding the dams sector. Publications include: Dams Sector Consequence-Based Top Screen Fact Sheet, Dams Sector Councils Fact Sheet, Dams Sector Crisis Management Handbook , Dams Sector Exercises Series Fact Sheet—2009, Dams Sector Overview Brochure, Dams Sector Security Awareness Guide, Security Awareness Guide for Levees, Security Awareness for Levee Owners Brochure, Dams Sector Standard Operating Procedures for Information Sharing, Waterside Barriers Guide, Suspicious Activity Reporting Fact Sheet, Personnel Screening Guide for Owners and Operators, and Physical Security Measures for Levees Brochure. These resources are available on the HSIN-CS Dams Portal, https://cs.hsin .gov/C2/DS/default.aspx, the CIKR Resource Center, www.dhs.gov/ criticalinfrastructure, and the Association of State Dam Safety Officials (ASDSO) Web site, www.damsafety.org. For more information, contact the Dams Sector-Specific Agency at dams@dhs.gov.

Dams Sector Resources (For Official Use Only): The *Dams Sector Security Awareness Handbook* assists owners/operators in identifying security concerns, coordinating proper response, and establishing effective partnerships with local law enforcement and first-responder communities. The *Dams Sector Protective Measures Handbook* assists owners/operators in selecting protective measures addressing the physical, cyber, and human elements and includes recommendations for developing site security plans. The *Dams Sector Research & Development Roadmap: Development of Validated Damage and Vulnerability Assessment Capabilities for Aircraft Impact Scenarios* is a collaborative effort involving multiple agencies focused on investigating vulnerabilities of concrete arch and embankment dams to aircraft impact scenarios. These For Official Use Only (FOUO) documents are available to vetted private sector critical infrastructure owners and operators with a demonstrated need to know. For more information, contact the Dams Sector-Specific Agency at dams@dhs.gov.

DHS Daily Open Source Infrastructure Report is collected each week day as a summary of open-source published information concerning significant critical infrastructure issues. Each Daily Report is divided by the critical infrastructure sectors and key assets defined in the National Infrastructure Protection Plan. The DHS Daily Open Source Infrastructure Report is available on DHS.gov and Homeland Security Information Network-Critical Sectors (HSIN-CS). See www.dhs.gov/files/programs/ editorial_0542.shtm. For more information, contact NICCReports@dhs .gov or CIKR.ISE@dhs.gov or (202) 312-3421.

DHS Retail Video: "What's in Store—Ordinary People/Extraordinary Events" is a multimedia training video for retail employees of commercial shopping venues alerting them to the signs of suspicious behavior in the workplace that might lead to a catastrophic act. See www.dhs.gov/ multimedia/dhs_retail_video.wmv. For more information, contact the Commercial Facilities Sector-Specific Agency at CFSteam@hq.dhs.gov.

Education, Outreach, and Awareness Snapshot The National Infrastructure Protection Plan (NIPP) provides the coordinated approach for establishing national priorities, goals, and requirements for critical infrastructure and key resources (CIKR) protection and resilience. The NIPP also establishes a framework that allows people and organizations to develop and maintain key CIKR protection expertise. This two-page snapshot describes the NIPP's approach to building national awareness and enabling education, training, and exercise programs. See www.dhs .gov/xlibrary/assets/nipp_education.pdf. For additional information, contact NIPP@dhs.gov.

Emergency Services Personal Readiness Guide for Responders and Their Families is a tri-fold handout providing a description of the Ready Campaign, the Emergency Services Sector-Specific Agency, a list of website resources and instructions on family preparedness that include suggestions on developing an emergency kit and family emergency plan. The Emergency Services Sector (ESS) Video is a three-minute video providing an overview of the ESS. The video is appropriate for conferences and events to grow awareness and participation in sector activities. For more information, or to request materials, contact the Emergency Services Sector-Specific Agency at ESSTeam@hq.dhs.gov.

Evacuation Planning Guide for Stadiums was developed to assist stadium owners and operators with preparing an Evacuation Plan and determining when and how to evacuate, conduct shelter-in-place operations, or relocate stadium spectators and participants. The NASCAR Mass Evacuation Planning Guide and Template was modified into an Evacuation Planning Guide for Stadiums by a working group composed of various federal agencies and members of the Commercial Facilities Sector Coordinating Council. See www.dhs.gov/xlibrary/assets/ip_cikr_ stadium_evac_guide.pdf. For more information, contact the Commercial Facilities Sector-Specific Agency at CFSteam@hq.dhs.gov.

Guide to Critical Infrastructure and Key Resources (CIKR) Protection at the State, Regional, Local, Tribal, & Territorial Level outlines the attributes, capabilities, needs, and processes that a state or local government entity should include in establishing its own CIKR protection function such that it integrates with the National Infrastructure Protection Plan (NIPP) and accomplishes the desired local benefits. This document is available by contacting the NIPP Program Management Office at NIPP@ dhs.gov.

Hotel and Lodging Advisory Poster was created for all staff throughout the U.S. Lodging Industry designed to increase awareness regarding a property's potential to be used for illicit purposes; suspicious behavior and items; and appropriate actions for employees to take if they notice suspicious activity. The poster was designed in tandem with the Commercial Facilities Sector Coordinating Council and the Lodging Subsector. See www.dhs.gov/xlibrary/assets/ip_cikr_hotel_advisory.pdf. For additional information, contact the Commercial Facilities Sector-Specific Agency at CFSteam@hq.dhs.gov.

Infrastructure Data Taxonomy (IDT) Critical infrastructure and key resources (CIKR) and their elements can be described and categorized in various ways, which can result in inconsistent communication and hinder timely decision making within the homeland security community. To prevent such problems, the Department of Homeland Security uses an Infrastructure Data Taxonomy to enable transparent and consistent communication about CIKR between government and private sector partners with its structured terminology, the Infrastructure Data Taxonomy allows its users to designate an asset as belonging to a particular group, and then apply additional, associated taxonomy levels to detail the specifics of the asset and describe its functions. By applying a detailed, structured system of categorization to assets that include sectors, subsectors, segments, sub-segments, and asset type, the Infrastructure Data Taxonomy minimizes potential confusion and enhances transparency about CIKR. See www.dhs.gov/files/publications/gc_1226595934574 .shtm. To request access to download, view, and comment on the Infrastructure Data Taxonomy please visit https://lens.iac.anl.gov/dana-na/ auth/url_31/welcome.cgi. Contact: IICD@dhs.gov.

Infrastructure Protection Report Series (IPRS) is a comprehensive series of For Official Use Only (FOUO) reports containing detailed information for all 18 critical infrastructure and key resources (CIKR) sectors focusing on infrastructure characteristics and common vulnerabilities, potential indicators of terrorist activity, potential threats, and associated protective measures. The IPRS is available to vetted private sector critical infrastructure owners and operators with a demonstrated need to know through the Homeland Security Information Network-Critical Sectors (HSIN-CS) (https://cs.hsin.gov/) online secure portal. For more information on the IPRS, private sector CIKR owners and operators should contact DHS Office of Infrastructure Protection Vulnerability Assessments Branch at IPassessments@dhs.gov or the DHS Protective Security Advisor (PSA) Field Operations Staff: PSAFieldOperationsStaff@hq.dhs.gov or (703) 235-5724.

International Issues for Critical Infrastructure and Key Resources (CIKR) Protection The National Infrastructure Protection Plan (NIPP) brings a new focus to international security cooperation and provides a risk-based framework for collaborative engagement with international partners and for measuring the effectiveness of international CIKR protection activities. This two-page snapshot describes the approach to international issues embodied in the NIPP and the Sector-Specific Plans. See www.dhs.gov/xlibrary/assets/nipp_consolidated_snapshot.pdf. For more information, contact NIPP@dhs.gov.

Multi-Jurisdiction Improvised Explosive Device (IED) Security Plan (MJIEDSP) An effective response to bombing threats and actual incidents requires the close coordination of many different public safety and law enforcement organizations and disciplines. MJIEDSP assists multi-jurisdiction areas in developing a detailed IED security plan that integrates the assets and capabilities of multiple jurisdictions and emergency service sectors. To request additional information, contact the DHS Office for Bombing Prevention at OBP@dhs.gov, (703) 235-5723.

National Critical Infrastructure and Key Resources (CIKR) Protection Annual Report Snapshot Homeland Security Presidential Directive 7, which directed the development of the National Infrastructure Protection Plan, also designated 17 federal sector-specific agencies (SSAs) and required each SSA to provide an annual report to the Secretary of Homeland Security on their efforts to identify, prioritize, and coordinate CIKR protection in their respective sectors. This two-page snapshot describes the National CIKR Protection Annual Report that is developed from the Sector Annual Reports. See www.dhs.gov/xlibrary/assets/nipp_annrpt .pdf. For more information, contact NIPP@dhs.gov.

National Infrastructure Protection Plan (NIPP) 2009 provides the unifying structure for the integration of a wide range of efforts for the enhanced protection and resiliency of the nation's critical infrastructure and key resources (CIKR) into a single national program. See www.dhs.gov/ files/programs/editorial_0827.shtm. The NIPP 2009 Overview Snapshot provides a brief overview of the NIPP risk management framework and the sector partnership model. See www.dhs.gov/xlibrary/assets/ nipp_consolidated_snapshot.pdf. The NIPP Brochure describes the national approach to achieving the goals articulated in the NIPP, the NIPP risk management framework, the NIPP value proposition, and the sector partnership model. The NIPP Information Sharing Snapshot describes the NIPP's approach to achieving active participation by government and private sector partners through robust multidirectional information sharing. It describes the networked approach to information sharing under the NIPP and the establishment of the CIKR Information-Sharing Environment (CIKR ISE). See www.dhs.gov/xlibrary/assets/NIPP_ InfoSharing.pdf. For more information or to request materials, contact the NIPP Program Management Office NIPP@dhs.gov.

NIPP in Action Stories are multimedia pieces highlighting successes in National Infrastructure Protection Plan (NIPP) and Sector Specific Plan (SSP) implementation; these stories can take the form of a printed snapshot, a short video, or a poster board. NIPP in Action stories are developed in concert with sector partners and are designed to promote cross-sector information sharing of best practices with government partners and infrastructure owners and operators. If you would like more information or are interested in developing a NIPP in Action story, contact NIPP@dhs.gov.

Planning for 2009 H1N1 Influenza: A Preparedness Guide for Small Business The Department of Homeland Security, the Centers for Disease Control (CDC), and the Small Business Administration have developed this booklet to help small businesses understand what impact a new influenza virus, like 2009 H1N1 flu, might have on their operations, and how important it is to have a written plan for guiding your business through a possible pandemic. See www.flu.gov/professional/business/smallbiz .html. For more information, contact IP_Education@hq.dhs.gov.

Protective Measures Guide for U.S. Sports Leagues provides an overview of best practices and protective measures designed to assist sports teams and owners/operators of sporting event venues with planning and managing security at their facility. The guide provides examples of successful planning, organization, coordination, communication, operations, and training activities that result in a safe sporting event experience. This document is For Official Use Only (FOUO) and is available to vetted critical infrastructure owners and operators on request based on a demonstrated need to know. For more information, contact the Commercial Facilities Sector-Specific Agency at CFSteam@hq.dhs.gov.

Sector Annual Reports The Sector-Specific Agency Executive Management Office (SSA EMO) Collaborates with state, local, tribal, and territorial government and the private sector to develop, maintain and update Sector Annual Reports for the chemical, commercial facilities, critical manufacturing, dams, emergency services, and nuclear sectors. These reports are For Official Use Only (FOUO) and available to vetted private sector critical infrastructure owners and operators with a demonstrated need to know. For more information, contact ssaexecsec@dhs.gov.

Sector-Specific Agency Executive Management Office (SSA EMO) Sector Snapshots, Fact Sheets and Brochures These documents provide a quick look at SSA EMO sectors and generally contain sector overviews; information on sector partnerships; information on key CIKR protection issues, and Priority Programs. The products bring awareness to CIKR issues and encourage sector participation in critical infrastructure protection risk management activities. These products include: fact sheets and brochures for the chemical, commercial facilities, critical manufacturing, dams, emergency services and nuclear sectors. Additional materials available on request. See www.dhs.gov/files/programs/gc_1189168948944 .shtm. For more information, contact NIPP@dhs.gov.

Sector-Specific Pandemic Influenza Guides (Sector-Specific Agency Executive Management Office (SSA EMO) Sectors) SSA EMO worked with Partnership and Outreach Division to develop sector-specific guides for pandemic influenza for the chemical, commercial facilities, dams, emergency services, and nuclear sectors. Available on request by contacting SSAexecsec@dhs.gov.

Sector-Specific Plans detail the application of the National Infrastructure Protection Plan (NIPP) risk management framework to the unique characteristics and risk landscape of each sector. The SSPs provide the means by which the NIPP is implemented across all the critical infrastructure and key resources (CIKR) sectors. Each sector-specific agency is responsible for developing and implementing an SSP through a coordinated effort involving their public and private sector CIKR partners. For publicly available plans, please visit www.dhs.gov/files/programs/gc_1179866197607.shtm. For more information, contact NIPP@dhs.gov.

State and Local Implementation Snapshot The National Infrastructure Protection Plan (NIPP) provides the coordinated approach for establishing national priorities, goals, and requirements for critical infrastructure and key resources protection so that federal funding and resources are applied in the most effective manner to reduce vulnerability, deter threats, and minimize the consequences of attacks and other incidents. This two-page snapshot describes the role of state and local governments in implementing the NIPP. This snapshot is available by contacting the NIPP Program Management Office at NIPP@dhs.gov.

Summary of the NIPP and SSPs provides the executive summary of the 2006 National Infrastructure Protection Plan (NIPP), as well as the executive summaries of each of the 17 supporting Sector-Specific Plans (SSPs). The 18th sector, critical manufacturing, is not included in this summary document. This document is available by contacting the NIPP Program Management Office at NIPP@dhs.gov.

Who's Who in Chemical Sector Security (October 2008) The document describes the roles and responsibilities of different DHS components with relation to chemical security. See http://training.fema.gov/EMIWeb/IS/IS860a/CIKR/assets/ChemicalSectorWhosWho.pdf. For more information, contact the Chemical Sector-Specific Agency at ChemicalSector@dhs.gov.

Who's Who in Emergency Services Sector describes the roles and responsibilities of the DHS components with relation to the emergency services sector. Contact the Emergency Services Sector-Specific Agency ESSTeam@hq.dhs.gov.

IP Programs/Services/Events

Bomb-making Materials Awareness Program (BMAP) Developed in cooperation with the Federal Bureau of Investigation, BMAP is designed to assist local law enforcement agencies engage a wide spectrum of private sector establishments within their jurisdictions that manufacture, distribute, or sell products that contain homemade explosives (HMEs) precursor materials. BMAP outreach materials, provided by law enforcement to these local businesses, help employees identify HME precursor chemicals and other critical improvised explosive devices (IED) components of concern, such as electronics, and recognize suspicious purchasing behavior that could indicate bomb-making activity. To request materials or additional information, contact the DHS Office for Bombing Prevention at OBP@dhs.gov, (703) 235-5723.

Buffer Zone Protection Program (BZPP) is a DHS-administered infrastructure protection grant program targeted to local law enforcement (LLE). The BZPP provides funding to LLE for equipment acquisition and planning activities to address gaps and enhance security capabilities. It is also designed to increase first-responder capabilities and preparedness by bringing together private sector security personnel and first responders in a collaborative security planning process that enhances the buffer zone—the area outside a facility that can be used by an adversary to conduct surveillance or launch an attack, around individual assets. Detailed BZPP annual grant guidance is available on the DHS/FEMA grants website (www.fema.gov/government/grant/bzpp/).

Cesium Chloride In-Device Delay (Irradiator Hardening) DHS, as the Nuclear Sector-Specific Agency, coordinates with Department of Energy's National Nuclear Security Administration (NNSA), which is collaborating with the private sector and other federal agencies to enhance the security of blood and research irradiators that use cesium chloride sources (Cs-137). This effort includes the three major domestic manufacturers and vendors of self-contained irradiators containing Cs-137. The security enhancements consist of adding an in-device delay (IDD) kit, which significantly increases the amount of time needed for the unauthorized removal of the radioactive material. The objective is to implement security enhancements that minimize impact to the user community. For more information, contact the Nuclear Sector-Specific Agency at nuclearSSA@hq.dhs.gov.

Chemical Facility Anti-Terrorism Standards (CFATS) Chemical Facility Security Tip Line Individuals who would like to report a possible security concern involving the CFATS regulation at their facility or at another facility may contact the CFATS Chemical Facility Security Tip Line. They are welcome to report these concerns on the voicemail anonymously, or, if they would like a return call, they may leave their name and contact number. See www.dhs.gov/chemicalsecurity or Contact the CFATS Chemical Facility Security Tip Line at (877) FYI-4-DHS (1-877-394-4347). To report a potential security incident that has already occurred, call the National Infrastructure Coordination Center at (202) 282-9201.

Chemical Security Summit is an annual industry benchmark event, co-sponsored by DHS and the Chemical Sector Coordinating Council. See www.dhs.gov/files/programs/gc_1176736485793.shtm. For more information, contact the Chemical Sector-Specific Agency at 1-877-CHEMSEC, ChemicalSector@dhs.gov.

Chemical Security Compliance Assistance Visit (CAV) Requests Upon request, the Infrastructure Security Compliance Division (ISCD) provides compliance assistance visits (CAV) to Chemical Facility Anti-Terrorism Standards (CFATS)-covered facilities. CAVs are designed to provide in-depth knowledge of and assistance in a facility's efforts to comply with CFATS. Those interested in a CAV can find more information about these visits at DHS's chemical security website: www.dhs.gov/chemicalsecurity. To request a CAV, contact cscd.ieb@hq.dhs.gov.

Chemical Sector Monthly Suspicious Activity Calls Employees of chemical companies, associations, and agencies who have a need to know information concerning potential physical and cyber threats and vulnerabilities to chemical infrastructure are eligible to listen in on the briefings. This monthly unclassified suspicious activity call for the chemical sector is scheduled for the first Wednesday of every month at 10:00AM EDT. The call-in information is as follows: DDI number: (800) 501-9384, Conference ID: 4754043. Contact the Chemical Sector-Specific Agency at ChemicalSector@dhs.gov.

Critical Infrastructure and Key Resource (CIKR) Asset Protection Technical Assistance Program (CAPTAP) helps state and local law enforcement, first responders, emergency management, and other homeland security officials understand the steps necessary to develop and implement a comprehensive CIKR protection program in their respective jurisdiction through the facilitated sharing of best practices and lessons learned. This includes understanding processes, methodologies, and resources necessary to identify, assess, prioritize, and protect CIKR assets, as well as those capabilities necessary to prevent and respond to incidents, should they occur. Through a partnership with the National Guard Bureau

(NGB); the U.S. Army Research, Development and Engineering Command (RDECOM); and the DHS Office of Infrastructure Protection (IP) Infrastructure Information Collection Division (IICD), this service also provides Web-based and instructor-led training on Protected Critical Infrastructure Information (PCII) and the use of the *Automated Critical Asset Management System* (ACAMS) and *Integrated Common Analytical Viewer* (iCAV) system. See www.dhs.gov/files/programs/gc_1195679577314 .shtm. For additional information, contact ACAMS-info@hq.dhs.gov, or (703) 235-3939.

Dams Sector Exercise Series (DSES) In collaboration with sector partners, including the Emergency Services SSA, the Dams SSA has developed an exercise series to test interoperability, preparedness, and regional resilience. DSES-09: Columbia River Basin was an effort undertaken in collaboration with the Pacific Northwest Economic Region, U.S. Army Corps of Engineers, and Pacific Northwest region stakeholders to conduct exercise series along the Columbia River Basin to develop an Integrated Regional Strategy to improve disaster resilience and preparedness for the Tri-Cities region of Washington State. See http://training.fema .gov/EMIWeb/IS/IS860a/CIKR/assets/2009DamsSectorExerciseSeries ColumbiaRiverBasinFactSheet.pdf. For more information, contact the Dams Sector-Specific Agency at dams@dhs.gov.

Enhanced Critical Infrastructure Protection (ECIP) Visits are conducted by protective security advisors (PSAs) in collaboration with critical infrastructure and key resources (CIKR) owners and operators to assess overall facility security and increase security awareness. ECIP Visits are augmented by the Infrastructure Survey Tool (IST), a Web-based tool that provides the ability to collect, process, and analyze ECIP survey data in near real time. Data collected during an ECIP visit is consolidated in the IST and then weighted and valued, which enables PSAs to develop ECIP metrics; conduct sector-by-sector and cross-sector vulnerability comparisons; identify security gaps and trends across CIKR sectors and sub-sectors; and establish sector baseline security survey scores. Private sector owners and operators interested in receiving an ECIP visit should contact the PSA Field Operations Staff PSAFieldOperationsStaff@hq.dhs .gov (703) 235-5724.

National Infrastructure Advisory Council (NIAC) provides the president through the secretary of homeland security advice on the security of the critical infrastructure sectors and their information systems. The council is composed of a maximum of 30 members, appointed by the president from private industry, academia, and state and local government. For more information, see www.dhs.gov/niac.

National Infrastructure Protection Plan (NIPP) Sector Partnership improves the protection and resilience of the nation's critical infrastructure. The partnership provides a forum for the designated 18 critical sectors to engage with the federal government regularly on national planning, risk mitigation program identification and implementation, and information sharing. Additional information for private sector owners and operators of critical infrastructure may be found at www.dhs.gov/cipac or by contacting Sector.Partnership@dhs.gov.

Office of Infrastructure Protection (IP) and National Infrastructure Protection Plan (NIPP) booths are available for exhibiting at national and sector-level events to promote awareness of the IP mission and the NIPP to government partners and infrastructure owners and operators. In addition, IP maintains a cadre of trained speakers who are available to speak on critical infrastructure protection and resilience issues at conferences and events. For more information, contact NIPP@dhs.gov.

Protected Critical Infrastructure Information (PCII) Program is an information-sharing resource designed to facilitate the flow and exchange of critical infrastructure information (CII) between the private sector; DHS; and federal, state and local government entities. Private sector entities can voluntarily submit their CII to the PCII Program for use in federal, state and local critical infrastructure protection efforts. Once the PCII Program has validated and marked the CII as PCII, the information will be safeguarded, disseminated, and used in accordance with PCII requirements established pursuant to the Critical Infrastructure Information Act of 2002 and the implementing Regulation. PCII is protected from disclosure under federal, state and local disclosure laws and from use in civil litigation and for regulatory purposes. Information about the PCII Program, including the CII Act of 2002, the implementing Regulation and the PCII Program Procedures Manual can be found on the program's website at www.dhs.gov/pcii. For additional information, contact pcii-info@dhs.gov, or (202) 360-3023.

Protective Security Advisor (PSA) Program Established in 2004, the PSA Program provides a locally based DHS infrastructure security expert as the link between state, local, tribal, territorial, and private sector organizations and DHS infrastructure protection resources. PSAs assist with ongoing state and local critical infrastructure and key resources (CIKR) security efforts, coordinate vulnerability assessments and training, support incident management, and serve as a vital channel of communication between private sector owners and operators of CIKR assets and DHS. Private sector owners and operators interested in contacting their PSA should contact the DHS Protective Security Advisor (PSA) Field Operations Staff: PSAFieldOperationsStaff@hq.dhs.gov or (703) 235-5724.

Radiological Voluntary Security Enhancements DHS, as the Nuclear Sector-Specific Agency, coordinates with security experts from the Department of Energy's national laboratories, led by National Nuclear Security Administration (NNSA) headquarters staff, to provide security assessments, share observations, and make recommendations for enhancing security at facilities that house high-risk radioactive sources. The security upgrades are aimed at improving deterrence, control, detection, delay, response, and sustainability. Contact the Nuclear Sector-Specific Agency at nuclearSSA@hq.dhs.gov.

Regional Resiliency Assessment Program (RRAP) is a cooperative DHS-led interagency assessment of specific critical infrastructure and key resources (CIKR) and regional analysis of the surrounding infrastructure, including key interdependencies. The emphasis for the RRAP is infrastructure "clusters," regions, and systems. The assessment and its final report are protected as Protected Critical Infrastructure Information (PCII). Regions are selected collaboratively by state and DHS Officials. Private sector CIKR owners and operators of infrastructure interested in receiving more information on the RRAP should contact the DHS Protective Security Advisor (PSA) Field Operations Staff: PSAFieldOperations Staff@hq.dhs.gov or (703) 235-5724.

Research and Test Reactors (RTRs) Voluntary Security Enhancement Program As chair of the Nuclear Government Coordinating Council (GCC) and a participant in the Joint GCC-Sector Coordinating Council (public-private) Research and Test Reactor (RTR) Subcouncil, the Nuclear Sector-Specific Agency coordinates with the Department of Energy's National Nuclear Security Administration on voluntary security enhancements at RTR facilities nationwide. Security enhancements are jointly determined by NNSA and the facility owner-operator and are funded by NNSA. These enhancements improve security beyond what is required by law and are consistent with RTR security regulations. For additional information, contact the Nuclear Sector-Specific Agency nuclearSSA@hq.dhs.gov.

Sector-Specific Agency Executive Management Office/Transportation Security Administration (TSA) Joint Exercise Programs Working with support and funding from TSA, this potentially multiyear program allows critical manufacturers with planning support by TSA's Intermodal Security Training and Exercise Program (ISTEP) to develop advanced table-top exercises that determine gaps and mitigate vulnerabilities in their respective transportation supply chains within the U.S. and cross border (particularly across Canadian and Mexican borders). For more information, contact the Critical Manufacturing Sector-Specific Agency, cm-ssa@dhs.gov.

Security Outreach and Awareness Program (SOAP) provides critical information to chemical facility managers, control engineers, and IT administrators working in cybersecurity management. Participating companies receive a free voluntary review of the security of their system networks and a summary of their cybersecurity policies and processes. For more information, contact the Chemical Sector-Specific Agency at ChemicalSector@dhs.gov.

Security Seminar Exercise Series with State Chemical Industry Councils This collaborative effort between the DHS Chemical Sector-Specific Agency and various state chemical industry councils fosters communication between facilities and their local emergency response teams by encouraging representatives to share their insight, knowledge, and experiences during a facilitated table-top exercise. The exercises can include a wide variety of topics and are catered toward the specific interests of the local chemical facilities. For more information, contact the Chemical Sector-Specific Agency at ChemicalSector@dhs.gov.

Site Assistance Visit (SAV) is a facility vulnerability assessment focused on identifying security gaps and providing options for consideration to enhance protective measures. The SAV uses analyses of critical assets and current security measures, and scenario-based approaches such as assault planning to identify vulnerabilities and develop mitigation strategies. Following the assessment, DHS provides critical infrastructure and key resources (CIKR) owners and operators with an SAV Report, protected as Protected Critical Infrastructure Information (PCII). The report details the facility information and offers options for consideration to increase the ability to detect and prevent terrorist attacks and reduce infrastructure vulnerabilities. Private sector owners and operators interested in receiving more information on the SAV should contact the DHS Protective

Security Advisor (PSA) Field Operations Staff: PSAFieldOperationsStaff@ hq.dhs.gov or (703) 235-5724.

IP Web-Based Resources

Automated Critical Asset Management System (ACAMS) is a secure, Web-based portal designed to help state and local emergency responders, such as infrastructure protection planners, homeland security officials, law enforcement personnel, and emergency managers, collect and organize critical infrastructure and key resource (CIKR) asset data as part of a comprehensive CIKR protection program. ACAMS is managed by the Office of Infrastructure Protection (IP) and continues to be developed in partnership with state and local communities. ACAMS benefits are provided at no cost for state and local use, it has public disclosure protections through the Protected Critical Infrastructure Information (PCII) program, and it is an integrated approach for collecting, protecting, and analyzing CIKR asset data. The Federal Emergency Management Agency's National Preparedness Directorate also supports critical infrastructure protection–related ACAMS training. See www.dhs.gov/ACAMS. For more information, contact ACAMS-info@hq.dhs.gov or (703) 235-3939.

Chemical Security Assessment Tool (CSAT) is an online tool developed by the Infrastructure Security Compliance Division (ISCD) to streamline the facility submittal and subsequent DHS analysis and interpretation of critical information used to (1) preliminarily determine facility risk, (2) assess high-risk facility's vulnerability, (3) describe security measures at high-risk sites, and (4) ultimately track compliance with the CFATS program. CSAT is a secure information portal that includes applications for completing the User Registration, Top-Screen, Security Vulnerability Assessment (SVA), and Site Security Plan (SSP). ISCD provides user guides to assist with each of these applications. See www.dhs.gov/files/programs/ gc_1169501486197.shtm. Contact the CFATS Help Desk at csat@dhs.gov, (866) 323-2957.

Computer-Based Assessment Tool (CBAT) is a cross-platform tool that integrates 360-degree geospherical video, geospatial, and aerial imagery of facilities, surrounding areas, routes, and other areas of interest with a wide variety of other facility data, including evacuation plans, vulnerability assessments, standard operating procedures, and schematic/floor plans. By integrating this disparate data, the CBAT provides a comprehensive visual guide of a site that assists facility owners and operators, local law enforcement, and emergency response personnel to prepare for and respond to an incident. This resource is protected at the Protected Critical Infrastructure (PCII) and For Official Use Only (FOUO) level and is available to vetted private sector critical infrastructure owners and operators with a demonstrated need to know. For more information, contact the DHS PSA Field Operations Staff: PSAFieldOperationsStaff@hq.dhs .gov or (703) 235-5724.

Critical Infrastructure and Key Resources (CIKR) Resource Center was designed to build awareness and understanding of each sector's scope and efforts to ensure CIKR protection and resiliency. The Center offers a centralized location page to find sector goals, plans, priorities, online training modules, activities and achievements, useful links, and other sector-based and cross-sector resources. See http://training.fema.gov/ emiweb/is/IS860a/CIKR/index.htm. For more information, contact IP_Education@hq.dhs.gov.

Dams Sector Consequence-Based Top Screen Methodology is an online tool based on the methodology developed to identify the subset of those high-consequence facilities whose failure or disruption could potentially lead to the most severe impacts. The Web-based tool was developed to support the implementation of the methodology across the sector. Available on LENS—https://lens.iac.anl.gov, for more information contact the Dams Sector-Specific Agency at dams@dhs.gov.

Dams Sector Suspicious Activity Reporting Tool is an online reporting tool within the Homeland Security Information Network—Critical Sectors Dams Portal that was established to provide sector stakeholders with the capability to report and retrieve information pertaining to suspicious activities that may potentially be associated with pre-incident surveillance, and those activities related to the exploration or targeting of a specific critical infrastructure facility or system. It is accompanied by a Fact Sheet/Brochure. For additional information, contact the Dams Sector-Specific Agency at dams@dhs.gov.

DHS 20-Minute Retail Security Webinar is a Web-based application dealing with security issues for all shopping center, mall, and retail employees. The webinar, produced by the Office of Infrastructure Protection's Protective Security Coordination Division (Office for Bombing Prevention), covers issues such as overall security awareness, suspicious purchases, and unattended or suspicious packages. To request, contact the Commercial Facilities Sector-Specific Agency at CFSteam@hq.dhs .gov.

DHS 90-Minute Retail Security Webinar is a Web-based application similar to the 20-minute Retail Security Webinar but designed for mall and retail professional security staff. The webinar, produced by the Office of Infrastructure Protection's Protective Security Coordination Division (Office for Bombing Prevention), offers greater detail on the topics covered in the 20-minute webinar, but with a greater scope and detail. Available on request. For additional information, please contact the Commercial Facilities Sector-Specific Agency at CFSteam@hq.dhs.gov.

General Information on Sector-Specific Agency Executive Management Office (SSA EMO) Critical Infrastructure and Key Resources (CIKR) Sectors and Programs provides an overview of the SSA EMO mission in CIKR risk management, and a description of SSA EMO Sectors. See www .dhs.gov/xabout/structure/gc_1204058503863.shtm. Contact the Sector-Specific Agency Executive Management Office at SSAexecsec@dhs.gov.

Homeland Security Information Network-Critical Sectors (HSIN-CS) is the primary information-sharing platform between the critical infrastructure/key resource sector stakeholders. HSIN-CS enables DHS and critical infrastructure owners and operators to communicate, coordinate, and share sensitive and sector-relevant information to protect their critical assets, systems, functions, and networks, at no charge to sector stakeholders. Vetted critical infrastructure private sector owners and operators are eligible to access HSIN-CS. To request access to HSIN-CS, please e-mail CIKRISEAccess@hq.dhs.gov. When requesting access, please indicate the critical infrastructure sector to which your company belongs and include your name, company, official e-mail address, and supervisor's name and phone number.

Integrated Common Analytical Viewer (iCAV) provides a suite of free, Web-based, infrastructure-focused, geospatial visualization and analysis tools managed by the DHS Office of Infrastructure Protection. The two primary tools in the iCAV suite are the iCAV Next Generation Web-based visualization and analysis platform and the DHS Earth data service, both of which provide authoritative infrastructure data and various dynamic situational awareness feeds in standard geographic information system (GIS) data formats to authorized Homeland Security Information Network (HSIN) users at the federal, state, and local levels and within the private sector. iCAV Next Generation is also the GIS platform for the *Automated Critical Asset Management System* (ACAMS). See www.dhs .gov/icav. For more information, contact iCAV.info@hq.dhs.gov, or (703) 235-4949.

Risk Self-Assessment Tool (RSAT) for Stadiums and Arenas is a secure, Web-based application designed to assist managers of stadiums and arenas with the identification and management of security vulnerabilities to reduce risk to their facilities. The RSAT application uses facility input in combination with threat and consequence estimates to conduct a comprehensive risk assessment and provides users with options for consideration to improve the security posture of their facility. Accompanied by a Fact Sheet/Brochure. See www.dhs.gov/files/programs/gc_1259861625248 .shtm. For additional information, please contact the Commercial Facilities Sector-Specific Agency at CFSteam@hq.dhs.gov.

Technical Resource for Incident Prevention (TRIPwire) (www.tripwire-dhs.net) is DHS's 24/7 online, collaborative, information-sharing network for bomb squads, law enforcement, and other first responders to learn about current terrorist improvised explosive device (IED) tactics, techniques, and procedures. The system combines expert analyses and reports with relevant documents, images, and videos gathered directly from terrorist sources to help law enforcement anticipate, identify, and prevent IED incidents. To request additional information, contact DHS Office for Bombing Prevention at OBP@dhs.gov, (703) 235-5723.

TRIPwire Community Gateway (TWCG) is a TRIP*wire* Web portal designed specifically for the Nation's CIKR owners, operators, and private security personnel. TWCG provides expert threat analyses, reports, and relevant planning documents to help key private sector partners anticipate, identify, and prevent improvised explosive device (IED) incidents. TWCG shares IED-related information tailored to each of the 18 CIKR sectors as well as a community sector for educational institutions, in accordance with the National Infrastructure Protection Plan (NIPP). TWCG information is currently available to vetted private sector critical infrastructure owners and operators with a demonstrated need to know through the Homeland Security Information Network-Critical Sectors (HSIN-CS) (https://cs.hsin.gov/) online secure portal. To request additional information, contact the DHS Office for Bombing Prevention at OBP@dhs.gov, (703) 235-5723.

Voluntary Chemical Assessment Tool (VCAT) is a secure, Web-based application that allows owners and operators to identify their facilities' current risk level using an all-hazards approach and facilitates a cost-benefit analysis by allowing them to select the best combination of physical security countermeasures and mitigation strategies to reduce overall risk. There is also a brochure that describes the features and benefits of VCAT and includes instructions on how to gain access to the tool. Accompanied by Fact Sheet/Brochure. Available on request. For more information, contact the Chemical Sector-Specific Agency at ChemicalSector@dhs.gov.

SCIENCE & TECHNOLOGY DIRECTORATE (S&T)

The S&T Directorate's mission is to improve homeland security by providing to customers state-of-the-art technology that helps them achieve their missions. S&T customers include the operating components of the department, state, local, tribal and territorial emergency responders and officials. www.dhs.gov/scienceandtechnology.

S&T Programs

S&T Collaboration in Data and Visual Analytics both internally within the DHS research community as well as externally enables S&T to leverage both its funding and technical expertise by taking advantage of research activities underway in government laboratories, industry laboratories, and in universities across the world. In 2008 S&T's Command, Control, and Interoperability Division (CCI) established a five-year joint program with the National Science Foundation (NSF) on the Foundations of Visual and Data Analytics. In 2009, CCI contributions were matched more than twofold by NSF, and 16 universities have been awarded research grants. Additionally, DHS has signed formal international collaboration agreements between Canada and Germany, and discussions with United Kingdom (UK) and France are underway. These efforts have resulted in the development of joint scientific and technical projects in visualization and data analytics. For more information, contact iVAC@dhs.gov.

Commercial Mobile Alert Service (CMAS) is a component of the Integrated Public Alert and Warning System. It is an alert system that will have the capability to deliver relevant, timely, effective, and targeted alert messages to the public through cell phones, blackberries, pagers, and other mobile devices. This national capability will ensure more people receive presidential, imminent threat, and AMBER alerts. In support of this effort, the first CMAS Forum was recently held. The purpose of the Forum was to convene the alerts and warnings community—including message originators, emergency responder organizations, industry organizations, academia, and organizations representing special needs populations-to address critical issues and determine next steps for the CMAS Research, Development, Test and Evaluation (RDT&E) program. Action teams based around the initiatives that came out of the CMAS Forum were created and are being populated. See www.cmasforum.com/, contact cmasforum@sra.com.

Commercialization Office is responsible for the development and implementation of a commercialization process and for the execution of two innovative public-private partnerships that leverage research and development efforts in the private sector that are aligned to detailed operational requirements from department stakeholders. The Commercialization Office also spearheads DHS S&T's outreach efforts that inform the private sector on "How to do business with DHS." See www.dhs.gov/xabout/structure/gc_1234194479267.shtm. Contact: SandT_Commercialization@hq.dhs.gov, 1-(202) 254-6749.

Cyber Security Research and Development Center (CSRDC) S&T has the mission to conduct research, development, test and evaluation, and timely transition (RDTE&T) of cybersecurity capabilities to operational units within DHS, as well as federal, state, local and critical infrastructure sector operational end users for homeland security purposes. As part of its cybersecurity mission, DHS/S&T has established the Cyber Security Research and Development Center (CSRDC). As part of its cybersecurity mission, DHS/S&T utilizes CSRDC to focus cybersecurity RDTE&T efforts and to involve the best practices and personnel from academic, private industry, and federal and national laboratories. The Cyber Security R&D Center was established by the Department of Homeland Security in 2004 to develop security technology for protection of the U.S. cyber infrastructure. For example, the Linking the Oil and Gas Industry to Improve Cyber Security (LOGIIC) project, which addresses security vulnerability issues related to the oil and gas industry's Process Control Systems (PCS) and Supervisory Control and Data Acquisition systems. The comprehensive monitoring system developed in LOGIIC provides an integrated, multi-component security solution that monitors a PCS for abnormal activity. The Center conducts its work through partnerships between government and private industry, the venture capital community, and the research community. This website provides information about this and other DHS S&T projects, workshop information and presentations, cybersecurity news, events and outreach information. See www.cyber.st.dhs.gov/, contact csrdc@dhs.gov.

Defense Technology Experimental Research (DETER) The DETER testbed was jointly funded by S&T and the National Science Foundation (NSF) and has been open to the research community since March 2004. The centerpiece of the experimental environment is a safe (quarantined), but realistic, network testbed based on a mesh of clusters of homogeneous experimental nodes. DETER is a critical national cybersecurity experimental infrastructure that enables users to study and evaluate a wide range of computer security technologies including encryption, pattern detection, intrusion-tolerant storage protocols, next generation network simulations; as well as develop and share educational material and tools to train the next generation of cybersecurity experts. Existing testing facilities cannot handle experiments on a large enough scale to represent today's operational networks or the portion of the Internet that might be involved in a security attack. Industry has only been able to test and validate new security technologies in small- to medium-scale private research laboratories that do not adequately simulate a real networking environment. Newsletters, published papers, videos and update presentations can be viewed at www.isi.edu/deter/. *Contact* testbed-ops@isi.deterlab.net.

Domain Name System Security Extensions (DNSSEC) Deployment Coordinating Initiative To strengthen the domain name system against attacks, S&T has initiated the DoDNSSEC Deployment Initiative. DNSSEC has been developed to provide cryptographic support for domain name system (DNS) data integrity and authenticity. DHS sponsors a community-based, international effort to transition the current state of DNSSEC to large-scale global deployment, including sponsorship of the DNSSEC Deployment Working Group, a group of experts active in the development or deployment of DNSSEC. It is open for anyone interested in participation. The DNSSEC website contains articles, published research papers, DNSSEC tools, case studies, workshop information and presentation materials. See www.dnssec-deployment.org/.

Emergency Data Exchange Language (EDXL) messaging standards help emergency responders exchange critical data, including alerts, hospital capacity, and availability of response personnel and equipment. Industry can leverage these standards to better ensure compliance and interoperability for their products. See www.oasis-open.org.

FutureTECH Program targets critical research/innovation focus areas that detailed the long-term needs of the department to partner with the private sector, university communities, and national labs in the development of technology for future use by department stakeholders. See www.dhs.gov/files/programs/gc_1242058794349.shtm. Contact SandT_Commercialization@hq.dhs.gov, (202) 254-6749.

Long-Range Broad Agency Announcement (BAA) is a funding mechanism for original research that addresses DHS capability gaps, which are specified in Part I of its announcement under Research Areas of Strategic Interest. It also funds original research that advances the foundations of technical knowledge in the basic sciences. Successful submissions to the Long-Range BAA answer questions such as, "What research problem do you propose to solve? How is your solution different from and superior to currently available solutions or from the efforts of others to achieve a similar solution? What data and analysis do you have to support the contention that funding your R&D project will result in a significant increase in capability for DHS?" All of S&T's divisions and special programs receive and evaluate submissions, as appropriate, through the Long-Range BAA. For submission instructions, evaluation criteria, and to apply online, visit: https://baa.st.dhs.gov/.

National Science and Technology Council (NSTC) Subcommittee on Biometrics and Identity Management (BIdM) encourages greater collaboration and sharing of information on biometric activities among government departments and agencies; commercial entities; state, regional, and international organizations; and the general public. See www.Biometrics .gov, contact info@biometrics.org.

Project 25 Compliance Assessment Program (P25 CAP) was established, in coordination with the National Institute of Standards and Technology (NIST), to provide a process for ensuring that equipment complies with P25 standards, meets performance requirements, and is capable of interoperating across manufacturers. P25 standards are focused on developing radios and other components that can interoperate regardless of manufacturer. P25 CAP allows emergency responders to confidently purchase and use P25-compliant products, and the program represents a critical step toward allowing responders to communicate with their own equipment. In 2009, the first eight laboratories were officially recognized by DHS as part of the P25 CAP. A DHS-approved laboratory is authorized to produce test reports for P25 equipment. NPPD/CS&C/OEC coordinates the implementation of P25 compliance standards with S&T to promote communications interoperability, and by encouraging grant recipients to purchase P25-compliant equipment and technologies with federal grant funding. See www.safecomprogram.gov/SAFECOM/currentprojects/ project25cap/, contact P25CAP@dhs.gov.

The Protected Repository for the Defense of Infrastructure against Cyber Threats (PREDICT) will facilitate the accessibility of computer and network operational data for use in cyber defense research and development through large-scale research datasets. PREDICT allows partners to pursue technical solutions to protect the public and private information infrastructure. It also provides researchers and developers with real network data to validate their technology and products before deploying them online. This initiative represents an important three-way partnership between the federal government, critical information infrastructure providers, and the security development community (both academic and commercial). Within this project, the Los Angeles Network Data Exchange and Repository (LANDER), Network Traffic Data Repository to Develop Secure Information Technology Infrastructure, Routing Topology and Network Reliability Dataset Project, and Virtual Center for Network and Security Data serve as data set collectors and hosts. The PREDICT Data Coordinating Center helps manage and coordinate the research data repository. See https://www.predict.org, contact PREDICT-contact@rti.org.

Science & Technology Basic Research Focus Areas represent the technological areas in which S&T seeks to create and/or exploit new scientific breakthroughs and help guide the direction of the S&T research portfolio, within resource constraints, to provide long-term science and technology advances for the benefit of homeland security. The focus areas identified by S&T's Research Council, with input from our customers and the research community, summarize the fundamental work needed to support the future protection of our nation. See www.dhs.gov/xabout/structure/gc_1242157296000.shtm. Contact the Director of Research, SandT .Research@dhs.gov , (202) 254-6068.

SECURE Program leverages the experience and resources of the private sector to develop fully deployable products/services based on department-generated and -vetted, detailed operational requirements documents (ORDs) and a conservative estimate of the potential available market of department stakeholders. See www.dhs.gov/files/programs/gc_1211996620526.shtm. Contact sandt_commercialization@hq.dhs.gov, (202) 254-6749.

Support Anti-Terrorism by Fostering Effective Technologies Act (SAFETY Act) is a program managed by the Office of SAFETY Act Implementation (OSAI). The program evaluates and qualifies technologies for liability protection in accordance with the Support Anti-Terrorism by Fostering Effective Technologies (SAFETY) Act of 2002 and the supporting regulations of the Final Rule (6 CFR Part 25) implemented on July 10, 2006. As part of the Homeland Security Act of 2002 (Public Law 107-296), the SAFETY Act provides risk management and liability protections for sellers of qualified antiterrorism technologies. The purpose of the SAFETY Act is to ensure that the threat of liability does not deter potential manufacturers or sellers of effective antiterrorism technologies from developing, deploying and commercializing these technologies that meet homeland security objectives. See www.SAFETYAct.gov. Contact SAFETYActHelpDesk@dhs.gov, (866) 788-9318.

Technologies for Critical Incident Preparedness (TCIP) Conference and Exposition TCIP highlights DoJ, DHS, and DoD technologies; RDT&E investments; and training tools for the emergency responder community. It provides a forum for emergency responders to discuss best practices and exchange information and offers a unique opportunity for emergency responders; business and industry; academia; and local, tribal, state, and federal stakeholders to network; exchange ideas; and address common critical incident technology, preparedness, response and recovery needs, protocols, and solutions. See www.tcipexpo.com.

DHS Technology Transfer Program serves as the focal point for technology transfer activities at the Department of Homeland Security. Currently, DHS operates from one centralized Office of Research and Technology Applications (ORTA) to manage technology transfers at each of its laboratories and throughout the department. The Technology Transfer Program promotes the transfer and/or exchange of technology with industry, state and local governments, academia, and other federal agencies. The technologies developed and evaluated within the DHS can have a tremendous potential for commercial applications throughout the nation and dramatically enhance the competitiveness of individual small businesses as well as expanding areas of exploration and cooperation for all non-federal partners. For more information, visit www.dhs.gov/xabout/structure/gc_1264538499667.shtm.

Voice over Internet Protocol (VoIP) project researches IP-enabled communication technologies and evaluates promising solutions. This project will enable the emergency response community to confidently deploy and use IP technologies and integrate video, cellular, and satellite communications. In FY 2009, the project initiated testing and evaluation of IP solutions and completed the first VoIP profile as prioritized by the emergency response community. Ultimately, the project will complete the development of a set of standards based on the needs of emergency responders. DHS and the U.S. Department of Commerce (DOC) gathered key stakeholders from both the public safety and industry communities to form a working group. Led by the DHS Office for Interoperability and Compatibility and DOC's Public Safety Communications Research Program, the Public Safety VoIP Working Group works to define and clarify the expectations for VoIP in the public safety environment. See www

.safecomprogram.gov/SAFECOM/currentprojects/voip/ and www
.pscr.gov/projects/broadband/voip/voip.php, contact VoIP_Working_
Group@sra.com.

Video Quality in Public Safety (VQiPS) As video technology has
evolved, the array of options for public safety practitioners has grown
and the interoperability challenges have become increasingly complex.
Thus the need has emerged for public safety to collectively articulate
their video quality needs to the manufacturing community. A VQiPS
Working Group was formed to focus on the major policy, technology, and
practical uses and challenges of public safety video systems. Comprised
of emergency responders, academics, federal partners, and vendors, the
working group is currently creating an end user guide to help practitioners articulate their needs to vendors when they look to purchase or
upgrade video systems. See www.safecomprogram.gov/SAFECOM/
currentprojects/videoquality/videoquality.htm and www.pscr.gov/
projects/video_quality/video_about.php. Contact VQiPS_Working_
Group@sra.com.

DHS Centers of Excellence

**DHS Center of Excellence: Awareness & Location of Explosives-Related
Threats (ALERT)** develops new means and methods to protect the nation
from explosives-related threats, focusing on detecting leave-behind improvised explosive devices, enhancing aviation cargo security, providing
next-generation baggage screening, detecting liquid explosives, and enhancing suspicious passenger identification. Resources include Training
Opportunities and courses in Explosives. See www.northeastern.edu/
alert/ and http://energetics.chm.uri.edu. For more information, contact
universityprograms@dhs.gov.

**DHS Center of Excellence: Preparedness and Catastrophic Event Re-
sponse (PACER)** optimizes our nation's preparedness in the event of
a high-consequence natural or man-made disaster, as well as develops
guidelines to best alleviate the effects of such an event. Resources available include a Modeling & Simulation Catalog, a Model Memorandum of
Understanding (MOU) between Hospitals during Declared Emergencies,
and the Electronic Mass Casualty Assessment and Planning Scenarios
Applet (EMCAPS). See www.pacercenter.org/. For more information,
contact universityprograms@dhs.gov.

**DHS Center of Excellence: National Center for Risk and Economic
Analysis of Terrorism Events (CREATE)** develops advanced tools to

evaluate the risks, costs and consequences of terrorism, and guides economically viable investments in countermeasures that will make our nation safer and more secure. Resources include: an Executive Program for Counter-Terrorism, Aviation Safety & Security Program covering the use of models and tools for evaluation of security and antiterrorism, Degree Specializations in Homeland Security Analysis, and the National Interstate Economic Model (NIEMO) an operational multiregional input-output economic impact model. See http://create.usc.edu/. For more information, contact universityprograms@dhs.gov.

DHS Center of Excellence: National Center for Food Protection and Defense (NCFPD) defends the safety and security of the food system from pre-farm inputs through consumption by establishing best practices; developing new tools; and attracting new researchers to prevent, manage, and respond to food contamination events. Resources include: Food and Agriculture Criticality Assessment Tool (FAS-CAT); FoodSHIELD, a Web-based system for communication, coordination, community-building, education, and training among the nation's food and agriculture sectors; Exercise Design and Facilitation; Event and Consequence Models; Continuous Tracking and Analyzing Consumer Confidence in the U.S. Food Supply Chain; Supply Chain Benchmarking Diagnostic Tool; Global Chronology of Incidents of Chemical, Biological, Radioactive and Nuclear Attacks 1961–2005; Mass Production of Detection and Neutralizing Antibodies; Biosensors Courses; The Biosecurity Research Institute (BRI); The Frontier Program; Food Protection and Food Safety and Defense Graduate Certificate Programs; The National Agricultural Biosecurity Center (NABC); Optimized Detection of Intentional Contamination using Simulation Modeling; Risk Communication, Message Development/Evaluation and Training; decontamination protocols; and Regulatory, Policy, Technical, and Practical Issues related to Contaminated Food Disposal. For more information, see www.ncfpd.umn.edu/ or contact universityprograms@dhs.gov.

DHS Center of Excellence: National Center for Foreign Animal and Zoonotic Disease Defense (FAZD) protects against the introduction of high-consequence foreign animal and zoonotic diseases into the United States, with an emphasis on prevention, surveillance, intervention and recovery. Resources include Courses on Foreign Animal and Zoonotic Diseases, Public and Private sector Awareness Materials, Field Guide to Handling Contaminated Animal and Plant Materials, Mass Livestock Carcass Management workshop, Specialists in Foreign Animal and Zoonotic Diseases, an Avian Influenza Study Curriculum, a Guide to Developing an Animal Issues Emergency Management Plan, and a compilation of materials pertaining to the Economic Impact of Foreign Animal Diseases to the United States. See http://fazd.tamu.edu/. For more information, contact universityprograms@dhs.gov.

DHS Center of Excellence: National Center for Command, Control, and Interoperability (C2I) creates the scientific basis and enduring technologies needed to analyze massive amounts of information from multiple sources to more reliably detect threats to the security of the nation, its infrastructures, and to the health and welfare of its populace. These new technologies will also improve the dissemination of both information and related technologies. Co-led by Purdue University and Rutgers University, available educational opportunities are geared toward educating the next generation of homeland security professionals with initiatives that span the entire career development pipeline, ranging from K–12 programs through undergraduate and graduate level work, to professional education and training. For more information, see www.purdue.edu/discoverypark/vaccine/ and www.ccicada.org/ or contact universityprograms@dhs.gov.

DHS Center of Excellence: Center for Maritime, Island, & Remote/Extreme Environment Security led by the University of Hawaii in Honolulu for maritime and island security and Stevens Institute of Technology in Hoboken, N.J., for port security, will strengthen maritime domain awareness and safeguard populations and properties unique to U.S. islands, ports, and remote and extreme environments. Programs include the MARCOOS High Frequency Radar Network and the New York /New Jersey Harbor Maritime Awareness System. See http://cimes.hawaii.edu/ and www.stevens.edu/csr/. For more information, contact universityprograms@dhs.gov.

DHS Center of Excellence: National Transportation Security Center of Excellence (NTSCOE) develops new technologies; tools; and advanced methods to defend, protect, and increase the resilience of the nation's multi-modal transportation infrastructure and education and training base lines for transportation security geared toward transit employees and professionals. Educational programs include H1N1 Training for transit agency managers and employees, Educational opportunities in transportation at the Mineta Transportation Institute (MTI), Online Master of Science in Homeland Security Management degree from the Homeland Security Management Institute of Long Island University. See www.cti.uconn.edu/, www.tougaloo.edu/, http://transportation.tsu.edu/NTSCE/home.htm, www.policy.rutgers.edu/centers/nti.php, www.southampton.liu.edu/homeland/index.html, http://transweb

.sjsu.edu/, and www.mackblackwell.org/. For more information, contact universityprograms@dhs.gov.

DHS Center of Excellence: National Consortium for the Study of Terrorism and Responses to Terrorism (START) informs decisions on how to disrupt terrorists and terrorist groups, while strengthening the resilience of U.S. citizens to terrorist attacks. Resources include the Minorities at Risk Organizational Behavior, an open-source dataset covering political organizations representing the interests of ethnic groups whose political status and behavior is tracked by the Minorities at Risk project; the Global Terrorism Database, an open-source database including information on terrorist events around the world from 1970 through 2007; Terrorist Organization Profiles; and Training Programs related to the Human Causes and Consequences of Terrorism. See www.start.umd.edu/start/. For more information, contact universityprograms@dhs.gov.

TRANSPORTATION SECURITY ADMINISTRATION (TSA)

The Transportation Security Administration protects the nation's transportation systems to ensure freedom of movement for people and commerce. www.tsa.gov.

TSA Training and Education

Airport Watch/AOPA Training TSA partnered with the Aircraft Owners and Pilots Association (AOPA) to develop a nationwide Airport Watch Program that uses the more than 650,000 pilots as eyes and ears for observing and reporting suspicious activity. The Airport Watch Program includes warning signs for airports, informational literature, and a training video to teach pilots and airport employees how to enhance security at their airports. For additional information including a training video, visit www.aopa.org/airportwatch/.

Alien Flight/Flight School Training The Interim Final Rule, Flight Training for Aliens and Other Designated Individuals and Security Awareness Training for Flight School Employees, requires flight schools to ensure that each of its flight school employees who has direct contact with students (including flight instructors, ground instructors, chief instructors, and administrative personnel who have direct contact with students) receive both initial and recurrent security awareness training. Flight schools may either choose to use TSA's security awareness training program or

Appendix D

develop their own program. For more information, see www.tsa.gov/
what_we_do/tsnm/general_aviation/flight_school_security.shtm.

First Observer Training TSA provides funding for the First Observer program under the Trucking Security Program grant. One component of First
Observer is a security awareness training program. The First Observer
website has online training modules for Trucking and School Bus, with
nine other modules planned. You can log on to the website for training at:
www.firstobserver.com/training/home.php. You can call (888) 217-5902
or E-mail (Firstobserver@hms-world.com) for more information.

Hazmat Motor Carrier Security Action Item Training (SAIT) Program
addresses the TSA recommended security actions that were developed
by the TSA for the hazmat transportation industry. For more information,
see www.tsa.gov/highway. Or contact TSA Highway and Motor Carrier
Division, highwaysecurity@dhs.gov.

Hazmat Motor Carrier Security Self-Assessment Training Program addresses the requirements contained in 49 Code of Federal Regulations
(CFR), Part 172.802, which requires motor carriers that transport plac-
arded amounts of hazardous materials to develop a plan that adequately
addresses security risks related to the transportation of hazardous materials. Training materials can be found at www.tsa.gov/what_we_do/
tsnm/highway/self_training.shtm. Contact TSA Highway and Motor
Carrier Division with any questions at: highwaysecurity@dhs.gov.

**IED Recognition and Detection for Railroad Industry Employees Train-
ing (CD)** is a self-paced program that leads users through four separate
modules which focus on heightening rail employees' awareness of suspicious activity. Topics covered include an overview of the terrorist threat,
high-risk targets, improvised explosive device recognition, and inspection and response procedures. See www.tsa.gov/what_we_do/tsnm/
freight_rail/training.shtm, or contact freightrailsecurity@dhs.gov.

Intermodal Security Training and Exercise Program (I-STEP) supports
TSA's Transportation Sector Network Management (TSNM) Modal Security Managers with exercises and training. The program is designed to
support all transportation security partners with security objectives and
training that has clear and consistent performance measures. See www
.tsa.gov/what_we_do/layers/istep/index.shtm, contact i-step@dhs.gov,
(571) 227-5150.

Land Transportation Antiterrorism Training Program (LTATP) is a joint
effort by TSA and the Federal Law Enforcement Training Center (FLETC)

to enhance knowledge, skills, and capabilities of law enforcement and security officials to prevent acts of terrorism. The program recognizes that security at most land transportation systems is accomplished by a cooperative effort of private sector and local, state, and federal government personnel. Through a curriculum focused on surface transportation security, this five-day program provides the participants with tools to protect the land transportation infrastructure, including rail; mass transit and bus operations; and most importantly, passengers and employees. See www.fletc.gov/training/programs/counterterrorism-division/land-transportation-antiterrorism-training-program-ltatp, contact: MassTransitSecurity@dhs.gov.

Maritime Passenger Security Courses TSA's Port & Intermodal Security Division creates and distributes training courses for passenger vessel employees. The courses address topics to improve passenger vessel employees' security awareness in their operating environments and to increase the effectiveness of their responses to suspicious items and persons that they might encounter. Courses available include: "Security Awareness for Passenger Vessel Employees," "IED/VBIED Recognition and Response," and "Crowd Control." To order, contact TSA Port & Intermodal Security Division at Maritime@dhs.gov, (571) 227-3556.

Mass Transit and Passenger Rail—Bomb Squad Response to Transportation Systems Through training and scenario-based exercises, this program expands regional capabilities to respond to a threat or incident involving a suspected explosive device in mass transit and passenger rail systems. Bomb technicians from law enforcement forces in the system's operating area are placed in the mass transit or passenger rail environment to confront exercise situations necessitating coordinated planning and execution of operations to identify; resolve; and, if appropriate, render harmless improvised explosive devices. These joint activities build relationships and skills in a challenging operational setting, advancing operational partnerships that enhance capabilities to accomplish the prevention and response missions. Contact: MassTransitSecurity@dhs.gov.

Mass Transit and Passenger Rail—Field Operational Risk and Criticality Evaluation (FORCE) The purpose of this process is to establish a threat-based, risk-managed protocol that is particularly effective for regional use. This risk assessment evaluates threat, vulnerability, and consequence from a variety of vantage points, focusing primarily on the rail and bus properties but also surveying intermodal and interdependent critical infrastructure and key resources. The approach for any given region will apply the methodology that best addresses the needs of the particular transit agencies. The results of this assessment aid agencies in setting risk mitigation priorities and completing requests for grant awards and advance regional security collaboration. It is also adaptable to assist with new start-up properties about to come online or transit agencies with aggressive future expansion initiatives as well as regions hosting special security events. For more information, contact MassTransitSecurity@dhs.gov.

Mass Transit Smart Security Practices In mass transit and passenger rail, TSA has produced a compilation of smart security practices drawn from the results of the comprehensive security assessments completed under the Baseline Assessment for Security Enhancement (BASE) program that evaluate agencies' posture in the Security and Emergency Management Actions Items. TSA coordinated the preparation of this compilation with each agency with one or more practices recognized in a BASE assessment, ensuring an accurate description of the practice the agency developed and implemented and securing contact information for an official in the agency that professional colleagues may consult for more information. This compilation fosters communication among security professionals in mass transit and passenger rail nationally with the specific objective of expanding adoption of these most effective practices, tailored as neces-sary to each agency's operating environment. With the December 2009 update, the compilation now consists of some 80 smart security practices, many of which focus on regional partnerships; random security patrols, sweeps, and surges; intelligence and security information sharing; and training and public awareness. For more information, please contact: MassTransitSecurity@dhs.gov.

Mass Transit Security Training Program Guidelines Recognizing the vital importance of training frontline employees, TSA developed and implemented a focused security training initiative under the Transit Security Grant Program (TSGP) in February 2007. TSA coordinated de-velopment of this initiative through the Mass Transit SCC and the PAG. The resulting Mass Transit Security Training Program provides guide-lines to mass transit and passenger rail agencies on the types of training to be provided by category of employee. The guidance further identifies specific courses developed under federal auspices through the FTA, the Federal Emergency Management Agency, and TSA that are available to ensure employees are trained in the designated areas. Finally, the de-partment revised the eligible costs under the TSGP to allow coverage of overtime expenses incurred when employees receive training courses. For Mass Transit Security Training Program Guidelines, see www.tsa.gov/assets/pdf/TSGP_Training_IB243.pdf; for TSGP-Approved Training

Programs List see www.tsa.gov/assets/pdf/approved_vendor_list.pdf. MassTransitSecurity@dhs.gov.

Operation Secure Transport (OST) is security awareness training for the Over-the-Road Bus industry. The training program will be available on CD and online. The training modules will be broken down into the following categories: Driver; Maintenance; Terminal Employees; Management; and Crisis Response. OST will have a link on the TSA Highway and Motor Carrier webpage in the near future: www.tsa.gov/highway. Contact TSA HMC with any questions at: highwaysecurity@dhs.gov.

Pipeline Security Awareness for the Pipeline Industry Employee Training CD and Brochures is a compact disc–based security awareness training program. The training is intended for distribution to interested pipeline companies and is centered on heightening pipeline employees' awareness of suspicious activity and their importance in keeping our nation's pipeline system secure. The training is useful to all pipeline company employees—administrative, operations, and security personnel—who need a basic level of awareness and understanding of pipeline security. To further enhance the information contained in the pipeline security awareness training CD, TSA produced the brochures "Pipeline Security Awareness for Employees" and "Good Neighbors! A Pipeline Security Neighborhood Watch." The CD and brochures may be requested on the TSA Pipeline Security website at www.tsa.gov/what_we_do/tsnm/pipelines/training.shtm. For more information contact the Pipeline Security Division at PipelineSecurity@dhs.gov.

Public Transportation Emergency Preparedness Workshop—Connecting Communities Program brings mass transit and passenger rail agencies' security and emergency management officials together with federal, state, local, and tribal government representatives and the local law enforcement and first-responder community to discuss security prevention and response efforts and ways to work together more effectively to prepare and protect their communities. The two-day workshops enable the participants to apply their knowledge and experiences to a range of security and emergency response scenarios. The overall purpose is to foster dialogue, advance cooperative planning efforts, review past experiences, analyze best practices, and improve overall interoperability, resource utilization, and prevention and response capabilities to address threats, security incidents, and natural disasters. See www.connectingcommunities.net, contact: MassTransitSecurity@dhs.gov.

Appendix D

School Transportation Security Awareness (STSA) was developed by TSA in conjunction with the National Association of State Directors of Pupil Transportation Services, the National Association of Pupil Transportation, and the National School Transportation Association to provide much needed security awareness information and training to the school transportation industry. STSA focuses on terrorist and criminal threats to school buses, bus passengers, and destination facilities. It is designed to provide school bus drivers, administrators, and staff members with information that will enable them to effectively identify and report perceived security threats, as well as the skills to appropriately react and respond to a security incident should it occur. See www.tsa.gov/what_we_do/ tsnm/highway/stsa.shtm, contact highwaysecurity@dhs.gov.

TSA Publications and Guidance

Federal Bureau of Investigation (FBI) Terrorism Vulnerability Self-Assessment (Appendix B of the FTA SEPP guide—pages 139 to 147). See http://transit-safety.volpe.dot.gov/publications/security/Planning Guide.pdf. Contact the TSA Highway and Motor Carrier offices with any questions at: highwaysecurity@dhs.gov.

Federal Motor Carrier Safety Administration: Guide to Developing an Effective Security Plan for the Highway Transportation of Hazardous Materials See www.fmcsa.dot.gov/safety-security/hazmat/security-plan-guide.htm. Contact the TSA Highway and Motor Carrier offices with any questions at: highwaysecurity@dhs.gov.

General Aviation Security Guidelines In April 2003, TSA requested that the Aviation Security Advisory Committee (ASAC) establish a working group made up of industry stakeholders to develop guidelines for security enhancements at the nation's privately and publicly owned and operated general aviation (GA) landing facilities. The resulting document constitutes a set of federally endorsed guidelines for enhancing airport security at GA facilities throughout the nation. It is intended to provide GA airport owners, operators, and users with guidelines and recommendations that address aviation security concepts, technology, and enhancements. For more information, visit: www.tsa.gov/what_we_do/tsnm/general_aviation/airport_security_guidelines.shtm.

Keep the Nation's Railroad Secure (Brochure) assists railroad employees to recognize signs of a potential terrorist act. It is to be used in conjunction with a railroad company's existing security policies and procedures and may be modified to display the company's emergency contact in-

formation for ease of reference. See www.tsa.gov/what_we_do/tsnm/
freight_rail/training.shtm or contact freightrailsecurity@dhs.gov.

Laminated Security Awareness Driver Tip Card contains the following
topics: Bus Operator Alerts; Hijacking; Evacuating the Vehicle; Awareness and What to Look For; and Possible Chemical/Biological Weapons.
See www.tsa.gov/what_we_do/tsnm/highway/documents_reports
.shtm. Any questions can be sent to highwaysecurity@dhs.gov.

**HAZMAT TRUCKING GUIDANCE: Highway Security-Sensitive Ma-
terials (HSSM) Security Action Items (SAIs)** See www.tsa.gov/what_
we_do/tsnm/highway/hssm_sai.shtm. Contact the TSA Highway and
Motor Carrier offices with any questions at: highwaysecurity@dhs.gov.

Highway and Motor Carrier Awareness Posters include Motorcoach
Awareness Posters for terminals: "Watch for Suspicious Items" and
"Watch for Suspicious Behaviors" for terminals as well as a School Transportation Employee Awareness poster. See www.tsa.gov/what_we_do/
tsnm/highway/documents_reports.shtm. Any questions can be sent to
highwaysecurity@dhs.gov.

Mass Transit Employee Vigilance Campaign The "NOT ON MY SHIFT"
program employs professionally designed posters to emphasize the essential role that mass transit and passenger rail employees play in security
and terrorism prevention in their systems. Adaptable templates enable
each transit agency to tailor the product to its operations by including the
system's logo; photographs of their own agency's employees at work; and
quotes from the senior leadership, law enforcement and security officials,
or frontline employees. The personalized approach has proven effective
in gaining employees' attention and interest, supporting the participating transit and rail agencies' efforts to maintain vigilance for indicators
of terrorist activity. TSA designs the posters based on the preferences of
the particular mass transit or passenger rail agency. For more information
contact: MassTransitSecurity@dhs.gov.

**Mass Transit and Passenger Rail—Additional Guidance on Back-
ground Checks, Redress, and Immigration Status** The additional guidance on background checks, redress, and immigration status supplement
item 14 of the Security and Emergency Management Action Items, which
recommends that the operators of mass transit conduct background
investigations, such as criminal history and motor vehicle records, on
all new frontline operations and maintenance employees and those employees and contractors with access to sensitive security information and

security-critical facilities and systems. This guidance addresses factors to consider on the recommended scope of and procedures for voluntarily conducted background checks. See www.tsa.gov/assets/pdf/guidance_employee_background_checks.pdf, contact: MassTransitSecurity@dhs.gov.

Motorcoach Guidance: Security and Emergency Preparedness Plan (SEPP) See www.tsa.gov/assets/doc/sepp.doc. Contact the TSA HMC offices with any questions at: highwaysecurity@dhs.gov.

Rail Security Rule Overview On November 26, 2008, the Department of Homeland Security published a regulation governing security in the freight rail industry. The regulation not only affects freight railroads, but their customers as well. This presentation provides a high-level overview of the Rail Security Rule and information regarding the requirements of the regulation. See www.tsa.gov/assets/pdf/rail_rule_overview_for_stakeholder_workshops_mar_09.pdf (pdf—229 KB); for more information contact: Scott.Gorton@dhs.gov.

Planning Guidelines and Design Standards (PGDS) for Checked Baggage Inspection Systems incorporate insights and experience of industry stakeholders, including airport and airline representatives, planners, architects, baggage handling system designers, and equipment manufacturers. The PGDS is intended to assist planners and designers in developing cost-effective solutions and to convey TSA requirements for checked baggage inspection systems. The PGDS emphasizes best practices associated with screening-system layouts and addresses other factors necessary to actively manage system costs and performance. For more information, see www.tsa.gov/press/happenings/updated_pgds.shtm or contact the TSA Contact Center, (866) 289-9673.

Pipeline and Hazardous Materials Safety Administration: Risk Management Self-Evaluation Framework (RMSEF) See www.phmsa.dot.gov/hazmat/risk/rmsef. Contact the TSA HMC offices with any questions at: highwaysecurity@dhs.gov.

Recommended General Aviation Security Action Items for General Aviation Aircraft Operators and Recommended Security Action Items for Fixed Base Operators. These voluntary action items are measures that aircraft operators and fixed base operators should consider when they develop, implement, or revise security plans or other efforts to enhance security. For more information, see www.tsa.gov/what_we_do/tsnm/general_aviation/security.shtm.

Safeguarding America's Transportation System Security Guides are available for highway passenger security motorcoach personnel, private and contract carrier company employees, Owner-Operator Independent Drivers Association (OOIDA) members, school transportation industry personnel, tank truck carrier employees, and truck rental company employees. You can access the guides by clicking on "Documents and Reports" on the main Highway and Motor Carrier page on the TSA website at: www.tsa.gov/highway. Any questions can be sent to highwaysecurity@dhs.gov.

Transportation Security Administration Counterterrorism Guides are highway security counterterrorism guides for highway transportation security partners in the trucking, highway infrastructure, motorcoach, and school transportation industries. These guides are small flip-charts containing the following topics: Pre-Incident Indicators; Targets; Threats to Highway; Insider Threat; Cloned Vehicle; Hijacking Prevention; Suspicious Packages; Information on Explosive Devices; Prevention/Mitigation; Security Planning; Security Inspection Checklist; Security Exercises; Chemical/Biological/Nuclear/Radiological Incidents; and federal, state and local POCs. You can contact TSA HMC to order a copy, pending available inventory at highwaysecurity@dhs.gov.

Transportation Sector Network Management Highway and Motor Carrier Division Annual Report TSA Highway and Motor Carrier Division publishes an Annual Report and posts the document on the following website: www.tsa.gov/what_we_do/tsnm/highway/documents_reports.shtm.

Transit Agency Security and Emergency Management Protective Measures is a compilation of recommended protective measures for threat levels under the Homeland Security Advisory System jointly developed by TSA and FTA. The current recommended protective measures reflect the advantages of improved threat and intelligence information, security assessments conducted by FTA and TSA, operational experience since the 9/11 attacks that prompted the original version, and collective subject matter expertise and experience of federal partners and the transit community. This product has been developed as a technical resource to transit agency executive management and senior staff assigned to develop security and emergency response plans and to implement protective measures for response to the HSAS threat conditions and emergencies that might affect a transit agency. See www.tsa.gov/assets/pdf/mass_transit_protective_measures.pdf, contact: MassTransitSecurity@dhs.gov.

User's Guide on Security Seals for Domestic Cargo provides information on the different types of security seals available for use in securing and controlling containers, doors, and equipment. While this guide is not intended as a precise procedure for developing a comprehensive seal control program, instead, the objective is to provide information and procedures that will support the development of a seal control program that will meet site-specific requirements. The "User's Guide on Security Seals" document can be obtained by accessing this link: https://portal .navfac.navy.mil/portal/page/portal/NAVFAC/NAVFAC_WW_PP/ NAVFAC_NFESC_PP/LOCKS/PDF_FILES/sealguid.pdf.

TSA Alerts and Newsletters

Highway ISAC The TSA Trucking Security Program funds the First Observer domain awareness program as well as a Call-Center and Information Sharing and Analysis Center (ISAC). The Highway ISAC creates products and bulletins and e-mails them to a distribution list from TSA Highway and Motor Carrier and the First Observer program. Contact First Observer at www.firstobserver.com.

TSA Alert System is an emergency notification alert system for Highway and Motor Carrier security partners. The system is capable of sending out a message via phone, e-mail, or SMS (text) based on the person's priority contact preference. Contact TSA by e-mail to become a TSA Alert subscriber at highwaysecurity@dhs.gov.

TSA Technical Assistance and Help

Comprehensive Security Assessments and Action Items encompass activities and measures that are critical to an effective security program. The 17 Action Items cover a range of areas including security program management and accountability, security and emergency response training, drills and exercises, public awareness, protective measures for the Homeland Security Advisory System threat levels, physical security, personnel security, and information sharing and security. TSA's Transportation Security Inspectors (Surface) conduct security assessments under the Baseline Assessment for Security Enhancement (BASE) program that evaluate the posture of mass transit and passenger rail agencies in the Action Items in a comprehensive and systematic approach to elevate baseline security posture and enhance security program management and implementation. The results of the security assessments inform development of risk mitigation programs and resource allocations, most notably security grants.

See www.tsa.gov/assets/pdf/mass_transit_action_items.pdf. For additional information, contact MassTransitSecurity@dhs.gov.

General Aviation Secure Hotline serves as a centralized reporting system for general aviation pilots, airport operators, and maintenance technicians wishing to report suspicious activity at their airfield. Hotline phone number: 1-866-GA-SECUR (1-866-427-3287).

Highway and Motor Carrier First Observer Call-Center "First Observer"–trained specialists serve as the first line of communication for all matters related to this antiterrorism and security awareness program. Well-trained responders will provide nationwide first-responder and law enforcement contact numbers and electronic linkage to registered participants. Reported caller information is entered into a fully secured reporting system that allows for an electronic transfer to the Information Sharing and Analysis Center (ISAC) for further investigation by industry analysts. The call center may also be utilized during an incident of national significance. Call the center 24/7 at (888) 217-5902. For more information see www.firstobserver.com.

Traveler Redress Inquiry Program (DHS TRIP) provides a single point of contact for individuals who have inquiries or seek resolution regarding difficulties they experienced during their travel screening at airports, train stations, or crossing U.S. borders. To initiate an inquiry, please log on to DHS TRIP's interactive website, www.dhs.gov/trip. For more information, contact the TSA Contact Center, (866) 289-9673.

TSA Programs and Services

Air Cargo Watch Program The likelihood that office staff or managers will uncover the next terrorist is not high. The likelihood that an employee or contractor will see something that is out of the normal routine, the odd out-of-place person, activity, or thing, is high. If it makes that employee feel uncomfortable or take notice, it should be reported to a supervisor immediately. The chance that a driver, dockworker, or cargo agent will be the person that uncovers the next attack is very likely. The Air Cargo Watch program involves all aspects of the supply chain reporting suspicious activity. TSA is collaborating with industry partners to increase security domain awareness so that individuals are empowered to detect, deter, and report potential or actual security threats. The resulting Air Cargo Watch campaign is consistent with U.S. Department of Homeland Security and TSA efforts. Air Cargo Watch has developed materials including a presentation, posters, and a two-page guide to encourage increased attention to potential security threats among several audiences. TSA encourages the display of posters and guides in public view to better attain its goal of maximizing security awareness along the entire air cargo supply chain. See www.tsa.gov/what_we_do/layers/aircargo/ watch.shtm.

Cargo Certified Cargo Screening Program Effective August 1, 2010, 100 percent of cargo flown on passenger aircraft originating in the United States must be screened, per an act passed by Congress and signed into law by former president Bush following the 9/11 Commission Act of 2007. In response, TSA created the Certified Cargo Screening Program (CCSP) to provide a mechanism by which industry may achieve 100 percent screening without impeding the flow of commerce. Informational materials include: one-page overview of CCSP, CCSF, and chain-of-custody standards, tri-fold brochure, supplemental CCSP program material with at-a-glance program overview of the program, and Quick Hits overview with impact of 100 percent screening. For more information visit: www. tsa.gov/ccsp, contact CCSP, ccsp@dhs.gov, or the TSA Contact Center, (866) 289-9673.

Airspace Waivers The Office of Airspace Waivers manages the process and assists with the review of general aviation aircraft operators who request to enter areas of restricted airspace. For each waiver applicant, to support the vetting requirements, last name, first name, social security number, passport number, date of birth, and place of birth are collected. For applications for aircraft operating into, out of, within or overflying the United States, the waiver review process includes an evaluation of the aircraft, crew, passengers, and purpose of flight. The office then adjudicates the application and provides a recommendation of approval or denial to the FAA System Operations Security. For more information, see www.tsa.gov/what_we_do/tsnm/general_aviation/programs_ aw.shtm#overview or contact (571) 227-2071.

DCA Access Standard Security Program (DASSP) TSA's Interim Final Rule, which was developed in coordination with other Department of Homeland Security agencies and the Department of Defense, takes into consideration the special security needs of Washington Reagan National Airport (DCA). Under TSA's security plan, a maximum of 48 flights in and out of DCA will be allowed each day. All aircraft will be required to meet the security measures set forth in the DCA Access Standard Security Program (DASSP). See www.tsa.gov/what_we_do/tsnm/general_avia- tion/programs_sp.shtm#dassp or contact (571) 227-2071.

General Aviation Maryland Three Program allows properly vetted private pilots to fly to, from, or between the three general aviation airports closest to the National Capital Region. These airports are collectively known as the Maryland Three airports, and include College Park Airport (CGS), Potomac Airfield (VKX), and Hyde Executive Field (W32.) These airports are all within the Washington, D.C., Air Defense Identification Zone (ADIZ) and the Washington, D.C., Flight Restricted Zone (FRZ). See www.tsa.gov/what_we_do/tsnm/general_aviation/programs_sp.shtm#maryland or contact (571) 227-2071.

Homeland Security Information Network (HSIN)—Freight Rail Portal has been designed to provide consistent, real-time information sharing capabilities in an integrated, *secure*, Web-based forum to coordinate and collaborate *directly* with our security partners. Membership to the Freight Rail portal is provided once vetted by portal administrators. If you have questions, or for access please contact the HSIN Helpdesk at (866) 430-0162 or send an e-mail to HSIN.helpdesk@dhs.gov or Linda.Lentini@dhs.gov.

Homeland Security Information Network (HSIN)—Highway and Motor Carrier Portal is part of the Critical Sector part of the HSIN system (HSIN-CS). Membership to the HMC portal is provided once vetted by portal administrators. If you have questions, please contact the HSIN Helpdesk at (866) 430-0162 or send an e-mail to HSIN.helpdesk@dhs.gov.

Homeland Security Information Network—Public Transit Portal (HSIN-PT) Intelligence sharing between mass transit and passenger rail agencies and their federal, state and local partners is further facilitated through TSA's Mass Transit Security Information Network's inter-agency communication and information sharing protocols. The HSIN-PT has been integrated into this network to provide one-stop security information sources and outlets for security advisories, alerts, and notices. TSA periodically produces and disseminates Mass Transit Security Awareness Messages that address developments related to terrorist activity and tactics against mass transit and passenger rail at the "for official use only" level. Additionally, TSA is actively involved in regional security forums and supports these collaborative efforts by sharing intelligence products and related security information. Finally, a preplanned alert notification system enables access to mass transit and passenger rail law enforcement and security officials nationally with timely notification of threats or developing security concerns. Membership to the Public Transit portal is provided once vetted by portal administrators, contact MassTransitSecurity@dhs.gov.

Joint DHS/FBI Classified Threat and Analysis Presentations A joint DHS Office of Intelligence and Analysis, TSA Office of Intelligence, and Federal Bureau of Investigation effort provides classified intelligence and analysis presentations to mass transit and passenger rail security directors and law enforcement chiefs in more than 20 metropolitan areas simultaneously through the Joint Terrorism Task Force (JTTF) network's secure video teleconferencing system. These briefings advance two key strategic objectives—providing intelligence and security information directly to mass transit and passenger rail law enforcement chiefs and security directors and enhancing regional collaboration by bringing these officials together with their federal partners to discuss the implications for their areas and coordinate to implement effective security solutions. The briefings occur on approximately a quarterly to semiannual basis, with additional sessions as threat developments may warrant. For more information, contact MassTransitSecurity@dhs.gov.

Mass Transit Security and Safety Roundtables TSA, The Federal Transit Administration (FTA), and the Federal Emergency Management Administration (FEMA) cosponsor the semiannual Transit Security and Safety Roundtables, bringing together law enforcement chiefs, security directors, and safety directors from the nation's 50 largest mass transit and passenger rail agencies and Amtrak with federal security partners to discuss specific terrorism prevention and response challenges and to work collaboratively in developing effective risk mitigation and security enhancement solutions. The roundtables also provide a forum for agency safety and security officials to share effective practices and develop relationships to improve coordination and collaboration. For additional information, contact MassTransitSecurity@dhs.gov.

Mass Transit Security Technology Testing In coordination with TSA's Office of Security Technology and DHS's Office of Science and Technology, the Mass Transit Division pursues development of multiple technologies to advance capabilities to detect and deter terrorist activity and prevent attacks. TSA partners with mass transit and passenger rail agencies to conduct pilot testing of various security technologies. These activities evaluate these capabilities in the varied operational environments that prevail in rail and bus operations across the country. Contact: MassTransitSecurity@dhs.gov.

Paperless Boarding Pass Pilot enables passengers to download their boarding pass on their cell phones or personal digital assistants (PDAs). This innovative approach streamlines the customer experience while heightening the ability to detect fraudulent boarding passes. For more information, see www.tsa.gov/approach/tech/paperless_boarding_pass_ expansion.shtm or contact the TSA Contact Center, (866) 289-9673.

Screening Partnership Program (SPP) also known as Opt-Out, is a unique approach to providing security screening services for air passengers and baggage. Under the program, an airport operator may apply to have security screening conducted by personnel from a qualified private contractor working under federal oversight. For more information, see www.tsa.gov/what_we_do/optout/index.shtm or contact the TSA Contact Center, (866) 289-9673.

Secure Fixed Base Operator is a public-private sector partnership program that allows fixed base operators (FBOs) to check passenger and crew identification against manifests or Electronic Advance Passenger Information System (eAPIS) filings for positive identification of passengers and crew onboard general aviation aircraft. See www.tsa.gov/assets/ pdf/sfbop_general_faq.pdf (pdf—35KB). For additional information, contact tsnmfbo@dhs.gov.

Secure Flight is a behind-the-scenes program that enhances the security of domestic and international commercial air travel through the use of improved watch list matching. By collecting additional passenger data, it will improve the travel experience for all airline passengers, including those who have been misidentified in the past. Resources available for aviation stakeholders include a communications toolkit, a brochure, privacy information, signage informational video. For more information, visit www.tsa.gov/what_we_do/layers/secureflight/index.shtm, or contact the TSA Contact Center, (866) 289-9673.

Transportation Security Grant Programs provides security grants to transit systems, intercity bus companies, freight railroad carriers, ferries, and the trucking industry to help protect the public and the nation's critical transportation infrastructure. The grants support high-impact security projects that have a high efficacy in reducing the most risk to our nation's transportation systems. See www.tsa.gov/grants. For more information, contact TSAGrants@tsa.dhs.gov.

Transportation Worker Identification Credential (TWIC) is a security program designed to ensure that individuals who pose a security threat do not gain unescorted access to secure areas of the nation's maritime transportation system. The credential is a biometric card that ensures only vetted workers can enter without an escort to secure transportation areas. The TWIC Program is jointly administered by TSA and the U.S. Coast

Guard. More information can be found at www.tsa.gov/what_we_do/ layers/twic/index.shtm, or by contacting the TWIC Hotline, (866) 347-8942.

3-1-1 Liquid Restriction is a travel tip for passengers to remind them to pack liquids/gels in 3.4-ounce bottles or less, to consolidate bottles into a one-quart baggie and place them in a bin, outside of their carry-on to send through the X-ray for screening. See www.tsa.gov/311/index.shtm or contact the TSA Contact Center, (866) 289-9673.

KEY CONTACTS

Table D.1.

Component	Contact	E-mail	Phone
CBP	ACE Help Desk		(800) 927-8729
CBP	Air & Marine Operations Center (AMOC)		(951) 656-8000
CBP	Carrier Liaison Program	CLP@dhs.gov	(202) 344-3440.
CBP	CBP INFO Center		(877) CBP-5511
CBP	Client Representative Office		(571) 468-5000
CBP	Electronic System for Travel Authorization (ESTA)		(202) 344-3710
CBP	Global Entry	cbp.goes.support@dhs.gov	(866) 530-4172
CBP	Industry Partnership Program	industry.partnership@dhs.gov	(202) 344-1180
CBP	Intellectual Property Rights Help Desk	ipr.helpdesk@dhs.gov	(562) 980-3119 ext. 252
CBP	Intellectual Property Rights Policy and Programs	iprpolicyprograms@dhs.gov	
CBP	National Gang Intelligence Center		(703) 414-8600
CBP	Private Aircraft Travel Entry Programs	Private.Aircraft.Support@dhs.gov	
CBP	Secure Freight Initiative	securefreightinitiative@dhs.gov	
CRCL	Training	crcltraining@dhs.gov	(202) 357-8258
CRCL	Disability Preparedness	Disability.preparedness@dhs.gov	(202) 357-8483
CS&C	Control Systems Security Program (CSSP)	CSSP@dhs.gov	
CS&C	Cybersecurity Evaluation Tool	CSET@dhs.gov	
CS&C	Information Techhnology Sector	ncsd_cipcs@hq.dhs.gov	
CS&C	Office of Emergency Communications	oec@hq.dhs.gov	
CS&C	Software Assurance Program	software.assurance@dhs.gov	
CS&C	U.S. Computer Emergency Readiness Team (US-CERT)	info@us-cert.gov	(888) 282-0870
CS&C	US-CERT Secure Operations Center	soc@us-cert.gov	(888) 282-0870
DHS	Center for Faith-based and Community Initiatives	Infofbci@dhs.gov.	
DHS	Homeland Security Information Network (HSIN)	hsin.helpdesk@dhs.gov	(866) 430-0162
DHS	Lessons Learned and Information Sharing (LLIS)	feedback@llis.dhs.gov	(866) 276-7001
DHS	National Information Exchange Model (NIEM) Program	NIEMPMO@NIEM.gov	

(Continued)

Table D.1. (Continued)

Component	Contact	E-mail	Phone
DHS	Office of Small and Disadvantaged Business Utilization		(202) 447-5555
DHS	Private Sector Office	Private.sector@dhs.gov	(202) 282-8484
FEMA	Center for Domestic Preparedness	Studentservices@cdpemail.dhs.gov	(866) 213-9553
FEMA	Centralized Scheduling and Information Desk	askcsid@dhs.gov	(800) 368-6498
FEMA	Citizen Corps	citizencorps@dhs.gov	
FEMA	Community Emergency Response Teams	cert@dhs.gov	
FEMA	Disaster Assistance		(800) 745-0243
FEMA	Emergency Lodging Assistance Program	femahousing@corplodging.com	(866) 545-9865
FEMA	FEMA Emergency Management Institute		(301) 447-1200
FEMA	FEMA Learning Resource Center	netclrc@dhs.gov	(800) 638-1821
FEMA	FEMA Private Sector Division	FEMA-Private-Sector-Web@dhs.gov	
FEMA	First Responder Training	askCSID@dhs.gov	(8000) 368-6498
FEMA	Industry Liaison Support Center (contracting)		(202) 646-1895
FEMA	Maps Assistance Center	FEMAMapSpecialist@riskmapcds.com	(877) 336-2627
FEMA	National Incident Management System	FEMA-NIMS@dhs.gov	(202) 646-3850
FEMA	Regulations	FEMA-RULES@dhs.gov	
FEMA	Small Business Program	FEMA-SB@dhs.gov	
FEMA	Technical Assistance Program	FEMA-TARequest@fema.gov	(800) 368-6498
FEMA	U.S. Fire Administration		(301) 447-1000
FEMA	U.S. Fire Administration Publications	usfa-publications@dhs.gov	(800) 561-3356
FLETC	CRADA Program Office	FLETC-CRADAProgramOffice@dhs.gov	(912) 267-2100
I&A	DHS Open Source Enterprise	OSINTBranchMailbox@hq.dhs.gov	
I&A	Office of Intelligence and Analysis Private Sector Partnership Program	I&APrivateSectorCoordinator@hq.dhs.gov	(202) 447-3517 or (202) 870-6087
ICE	Victim Assistance Program		(866) 872-4973
ICE	Human Rights Violators and War Crimes Center	HRV.ICE@DHS.GOV	
ICE	ICE 24/7 Hotline		(866) DHS-2-ICE
ICE	ICE Mutual Agreement between Government and Employers Program (IMAGE)	IMAGE@dhs.gov	(202) 732-3064

ICE	Intellectual Property Rights Center	niru@dhs.gov	(866) IPR-2060 or (866) 477-2060
ICE	National Incident Response Unit (NIRU)		
ICE	Privacy Office	ICEPrivacy@dhs.gov	(202) 732-3300
ICE	Public Affairs	PublicAffairs.IceOfficeOf@dhs.gov	(202) 732-4242
ICE	Student and Exchange Visitor Program (SEVP) Response Center	SEVIS.Source@DHS.gov	(703) 603-3400
IP	Chemical Facility Anti-Terrorism Standards (CFATS) Help Desk	csat@dhs.gov	(866) 323-2957
IP	Chemical Facility Anti-Terrorism Standards Compliance Assistance Visit Requests	cscd.ieb@hq.dhs.gov	
IP	Chemical Sector Specific Agency	ChemicalSector@dhs.gov	(877) CHEMSEC
IP	CIKR Asset Protection Technical Assistance Program (CAPTAP)	ACAMS-info@hq.dhs.gov	(703) 235-3939
IP	Commercial Facilities Sector-Specific Agency	CFSteam@hq.dhs.gov	
IP	Critical Manufacturing Sector-Specific Agency	cm-ssa@dhs.gov	
IP	Dams Sector-Specific Agency	dams@dhs.gov	
IP	Emergency Services Sector-Specific Agency	ESSTeam@hq.dhs.gov	
IP	Infrastructure Data Taxonomy (IDT)	IICD@dhs.gov	
IP	Integrated Common Analytical Viewer (iCAV)	iCAV.info@hq.dhs.gov	(703) 235-4949
IP	IP Education and Learning Series	IP_Education@hq.dhs.gov	
IP	National Infrastructure Coordination Center (NICC)	NIPP@dhs.gov	(202) 282-9201
IP	National Infrastructure Protection Plan (NIPP)	nuclearSSA@hq.dhs.gov	(703) 603-5069
IP	Nuclear Sector-Specific Agency	OBP@dhs.gov	
IP	Office for Bombing Prevention	pcii-info@dhs.gov	(703) 235-5723
IP	Protected Critical Infrastructure Information (PCII) Program	PSAFieldOperationsStaff@hq.dhs.gov	(202) 360-3023
IP	Protective Security Advisor (PSA) Field Operations Staff	SSAexecsec@dhs.gov	(703) 235-5724
IP	Sector Specific Agency Executive Management Office	IPassessments@dhs.gov.	
IP	Vulnerability Assessments Branch		
S&T	Commercialization Office	SandT_Commercialization@hq.dhs.gov	(202) 254-6749

(Continued)

Table D.1. (Continued)

Component	Contact	E-mail	Phone
S&T	Cyber Security Research and Development Center	csrdc@dhs.gov	(202) 254-6934
S&T	Office of University Programs	universityprograms@dhs.gov	
S&T	Project 25 Compliance Assessment Program (P25 CAP)	P25CAP@dhs.gov	
S&T	SAFECOM Program	SAFECOM@dhs.gov	
S&T	SAFETY Act	SAFETYActHelpDesk@dhs.gov	(866) 788-9318
TSA	Cargo Certified Cargo Screening Program	ccsp@dhs.gov	
TSA	Freight and Rail	freightrailsecurity@dhs.gov	
TSA	General Aviation Secure Hotline		1-866-GA-SECUR (1-866-427-3287)
TSA	Highway and Motor Carrier Division	highwaysecurity@dhs.gov	
TSA	Intermodal Security Training and Exercise Program (I-STEP)	i-step@dhs.gov	(571) 227-5150
TSA	Mass Transit	MassTransitSecurity@dhs.gov	
TSA	Office of Airspace Waivers		(571) 227-2071
TSA	Pipeline Security Division	PipelineSecurity@dhs.gov	
TSA	Port & Intermodal Security Division	Maritime@dhs.gov	(571) 227-3556
TSA	Transportation Security Grant Programs	TSAGrants@tsa.dhs.gov	
TSA	TSA Contact Center		1-866-289-9673
CIS Ombudsman	CIS Ombudsman	cisombudsman@dhs.gov	
USCIS	E-Verify	E-Verify@dhs.gov	(888) 464-4218
USCIS	Office of Public Engagement	Public.Engagement@dhs.gov	

Bibliography

AntFarm, Inc. "Uncovering Hidden Customer Needs to Grow Your Services Business." 2007. Available online: www.antfarm-inc.com/docs/Growing_Services.pdf.

Byrd, T. A., K. L. Cossick, and R. W. Zmud. "A Synthesis of Research of Requirements Analysis and Knowledge Acquisition Techniques." *MIS Quarterly* 16 (1): 117–38.

Cellucci, Thomas A. "Bridging the 'Communications Gap' between the Public and Private Sector—Making It Easier to Do Business with DHS." U.S. Department of Homeland Security, October 2008. Available online: www.dhs.gov/xlibrary/assets/bridging_the_communication_gap.pdf.

———. "Commercialization Office: Offering Transformational Change beyond DHS." U.S. Department of Homeland Security, June 2009.

———. "Commercialization Office: Providing Value through Efficiency and Cost-Effectiveness." U.S. Department of Homeland Security, April 2009.

———. "Commercialization: The First Responders' Best Friend." U.S. Department of Homeland Security, January 2009. Available online: www.dhs.gov/xlibrary/assets/st_first_responder_commercialization_article.pdf.

———. "Conservative Estimates of Potential Available Market(s)." U.S. Department of Homeland Security, December 2008. Available online: www.dhs.gov/xlibrary/assets/st_potential_available_market_final.pdf.

———. "Creating and Demonstrating Value." U.S. Department of Homeland Security, 2009. Available online: www.dhs.gov/xlibrary/assets/st_why_a_commercialization_office_creating_and_demonstrating_value.pdf.

———. "Creating Change to Drive Results: A Journey into Creating a 'Commercialization Mindset' at DHS." U.S. Department of Homeland Security, April 2009.

———. *Developing Operational Requirements.* U.S. Department of Homeland Security, May 2008.

———. *Developing Operational Requirements, Version 2.0.* U.S. Department of Homeland Security, November 2008. Available online: www.dhs.gov/xlibrary/assets/Developing_Operational_Requirements_Guides.pdf.

———. "DHS Global Outreach Efforts: Looking for the Best Technology and Products—Period." U.S. Department of Homeland Security, November 2008. Available online: www.dhs.gov/xlibrary/assets/st_dhs_global_outreach_effots_looking_for_the_best_technologies_and_products.pdf.

———. "DHS Implements Commercialization Process." U.S. Department of Homeland Security, August 2008. Available online: www.dhs.gov/xlibrary/assets/DHS_Commercialization.pdf.

———. "DHS: Leading the way to Help the Private Sector Help Itself." U.S. Department of Homeland Security, February 2009. Available online: www.dhs.gov/xlibrary/assets/st_critical_infrastructure_key_resources_article.pdf.

———. "DHS Makes Transition from Acquisition to Commercialization." U.S. Department of Homeland Security, August 2008.

———. "Focus on Small Business: Opportunities Abound for the Engines of Innovation." U.S. Department of Homeland Security, March 2009. Available online: www.dhs.gov/xlibrary/assets/st_focus_on_small_business.pdf

———. "FutureTECH: Guidance to Understanding Future DHS S&T Critical Research/Innovation Focus Areas." U.S. Department of Homeland Security, April 2009.

———. "FutureTECH™ Program: Public-Private Technology Certification Process." U.S. Department of Homeland Security, June 2010.

———. "FutureTECH™ Program: Roles and Responsibilities." U.S. Department of Homeland Security, June 2010.

———. "FutureTECH™ Program Swim Lane Chart." U.S. Department of Homeland Security, June 2010.

———. *Harnessing the Valuable Experience and Resources of the Private Sector for the Public Good: DHS' Entry into Commercialization.* U.S. Department of Homeland Security, February 2009.

———. "Innovative Commercialization Process Delivers Cost-Effective and Efficient Product Development at DHS with Unparalleled Speed-of-Execution." U.S. Department of Homeland Security, November 2008.

———. "Innovative New Partnership Program Creates 'Wins' for Taxpayers and the Private & Public Sectors." U.S. Department of Homeland Security, September 2008.

———. *Innovative Public-Private Partnerships: Pathway to Effectively Solving Problems.* U.S. Department of Homeland Security, July 2010. Available online: www.dhs.gov/xlibrary/assets/st_innovative_public_private_partnerships_0710_version_2.pdf.

———. "Making It Easier to Work with DHS: The Critical Role of Detailed Operational Requirements." U.S. Department of Homeland Security, September 2008. Available online: www.dhs.gov/xlibrary/assets/making_it_easier_to_work_with_dhs.pdf.

———. "Opportunities for the Private Sector." U.S. Department of Homeland Security, May 2009. Available online: www.dhs.gov/xlibrary/assets/st_opportunities_for_the_private_sector.pdf.

———. "Partnership Program Benefits Taxpayers as Well as Private and Public Sectors." U.S. Department of Homeland Security, September 2008. Available online: www.dhs.gov/xlibrary/assets/Partnership_Program_Benefits_Tax_Payers_Public_and_Private_Sector.pdf.

———. "Private Sector Outreach Statistics." U.S. Department of Homeland Security, May 2009. Available online: www.dhs.gov/xlibrary/assets/st_private_sector_outreach_statistics.pdf.

———. "Product Realization Chart." U.S. Department of Homeland Security, March 2008. Available online: www.dhs.gov/xlibrary/assets/st_product_realization_chart_version_1-4.pdf.

———. "Program Prioritization Index." U.S. Department of Homeland Security, August 2010. Available online: www.dhs.gov/xlibrary/assets/sandt-program-prioritization-index-august-2010.pdf.

———. *Requirements Development Guide.* U.S. Department of Homeland Security, April 2008.

———. "SECURE Program: Concept of Operations." U.S. Department of Homeland Security, 2008. Available online: www.dhs.gov/xlibrary/assets/secure_program_overview_and_concept_of_operations.pdf.

———. "SECURE™ Program: Public-Private Product Certification Process." U.S. Department of Homeland Security, June 2010.

———. "SECURE™: Program Swim Lane Chart." U.S. Department of Homeland Security, June 2010.

———. "SECURE™: System Efficacy through Commercialization Utilization Relevance and Evaluation: Program Roles and Responsibilities." U.S. Department of Homeland Security, June 2010.

———. "Speed of Execution in Government? You Bet." U.S. Department of Homeland Security, October 2008.

———. "Uncovering Requirements: How to Start the Conversation . . ." U.S. Department of Homeland Security, January 2008.

Connecticut State Library, History and Genealogy Unit. "John Winthrop, Jr." April 1999. Available online: www.cslib.org/gov/winthropj.htm.

Coplenish Consulting Group. "New Product Best Practices: Over 100 Ideas for Better NPD." 2004. Available online: www.coplenish.com/FreeStuffPages/npdbp.pdf.

David T. "Undreamt Requirements." *David's Software Development Survival Guide.* March 12, 2007. Available online: http://softwaresurvival.blogspot.com/2007/03/undreamt-requirements.html.

Davis, Alan. "Just Enough Requirements Management, Part I." *CodeGear*, November 10, 2004. Available online: http://conferences.codegear.com/print/32301.

Defense Acquisition University. "Assessing Manufacturing Risk." Available online: https://acc.dau.mil/CommunityBrowser.aspx?id=18231.

———. "Manufacturing Readiness Assessment (MRA) Deskbook." May 2009. Available online: https://acc.dau.mil/CommunityBrowser.aspx?id=182129.

———. "Technology Readiness Assessment (TRA) Deskbook." July 2009. Available online: https://acc.dau.mil/CommunityBrowser.aspx?id=18545.

———. "TRL Calculator." Available online: https://acc.dau.mil/CommunityBrowser.aspx?id=25811.

Derby, Esther. "Building a Requirements Foundation through Customer Interviews." *Amplifying Your Effectiveness*. 2004. Available online: www.ayeconference
.com/buildingreqtsfoundation/.

Francis, Samuel. "Acquisition and Commercialization: How DHS Develops End-
User Capabilities." U.S. Department of Homeland Security, April 2009.

———. "Acquisition: What It Is and How S&T Supports it." U.S. Department of
Homeland Security, March 2008.

———. "Requirements: Types of Requirements and Their Development." U.S. Department of Homeland Security, March 2008.

———. "Technology Commercialization: The Other Path to the User." U.S. Department of Homeland Security, March 2008.

Graettinger, Caroline P., et al. "Using the Technology Readiness Levels Scale to
Support Technology Management in the DoD's ATD/STO Environments."
September 2002. Available online: www.sei.cmu.edu/reports/02sr027.pdf.

Graham, Ian. *Requirements Engineering and Rapid Development: An Object Oriented
Approach.* Reading MA: Addison-Wesley Professional, 1999.

Hearne, Rory. "Origins, Development and Outcomes of Public Private Partnerships in Ireland: The Case of PPPs in Social Housing Regeneration." September
2007. Available online: www.cpa.ie/publications/workingpapers/2009-07_
WP_PPPsInSocialHousingRegeneration.pdf.

Hooks, Robert R., and Thomas A. Cellucci. "Commercialization: It's Not Business
as Usual at the Department of Homeland Security." U.S. Department of Homeland Security, April 2008.

International Institute of Business Analysis. *A Guide to the Business Analyst Body of Knowledge*, Release 1.6. 2006. Available online: www.theiiba
.org/Content/NavigationMenu/Learning/BodyofKnowledge/Version16/
BOKV1_6.pdf.

Japenga, Robert. "How to Write a Software Requirements Specification." Micro
Tools, Inc. 2003. Available online: www.microtoolsinc.com/Howsrs.php.

Kar, Pradip, and Michelle Bailey. "Characteristics of Good Requirements," Inter-
national Council of Systems Engineers, Requirements Working Group: INCOSE
Symposium. 1996. Available online: www.afis.fr/nav/gt/ie/doc/Articles/
CHARACTE.HTM.

Kiel, Todd, and Thomas A. Cellucci. *Critical Infrastructure & Key Resources: Using
Commercialization to Develop Solutions Efficiently and Effectively.* U.S. Department
of Homeland Security, January 2010. Available online: www.dhs.gov/xlibrary/
assets/st_cikr_requirements_book_jan_2010.pdf.

Kikla, Richard V., and Thomas A. Cellucci. "Capstone IPTs and Beyond . . ." U.S.
Department of Homeland Security, December 2009.

Kikla, Richard V., and Thomas A. Cellucci. "Capstone IPTs: Even in Government
the Customer Comes First." U.S. Department of Homeland Security, April 2008.

Korman, Jonathan. "Putting People Together to Create New Products." *Cooper*,
2001. Available online: www.cooper.com/insights/journal_of_design/articles/
putting_people_together_to_cre.html.

Kotonya, G., and I. Sommerville. *Requirements Engineering: Processes and Techniques.* New York: John Wiley & Sons, 1998.

Larson, Elizabeth, and Richard Larson. "Projects without Borders: Gathering Requirements on a Multi-Cultural Project." *The Project Manager Homepage.* August 3, 2006. Available online: www.allpm.com/print.php?sid=1587.

Link, Albert N. "The History of Public/Private Partnerships." In *Public/Private Partnerships: Innovation Strategies and Policy Alternatives.* New York: Springer, 2006.

Margetta, R. "S&T Official Working to Move Product Development Out of DHS, into Private Sector." *Congressional Quarterly Homeland Security.* June 27, 2008.

Mcquarrie, Edward F. *The Market Research Toolbox: A Concise Guide for Beginners.* Thousand Oaks, CA: Sage Publications, Inc, 2005.

Medalye, Jacqueline. "Support and Opposition of Public-Private Partnerships." *Encyclopedia of Earth.* November 2006. Available online: www.eoearth.org/article/Support_and_opposition_of_public-private_partnerships.

Meer, David, and Daniel Yankelovich. *Rediscovering Market Segmentation.* Boston: Harvard Business Review, 2006.

Miller, Hal. "Customer Requirements Specifications." The Usenix Magazine 30 (2). Available online: www.usenix.org/publications/login/2005-04/pdfs/miller0504.pdf.

Myers, James H. *Segmentation & Positioning for Strategic Marketing Decisions.* Cincinnati, OH: South-Western Educational Pub, 1996.

National Aeronautics and Space Administration. "National Definition of Technology Readiness Levels." Available online: http://esto.nasa.gov/files/TRL_definitions.pdf.

———. "Technology Readiness Levels." April 1995 Available online: www.hq.nasa.gov/office/codeq/trl/trl.pdf.

National Council for Public-Private Partnerships. Available online: http://ncppp.org/.

National Science and Technology Council—Domestic Improvised Explosive Devices Subcommittee. "Research Challenges in Combating Terrorist Use of Explosives in the United States." December 2008. Available online: www.dtic.mil/cgi-bin/GetTRDoc?Location=U2&doc=GetTRDoc.pdf&AD=ADA505299.

Olshavsky, Ryan. "Bridging the Gap with Requirements Definition." *Cooper,* 2002. Available online: www.cooper.com/insights/journal_of_design/articles/bridging_the_gap_with_requirem_1.html.

Pande, Peter S., Robert Neuman, and Roland Cavanagh. "Defining Customer Requirements: Six Sigma Roadmap Step 2." In *The Six Sigma Way: How GE, Motorola, and Other Top Companies Are Honing Their Performance.* New York: McGraw-Hill, 2000. Available online: www.sixsig.info/research/chapter13.php.

Sehlhorst, Scott. "Elicitation Techniques for Processes, Rules, and Requirements." *Tyner Blain,* September 13, 2007. Available online: http://tynerblain.com/blog/2007/09/13/elicitation-techniques-2/.

———. "Ten Requirements Gathering Techniques." *Tyner Blain,* November 21, 2006. Available online: http://tynerblain.com/blog/2006/11/21/ten-requirements-gathering-techniques/.

Silverman, Lori L., "Customers or Consumers? Focus or Obsession?" Partners for Progress, 2000. Available online: www.partnersforprogress.com/Articles/Customers%20or%20Consumers.pdf.

Sisson, Derek. "Requirements and Specifications." Philosophe.com, January 9, 2000. Available online: www.philosophe.com/design/requirements.html.

Smith, Douglas A., and Thomas A. Cellucci. *Harnessing the Valuable Experience and Resources of the Private Sector for the Public Good: Innovative Public-Private Partnerships.* June 2010 Available online: www.dhs.gov/xlibrary/assets/st_harnessing_the_value_of_the_private_sector2.pdf.

Turner, Arch. "Homeland Security Capabilities." U.S. Department of Homeland Security, May 2009.

U.S. Department of Defense. *Defense Acquisition Guidebook.* Chapter 4. December 2004. Available online: https://akss.dau.mil/DAG/TOC_GuideBook.asp?sNode=R&Exp=Y.

U.S. Department of Energy. "NETL: Cooperative Research and Development Agreement." Available online: www.netl.doe.gov/business/crada/crada.html.

U.S. Department of Homeland Security. "Acquisition Management Directive." Available online: www.dhs.gov/xlibrary/assets/foia/mgmt_directive_102-01_acquisition_management_directive.pdf.

———. "Essential Technology Task Force: Homeland Security Advisory Council." June 2008. Available online: www.dhs.gov/xlibrary/assets/hsac_dhs_ettf_report_update.pdf.

———. "High Priority Technology Needs." May 2009. Available online: www.dhs.gov/xlibrary/assets/High_Priority_Technology_Needs.pdf.

———. "National Infrastructure Protection Plan: Partnering to Enhance Protection and Resiliency." 2009. Available online: www.dhs.gov/xlibrary/assets/NIPP_Plan.pdf.

———. "Quadrennial Homeland Security Review Report: A Strategic Framework for a Secure Homeland." February 2010. Available online: www.whitehouse.gov/sites/default/files/rss_viewer/STSA.pdf.

U.S. Department of Homeland Security: Science & Technology Directorate. "High-Priority Technology Needs." May 2009. Available online: www.dhs.gov/xlibrary/assets/High_Priority_Technology_Needs.pdf.

U.S. Department of the Interior. "What Is a CRADA?" Available online: www.usbr.gov/research/tech-transfer/crada/whatcrada.html.

U.S. Government Accountability Office. "Defense Acquisitions: Assessment of Selected Major Weapons Programs." March 2006. Available online: www.gao.gov/new.items/d06391.pdf.

Ward, James. "It Is Still the Requirements: Getting Software Requirements Right." *Sticky Minds,* June 7, 2005. Available online: www.stickyminds.com/s.asp?F=S9150_ART_2.

The White House. "Surface Transportation Security Assessment." March 2010. Available online: www.whitehouse.gov/sites/default/files/rss_viewer/STSA.pdf.

Wiegers, Karl E., and Sandra McKinsey. "Accelerate Development by Getting Requirements Right." 2007. Available online: www.serena.com/docs/repository/products/dimensions/accelerate-developme.pdf.

Wikipedia: The Free Encyclopedia. "Requirements Analysis." April 8, 2008. Available online: http://en.wikipedia.org/w/index.php?title=Requirements_analysis&oldid=204196812.

Wilson, William. "Writing Effective Requirements Specifications." April 1997. Available online: http://satc.gsfc.nasa.gov/support/STC_APR97/write/writert .html.

Winant, Becky. "Requirement #1: Ask Honest Questions." *Sticky Minds*, April 3, 2002. Available online : www.stickyminds.com/s.asp?F=S3264_COL_2.

Wright-Patterson Air Force Base. "About Manufacturing Readiness Assessments." Available online: www.wpafb.af.mil/library/factsheets/factsheet .asp?id=9757.

Zeller, Randel. "DHS Science & Technology Directorate Brief—Capstone IPT: First Responders." U.S. Department of Homeland Security, May 2009.

Zeller, Randel L., and Thomas A. Cellucci. *First Responder Capstone IPT: Delivering Solutions to First Responders*. U.S. Department of Homeland Security, May 2009. Available online: www.dhs.gov/xlibrary/assets/st_comm_first_responder_ capstone_ipt_book.pdf.

Index

acquisition, 111, 124–27, 129, 130, 135,139, 146, 259, 269, 329, 382, 393

Acquisition Management Directive, 13, 89, 111

analyses of alternatives (AoAs), 44, 78

ancillary markets, 1, 5, 7, 14, 17, 19, 21, 23, 27, 77, 92, 95, 103, 104, 107, 113, 119, 128, 147, 148, 249, 259

angel investor, 48, 76, 107, 108, 304

applications, 5, 8, 25, 47, 76, 92, 95, 104, 114, 120, 125, 131, 140, 155, 172, 195, 206, 209, 214, 15, 249, 250, 251, 263, 275, 279, 280, 341, 348, 358, 388, 397, 412

benefit analysis, 27, 77, 108, 152, 391

blast resistant autonomous video equipment (BRAVE), 248, 251–55

Borders and Maritime Security (BMD), 38, 136

business case, 5, 13, 14, 22, 23, 73, 104, 107, 128, 129, 148

buy, 76, 82, 97, 157, 162, 187, 189, 232

CAL FIRE, 20

capability gap, 1, 7, 10–12, 14, 17, 25, 35, 37–38, 40, 42–44, 47, 49–50, 53, 75, 95, 100, 103–4, 106, 124, 129, 135–39, 143, 154, 164, 176–77, 179–80, 211, 236–38, 250, 261, 270, 284, 292, 296, 300

Capstone Integrated Product Team (IPT), 12, 25, 27, 37, 38, 40, 44–50, 53, 102, 103, 133, 135–42, 261, 286, 372

certification, 82, 83, 184

chemical/biological, 38, 135, 136, 407

chief commercialization officer, 9, 13, 19

Citizenship and Immigration Service, 1, 78

Coast Guard, 1, 21, 24, 30, 78, 111, 114, 124, 133, 175, 178, 236, 292, 335, 336

Command, Control, and Interoperability Division, 392

commercialization, 3, 5, 7, 8, 9–20, 18, 21, 22–28, 40, 45, 47, 53, 55, 73, 74, 77, 78, 82, 89, 95, 99, 101, 104, 111, 112, 118, 123–35, 140, 146–48, 163, 178, 251, 259, 267, 269, 303, 326, 393

Commercialization Office, 9, 13–22, 82, 99, 102–3, 106–7, 123, 131, 259, 267, 304, 326, 393

Commercialization Operational Requirements Document (C-ORD), 3, 5, 7, 11, 13, 14, 23, 31, 44, 47, 53,

54–56, 62, 78, 83, 103, 104, 106, 119, 125, 139, 140, 143, 146, 147, 152, 153, 162, 163, 175, 178–80, 187, 188, 206, 209, 212, 234, 248, 251, 259, 261, 267, 268

commercial off-the-shelf (COTS), 1, 9, 22, 27, 45, 77, 82, 108, 127, 131, 139, 147, 152, 181, 195, 214, 234, 238–39, 244, 245

Committee on Requirements, 42

Community of Practitioners (CoP), 47, 92, 95, 113, 114

Cooperative Research and Development Agreement (CRADA), 7, 16, 83, 89, 129, 267–70, 326, 327

critical infrastructure/key resources (CIKR), 1, 16, 17, 18, 22, 24, 25, 27, 29–35, 37, 42, 46, 48, 49, 78, 79, 82, 92, 101, 102, 107, 111, 119, 133, 135, 147, 234, 236, 238, 248, 259, 261, 270, 293, 296, 304, 350, 351, 365, 367, 369, 371–73, 375, 376–91

cross-cutting, 92, 113

customer, 3, 5, 7, 8, 18, 27, 35, 37, 38, 40–47, 53, 55, 61, 73, 76, 77, 99, 102, 104, 108, 120, 124, 125, 127, 129, 130, 133, 135–36, 139, 141, 147, 152, 161, 208, 261, 330, 332–34, 336, 339, 344, 360, 392, 396, 408, 414

Customs and Border Protection (CBP), 1, 21, 24, 30, 78, 111, 124, 133, 236, 263, 336, 337–66

Cyber Security and Communications (CS&C), 32, 345, 346, 349–51, 395

Department of Defense (DOD), 47, 48, 92, 113, 140, 263, 265, 288, 294, 394, 397

Department of Energy (DOE), 48

Department of Homeland Security (DHS), 1, 3, 5, 7, 8, 9, 13, 21, 24, 25, 28, 30, 31, 35, 37–38, 40, 42–50, 53, 55, 63, 73, 77, 78–79, 82, 89, 91–92, 95–96, 99–104, 106–7, 109, 111–16, 119, 123–31, 133, 135–41, 143, 146–48, 152, 162, 166, 175, 183, 213, 235, 236, 238, 250, 251, 257, 259–61, 265–70, 272, 273, 275, 276, 284, 287, 289, 292–94, 296–301, 304, 325–35, 347, 351, 368, 376, 381–92, 393–401, 411; Science and Technology Directorate (S&T), 3, 5, 7, 8, 9, 10, 11, 15, 16, 17, 18, 27, 31, 37, 38, 43–47, 50, 53, 78, 79, 92, 103–4, 106, 111, 124, 129, 135–39, 141, 213, 251, 259–61, 267–71, 273, 276, 279, 280, 283, 284, 286, 287, 289, 292, 296, 300, 304, 326, 392–96

design specifications, 54

development, 1, 3, 5–8, 9–18, 21, 23–25, 27, 28, 33, 35, 37, 40, 42–47, 49–52, 53, 55, 56, 58, 62, 71–73, 76, 77, 78, 83, 91, 92, 96, 99, 100, 102–4, 106, 112, 114, 118, 123, 125, 127, 129–31, 133, 135–36, 138–41, 146, 147, 166, 168, 195, 204, 232, 249, 251, 259, 260, 261, 266–69, 271, 274, 280, 281, 287, 290, 291, 293, 294, 297, 298, 300, 326, 327, 346, 347, 352, 353, 361, 368, 375, 379, 392, 393–94, 395, 396, 397, 399, 400, 404, 410, 413, 414

developmental test and evaluation (DT&E), 27, 38, 51, 135, 137, 397

effectiveness, 42, 50, 75, 92, 137, 179, 215, 235, 244, 262, 301, 351, 368, 369, 378, 403

efficiency, 47, 67, 102, 175, 333

Enabling Homeland Capabilities (EHCs), 43–45, 139

estimate, 3, 5, 11, 13, 14, 18, 19, 23, 28, 74, 79, 91, 99, 102, 104, 106, 107, 111, 119, 125, 128, 143, 147, 148, 161, 175, 259, 391, 396

evaluation, 3, 5, 7, 10, 13, 14, 15, 17, 22, 27, 38, 44, 51, 78, 79, 82, 82, 106, 111, 126, 128, 135, 146, 148, 260, 261, 263, 264, 268, 270, 291, 346, 350, 352, 392, 393, 395, 397, 399, 403, 408, 412

explosives, 38, 135, 265–66, 273, 274, 275, 277, 279, 280–82, 287, 290–92, 293, 296, 299, 301, 360, 370, 371, 374, 382, 398

Federal Acquisition Regulation (FAR), 8

Federal Emergency Management Agency (FEMA), 1, 21, 24, 30, 78, 111, 124, 133, 190, 236, 237, 297, 327, 350, 353–58, 362, 369, 382, 414

Federally Funded Research and Development Center (FFRDC), 17

Federal Protective Service (FPS), 32

first responder(s), 1, 9, 12, 13, 14, 16, 17, 18, 19, 20, 24, 25, 27, 28, 30, 31, 35, 37, 38, 40, 47, 49, 78, 79, 92, 101, 102, 103, 111, 119, 124, 127, 131, 133, 135, 136, 140, 143, 146, 147, 148, 152, 154, 155, 163, 175, 179, 209, 211–14, 216, 236, 237, 259, 261, 276, 298, 304, 328, 353, 354, 370, 382, 383, 391

free market system, 7, 13, 18, 25, 73, 74, 99, 108, 152, 268

functional specifications, 54

FutureTECH, 11, 14, 15, 16, 17, 79, 82, 91, 99, 100, 106, 107, 111, 141, 259, 261, 267, 268, 270, 273, 303, 394

Government Coordinating Council (GCC), 35, 347, 386

Homeland Security Enterprise (HME), 24, 92, 118, 326

HUBZone, 11, 19, 97

hybrid model, 22, 127, 151

independent operational testing and evaluation (IOT&E), 83

independent research and development (IRAD), 15, 266, 267

Infrastructure and Geophysical Division (IGD), 38, 136, 264

infrastructure protection, 29, 30, 31, 32, 33, 35, 38, 42, 46, 136, 236, 237, 238, 251, 367, 369, 371, 376, 377, 378, 379, 380, 381, 382, 384, 385, 388, 389, 390, 391

Immigrations and Customs Enforcement (ICE), 1, 30, 114, 133, 263, 362, 366

innovation, 11, 15, 16, 17, 79, 106, 108, 123, 259, 260–61, 264, 266–69, 270, 273, 276, 279, 283, 286, 287, 289, 292, 296, 300, 342, 394

intellectual property, 83, 99, 337, 338, 342, 343, 366

investment, 17, 27, 37, 45, 73, 74, 76, 77, 89, 99, 108, 112, 115, 116, 135, 152, 177, 236, 237, 348, 397, 399

justification, 116

key performance parameters (KPP), 64, 65, 144, 145, 146, 153, 159, 176, 193, 200, 204, 210, 229, 234, 235, 244, 248, 254

know-how, 270

large business, 11, 19, 27, 77, 108, 152

Manufacturing Readiness Level (MRL), 6, 130

market(s), 1, 3, 5, 7, 8, 9, 14, 17, 18, 19, 21, 23, 24, 25, 28, 35, 55, 73, 74, 76, 79, 92, 95, 102, 103, 104, 107, 108, 113, 119, 127, 128, 143, 147, 148, 152, 249, 259, 304

market "pull" versus "push," 51

material specifications, 54

merger and acquisitions (M&A), 21, 101

metrics, 11, 43, 50, 75, 82, 115, 259, 269, 352, 384, 395

mission needs statement (MNS), 53, 125

model, 5, 6, 16, 17, 21, 22, 23, 24, 32, 33, 34, 35, 38, 53, 75, 89, 91, 96, 99, 100, 104, 111, 113, 115, 118, 125, 126, 128, 146, 147, 163, 170, 187, 264, 271, 272, 298, 300, 301, 303, 330, 350, 361, 379, 398, 399

mutually beneficial partnerships, 11, 14

National Infrastructure Protection Plan (NIPP), 29, 32, 33, 34, 42, 348, 351, 369, 371, 376, 377, 378, 379, 381, 385, 391

national labs, 308, 394
National Protection and Programs
    Directorate (NPPD), 29, 30, 31, 236,
    395
National Response Framework (NRF),
    32, 359
new product development, 7, 12, 103

Office of Infrastructure Protection, 29,
    31, 38, 42, 46, 236, 237, 327, 328, 367,
    378, 384, 385, 388, 389, 390
Office of Public Affairs, 13, 365
Office of Public-Private Partnerships,
    18
operating components, 1, 3, 5, 9, 10,
    11, 12, 14, 17, 18, 19, 21, 22, 24, 27,
    30, 37, 38, 40, 49, 50, 78, 79, 102, 104,
    106, 111, 114, 119, 124, 127, 131, 133,
    135, 136, 143, 146, 147, 152, 162, 259,
    261, 270, 392
operational requirements, 1, 3, 5, 9, 10,
    11, 12, 13, 15, 17, 20, 23, 28, 30, 31,
    37, 38, 40, 43, 44, 47, 50, 51, 52, 53,
    54, 55, 56, 62, 75, 78, 79, 82, 91, 92,
    99, 102, 103, 104, 106, 107, 111, 112,
    114, 119, 125, 126, 128, 129, 131,
    135, 136, 140, 141, 143, 147, 148,
    152, 153, 163, 259, 261, 268, 326,
    393, 396
operational test and evaluation
    (OT&E), 13, 51, 52, 79, 83
organizational elements, 1, 30, 31, 35,
    37, 79, 106, 259
outreach, 3, 8, 9, 10, 11, 18, 19, 29, 31,
    55, 89, 103, 107, 111, 123, 128, 131,
    141, 147, 266, 267, 268, 308, 326, 329,
    332, 345, 351, 358, 363, 364, 365, 374,
    376, 381, 382, 387, 393

partnership(s), 3, 8, 9, 10, 11,14, 15, 17,
    18, 19, 20, 21, 22, 23, 29, 32, 33, 34,
    35, 48, 67, 68, 69, 71, 72, 73–76, 77,
    79, 82, 83, 89, 91, 92, 95, 96, 99, 100,
    101–3, 106–9, 111–12, 117, 123, 126,
    128, 131, 141, 143, 146, 148, 266, 267,
    269, 326, 327, 329, 340, 341, 342, 344,
    345, 347, 351, 355, 359, 366, 367, 375,

379, 380, 381, 383, 385, 388, 393, 396,
    403, 404, 415
performance requirements, 53, 54, 395
potential available market(s) (PAM), 1,
    3, 11, 13, 14, 17, 18, 23, 25, 28, 47, 48,
    73, 79, 91, 92, 99, 102, 103, 104, 106,
    107, 111, 112, 114, 119, 120, 128, 140,
    143, 147, 148, 161, 259, 304, 396
prioritization, 35, 37, 43, 78, 82, 114–16,
    135, 136, 261, 271, 272
private sector, 1, 3, 5, 6, 7, 8, 9–20,
    21–25, 28, 30, 32, 33, 42, 45, 47, 48,
    50, 68, 69, 70, 72–77, 78, 79, 82, 83,
    89, 91, 92, 96, 99, 100–104, 106–9,
    111, 112, 114, 120, 122, 123–29,
    130–31, 140–41, 147–48, 177, 178,
    180, 190, 205, 207, 257, 259, 261,
    267–70, 296, 297, 304, 308, 325–26,
    327, 328, 329, 330, 340, 345, 346, 347,
    348, 351, 354, 355, 356, 358, 359, 361,
    365, 366, 368, 369, 370, 372, 373, 376,
    378, 379, 380, 381, 382, 384, 385, 386,
    387, 389, 390, 391, 393, 394, 396, 399,
    403, 415
Private Sector Office, 13, 14, 17, 326,
    327
procurement, 9, 12, 17, 55, 79, 83
product, 1, 3, 5, 6, 7, 8, 9, 10, 11, 12,
    13, 14, 15–18, 19, 21, 22, 23, 24–25,
    27, 28, 31, 35, 37–38, 40, 42, 44–47,
    48–50, 51–54, 57, 58, 61, 62, 67, 69,
    71, 72, 73–77, 78, 79, 82, 83, 89, 91,
    96, 99, 101–4, 106–9, 111, 112, 118,
    119, 120, 123–31, 133, 135, 136, 138,
    139, 141, 142, 146, 147, 154, 162, 167,
    175, 187, 234, 238, 241, 244, 247, 254,
    259, 261, 267, 268, 293, 294, 304, 305,
    329, 342–46, 351, 352, 363, 375, 380,
    382, 394, 395, 396, 399, 407, 409, 410,
    413
product realization, 31, 48, 49, 50, 52,
    62, 109, 123, 124, 125, 126, 131
Project Integrated Product Team (IPT),
    12, 27, 37, 38, 40, 42, 43, 44–46, 49,
    50, 53, 63, 102, 103, 133, 135, 136–41,
    143, 261, 270, 273, 276, 279, 283, 284,
    286, 287, 289, 292, 296, 300

public-private partnerships, 18, 32, 67, 68, 72, 73, 74, 77, 78, 83, 89, 96, 99, 102, 103, 108, 109, 112, 141, 143, 326, 355, 367, 393

public sector, 3, 14, 27, 67, 73–76, 77, 82, 83, 89, 91, 96, 99, 100, 102, 106, 112, 123, 141, 148, 208, 267, 296, 357

quality control/assurance, 125

requirements, 1, 3, 5, 7, 9, 10, 11, 12–15, 17, 18, 19, 20, 22, 23, 25, 27–28, 30–31, 33–35, 37–40, 43–44, 47–62, 67, 72, 74–79, 82, 83, 91, 92, 95, 99, 101, 102–4, 106–7, 111–15, 119, 120, 122, 124–29, 131, 133, 135, 136–41, 143, 147, 148, 152, 153, 156, 160, 163, 167, 168, 173, 175, 178, 180, 183, 186, 189, 190, 195, 206, 210, 214, 215, 216, 217, 228, 230, 246, 247, 249, 250, 252, 269, 261, 267, 269, 272, 280, 297, 304, 305, 326, 336, 339, 342, 344, 348, 358, 364, 371, 376, 381, 385, 393, 395, 396, 402, 408, 410, 412

research, 3, 5, 7, 11, 15–18, 25, 27, 29, 31, 33, 37, 38, 42, 68–72, 74, 76, 77, 79, 83, 100, 106, 119, 124, 125, 129, 135, 164, 168, 251, 259, 260–61, 266, 267–70, 273, 274, 276, 279, 283, 286, 289, 292, 296, 300, 326, 327, 331, 332, 338, 347, 352, 353, 355, 357, 362, 376, 382, 384, 386, 392–99

research and development, 5, 7, 11, 15, 25, 29, 33, 38, 42, 70, 71, 73, 76, 77, 78, 83, 100, 125, 129, 260, 261, 267, 326, 327, 347, 353, 393, 395, 399

return-on-investment (ROI), 73, 89, 90, 99, 112, 113

risk management and analysis (RMA), 32

Science and Technology Directorate (S&T), 3, 5, 7, 8, 9, 10, 11, 15, 16, 17, 18, 27, 31, 37, 38, 43–47, 50, 53, 78, 79, 92, 103–4, 106, 111, 124, 129, 135–39, 141, 213, 251, 259–61, 267–71, 273, 276, 279, 280, 283, 284, 286, 287, 289, 292, 296, 300, 304, 326, 392–96

Secret Service, 1, 24, 30, 78, 111, 114, 124, 133, 270, 273, 276, 279, 284, 287, 289, 292, 296, 300, 328, 396

Sector Coordinating Council (SCC), 35, 203, 347, 404

sector-specific agency (SSA), 33, 34, 368, 369, 370, 371, 373, 374, 375, 376, 377, 380, 381, 382, 383, 384, 386, 387, 389, 390, 391, 392

segment, 74, 119, 120, 122, 147, 378

Small Business Innovative Research (SBIR), 3, 97, 98

strategic partnerships, 3, 76, 96, 108

subject matter experts (SMEs), 16, 44, 83, 263, 409

Support Anti-Terrorism by Fostering Effective Technologies (SAFETY) Act, 96, 98, 304, 396, 397

synchronization, 5

System Efficacy through Commercialization, Utilization, Relevance, and Evaluation (SECURE), 10, 13, 14, 15, 16, 18, 20, 22, 23, 78–79, 82, 91, 99, 100, 106–7, 111, 119, 124, 128–29, 141, 146, 148, 161, 233, 259, 266, 267–69, 303, 304, 396

technology, 3, 5–9, 11–16, 18, 20, 25, 31, 34, 35, 37–38, 40, 42–47, 61, 60, 62, 63, 64, 69, 70, 72, 73, 76, 79, 91, 92, 95, 96, 99, 100, 102, 103, 104, 107, 111, 113, 115, 118, 123, 125–27, 129–31, 133, 135–41, 154, 157, 158, 168, 177, 179, 187, 189, 190, 207, 208, 236, 237, 239, 242, 251, 259–61, 266–69, 276, 279, 280, 282, 284, 289, 290, 292, 293, 296, 297, 300, 328, 347, 348, 351, 359, 366, 392–98, 406, 414

technology push, 51

Technology Readiness Level (TRL), 6, 7, 11, 15, 16, 47, 80, 106, 123, 126, 129–30, 175, 259, 267–69

technology requirements, 53, 137

Technology Transition Agreements
  (TTAs), 45, 46, 126
test and evaluation (T&E), 7, 13, 16, 17,
  27, 38, 51, 52, 79, 83, 126, 135, 137,
  270, 392, 397
third party, 3, 7, 13, 79, 83, 106, 111,
  129, 178, 218, 268, 270, 335
transition, 5, 9, 18, 30, 37, 40, 45, 50, 51,
  103, 104, 118, 123, 126, 129, 130, 136,
  139, 221, 261, 393, 394
Transition Office, 45
Transport Security Administration
  (TSA), 1, 21, 24, 30, 78, 111, 124,
  133, 236, 330, 387, 401–16

undersecretary, 261
U.S. Visitor and Immigrant Status
  Indicator Technology (US-VISIT), 32
utilitarian approach, 116

vendors, 78, 79, 96, 127, 156, 157, 174,
  187, 207, 232, 233, 246, 248, 255, 329,
  340, 349, 351, 352, 357, 358, 382, 398,
  405
venture capitalist (VC), 76, 108, 304

widely distributed products, 9, 10, 17,
  21, 25, 35, 45, 53, 101, 103, 125, 139,
  146
win-win-win, 27, 74, 77, 79, 99, 106,
  108, 148, 152
working group, 14, 16, 34, 55, 65,
  131, 137, 328, 377, 394, 397, 398,
  406

x-ray, 266, 282, 416

yields, 15, 267, 304

About the Author

Thomas A. Cellucci, PhD, MBA, accepted a five-year appointment in 2007 from the Department of Homeland Security to serve as its first chief commercialization officer. He is responsible for initiatives that identify, evaluate, and commercialize technology for the specific goal of rapidly developing and deploying products and services that meet the specific operational requirements of the Department of Homeland Security's operating components, first responders, and critical infrastructure/key resources owners and operators. Cellucci conducts DHS-S&T's outreach with both the private and public sectors to establish and foster mutually beneficial working relationships that facilitate cost-effective and -efficient product/service and technology development efforts. He has published eight comprehensive books dealing with the development of operational requirements and innovative public-private partnerships, developed and implemented a commercialization process for the entire department, and established both the SECURE and FutureTECH programs—innovative public-private partnerships to cost-effectively and -efficiently develop products/services and technologies for DHS's Operating Components, the First Responder community, and other DHS stakeholders.

In 2010, while continuing to serve as chief commercialization officer, Cellucci was appointed the director of the Office of Public-Private Partnerships which oversees the Long Range Broad Agency Announcement (LRBAA) procurement process, Office of SAFETY Act Implementation (OSAI), Small Business Innovation Research (SBIR) Office, as well as the Commercialization Office. In addition, he was named director of Research and Development (R&D) Partnerships Group (Acting) responsible to leverage the billions of dollars in assets and the expertise of more than

1,400 team members through the group's investments in national labs, universities, international partners, the private sector, and government interagency partners to develop technologies, products, and services for the Homeland Security Enterprise (HSE).

Cellucci is an accomplished entrepreneur, seasoned senior executive, and board member possessing extensive corporate and VC experience across a number of worldwide industries. Profitably growing high-technology firms at the start-up, mid-range, and large corporate level has been his trademark. In 1999, he founded a highly successful management consulting firm, Cellucci Associates, Inc. He has authored or coauthored over 160 articles on requirements development, commercialization, nano-technology, laser physics, photonics, environmental disturbance control, MEMS test and measurement, and mistake-proofing processes. Cellucci coauthored ANSI Standard Z136.5 "The Safe Use of Lasers in Educational Institutions." He has also held the rank of professor or lecturer at institutions like Princeton University, University of Pennsylvania, and Camden Community College.

As a result of his consistent achievement in the commercialization of technologies and role as DHS's first chief commercialization officer, Cellucci has received numerous awards from industry, government, and business. In addition, he has had the opportunity to interact with high-ranking members of the U.S. government—including the White House, U.S. Senate, and U.S. House of Representatives—having provided several executive briefs to three presidents of the United States and ranking members of Congress.

Cellucci earned a PhD in physical chemistry from the University of Pennsylvania, an MBA from Rutgers University, and a BS in chemistry from Fordham University. He has also attended and lectured at executive programs at the Harvard Business School, MIT Sloan School, Kellogg School, and others.